The Making of a Savior Bodhisattva

STUDIES IN EAST ASIAN BUDDHISM 21

The Making of a Savior Bodhisattva

Dizang in Medieval China

Zhiru

A Kuroda Institute Book
University of Hawai'i Press
Honolulu

Paperback edition 2017

Printed in the United States of America

22 21 20 19 18 17 6 5 4 3 2 1

Library of Congress Cataloging-in-Publication Data

Ng, Zhiru, 1964-
The making of a savior bodhisattva Dizang in medieval China / Zhiru.
p. cm. — (Studies in East Asian Buddhism ; 21)
"A Kuroda Institute book."
Includes bibliographical references and index.
ISBN 978-0-8248-3045-8 (hardcover : alk. paper)
1. Ksitigarbha (Buddhist deity)—Cult—China—History. I. Title.
BQ4710.K74C476 2007
294.3'42113—dc22
2007011059

ISBN 978-0-8248-6758-4 (pbk.)

The Kuroda Institute for the Study of Buddhism and Human Values is a nonprofit, educational corporation founded in 1976. One of its primary objectives is to promote scholarship on the historical, philosophical, and cultural ramifications of Buddhism. In association with the University of Hawai'i Press, the Institute also publishes Classics in East Asian Buddhism, a series devoted to the translation of significant texts in the East Asian Buddhist tradition.

University of Hawai'i Press books are printed on acid-free paper and meet the guidelines for permanence and durability of the Council on Library Resources.

Designed by Kenneth Miyamoto

In gratitude to all the donors
in the ten directions
who have supported my
study and practice

Contents

Figures

Acknowledgments

THIS BOOK GREW out of my doctoral dissertation, which was submitted to the Department of East Asian Studies at the University of Arizona. I am tremendously grateful to the Reverend Hou Zhong for his broad vision of monastic education and to the congregation at the Mahāprajñā Buddhist Society for their unstinting support of my graduate studies. In a similar vein I should thank my grand teacher Master Yinshun for modeling to a younger generation of monastics like myself how to fruitfully combine modern scholarship and religious ideals with uncompromising integrity. I was most fortunate to receive tutelage from a team of fine scholars and inspiring teachers at the University of Arizona, all of whom helped shape this book. Robert Gimello, the chair of my dissertation committee, provided a model of unexcelled scholarship; his erudition and rigorous standards are exceeded only by the depth of his concern for his students. His study on Mañjuśrī and Mount Wutai was the inspiration behind this book. Donald Harper taught me to question canonical orthodoxy; Beth Harrison shared her knowledge of Mizuko Jizō; Alan Bernstein's passion for history was simply contagious, his work on hells always thought-provoking.

Several scholars have contributed to this book. Françoise Wang-Toutain of the École Française d'Extrême-Orient graciously made her manuscript on Dizang accessible to me before its publication. My study is greatly indebted to her rigorous philology and the wealth of material she amassed and examined. The reviewers for the Kuroda Institute—Robert Campany, John Kieschnick, and Kyoko Tokuno—offered indispensible feedback. Peter Gregory, editor of the Kuroda series, made astute comments on my manuscript and kindly steered me through the publication process. Stephen Teiser shared insightful remarks on sections of the manuscript during its previous "incarnations." Margaret Dornish patiently edited an early version of the manuscript. Many others, too numerous to name, have offered encouragement and corrections and thus saved me from making countless errors of fact and expression. I alone am responsible for whatever shortcomings remain.

Without assistance from Hu Wenhe (Sichuan Academy), Li Li'an

(Northwest University, Xi'an), Wang Huimin (Dunhuang Research Institute), and Zhang Naizhu (Longmen Grottoes Research Institute), I would not have been able to collect pictures of images or even given access to certain art-historical sites in China. My Dharma-sister and ex-classmate Shi Zhihui was a spiritual and intellectual companion during my field research; her eye for detail was indispensable in locating images and making out inscriptions. She tirelessly contributed all manner of support and assistance to this project from conception to completion as a book manuscript. Morgan Huang and Lü Hui-tzu good-naturedly tracked down and photocopied materials for my use on various occasions. I am also very grateful to Patricia Crosby and Keith Leber for taking the book seriously and seeing it through to publication.

I am grateful to Pomona College for providing generous funding at different stages: first in the form of a sabbatical fellowship that enabled me to complete the writing of this book in a timely manner and then a generous subvention toward its publication. Finally, I owe an enormous debt to my mother, whose life embodies an exemplary spirit of dedication and perseverance. An unfailing source of inspiration, she has sustained me throughout my years of graduate training and the completion of this book.

Abbreviations

DHBZ — *Dunhuang baozang* 敦煌寶藏

HY — *Daozang zimu yinde* 道藏子目引得 (Harvard-Yenching Index to the Daoist Canon)

P — Pelliot collection of Dunhuang manuscripts at La Bibliothèque nationale de France, Paris

S — Stein collection of Dunhuang manuscripts at The British Library, London

T — *Taishō shinshū daizōkyō* 大正新修大蔵経

XZ — *Xinbian wanzi xuzang jing* 新編卍字續藏經

ZZ — *Dainihon zokuzōkyō* 大日本続蔵経

INTRODUCTION
Problems and Perspectives

My first encounter with the Bodhisattva Dizang 地藏 (Kṣitigarbha) took place more than two decades ago at the Chinese temple of a lay Buddhist society in Singapore called the Buddhist Lodge (Jushi lin 居士林). It was the last night of the seventh lunar month of the Chinese calendar, a month traditionally consecrated to the welfare of deceased relatives, especially those reborn in the unfortunate realms of hungry ghosts and hell beings.[1] An elaborate festival brought to a close the month-long communal recitation of the *Dizang pusa benyuan jing* 地藏菩薩本願經 (Scripture on the Past Vows of Dizang Bodhisattva).[2] At the heart of this festival was a ritual dramatization of the feeding the hungry ghosts ceremony (*shishi* 施食).[3] The monk who headed the performance wore fine, colorful robes and a golden five-buddha crown to signify his sovereignty over the infernal realm. A small statue of Dizang Bodhisattva sat on the ritual table.[4] Uttering a sequence of *dhāraṇīs* and liturgical prayers, the monk sprinkled water on the

1. The thirtieth day of the seventh lunar month is celebrated as the day when Dizang Bodhisattva achieved awakening during his incarnation as the Silla monk the Golden Dizang (Jin Dizang 金地藏). Jin is said to have resided at Mount Jiuhua (Jiuhua shan 九華山), now famed as the pilgrimage site for the Bodhisattva Dizang. Throughout the seventh lunar month rituals are held at Mount Jiuhua, culminating in mass ceremonies on the last day of the month. Devotees and pilgrims flock to the mountain to participate in the final rites. Local temples and monasteries around China, as well as immigrant societies outside of the country, also observe the rituals of the seventh lunar month honoring Dizang Bodhisattva.

2. *Dizang pusa benyuan jing*, T412:13.777c–790a, attributed to Śikṣānanda (Shicha'nantuo 實叉難陀, 652–710). Today Chinese Buddhists frequently employ this scripture at Dizang ritual assemblies. However, in premodern times, a small body of Dizang liturgical works was used in conjunction with confession rites addressed to Dizang Bodhisattva. For a discussion of these premodern repentance rituals, see Wang 1999.

3. This is basically the ritual performance of an esoteric ceremony introduced in the Tang period (618–907). For studies on *shishi*, see Orzech 1994; Lye 2003. The earliest versions in the corpus of ritual texts on feeding the hungry ghosts as it exists today date to the Yuan period (1280–1368). However, the ritual can be traced to esoteric Buddhist practices of the eighth century. For a translation of the portion of the ritual that can be traced to the Tang period, see Orzech 1996; for a translation of a version dating to the Yuan, see Stevenson 2004.

4. The ritual specialist wears the red and yellow ritual robes of an abbot. On the symbolism of monastic robes, see Kieschnick 1999. At the Buddhist Lodge, a statue of Dizang is always placed on the ritual table. (However, a statue of Guanyin may also be used.) One ritualist I interviewed informed me that the statue represents the principal deity (*benzun* 本尊) for the ritual, which is determined by the choice of deity for the visualization. However, as I will clarify later, in the ritual text Guanyin is the principal deity.

ground to sanctify the ritual space then symbolically enacted the closing of the gates of hell. Engulfed in incense smoke, candlelight, and mesmerizing incantations, the room was dramatically transformed into the desolate underworld of the damned. Excitement ran through the crowd of lay participants and observers as they stood on their toes and craned their necks to catch sight of the ritualist's every hand gesture (Ch. *shouyin* 手印; Skt. *mudrā*). I heard it murmured that he was impersonating Dizang returning the spirits of the deceased to their subterranean confines after a month in the world of the living. This then was my introduction to Dizang Bodhisattva—an impressive, shaman-like figure who oversees the affairs of the dead, an afterlife deity inextricably bound to the terrifying ethos of the underworld, a symbol of light and salvation for the lost and condemned souls of the deceased.

Years later I realized that the ritual I had witnessed was a modified enactment of a long ritual text, the *Yuqie jiyao jiu Anan tuoluoni yankou guiyi jing* 瑜伽集要救阿難陀羅尼焰口軌儀經 (The Scripture from the Essentials of Yoga Teachings on the Dhāraṇī Flaming-Mouth Rites for Saving Ānanda), ascribed to the esoteric Buddhist teacher Amoghavajra (Bukong jingang 不空金剛, 705–774).[5] This eighth-century text represents an esoteric articulation of a Buddhist rite conjured up to accommodate the indigenous Chinese practice of presenting offerings to honor ancestors. It is commonly known as the liberating the flaming-mouths (*fang yankou* 放焰口), or feeding the hungry ghosts, ceremony. According to Amoghavajra's text, the purgatories are crushed, the hungry ghosts summoned, and their transgressions evaluated. Following their confession and redemption, the ghosts receive sweet nectar, and the scorching flames in their throats are quenched. In the ritual text the main deity is Guanyin 觀音 (Avalokiteśvara), not Dizang. It contains only a short segment where the ritualist, having first visualized himself as Guanyin, briefly transforms into Dizang.[6]

The theme of feeding hungry ghosts (frequently understood as ancestral ghosts) is present in Tang (618–907) and Song (960–1279) afterlife rituals like the Avalambana, or Ullambana (Yulanpen 盂蘭盆), a ceremonial offering to the monastic establishment on the behalf of one's deceased ancestors; the Daoist version of the Avalambana, the Middle Primordial (*zhongyuan* 中元) festival; and the Buddho-Daoist purgatorial rites known as Universal Salvation (*pudu* 普度).[7] In a popular temple setting like the Buddhist Lodge,

5. *Yuqie jiyao jiu Anan tuoluoni yankou guiyi jing*, T1318:21.468c–472b; cf. *Yuqie jiyao yankou shishi yi* 瑜伽集要焰口施食儀, T1320:21.473c–484a. Also see n. 3.

6. Hun Yun Lye first brought to my attention the lack of textual support for the relationship between the ritual and Dizang Bodhisattva. The visualization procedure is more clearly delineated in the *Yuqie jiyao yankou shishi yi*, where the ritualist first envisions Guanyin (T1320:21.476b–c), then, having assumed the form of Guanyin, visualizes Dizang, who has aspired to release all beings from hell (T1320:21.476c).

7. The Sanskrit word *avalambana* (*ullambana* in Pāli) literally means "hanging upside down" and is associated with a physically afflictive condition in hell. The Chinese term *yulan-*

these various rites of feeding and liberating ancestral ghosts are drawn into the final rites of *fang yankou,* over which is transposed the imagery of Dizang Bodhisattva, who is invoked especially in scriptural and liturgical recitations throughout the seventh lunar month. In temple observances of holy days, the thirtieth day of the seventh lunar month is today celebrated as Dizang Bodhisattva's birthday.[8] Lay Buddhists make monetary donations to have the names of their departed loved ones written on pieces of paper, which are then pasted on makeshift memorial tablets housed in tents erected on the temple grounds during the seventh month.[9] Upon completion of the rites on the last day of the month, the paper tablets are burned in a bonfire, and the lay sponsors return to their homes satisfied with the knowledge that they have taken care of their deceased family members.

Dizang is best known in Chinese religion today as the savior par excellence of the dead, especially of those undergoing torments in hell because of their wicked ways. In Chinese monasteries and temples, Dizang Bodhisattva is frequently enshrined separately—away from the main shrine hall—in an adjunct Merit Cloister (Gongde yuan 功德院), which houses the memorial tablets of the dead ancestors and relatives of lay patrons. Dizang is often portrayed as a crowned sovereign, wearing monastic robes and a five-petaled golden crown (see Figure 1). He is also represented as a golden-bodied monk with a shaven head dressed in somber robes, his face serene and eyes downcast in silent contemplation (see Figures 2 and 3).[10]

In both cases Dizang is usually shown holding a staff in one hand and a jewel in the other, a configuration of attributes connected to his role as "Lord

---

pen is a euphonic transliteration of the Sanskirt words and does not quite communicate the semantics of the Indian phrase. For a study in English of the Ghost Festival in medieval China, see Teiser 1988b; also see Teiser 1986. The Avalambana focuses on ceremonial offerings to the *saṅgha* after the rain retreat. Especially in China, the ceremony focuses on transferring merit to dead ancestral ghosts who can partake of food offerings as a result of merit from making offerings to the monastic community. The mythological foundation for the Ghost Festival is based on the legend of Maudgalyāyana (Ch. Mulian 目蓮; J. Mokuren), who through the Buddha's aid and by virtue of offerings made to the monastic community, saved his deceased mother from the sufferings of hell. For a translation of one Japanese version of the legend and a discussion of the Ghost Festival in Japan known as *urabon,* see Glassman 1999.

On the fifteenth day of the seventh lunar month, Daoists hold a festival similar to the Ullambana known as *zhongyuan,* designating the day on which the Middle Primordial (that is, *zhongyuan*) descends to earth to judge the deeds of the people. Offerings are made to gods and ancestors by way of the Daoist temple and its priests, and consequently hungry ghosts are able to eat their fill on this day. For a discussion of the medieval sources on the *zhongyuan* festival, see Teiser 1988b: 35–40. On Daoist purgatorial rites in connection with a twelfth-century Daoist visualization text that discusses the interrelation between Buddhist and Daoist expressions of the rites of feeding the hungry ghosts, see Boltz 1983 (esp. 508–509). For a comparative study of *fang yankou* and *pudu,* see Orzech 2002.

8. For a listing of buddha and bodhisattva birthdays, see Zhong 2000: 186.

9. This practice is commonly known as *chaodu* 超度, or "to bring [the deceased] over [to better states of rebirth]."

10. Dizang is first depicted as a monk in the *Shilun jing* 十輪經, a text discussed in Chapter 1.

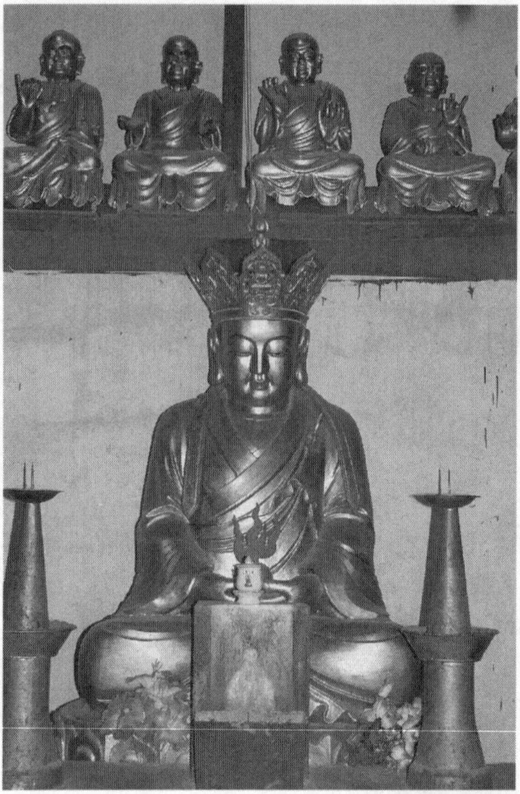

FIGURE 1. Crowned Dizang. Tiantai shan Fangguang si, Zhejiang.

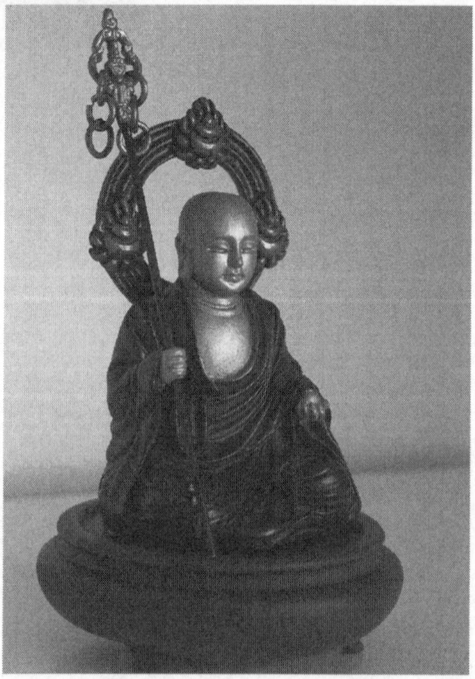

FIGURE 2. Dizang, modern statue.

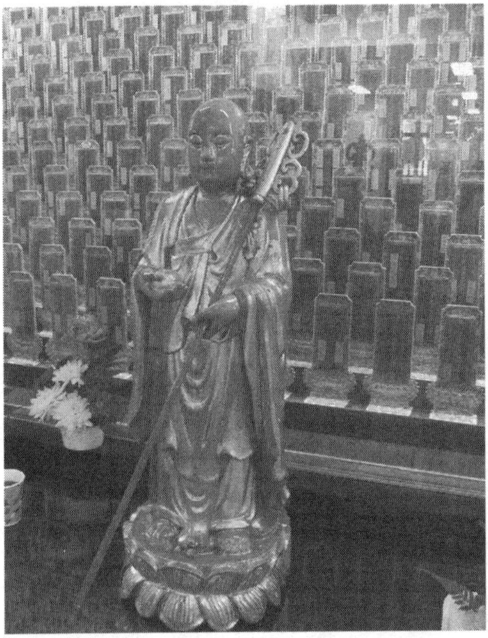

FIGURE 3. Dizang, modern statue. Buddhist Lodge Memorial Hall, Singapore.

Teacher of the Desolate Darkness" (*youming jiaozhu* 幽冥教主). Hence, the *Hymn to Dizang* (*Dizang zan* 地藏讚) states:

> His resplendent jewel illumines completely the road to heaven;
> His golden staff quakes open the gates of hell.
> He welcomes and leads inexhaustible generations of families and relatives;
> And on the bank of [the lake of] the throne of the nine [grades of] lotus,[11]
> they prostrate themselves to the compassionate lord.
>
> 明珠照徹天堂路　　金錫振開地獄門
> 累世親姻蒙接引　　九蓮臺畔禮慈尊[12]

Given Dizang's dominance in the cult of the dead in modern Chinese religion, it is only natural that participants and observers alike equate Dizang with the ritualist in his monastic robes and crown enacting the scene of closing the gates of hell. He is, in short, the sovereign of the underworld.[13]

---

11. The nine grades of lotus occur in the *Foshuo guan wuliangshou fo jing* 佛說觀無量壽佛經 (also known as the *Guan jing*), T365:12.344c–346a. The *Guan jing* enumerates sixteen visualizations that a practitioner should observe to attain rebirth in Amitābha's Pure Land in the west. In visualizations 13–16, the practitioner envisions himself being reborn on a different grade of lotus (superior, middling, or inferior of the superior grade; superior, middling, or inferior of the middling grade; superior, middling, or inferior of the inferior grade).

12. The *Hymn to Dizang* is recited during liturgies addressed to Dizang Bodhisattva.

13. In oral interviews, one ritualist at a rural temple in Xinzhu 新竹 (Taiwan), an expert in performing the *fang yankou,* informed me that it is possible to visualize Dizang or Guan-

In present-day Chinese Buddhism, Dizang is moreover known as one of the four great bodhisattvas (*si da pusa* 四大菩薩), together with Guanyin, Puxian 普賢 (Samantabhadra), and Wenshu 文殊 (Mañjuśrī). Each bodhisattva presides over one of four mountain cults, which constitute the tradition of Buddhist pilgrimages hailed as the "four famous great mountains" (*si da mingshan* 四大名山).[14] Dizang Bodhisattva reigns over the Mountain of Nine Flowers (Jiuhua shan 九華山), where he supposedly resided in the late eighth century in his earthly incarnation as a Korean prince-turned-monk known as the Golden Dizang (Ch. Jin Dizang 金地藏; Kor. Kim Chijang).[15] The pilgrimage cult of Mount Jiuhua and its mythology are today considered central to the Dizang cult.

The iconography, myths, sites, rituals, and roles associated with Dizang as they are known today developed over several centuries; they do not always render the complex and shifting vicissitudes this deity has undergone, especially during the medieval period. For instance, Mount Jiuhua emerged visibly as the *cultus locus* of Dizang devotion only in the late imperial period, long after Dizang's introduction into Chinese society no later than the sixth century.[16] It is thus important to study the emergence of the Dizang cult in its historical and social reality to recomplexify Dizang and so help to restore to life (as much as possible from the surviving fragmented historical sources) what this figure meant to Chinese Buddhists from the sixth to tenth centuries.

Unveiling the Presuppositions

Modern scholarly perceptions of Dizang Bodhisattva are shaped largely by two sets of assumptions, each linked to a methodological presupposition in the study of Chinese Buddhism. On the one hand, scholars tend to contrast the early obscurity of this bodhisattva in India, where he was known as Kṣitigarbha, with his subsequent ascendancy in China as a major Buddhist deity commanding widespread veneration. This contrast of roles in the two geographical regions leads to the assumption that a radical transformation must have taken place during the introduction of Kṣitigarbha as Dizang to China. For scholars, the radical changes that this bodhisattva seems to have undergone in China make him a natural candidate for studying patterns of sinicization in Chinese Buddhism. The history of Dizang is then a tale of how and why he fired the Chinese imagination, and the reconstruction of

---

yin as the principal deity. The choice of deity is decided by the *daochang* 道場, or ritual sanctuary, that is, the monastery or temple hosting the ritual.

14. The four pilgrimage centers are: for Guanyin, Putuo shan 普陀山 (Zhejiang); for Dizang, Jiuhua shan 九華山 (Anhui); for Puxian, Emei shan 峨嵋山 (Sichuan); for Wenshu, Wutai shan 五台山 (Shanxi). For a study of the four mountain sites in Chinese Buddhism, see Kamata 1987. The phrase "four famous great mountains" evidently was used only during the reign of the Qing emperor Kangxi 康熙 (1662–1722); see Pan 2000: 820. For further discussion on the emergence of the tradition of the four famous great mountains, see the Conclusion.

15. For studies on Mount Jiuhua, see Powell 1987, 1993; Wang-Toutain 2001.

16. See the Conclusion for further discussion on Mount Jiuhua and Dizang worship.

his cult becomes an opportunity to demonstrate the Buddhist assimilation of indigenous Chinese elements—just as scholars have shown Guanyin to be a Chinese transformation of the Indian Avalokiteśvara.[17] In other words, Dizang is regarded as the Chinese bodhisattva par excellence, and the study of Dizang is inevitably linked to the model of Buddhist sinicization that has characterized much of modern scholarship on Chinese Buddhist history.

Studies of Dizang also tend to emphasize his role as "Supreme Lord of the Underworld," the function for which he is most widely known today. Scholars have for the most part accepted this unidimensional portrayal of Dizang as true not only in the modern period, but also earlier. Consequently, the study of Dizang's history is presented largely as tracing a trajectory culminating in his consecration as the Buddhist sovereign of the underworld—a process that necessarily casts Dizang a product of folklorization or vulgarization (*minjian hua* 民間化) through which Buddhism infiltrated into the heart of everyday religion in medieval Chinese society. Viewed through this lens, Dizang has all but lost the character of a bodhisattva. Instead he has joined the complex bureaucracy of Chinese afterlife deities who maintain the records of life and death, judge the actions of the deceased, and pass sentence on their next rebirth.

Furthermore, scholars tend to synthesize the two sets of assumptions and so regard the culmination and success of the sinicization process to be the transformation of the Indian Kṣitigarbha Bodhisattva into the Chinese Dizang, Lord of the Underworld, and his penetration into the everyday religion of medieval Chinese society, which emphasizes the family structure in religion, particularly the obligations of descendants to procure salvation for deceased ancestors and relatives and to pacify those restless spirits threatening domestic bliss. In other words, Dizang, as Lord of the Underworld, is considered a paradigmatic sinicized bodhisattva. Certainly, broaching the study of Dizang through questions of sinicization and folklorization of Buddhism in China does offer salient insights into the rise of Dizang worship. But because these approaches exclude other roles Dizang may have played in medieval Chinese religion, they in fact restrict our understanding of the Dizang cult in China.

A Sinicized Bodhisattva?

First, let us examine the assumption that this bodhisattva underwent a radical transformation after his introduction to China and that he should be

17. The sinicization of the bodhisattva ideal has been discussed in past scholarship. For example, Robert Gimello (1978) examined the early medieval Chinese amalgamation of the Confucian sage and the bodhisattva ideal through figures like Vimalakīrti. Jan Yün-hua (1981) studied the sinicization of the bodhisattva in Chinese Buddhist literature through its typology and significance. Lewis Lancaster (1981) analyzed the bodhisattva doctrine as presented in the Chinese Buddhist canon. Studies have also focused on specific bodhisattvas, especially the savior bodhisattvas. A recent example (2001) is Yü Chün-fang's *Kuan-yin: The Chinese Transformation of Avalokiteśvara*. Also see Yü 1992, 1994.

regarded as a sinicized bodhisattva. When tracing his origin to pre-Chinese sources, one immediately encounters an anomaly: The earliest evidence for Kṣitigarbha in India dates no earlier than the eighth century, by which time, as documented in textual and visual materials, Dizang worship was already present in China, replete with iconography, mythology, texts, and practices. In fact, the earliest scripture on this bodhisattva is a Chinese text, the *Shilun jing* 十輪經, or the *Daśacakra-sūtra* (Scripture on the Ten Wheels), purported to be an anonymous translation from the Northern Liang (397–439) but only dated firmly to the sixth century. (See Appendix 1 for arguments on the text's dating.) In addition to the paucity of Indian sources, scholars have also called attention to the fact that, in travelogues of the sixth and seventh centuries, Chinese pilgrims make no mention of the worship of Kṣitigarbha at the Indian sites they visited.[18] In the pantheon of Indian Mahāyāna, moreover, little is known about Kṣitigarbha beyond his appearance as one of the eight bodhisattvas. Hence, scholars have concluded that Kṣitigarbha was either a minor figure or had only a nominal existence in Indian Buddhism. From this perspective, the *Scripture on the Ten Wheels* is accepted as a plausible pre-Chinese source for Kṣitigarbha that functioned as the "substratum" for the sinicization processes that produced the Bodhisattva Dizang. Another hypothesis argues that Dizang originally existed as an audience bodhisattva—that is, a bystander present at a buddha's sermon—in the long directories of bodhisattva names preserved in Mahāyāna scriptures.[19] Shortly after his introduction in China in the fourth century, Chinese Buddhists appropriated the name and fleshed out Dizang's character so that he became a major object of Buddhist worship, second in popularity only to Guanyin. The origin of the *Scripture on the Ten Wheels* remains uncertain. The Tibetan version was translated from a Chinese text, so one cannot completely rule out the possibility that this scripture was composed in China.[20] From such a perspective, Dizang is better understood as a Chinese bodhisattva who, except perhaps for his name, was engendered almost entirely in Chinese culture and society. Thus it is assumed that the character of this bodhisattva, as well as the iconography, mythology, rituals, and texts of his cult, was largely elaborated in China.

Both of these hypotheses accentuate sinicization as the process that created the Bodhisattva Dizang we know today. Yet examining Dizang through the lens of Buddhist sinicization locks us into a stalemate because his rela-

18. Both the *Datang xiyu ji* 大唐西域記, by the famous Chinese pilgrim-monk Xuanzang 玄奘 (602–664), and the *Nanhai jigui neifa zhuan* 南海寄歸內法傳, by Yijing 義淨 (634–713), contain no mention of Kṣitigarbha worship.

19. Lancaster 1981: 155–156. For a discussion of examples, see Appendix 2.

20. In Sanskrit, the title is reconstructed as **Daśacakrakṣitigarbha-sūtra*. A colophon appended to the extant Tibetan translation announces it to be based on a Chinese original. The Tibetan title is given as *Dus-pa chen-po las Sa'i snyning-po'i 'khor-lo bcu-pa zhes-bya-ba then-pa chen-po'i mdo*. The colophon mentions that the text was translated from the Chinese by Hoshang zab-mo, Rnam-par mi-tog, and others.

tionship to his Indian counterpart, Kṣitigarbha, is fraught with ambiguity (see Appendix 2). The *Śikṣāsammucaya*, attributed to the eighth-century Nalanda monk Śāntideva, cites passages from one *Aryakṣitigarbha-sūtra*, which was evidently some version of the *Scripture on the Ten Wheels*.[21] Śāntideva knew of Kṣitigarbha Bodhisattva and he explicitly invokes Kṣitigarbha as a member in the retinue of great bodhisattvas.[22] By the eighth century in India, Kṣitigarbha was incorporated into the cult of the eight great bodhisattvas (Ch. *ba da pusa* 八大菩薩; Skt. *Aṣṭamahābodhisattva*), which was in turn integrated into esoteric Buddhism. However, the paucity of dated evidence means that the process by which Kṣitigarbha became one of these eight bodhisattvas is lost to us. Some scholars suggest that this bodhisattva may have originated in Central Asia, but again the evidence is hardly conclusive. There is a dearth of datable evidence of Kṣitigarbha in Central Asia, and the earliest materials date no earlier than the eighth century.[23] The early history of Kṣitigarbha in India and Central Asia remains largely unknown to us, so the task of ascertaining what elements of the Dizang cult were originally derived from India and Central Asia is necessarily doomed from the beginning. Thus it is impossible to determine conclusively whether Dizang is a sinicized bodhisattva.

Sinicization Problematized

In addition to the problems of the evidence, there are also the methodological problems associated with studying Chinese Buddhist history through the lens of sinicization. The traditional approach to sinicization can be polarized into the "transformation" and "conquest" models, represented respectively by Erik Zürcher's *The Buddhist Conquest of China* and Kenneth Ch'en's *The Chinese Transformation of Buddhism*.[24] The conquest model argues that from the beginning of the common era, Buddhism began to infiltrate China

21. The *Aryakṣitigarbha-sūtra* is no longer extant. The Chinese text obviously predates the *Śikṣāsammucaya*.

22. Śāntideva invokes Ākāśagarbha and Kṣitigarbha, together with Samantabhadra, Mañjughoṣa, and Avalokita, as the great bodhisattvas; see *Bodhicaryāvatāra* 3.52, translated in Crosby and Skilton 1996: 18.

23. One argument for the Central Asian origin is the attribution of the *Benyuan jing* to the Khotanese monk Śikṣānanda. However, because the textual history of the *Benyuan jing* is itself problematic, it offers little confirmation of the Central Asian origin for Kṣitigarbha. See the discussion on the Central Asian sources in Appendix 1.

24. Zürcher 1972; Ch'en 1973. Several studies have examined various aspects of Chinese Buddhist history through the perspective of Buddhist sinicization in China. An early example is by Tso Sze-bong (1982), who traced the Chinese transformation of the *vinaya*. Peter Gregory (1991) investigated the sinicization of Buddhist doctrine in the major Huayan thinker Zongmi 宗密 (780–841). In a dissertation study, Kyoko Tokuno (1994) explored the patterns of sinicization that produced the indigenous Chinese scripture *Tiwei boli jing* 提謂波利經. Kuo Li-ying (1994a) discussed patterns of sinicization in Buddhist confession and contrition rites from the fifth to the tenth centuries. As mentioned earlier, Yü Chün-fang's recent study (2001) examined the transformation of Guanyin in China.

so pervasively that what was originally a foreign religion became part and parcel of Chinese culture and society. The transformation model asserts that indigenous culture and institutions so radically changed Buddhist teachings and practices in China that Chinese Buddhism must be recognized as a product of sinitic civilization. Robert Sharf has challenged both of these approaches, which, as he accurately points out, have cast the study of Chinese Buddhism permanently in the shadow of Indian Buddhism so that Chinese Buddhist expressions are always evaluated against some pristine Indian original. Sharf argues that the Buddhism medieval Chinese encountered in the translated texts was "already sinified if only by virtue of being rendered . . . into the native tongue."[25] The Chinese, moreover, "approached translations of Buddhist texts not as glosses on the Indic originals, but as valuable resources that addressed their own immediate conceptual, social, and existential concerns."[26] When Chinese Buddhism is understood in these terms, knowing the Indian antecedents proves far less urgent than knowing the questions Chinese readers of Buddhist texts were asking—"questions whose historical, linguistic, and conceptual genealogy was largely Chinese."[27]

At first glance, my study seems to adopt Sharf's perspective as its framework because it opens directly with Dizang's manifestations in Chinese contexts and explores this bodhisattva cult from the perspective of medieval Chinese culture, religion, and society. I want to clarify at the outset that this study does not share Sharf's presumptions or conclusions about the nature of Chinese Buddhism. Sharf's perspective has salient merits—not the least of which is questioning the scholarly use of Indian Buddhism as the authoritative standard for evaluating Buddhist developments in China as well as reiterating the urgency to study and contextualize Chinese Buddhism within the local social and institutional structures and what he calls the "local *episteme*."[28] Nonetheless, brought to its logical implication, Sharf's polemical arguments run the risk of implying a Chinese Buddhism that is culturally self-contained, impermeable, and relatively isolated from other Buddhist geographical regions. This is surely a problematic reductionist rendition because it belies the regular contacts and mutual influences across the land and sea routes that continued throughout the history of Chinese Buddhism, long after the initial transmission.[29] Medieval Buddhists in China for the

25. Sharf 2002a: 19.

26. Ibid.: 12.

27. Ibid.

28. Ibid.: 23.

29. On the transcultural interactions along the Silk Road and other trans-Himalayan trade routes, see Strickmann 1982. For examples of northwestern Chinese monks heading for the western regions in early medieval China and the resultant exchanges, see Du 1995: 103–113. Sharf acknowledges the routes of exchange connecting South and Central Asia to China but immediately dismisses their significance because "travel between these two regions was difficult if not impossible." Furthermore, he argues that "foreign monks with mastery over Buddhist scripture and doctrine . . . were relatively few in number, and their command of Chinese was often wanting. And while some Chinese pilgrims did successfully

most part did not see themselves as so culturally isolated that they could not comprehend Buddhism as it was understood in India, even if they were reading only Chinese translations of Indic scriptures. In fact, early Chinese Buddhists were frequently dissatisfied with translations of Buddhist texts and sought to improve translation techniques.[30] Although it is senseless to speak of an unchanging core of Buddhism perpetuated across cultural and geographical boundaries, it is equally problematic to negate the meaningful relationships and rich interchanges that existed among different Buddhist cultures and end up implying the existence of pockets of relatively isolated "Buddhisms" that were culturally severed from one another and virtually inaccessible to one another.

My investigation begins directly with Dizang's appearance in fifth-century China. However, the Indian and Central Asian evidence of Kṣitigarbha is discussed in the appendices so that meaningful connections (or their lack) can be considered in relation to the making of Dizang Bodhisattva. This structural organization is a strategy to circumvent the kind of "master narrative" Sharf critiques, which always opens the historical account of Chinese Buddhism with its Indian origins, followed by its subsequent domestication in China. On the other hand, modern scholarship has already witnessed the critical flaw of sinological readings that do not sufficiently attend to the pre-Chinese Buddhist elements and are overly quick to seize on the indigenous cultural conditionings in Chinese Buddhism. A classic example is the case of Buddhist filial piety, touted for a time as a Chinese Buddhist innovation, until Indologists called attention to antecedent practices in Indian Buddhism and shattered the myth that Buddhist filial piety was unique to China.[31] By presenting relevant Indian and Central Asian Buddhist examples in the appendices, I attempt to avoid the pitfalls of either studying Chinese Buddhism in a contextual void or overly emphasizing the role of earlier Buddhist cultures.

Although the danger of indiscriminately filtering Chinese Buddhism through Indian lenses should be acknowledged, the encounter metaphor is really problematic only when it presumes a linear one-way evolution of Bud-

---

journey to India . . . only a handful are remembered in the historical record for their contributions to the transmission of Buddhism to China" (2002a: 18). Hence he concludes, "[T]he educated Chinese elite, not to mention the unlettered masses, remained largely ignorant of the vast linguistic and conceptual divide that separated them from the world of Indian Buddhism" (ibid.: 21).

30. For a discussion in Chinese on issues in the translation of texts in early Buddhist China, see Tso 1992. Tso Sze-bong explores the extent and quality of Sanskrit language skills, the dynamics of translation teams, and the evolution of translation practices over time. For English discussions of translation activities in early Chinese Buddhism, see Boucher 1996, 1998; Zürcher 1977, 1991.

31. For classic treatments of filial piety as a patently Chinese Buddhist practice, see Ch'en 1968; 1973: 14–64; Jan 1995. Schopen (1984) and Strong (1983) countered the assumption that Buddhist filial piety was largely a sinitic development by highlighting examples of filial behavior in Indian Buddhism. On the cult of filial piety in medieval China, see Knapp 2005. On filial piety in Chinese history, mythology, and thought, see the essays in Chan and Tan 2004; Ching and Guisso 1991.

dhist history whereby Chinese Buddhist developments are always traced to some Indian original. As previous scholarship has pointed out, the medieval interaction between non-Chinese and Chinese Buddhist cultures involved movements in multiple directions that included "retroactive" influxes of artifacts, ideas, practices, and texts traveling out from China along the Silk Road.[32] One example is the *Prajñāpāramitāhṛdāya-sūtra* (*Bore poluomiduo xin jing* 般若波羅密多心經, Scripture on the Heart of the Perfection of Wisdom), which Jan Nattier has argued could have been composed in China and transmitted "back" along the Central Asian trade routes.[33] Vestiges of Chinese Buddhism were present in Turfan during the ninth century, and cave art in Khara Khoto (Heishui cheng 黑水城), dating from the eleventh century onward, further documents sinitic presences.[34] Any discussion of the Dizang cult should thus account for relevant elements in this fertile cross-cultural interchange, even while acknowledging that Dizang's mythology and individuality were largely defined in the cultural and social contexts of China. For example, Indian elaboration of Kṣitigarbha in the form of esoteric Buddhist iconography, practice, and texts made its way into China around the eighth century, after the Dizang cult had gained a firm foothold in the Chinese environment. Originating outside of China, these expressions of the bodhisattva evidently intermingled and melded with the extant art, history, mythology, ritual, and texts of the Dizang cult. Ultimately, these diverse religio-cultural

32. See Nattier 1990. Also see Du 1995: 142–150, for the impact of Northern Liang Buddhism on religion in Kharakhoja (Gaochang 高昌). Kharakhoja was the capital of the Üighurs when they moved into the Xinjiang region from Mongolia in the ninth century.

33. Nattier (1992) points out that the *Heart Scripture* gained popularity in China well before it became the subject of commentarial attention in India and that it has maintained a central role in East Asian Buddhism from the seventh century to the present. Reconstructing its textual history, Nattier argues that the *Heart Scripture* may be "a Chinese apocryphal text" composed of an extract from the *Large Sūtra* of Kumārajīva (itself a translation of the Indian *Pañcaviṃśati-prajñāpāramitā-sūtra*) together with an introduction and conclusion composed in China. According to Nattier, the scripture might have made its way back to the Sanskrit milieu through Buddhist pilgrims to the west.

34. The existence of snippets of a Üighur manuscript that contain excerpts from the *Dizang pusa benyuan jing* suggests that this scripture made its way from China to Turfan; see Zieme 1990: 379–384; facsimiles: plates I–II. Leaflets from a Tangut manuscript of the scripture were also found recently in the northern section of the Mogao 莫高 caves at Dunhuang. Maria Rudova (1993) argues that Chinese-style paintings from Khara Khoto in the State Hermitage Museum, especially those associated with the Amitābha and Guanyin cults, were executed under the influence of Chinese art of the Song period, when relations between China and the Tangut empire were at their peak. Khara Khoto (Mongolian for "Black City") was an important city of the Tanguts, a tribe of Tibetan origin whose homeland was originally in the highlands of western Sichuan. In the eleventh century the Tanguts took control of the Hexi corridor, the section of the Silk Road leading west from central China; by the 1070s, Tangut rule had extended to Dunhuang. Khara Khoto was excavated from the sands of what is now a largely uninhabited region of the Gobi by Russian expeditions led by P. K. Kozlov in 1908–1909 and 1923–1926. Among the city ruins was a large *stūpa;* its base contained a treasure trove of Buddhist sculpture, scriptures, and painted silk banners, all of which are now in the collection of the State Hermitage Museum in St. Petersburg. For a study of Khara Khoto, see Piotrovsky 1993.

strands became so tightly interwoven into the complicated fabric of the Dizang cult that they can seldom be clearly differentiated into disparate cultural threads. Hence, when references in this study are made to Indian, Central Asian, or Chinese elements, they should always be understood to be embedded in the expressions of Chinese Buddhism.

Lord of the Underworld

Dizang's connection with the infernal realm is taken so much for granted in Chinese religion today that, as we saw, the ritual participants and observers at the Buddhist Lodge simply assumed that the ritualist was enacting Dizang's descent into hell. For many Chinese, Dizang Bodhisattva holds out the promise of divine intercession for the welfare of deceased relatives and for the pacification of the dead in general. At the same time, because of Dizang's intimate association with the realm of the dead, this bodhisattva is regarded with some ambivalence. In temples, his isolation in a separate cloister reserved for the tablets of the deceased, away from the main shrine hall, spatially symbolizes the curious stigma attached to him. Despite his evident popularity, he is rarely enshrined in household altars, and lay Buddhists are hesitant when it comes to reciting the *Scripture on the Past Vows* in their homes.[35] It is feared his presence might invite into the household malignant forces causing illness, mishap, death, and ghost possessions.[36]

---

35. So dominant is the underworld Dizang in contemporary Taiwan that Buddhist leaders have taken measures to "correct" what they deem to be misconceptions about him. In an effort to reinstate his proper status as a bodhisattva, Buddhist modernist intellectuals in Taiwan have reinterpreted Dizang in terms of the this-worldly ideals of so-called Humanistic Buddhism (*renjian fojiao* 人間佛教). A prominent example is Yinshun 印順 (1906–2005), one of the foremost proponents of Humanistic Buddhism, who composed an essay titled "Dizang pusa zhi shengde ji qi famen 地藏菩薩之聖德及其法門". His writing seeks to dispel "widespread misconceptions" about Dizang and reasserts the bodhisattva's vows and altruism; see Yinshun 1989. Another example is the nun Zhengyan 證嚴 (1937–), the founder of the Buddhist Compassion Relief Meritorious Association (Fojiao Ciji gongdehui 佛教慈濟功德會), a transnational Buddhist charity organization. Under her leadership, an image of Dizang is placed together with those of Śākyamuni Buddha and Guanyin in the main shrine at Ciji's monastery, the Abode of Still Thoughts (Jingsi tang 靜思堂), located in Hualian 花蓮, eastern Taiwan. In Zhengyan's interpretation, Dizang represents the great vows of the bodhisattva mentioned in the *Scripture on the Past Vows* and is intimately related to this world; see Zhengyan 2003. Elsewhere I have argued that the appearance of the so-called Sahā Triad (*suopo sansheng* 娑婆三聖), consisting of Śākyamuni flanked by Guanyin and Dizang, in contemporary Taiwan, should be understood as furnishing appropriate visual imagery and devotional practice to embody the "this-worldliness" of Buddhist saints; see Zhiru 2000.

36. On the phenomenon of avenging ghosts in Chinese religion and society, see Feuchtwang 2003; Nickerson 1997; Poo 1998: 41–68. Vengeful spirits (*yuanhun* 冤魂), that is, the spirits of those unjustly killed who return to seek vengeance on their killers, is a pre-Buddhist Chinese concept. With the coming of Buddhism, this indigenous belief in vengeful spirits was combined with the doctrine of *karma* and retributive rebirth. Stories dealing with avenging spirits appear early in the *Soushen ji* 搜神記 composed in 335–345. For a study of the *Soushen ji*, see Dewoskin and Crump 1996. An important compilation of stories on aveng-

Uncritical acceptance of this underworld imagery on the part of modern scholarship is partially responsible for the curious paucity of research on Dizang in China. Except for Marinus Willem de Visser's now-dated survey (1914), no book-length study was undertaken until the last decade.[37] Dizang has received minimal attention from Buddhologists, even though he is an exemplar of the bodhisattva ideal, a core Buddhist doctrine. His association with the realm of the dead places Dizang, more so than the other major bodhisattvas, in an uncomfortable fuzzy zone that crosses the threshold of grassroots Chinese religion, tying him inseparably to the afterlife and the pacification of restless spirits and fiendish demons.[38]

Consequently, Buddhologists tend to relegate Dizang to the category of folk or popular religion, where Buddhism has lost its distinctive contours and exists more or less as amorphous phenomena frequently subsumed under indigenous religions.[39] They view the Dizang cult as a marginal topic—a "stepchild" of Buddhology—irrelevant to the study of "orthodox" or "mainstream" Buddhism and only pertinent to studying diffused religious culture in China. This attitude harks back to the distinction between so-called great and little traditions first proposed in 1956 by the anthropologist Robert Redfield. The great tradition is considered a construct of the elite and literate, who consciously transmitted it to their successors, whereas the little tradition is perpetuated unwittingly by the largely illiterate peasants in traditional society. This two-tier paradigm is associated with a bifurcation of culture and society and enforces a polarization of the religion of the elite versus that of the popu-

---

ing ghosts, the *Yuanhun ji* 冤魂記, is attributed to the sixth-century writer Yan Zhitui 顏之推 (531–591). For an English translation of these stories, see Cohen 1982.

37. I will return to survey trends in modern scholarship on Dizang Bodhisattva later in this chapter. In China, Dizang is the most popular Buddhist deity next to Guanyin, but he has attracted relatively few studies compared to the voluminous scholarship on the Guanyin cult. In western scholarship alone, several studies on Guanyin exist: for example, the early overview by de Mallman (1948); a close investigation of the Miao-shan legend by Dudbridge (1978); a cross-cultural study of the thousand-armed Guanyin by Chandra (1988); and the previously mentioned work by Yü (2001). Guanyin is also an exceedingly popular subject in art history; for a recent study in English, see Karetzky 2004; for a study of the water-moon Guanyin, see the unpublished dissertation by Chan (1996) and the unpublished paper by the German art historian Petra Rösch (2006). Also see Guoli gugong bowuyuan 2000 for the catalog of a special exhibition of Guanyin images held at the National Museum of Taiwan in Taipei. Several important monograph articles on Guanyin have been published: for example, Stein (1986) investigated the emergence of Guanyin as a female deity; Angela Howard (1990) studied Guanyin iconography during the Tang and Song periods; Robert Campany (1996b) translated early miracle tales on Guanyin. There also exists an overwhelming body of research on Guanyin in Chinese and Japanese that cannot be listed here.

38. To a greater or lesser extent, the major bodhisattvas perform functions connected with death and the afterlife. For example, Guanyin appears frequently as a savior in the realm of death and the afterlife. In the *Xiangshan baojuan* 香山寶卷, dated to the sixteenth century, Guanyin is led on a tour of hells. See Dudbridge 1978; Yü 2001: 320–333; Overmyer 1999: 34–47.

39. For discussions of folk religion, especially in relation to Buddhism, see Overmyer 1990; Teiser 1995, 2004. On popular religion in China, see Bell 1989; Feuchtwang 2001.

lace.[40] Scholars have repeatedly flagged this problematic bifurcation and the stereotypical characterization of religion and culture it engenders, but the rippling effects continue to be felt in the study of religion. One example is the tacit assumption that the Dizang cult is some form of "religion for the masses" and not quite on the same footing as "elite" Buddhism. This perspective overlooks the crucial fact that Dizang is a bodhisattva who has retained throughout his career obvious orthodox doctrinal overtones. Dizang thus defies any attempt to segregate elite doctrine from cultic practice; rather, he exemplifies and demonstrates continuity not only between doctrinal and devotional elements, but also between so-called elite and folk religion. Although it is true that Dizang is the focus of cultic practice, it is also the case that he draws power from his association with core doctrinal concepts of elite Buddhism. To label him univocally as either "elite" or "folk" cannot convey fully the complex dynamic in the making of the Dizang cult—or for that matter, the making of any Buddhist cult. For example, as discussed in Chapter 5 of this study, Dizang's underworld character may have initially appeared in narratives associated with Yogācāra and Avataṃsaka (Huayan 華嚴) teachings, in which the three realms of existence, including hells, are created by the mind alone.

Representing Dizang solely as an underworld sovereign reduces the complex dynamic of his cult's history to a more or less linear development of his underworld aspect. From this perspective, the rise of Dizang worship is interpreted as a folklorization of the bodhisattva ideal. But the image of Dizang as savior of the damned hardly exhausts his many functions in Chinese religion and society. In medieval religion, he was a multivalent figure situated at the nexus of religious experimentation, and the medieval cult of Dizang embodied a broad spectrum of elements extrapolated from diverse religious sources.[41]

Even in the modern period, Dizang, as savior of the damned, cannot account for the range of practices associated with his cult. The tremendous output of Buddhist literature in Taiwan today includes a series of liturgical manuals known as the *Fojing xiuchi fa* 佛經修持法 (Method of Upholding

40. Note that Redfield himself cautiously qualified his paradigm with an observation that in many traditional societies, China included, there existed overlaps and mutual exchanges between the two traditions. For application of this two-tier paradigm to Chinese religion, see Sangren 1984 and Jochim 1988. Applying the paradigm to Theravada Buddhism, Spiro (1970) distinguishes between "*kammatic* Buddhism" and "*nibbanic* Buddhism," which are then correlated to folk and elite expressions.

41. In fact, several short studies have already called attention to salient aspects of Dizang Bodhisattva apart from his underworld function: Yabuki (1927) argued for an early connection with the medieval Buddhist school Sanjie jiao; as part of his investigation of esoteric Buddhism, Osabe (1982) studied a hybrid Buddho-Daoist exorcism formula attributed to Dizang; Powell (1987, 1993) investigated the pilgrimage cult of the Golden Dizang on Mount Jiuhua; Lai (1990) and Kuo (1994b) analyzed the *Zhancha jing* 占察經 to illustrate Buddhist integration of indigenous Chinese practices; most recently, Zhiru (2001–2002, 2005) traced the medieval associations of Dizang worship with the cults of Amitābha and Maitreya.

Buddhist Scriptures), formulated for daily Buddhist practice. Volume 12 in this series focuses on the Bodhisattva Dizang.[42] The prescribed daily practice consists of a liturgical sequence commonly found in Chinese Buddhist rituals plus a two-step meditation procedure of calm and insight (Ch. *zhiguan* 止觀; Skt. *śamatha-vipaśyanā*) featuring Dizang as the object of meditation.[43] In addition, contemporary Buddhist preachers in China continue to deliver sermons on the *Zhancha shan'e yebao jing* 占察善惡業報經 (Scripture on Divining the Retribution of Skillful and Negative Actions), a sixth-century text on Dizang worship, popular divination, and *karma* composed prior to the emergence of his underworld aspect.[44] Esoteric echoes of Dizang also reverberate in religious milieux where Chinese and Tibetan Buddhism are increasingly interfused; Tibetan monks in exile, for example, preside over Dizang repentance ceremonies when addressing the needs of Taiwanese society and immigrant Chinese communities in Southeast Asia. The savior of the damned image thus obscures the multivalent character of Dizang worship.

The Study of Bodhisattva Cults

Although monographs have occasionally appeared—for instance, Marinus Willem de Visser's studies of Dizang (1914) and Ākāśagarbha (1931); Raoul Birnbaum's study of Mañjuśrī (1983); and Alan Sponberg and Helen Hardacre's edited volume on Maitreya (1988)—the investigation of bodhisattva cults and their significance in Buddhist history has been curiously marginalized in Buddhist studies and remains largely the province of art historians.[45] In recent decades, however, an exciting shift in the study of Chinese Buddhism has brought about a welcome surge of scholarly interest in Buddhist cults. Endeavoring to apply cross-disciplinary approaches, Buddhologists have increasingly engaged in dialogue with art historians and undertaken serious investigation of Buddhist art and epigraphy in their research and writing. In the subfield of Chinese Buddhism, this trend is further expedited by the growing opportunities for scholars outside of China to conduct field investigations at Chinese archaeological and cave sites. One heartening result

---

42. The volume is titled *Ruhe xiuchi Dizang jing* 如何修持地藏經; see the listing of primary sources in Works Cited. This manual invokes the *Scripture on the Past Vows of Dizang Bodhisattva*—not for its connection with the cult of the dead, but for its presentation of the bodhisattva ideal and the practice of filial piety.

43. *Ruhe xiuchi Dizang jing*, 56–60, 67–71.

44. *Zhancha shan'e yebao jing*, T839:17.901c–910c, ascribed to Putideng 菩提燈 (Bodhidīpa?). I will return to discuss this scripture in Chapter 3. A contemporary Chinese preacher, widely known as the monk elder Mengcan 夢參, delivered a sermon on the text, which has been recorded, printed, and circulated under the title *Zhancha shan'e yebao jing jiangji* 占察善惡業報經講記. One of his lectures is also printed in the form of a tract manual titled *Dizang zhancha lun xiuxing shouce* 地藏占察輪修行手冊, which comes with a packet of nineteen hexagon-shaped wheels to be used for Dizang divination.

45. Buddhist art history produces the bulk of the studies on buddha and bodhisattva cults. For early studies of Avalokiteśvara and Mañjuśrī, see de Mallmann 1948, 1964.

is a flowering of scholarship on the bodhisattva cults, many of whose histories are best documented using visual and material evidence. Yü Chün-fang's tome on Guanyin, Françoise Wang-Toutain's monograph on the Bodhisattva Dizang, and Robert Gimello's research on Mañjuśrī and Cundī (Zhunti 準提) all include investigations of visual materials.[46]

The significance of studying bodhisattva cults is perhaps best understood in light of the reasons for its relative neglect in past scholarship. One reason is the previously mentioned tendency to regard religious history as the progression of ideas and texts.[47] From this perspective, the bodhisattva is viewed largely as a doctrinal expression and the focus is on mapping typologies for its changing explications in scriptural writings and philosophical treatises.[48] This regnant tendency in older Buddhist studies scholarship also meant that the bodhisattva category attracting the most scholarly attention was the *jātaka* bodhisattva (*bensheng pusa* 本生菩薩) and the stages on the path entailed in its conceptualization.[49] The superhuman savior bodhisattva was treated only as the culmination of bodhisattva practice. Moreover, textbook accounts too often bifurcate the presentation of the bodhisattva ideal into doctrinal statements of the bodhisattva path and devotional practices pertaining to the cults of savior bodhisattvas, mistakenly engendering the impression that doctrine and devotion are mutually exclusive aspects of religion.[50] In fact, the

46. Yü 2001; Wang-Toutain 1998; Gimello 1997, 2004.

47. On the primacy of text in the study of culture and religion, see Sullivan 1990: 41–59. The necessity to integrate the study of Buddhism in China more fully within Chinese studies as a whole has been noted by several Buddhologists; see Buswell 1990: 1–3; Gregory 1999: 19–20.

48. One typology of the bodhisattva doctrine is Lewis Lancaster's fourfold stratification, enumerated as follows: (1) the *jātaka* bodhisattva, or the aspiring bodhisattva on the arduous path to buddhahood; (2) the phantasma bodhisattva, represented as a savior figure larger than life; (3) the audience bodhisattva, who graces the buddha assemblies; and (4) the living bodhisattva, who appears as an incarnation in this world. See Lancaster 1981: 153–161. To some extent, the four categories often overlap. In early medieval China, Dizang seems to have appeared first as an audience bodhisattva, who then fired the religious imagination of Chinese Buddhists so much so that he was rapidly transformed into a focus of worship, a savior bodhisattva. The *Scripture on the Past Vows* contains "flashbacks" into the past lives of this bodhisattva—that is, his career as a *jātaka* bodhisattva. Finally, the cult of the Golden Dizang at Mount Jiuhua is centered on his manifestation as an "incarnated," or living, bodhisattva, the Korean ascetic Kim Chijang.

49. For a classic example, see Jaini 1988. Drawing from different texts, Jaini pieces together a cogent presentation of Maitreya's bodhisattva path. For a survey of textual presentations on the bodhisattva doctrine, see Dayal 1970. The same can be said for most of the papers in the volume on the bodhisattva doctrine edited by Kawamura (1981).

50. The classic example is Paul Williams's (1989) excellent survey of Mahāyāna Buddhism. In Chapter 9, titled "The Path of the Bodhisattva," Williams highlights the doctrinal aspects of the bodhisattva ideal, whereas Chapter 10 is titled "Faith and Devotion: The Cults of Buddhas and Bodhisattvas." Another textbook survey of Buddhism (Harvey 1990) dedicates seven chapters to Buddhist doctrine and four chapters to Buddhist practice. The cults of Avalokiteśvara, Amitābha, and Bhaiṣajyaguru are treated in a chapter titled "Buddhist Practice: Devotion." In an essay, F. V. Tiso (1993) discusses the emergence of the bodhisattva in terms of the Mahāyānist systematized presentation of the bodhisattva path.

very phenomenon of the savior bodhisattva already implies a relationship between bodhisattva doctrine and cultic practice.[51]

In part, the marginalization of religious devotion can be traced to Protestant rhetoric that condemns "Catholic excesses" meant to satiate the ritualistic and emotional needs of the "uncritical masses" in presumed opposition to the "basic spirituality" of Protestant Christianity.[52] This disdain of devotional practice and the bifurcation of doctrine and devotion are hardly true of medieval Christianity, much less of Buddhist cultures, and western scholars have increasingly called attention to the Protestant biases in western scholarship on Buddhism.[53] David Snellgrove, for instance, has identified the problem of exaggerating the historical Buddha's humanity, cautioning that the Buddha is always "more than human" to his followers in Asia, who do not view the humanity and transcendence of the Buddha as mutually incompatible.[54] In other words, the Buddha does not fit the polarized paradigm of "human" and "divine" that underlies Christian discourse. Accordingly, scholars must exercise caution in applying to the Buddha those religious categories styled after western models of religion.

I would argue that the same should be said for the savior bodhisattvas: The tendency to separate the doctrine of the bodhisattva ideal from the devotional cult of the savior bodhisattva is misleading. Confining these cults to the overarching category of "devotionalism" as understood in modern western discourse fails to capture the complex array of religious attitudes associated with this Buddhist phenomenon or its historical significance. Interpreting the deification of the bodhisattva largely as a strategy to broaden the appeal of the bodhisattva ideal reduces the concept of the savior bodhisattva to a secondary expression.[55] Instead, the concept of the savior bodhisattva should be under-

51. Bielefeldt (2005) surveys the term "practice" (including "cultic practice") as understood by the Buddhist traditions and Buddhist studies; his observations on the nuanced (and often embedded) relationships between practice on the one hand and theory (principle) or ideal on the other are also applicable to the problem of separating the bodhisattva doctrine from the cult of the savior bodhisattva.

52. Art historians studying American Protestant art have shown that despite Protestant criticisms of icons and devotionalism, the use of religious art persisted in church and domestic settings in conjunction with worship; see Morgan 1996, 1998, 2001; Morgan and Promey 2001. Also see Finney 1999 for essays on the role of visual arts in the Calvinist tradition.

53. Anthropologists first called attention to the Protestant (and Orientalist) biases in the study of Buddhism; see Almond 1988; Gombrich and Obeyesekere 1988: 202–240. Subsequently, scholars in Buddhist studies have discussed Protestant implications in the study of Buddhism in the west: see Schopen 1991a; Lopez 1995; Strong 2004: 1–5.

54. Snellgrove 1987: 29–35. On the representation of the Buddha, particularly in the west, see Lopez 2005.

55. The demythologization of the savior buddha and bodhisattva is certainly present in Buddhist discourse, particularly in modernist Buddhist discourse that emphasizes the goal of buddhahood as a humanistic endeavor, but also in Chan Buddhist rhetoric. However, as Faure (1991, 1992) has shown, Chan Buddhists were associated with cultic practices in the mummification and veneration of awakened Chan teachers. On the ritual aspects of Chan Buddhism, see Foulk 1993; Foulk and Sharf 1993–1994. On the role of Confucian ritual and

stood as richly complex, drawing its power precisely from juxtaposing multiple strains of religious expression (art, doctrine, institution, myth, praxis, ritual) and thus rendering the bodhisattva ideal accessible to an audience of diverse backgrounds and applicable to a variety of social contexts. Rather than a "degeneration" of Buddhist doctrine into some kind of secondary religion for the gratification of the masses, the cult of the savior bodhisattva transforms the abstraction of the bodhisattva doctrine into a concrete, everyday reality—a "living presence" that believers can tangibly experience through iconography, myth, ritual, and social institutions.[56] Doctrine and devotion, transcendence and humanity, are inextricably entwined to create a potent religious expression that cannot be reduced to any single dimension of religion.

Another reason for past scholarly neglect of bodhisattva cults is also a component of the "master narrative" of the history of Chinese Buddhism to which Sharf calls attention, namely, undue fixation on lineages, schools, and sects and the persistent representation of Chinese Buddhist history in terms of their vicissitudes.[57] Sharf argues, first of all, that the boundaries were never as clear as once thought; and second, that in several cases the lineages and schools do not correlate to actual social institutions but are products of sectarian polemics and loose retrospective classifications, many of which derive from the sectarian structure of Japanese Buddhism. More often than not, bodhisattva cults are looked upon as marginal forms that evolved on the periphery of doctrinal explication, relevant only insofar as they render the teachings of a lineage or school more accessible to a larger audience. Moreover, cultic expressions often undermine the reified demarcations of lineages and schools. In fact, precisely because bodhisattva cults are prone to blur such proposed boundaries, the study of these cults should have corrective ramifications for the "old" understanding of Chinese Buddhist history. Cults better document the complex dialectics and interrelationships underscoring East Asian Buddhism than do the loose typologies traditionally deployed. For instance, as the present study shows, the medieval cult of Dizang presented an array of relationships with diverse forms of Buddhism at various junctures in its history. In the eighth and ninth centuries, the Dizang cult appears to have possessed simultaneous alliances with Teaching of Three Levels (Sanjie jiao 三階教) and Pure Land (Jingtu 淨土), although polemical literature pits these two schools as rivals with clearly demarcated objects of worship and practices.[58] Buddhist cults thus provide material evidence for Sharf's argument that lineages, schools, and traditions did not exist as discrete entities. However, one must be careful not to overstate the case and deconstruct the lineages in China altogether. They did exist insofar as they represented accepted doctrinal or soteriological distinctions for particular

ancestor worship in Chan Buddhism, see Jorgensen 1987. For the veneration of images in modernist expressions of Taiwanese Buddhism, see Zhiru 2000.

56. See Campany 1993b.

57. Sharf 2002a: 7–8.

58. See Zhiru 2001–2002: 80–85.

groups of Buddhists in China (especially after the Song period), even if they did not always correlate with institutional or social realities.

The Study of Dizang Bodhisattva

Until the late 1990s, Japanese scholars produced the bulk of scholarship on Dizang Bodhisattva. In his manifestation as Jizō 地藏, Dizang pervades Japanese society to such an extent that his fame surpasses that of Guanyin, known as Kannon in Japan, who is usually the more popular of the two in East Asia. From the late Heian period (898–1185), Jizō worship increasingly permeated Japanese culture and society, generating a broad range of Jizō manifestations endowed with specific names and sometimes peculiar iconographies. Hence, the religious landscape of Japan is dotted with shrines and temples dedicated to Anzan Jizō 安産地蔵 ("Easy Birth" Jizō), Hara-obi Jizō 腹帯地蔵 ("Belly-girdle" Jizō), Enmei Jizō 延命地蔵 ("Life Prolonging" Jizō), Indō Jizō 引導地蔵 (Jizō Who Guides [the Deceased to Their Afterlife Destinations]), and Roku Jizō 六地蔵 (Six Jizōs), to name just a few.[59] Although Dizang iconography in medieval China was wide-ranging—sometimes he appears as a monk, a sovereign, or even a royal householder—medieval Japanese exhibited an early preference for Jizō the monk, who over time became Jizō the novice. In a sense, Jizō in Japan was deliberately downscaled from the remote, otherworldly bodhisattva to the friendly, approachable little monk whom one could expect to run into on the next street corner.[60] Given the preeminence of Jizō in Japanese culture, religion, and society, it is not surprising that Japanese scholars should be fascinated with this bodhisattva and should have produced a wealth of excellent research on him.[61] This large corpus of scholarship, however, is interested in the Chinese development only insofar as it relates to the origins of the Jizō cult. Given that the Japanese Jizō and the Chinese Dizang are in many respects quite different, this tendency frequently alters the Japanese presentation of the Chinese historical reality. An important exception is the pioneering scholarship Japanese have produced on Dunhuang art that includes studies of Dizang iconography, notably the seminal contributions of Matsumoto Eiichi (1933, 1937).

Although there has been a lack of scholarship on Dizang Bodhisattva in China, the past decade has witnessed a welcome shift in scholarly interest that reflects a heightened awareness of the significance of this bodhisattva in Chinese religion. Besides a multiplying collection of articles, mostly on Dizang art in China, four book-length publications have appeared: (1) Françoise Wang-Toutain's *Le Bodhisattva Kṣitigarbha en Chine du Ve au XIIe siècle*; (2) Pan Liangwen's 潘亮文 *Zhongguo Dizang pusa xiang chutan* 中國地藏菩薩像初探; (3) Zhuang Mingxing's 莊明興 *Zhongguo zhonggu de Dizang xinyang* 中國中古的地

59. For studies on Jizō in Japan, see Fuji 1974; Hayami 1975; Ishikawa 1995; Tanaka 1989.
60. Lafleur 1992: 47.
61. See Manabe 1960; Sakurai 1983; Mochizuki 1989; Ishikawa 1995.

藏信仰; and (4) Zhang Zong's 張總 *Dizang xinyang yanjiu* 地藏信仰研究.[62] Although these studies on Dizang were all published within a five-year period, they were apparently conducted independently and in relative isolation—with the exception of Zhang's study, which does cite the other Chinese works.

Trained as an art historian, Pan Liangwen has collected the visual evidence and produced a slim volume surveying Dizang art and inscriptions in China. Zhuang Mingxing's publication, based on his M.A. thesis, discusses a range of materials that are often treated more substantively in the other publications. Zhang Zong, a mainland Chinese scholar, exhibits a superb mastery of the archaeological and art-historical materials, and he provides an exhaustive survey of Dizang sculpture, paintings, and cave art in China and Central Asia. His contribution is especially important for its inclusion of recent archaeological findings that have not been published outside of China. In addition, his survey of texts includes a section in which he discusses the *Dizang baojuan* 地藏寶卷 (Precious Scrolls on Dizang), a relatively unstudied collection of literature especially crucial for exploring Dizang in late imperial China.[63] Of the studies on Dizang, Zhang's work is the most ambitious in scope—not only in terms of geography and chronology, but also in the staggering wealth of literary and visual sources he has assembled.[64]

The French scholar Françoise Wang-Toutain traces the development of Dizang Bodhisattva up to the twelfth century. Possessing an excellent command of Buddhist art, philology, and history, she analyzes a substantial corpus of canonical and noncanonical literature, the bulk of which is scriptural. A major contribution is her extensive cross-comparison of Dunhuang manuscripts, which sheds light on the complicated and often ambiguous histories of Dizang texts. Her cataloging of Dunhuang manuscript copies of scriptures on Dizang will remain an immensely valuable resource for all subsequent studies. Wang-Toutain's monograph is divided into four sections: texts (scriptures), personality, cult, and iconography. The chapter on Dizang iconography is based largely on Dunhuang art, although examples from other regions are included where relevant. For Wang-Toutain, Dizang iconography is chiefly used as collaborative evidence for the conclusions she has already

62. Art historians, mostly from China but also from Taiwan, have increasingly studied Dizang art, particularly from Chinese Buddhist cave sites. Meriting special mention is an essay by Paul Katz (2003), who offers an anthropological study of the growth of the Dizang temple (Dizang an 地藏庵) in Taiwan during the period of Japanese occupation. His study is largely a statistical investigation that focuses on economic and political conditions shaping the local development of the Dizang temple and does not treat Dizang Bodhisattva or the religious practices in any significant manner. But its focus on the modern period takes Dizang study in a new direction.

63. The literary genre *baojuan*, or "precious scrolls," is relatively less studied in western scholarship. For an important volume on the precious scrolls in the sixteenth and seventeenth centuries, see Overmyer 1999.

64. Although his principal focus is China, Zhang also surveys historical evidence from Central Asia, Korea, Japan, Vietnam, and Tibet. His work thus serves as an invaluable guide to the resources for studying Dizang Bodhisattva.

reached in her textual analysis.[65] Although the monograph is not organized chronologically, her solid investigation does map a more or less linear trajectory whereby venerating Dizang originates in the cult of eight bodhisattvas in Central Asia and culminates in its Chinese underworld expression. One can thus isolate three phases in her mapping of Dizang's history. The first phase is a connection with the concept of the decline of Buddhism, apparent in the *Scripture on the Ten Wheels*, which she traces to Central Asia through scriptures ascribed to the translator Narendrayaśa (Naliantiyeshe 那連提耶舍, 517–589). The second phase is the dissemination of Dizang worship in the seventh century due to Sanjie jiao's promotion of the *Scripture on the Ten Wheels* and the teaching of the Final Dharma. The third phase is the ascendancy of Dizang worship after Sanjie jiao's disappearance from the religious scene in the ninth century, at which time the Dizang cult increasingly blended with other cults, notably those of Amitābha and Guanyin. Within this context, Dizang steadily emerged as *the* Buddhist savior of the damned, superceding claims to this role by other bodhisattvas, including the popular Guanyin Bodhisattva. It is telling that the chapters in which Wang-Toutain discusses Dizang's personality and cult focus largely on his underworld role. Although I hesitate to oversimplify what is an exceedingly rich investigation of complex developments surrounding the three phases of Dizang's history, Wang-Toutain's study clearly assumes that the development of Dizang was a steady folklorization resulting in his role as savior of the damned.

Why this sudden scholarly interest in the Dizang cult? Given the considerably smaller corpus of writings on Dizang relative to those on other major bodhisattvas, archaeological and art-historical findings have been especially instrumental in illuminating neglected aspects of his cult and expanding our understanding of Dizang's history. Although the potential of Dunhuang art and texts in this regard has been acknowledged for some time, the wealth of evidence found at other Buddhist sites has been relatively unstudied until recently. The art at these sites turns out to reveal fascinating and rarely recorded manifestations of Dizang worship. For instance, I have shown elsewhere that art and epigraphy at Sichuan and Dragon Gate (Longmen 龍門) indicate Dizang's link to the Amitābha Pure Land, while Shaanxi iconography hints at a plausible connection to the Maitreya cult.[66] As an object of study, Dizang worship constitutes a window for glimpsing the interrelationships between divergent religious expressions, otherwise mistakenly regarded as discrete and separate strands. Hence, the study of Dizang potentially has larger implications for the study of Chinese Buddhist history.

Because modern scholarship analyzes Dizang Bodhisattva largely from the *single* perspective of his popularized role as savior of the damned, it achieves only a *partial* reconstruction of the medieval Dizang cult.[67] The need for a study

65. Wang-Toutain 1998: 259.

66. Zhiru 2000–2001; 2005.

67. Wang-Toutain introduces her study as an investigation of the Bodhisattva Dizang as the "Teacher of the Desolate and Dark [Region]"—or, in other words, the savior of the damned (1998: 5–7).

of Dizang in medieval China that explicitly addresses the implications of the richly varied expressions of Dizang worship and so reconsiders its role in Chinese Buddhism is thus imperative. The Dizang cult intersected not just with different forms of indigenous religion (religious Daoism, Confucianism, Chinese divinatory and shamanic practices), but also with diversified strands of Chinese Buddhism (esoteric Buddhism, Maitreya mythology, Pure Land, Sanjie jiao). The process of cross-cultural assimilation that the Dizang cult embodies was frequently punctuated by tension and conflict. Against this complicated religious background, the image of Dizang as Lord of the Underworld came to the forefront in the late eighth or early ninth century. Yet this aspect never completely subsumed the others, which persisted into the tenth century and after.

Methods and Sources

Whereas historical documentation is scarce in India, scholars of Chinese Buddhism are fortunate to have at their disposal an abundance of historical records, ranging from catalogues to Buddhist historical writings. Risking an overgeneralization, one may say a preoccupation with historical documentation has always been an outstanding feature of Chinese culture. Nonetheless, the substantive corpus of literary materials is a mixed blessing, for it quite frequently conceals as much as it reveals.[68] The majority of surviving written records in the various archives of the Chinese Buddhist canon were composed by elite clerics, who defined "normative" or "mainstream" Buddhism and oversaw its transmission. These "official" historical records should thus be perused with caution, and the task of the modern historian is much like that of an archaeologist, excavating the embedded layers of discourse with an eye to extricating silenced or misrepresented elements. The scholar must endeavor to explore variant expressions that unfolded outside the "orthodoxy" articulated in the transmitted archives of canonical works.[69]

In this regard, the recent flowering of activities and studies based on archaeological and art-historical material is a boon to the study of Chinese Buddhist history. The recovery of Dunhuang archival manuscripts and art has already taught us that what we know about Chinese religious history is precious little in the face of what we do not know. It is not an overstatement to say that scholarly understanding of Chinese Buddhist history has drastically changed since the landmark discovery of the hidden archival chamber

68. As Erik Zürcher put it, "Our view of Chinese Buddhism as a historical phenomenon is greatly *obscured* by the abundance of our source materials" (1982b: 161).

69. Erik Zürcher also highlighted this point when he cautioned that "the Buddhist Canon is the final product of many centuries of clerical censorship" after "a constant process of expurgation (or even wholesale destruction) of . . . 'heretical' texts" (1982a: 168). As a corrective, Zürcher emphasized the need to investigate Chinese Buddhism in relation to indigenous religion particularly through the study of what he calls "Chinese apocryphal literature." For a discussion on the polemical intentions that underscored and critically shaped the articulation of "normative" stances in Chinese Buddhist history, see Sharf 2002a: 12–13.

in Dunhuang's Mogao grotto 16 alone. For instance, our views of Sanjie jiao would still be confined to the glimpses available through polemical Buddhist literature if the Dunhuang manuscripts had not yielded a stack of Sanjie jiao writings. A recently discovered cave in Shaanxi where Sanjie jiao texts are inscribed on the walls promises to shed crucial light on the practices of that movement.[70] Although we may not chance on another cache of manuscripts, scholars can look to the steady stream of reports on archaeological and art-historical findings from elsewhere in China that are regularly published by the regional academies. The numerous Buddhist sites that house enormous collections of iconography and epigraphy furnish a wealth of data that can expand, or even revise, our perception of Chinese Buddhist history. As material embodiments of religion, archaeological and visual artifacts encapsulate actual religious practices in ways that written texts rarely do and frequently elucidate patterns of religion apart from the "orthodoxy" preserved in the received archives of transmitted writings.

Accordingly, the principal thrust of my study of Dizang is to use extracanonical and visual materials to recover relatively neglected aspects of the cult's history. This reconstruction is based on a close analysis of three categories of evidence:

1. Scriptures are undoubtedly a "staple" item in the study of religion. In my study, however, I have broadened the scope of "scripture" to include extracanonical as well as canonical texts. Especially central to this project is a genre of para- or noncanonical texts referred to as "indigenous scriptures." The majority of texts about Dizang Bodhisattva, according to scholarly consensus, were composed in China. Particularly important are those scriptures recovered in the twentieth century from Chinese archaeological sites and from the archives of Japanese monasteries. Fortunately, some of these manuscripts are now published and accessible in modern editions.[71] One key text is the *Dizang pusa jing* 地藏菩薩經 (Scripture on the Bodhisattva Dizang). Another important but less studied scripture is the *Dizang dadao xin quce fa* 埊[illegible]大道心驅策法 (The Exorcism Method of Dizang's Aspiration Toward Great Awakening).[72]
2. As mentioned previously, Buddhologists have only recently paid attention to art and epigraphy. An important source of Buddhist art is

70. The cave is located at Jinchuan wan 金川灣 in Chunhua 淳化, Shaanxi, and is discussed in Chapter 2. For a preliminary investigation of the cave and its contents, see Zhang and Wang 2003.

71. Many of the texts recovered from Japanese monastery archives have been printed in modern editions of the Chinese Buddhist canon: the *Dainihon zokuzōkyō* 大日本続蔵経 and the *Taishō shinshū daizōkyō* 大正新修大蔵経.

72. The *Dizang dadao xin quce fa* has often escaped the attention of Dizang specialists because the text uses deviant characters for the name of Dizang invented during Empress Wu's 武 rule (r. 684–704).

Dunhuang, which has yielded a sizeable collection of art pertaining to the underworld Dizang. For a more comprehensive understanding of the forms of Dizang worship, however, other art-historical sites must also be studied. For example, Longmen is important as a site housing the earliest Dizang art, while Shaanxi has yielded evidence of early visualizations of Dizang in connection to the *Scripture on the Ten Wheels* and possibly the medieval Buddhist movement Sanjie jiao. The art and epigraphy at Sichuan, a region that has attracted considerable attention from art historians in recent decades, conveys the broadest range of Dizang worship, some examples of which are exceptionally significant because they embody religious strains documented in neither Dunhuang art nor textual sources.

3. The genre of popular narratives known as miracle tales, both Buddhist and non-Buddhist, allows us to reconstruct medieval attitudes toward Dizang in the larger religious milieu. In this regard, the non-Buddhist miracle tales are especially valuable because they reflect both a religious sensibility common across different segments of society and a diverse array of religious elements associated with Dizang worship. Especially important among the Buddhist collections of narratives is the canonical tenth-century compilation of Dizang miracle tales titled *Dizang pusa xiang lingyan ji* 地藏菩薩像靈驗記 (A Record of Numinous Verifications of Images of Dizang Bodhisattva; henceforth, A Record of Numinous Verifications), completed in 989 by a member of the clerical elite.[73] Compilations of miracle tales play a unique role in the religious canon by functioning as sub-texts articulating—albeit in an edited and domesticated form—the beliefs and practices of the larger populace as they existed alongside the dominant traditions of elite orthodoxy.

Although these three genres of evidence are by no means exhaustive, they do constitute the major sources for the study of Dizang Bodhisattva in medieval China. Other sources of documentation, such as liturgical works and gazetteer records, are also mentioned when relevant. Although the present study adopts a historical framework as the main organizational principle, my approach is essentially interdisciplinary and explores the topic from as many perspectives as the scope of examined evidence allows.

Organization and Terminology

This study is divided into two parts and a concluding chapter. Part 1 introduces and analyzes the early manifestations of Dizang in China from the sixth to eighth centuries based on the early scriptural representations of Dizang in the *Scripture on the Ten Wheels* and the *Xumizang fen* 須彌藏分 (Section

73. The English translation of the title is derived from Teiser 1994: 43.

on the Sumeru Treasury). The *Scripture on the Ten Wheels* inspired the basis for early cultic beginnings, including links to Sanjie jiao. In this early phase of the Dizang cult, the Chinese religious imagination was already at work crafting the identity and history of the bodhisattva, particularly in response to the socio-political conditions of fifth- and sixth-century China. The *Scripture on the Ten Wheels* inspired innovative visual imagery, including the Shaanxi representation of Dizang as a buddha surrounded by the six paths of rebirth. Part 2 explores new directions in Dizang worship from the sixth to the tenth centuries, arguing that the array of Dizang images places him at the interstices of multiple religious trends during that period. Three categories of sources (scriptural writings, art and epigraphy, narrative literature) are investigated. Scrutiny of the evidence reveals that Dizang's history was hardly a straightforward evolution of his underworld function. Although this function was growing more visible, it remained one of several—a testament to the vibrant diversity and rich complexity of Dizang cults. The Conclusion critically reexamines Dizang's role as Lord of the Underworld and affirms that Dizang was connected to several afterlife cults—not just that of the underworld. In addition, Dizang formed important alliances with other religious expressions that did not fall under the rubric of afterlife practice, which suggests that Dizang may have had a larger role in the medieval history of Chinese Buddhism.

Before embarking on the study proper, a few clarifications concerning terms and concepts used in this study are in order. First among these is the potentially problematic designation "medieval China." The phrase is employed simply as a term of convenience to avoid cumbersome repetitions of centuries or dynasties and should not be taken too literally.[74] It does not intend any stance concerning the thorny issue of when the medieval period ended and the premodern, early modern, or late imperial periods began in China. Also, as may by now be clear, Dizang and Kṣitigarbha are alternative names for the same bodhisattva: The former name is used in the Chinese context; its Sanskrit counterpart is used with reference to Indian and Central Asian contexts.

The chronological overlap of Part 1 (from the sixth to eighth centuries) and Part 2 (from the sixth to tenth centuries) also requires some explanation. Historical studies of religion tend to oversimplify the dynamic complexity of actual historical circumstances by presenting religious phenomena in a sequence of successive developments. A linear chronology does not do justice to the fact that older and innovative religious trends frequently share the same time and space. The arrangement of Parts 1 and 2 is thus intended to acknowledge the temporal overlap between the early expressions of Dizang worship, centered on the *Scripture on the Ten Wheels,* and their eventual extension.

74. The term is not intended to reflect a kind of teleological view of history—that is, history "on the way to" some destined "modernity." Nor is it intended to imply a western model that conceives of "medieval" as "postclassical" and "prerenaissance."

PART 1

Early Images

The Bodhisattva of This Defiled World

CHAPTER 1
Early Scriptural Representations
Texts and Contexts

IMAGINE BEING TRANSPORTED across vast expanses of time to early medieval China. What would be one's initial impressions of the Bodhisattva Dizang? Literary sources suggest that Dizang first appeared in China sometime in the late fourth or early fifth century, first as an audience bodhisattva—that is, a member of the entourage gracing the Buddha's assemblies in the scriptures.[1] One also finds examples of Dizang's appearance as an interlocutor posing questions to the person preaching a scripture.[2] However, in these passing references, Dizang exists only in name and no significant information is disclosed about him. The first substantive glimpses of Dizang should thus be traced to the images in the *Scripture on the Ten Wheels* and the *Section on the Sumeru Treasury*, both of which can be firmly dated to the second half of the sixth century.[3]

The *Scripture on the Ten Wheels* sets forth the foundational mythology and iconography for Dizang Bodhisattva and remains today one of the core scriptures for the Dizang cult. The *Section on the Sumeru Treasury* contains further glimpses of Dizang that resonated with the representation in the *Scripture on the Ten Wheels.* The two texts share a set of common themes that at first may not seem connected to Dizang Bodhisattva but, on close scrutiny, turn out to be crucial indicators of how Dizang worship initially gained a foothold in the religious and socio-political environment of the sixth century.

The *Scripture on the Ten Wheels*

This scripture exists in two versions. The earlier version is titled *Da fangguang shilun jing* 大方廣十輪經 (The Great Extended Scripture on the Ten Wheels), which traditional Buddhist scholarship characterizes as an anonymous Northern Liang translation. However, an investigation of the catalogs of Buddhist scriptures reveals that this title was first assigned to the Northern Liang period only toward the end of the sixth century. Further examina-

1. For examples of Dizang as an audience bodhisattva, see Appendix 2.

2. The *Vajrasamādhi-sūtra,* or *Jingang sanmei jing* 金剛三昧經 (T273), dated to the Northern Liang, is cited as an early example of Dizang in the interlocuter's role. However, Robert Buswell (1989) has argued that this text is more likely a seventh-century Korean composition that was retroactively ascribed Chinese authorship and reintroduced to China.

3. For the problem inherent in the traditional dating of the *Scripture on the Ten Wheels,* see Appendix 1.

tion of Sanjie jiao's use of the scripture confirms that this version of the *Scripture on the Ten Wheels* was known to north central Chinese no later than the early part of the second half of the sixth century. The second version, titled *Dasheng daji Dizang shilun jing* 大乘大集地藏十輪經 (The Scripture on Dizang and the Ten Wheels in the Great Mahāyāna Compendium), is a revised translation attributed to the famous pilgrim and translator monk Xuanzang 玄奘 (600–664). Broadly speaking, because the two versions are sufficiently similar in content, my analysis is based largely on the *Da fangguang shilun jing*; however, the *Dasheng daji Dizang shilun jing* is also discussed when relevant. Thematically, the *Scripture on the Ten Wheels* can be divided into two parts: the preface (Chapters 1–2 in the anonymous edition; Chapter 1 in the Tang edition), which introduces and eulogizes Dizang Bodhisattva, and the remaining core of the text (Chapters 3–15 in the anonymous edition; Chapters 2–8 in the Tang edition), which elucidates the teaching of the Ten Wheels.

The preface to the *Scripture on the Ten Wheels* serves as the chief source of information on the Bodhisattva Dizang. The scripture was preached on Mount Khalatika (Kharostha?), and it was said to have taken place after a discourse on the *Candragarbha-sūtra*.[4] Dizang comes with his retinue from the south, his arrival accompanied by a dazzling spectacle of wondrous rain, sounds, and lights.[5] The members of the audience find themselves miraculously adorned, each hand grasping a luminous wish-granting jewel (Ch. *ruyi zhu* 如意珠; Skt. *cintāmaṇi*) that emits rays of light illuminating various buddha-lands, and accompanied by miracles of healing, allayed suffering, and so forth.[6] (This scene may have inspired the wish-granting jewel in Dizang's iconography.)[7] The text introduces Dizang as a *śramaṇa* (*shamen* 沙門) or *śrāvaka* (*shengwen* 聲聞), an image of the bodhisattva that would later flourish in East Asian art.[8] The *Scripture on the Ten Wheels* further points out that for countless aeons Dizang has been liberating living beings in the "vile age of the five turbulences" (*wuzhuo eshi* 五濁惡世).[9]

---

4. *Da fangguang shilun jing*, T410:13.681a; cf. *Dasheng daji Dizang shilun jing*, T411:13.721a. It is odd that a specific reference is made in one scripture to the preaching of another. Did the author of the *Scripture on the Ten Wheels* feel the need to authenticate his composition by referencing another extant scripture? As I will show later in this chapter, the *Scripture on the Ten Wheels* reflects concerns similar to those found in other scriptures, including the *Candragarbha-sūtra*, which is also associated with the Central Asian monk Narendrayaśas. Also see Appendix 2.

5. *Da fangguang shilun jing*, T410:13.681a–b; cf. *Dasheng daji Dizang shilun jing*, T411:13.723b.

6. *Da fangguang shilun jing*, T410:13.681a–b; cf. *Dasheng daji Dizang shilun jing*, T411:13.721a–b.

7. As discussed in Chapter 4, the earliest extant Dizang art is found at Longmen and dates to the second half of the seventh century. The wish-granting jewel already appears in this early phase of Dizang art, and it remains typical of Dizang iconography to this day. Usually the bodhisattva is shown with a jewel in one hand, but some representations (for example, at Sichuan) depict him with a jewel in each hand.

8. The *Da fangguang shilun jing* states that Dizang appears as a *śramaṇa* (T410:13.681c); in the *Dasheng daji Dizang shilun jing* he is depicted as a *śrāvaka* (T411:13.721c).

9. *Da fangguang shilun jing*, T410:13.681c; cf. mention of the "buddha-less world" 無佛世界 in the *Dasheng daji Dizang shilun jing*, T411:13.721c. The five turbulences are: (1) *jiezhuo* 劫濁

Except for a few distinctive attributes, this portrayal of Dizang is derived mostly from stock descriptions of the bodhisattva ideal in early Mahāyāna literature. The text strings together a protracted list of analogies in praise of Dizang's salvific abilities:

> He is just like a wish-fulfilling pearl that satiates all of one's desires . . . the great earth that can produce good roots. . . . He is the sun or the moon that illuminates the path. . . . He is the source of the field of great merits. . . . He cures all maladies like a wondrous medicine king. . . . For the fearful he is the great relative or friend, warding off all foes and enemies like a solid city moat. He is able to quench one's thirst like cool purified water, relieve all hunger and starvation like sweet fruits, and is also the best garment for the naked.[10]

Because of his inconceivable merits, Dizang has mastered a range of *samādhi*: At each dawn, he enters into different forms of meditative concentration to assist living beings in an array of buddha-lands.[11] As with other great bodhisattvas, the intonation of Dizang's name will bring numinous efficacies when encountering hardship (starvation, thirst, etc.), perils (attacks by venomous snakes or insects, spirit possession, etc.), or calamities (fire, floods, etc.).[12] And like other savior bodhisattvas, Dizang is able to assume any one of a number of forms, beginning with the gods (from Brahmā down to the Four Lokapalas) and the Buddhist saints, continuing through the human hierarchy to demigods or demons, and entering the realm of animals and finally the underworld bureaucracy.[13] In short, Dizang is cast as the paradigmatic savior, and the merit of making offerings to him far exceeds that of making offerings to other great bodhisattvas like Avalokiteśvara, Maitreya, Mañjuśrī, and Samantabhadra.[14] This allusion to other great bodhisattvas suggests that Dizang was a latecomer to the Mahāyāna pantheon, probably appearing after the others were introduced to China.

The text then tells us that the teaching disseminated by the various emanations of Dizang is the Three Vehicles (Ch. *sansheng* 三乘; Skt. *Triyāna*). As

(kalpakaṣāya), the turbulent aeon when wars, natural disasters, famines, and pestilences occur; (2) *jianzhuo* 見濁 *(dṛṣṭikaṣāya),* the turbulence of viewpoints, when confused and deluded concepts prevail; (3) *fannaozhuo* 煩惱濁 *(kleśakaṣāya),* the turbulence of mental defilements due to greed, hatred, and ignorance; (4) *zhongshengzhuo* 眾生濁 *(sattvakaṣāya),* the turbulence of living beings, when the body is wracked with misery, the mind is weak, and one is plagued with infirmities; and (5) *mingzhuo* 命濁 *(āyuṣkaṣāya),* the turbulence of life span, when it diminishes to ten years.

10. *Da fangguang shilun jing,* T410:13.681c–682a.

11. *Da fangguang shilun jing,* T410:13.683a–684a; *Dasheng daji Dizang shilun jing,* T411:13.723b–724b.

12. *Da fangguang shilun jing,* T410:13.684c17–685b; *Dasheng daji Dizang shilun jing,* T411:13.724b–725c.

13. *Da fangguang shilun jing,* T410:13.684a–c; *Dasheng daji Dizang shilun jing,* T411:13.725c–726a.

14. *Da fangguang shilun jing,* T410:13.685a; *Dasheng daji Dizang shilun jing,* T411.13.726a.

defined in the *Saddharmapuṇḍarīka-sūtra* (*Miaofa lianhua jing* 妙法蓮華經, Scripture on the Lotus of the Wondrous Dharma), the Three Vehicles refer to the teachings shared by *śrāvakas*, solitary buddhas (Ch. *bizhifo* 辟支佛; Skt. *pratyekabuddhas*), and bodhisattvas—as opposed to the Great Vehicle (Ch. *dasheng* 大乘; Skt. *Mahāyāna*) or One Vehicle (Ch. *yisheng* 一乘; Skt. *Ekayāna*), that is, the teachings exclusive to the bodhisattva. Unfortunately, the *Scripture on the Ten Wheels* does not elaborate on the significance of its association with the Three Vehicles. An apparent link is Dizang's manifestation as a monk in the *Scripture on the Ten Wheels*, which certainly aligns him with the *śrāvaka* ideal at the heart of the Three Vehicles teachings, and perhaps with a phase of Mahāyāna development when the *śrāvaka* and bodhisattva are not regarded as contrary goals.[15] Research on Indian Buddhist history has established that Mahāyāna most probably originated in monastic communities that elaborated and promoted the ideals of the monastic and lay bodhisattva.[16] However, the ambiguous origin of the *Scripture on the Ten Wheels* makes it difficult to make any conclusive connection in this respect.

Finally, the *Scripture on the Ten Wheels* ascribes a *dhāraṇī* to Dizang:

Da fangguang shilun jing (T410)	*Dasheng daji Dizang shilun jing* (T411)
In the past, at the abodes of buddhas [numerous as] the grains of sand in the Ganges [River], I received from all and practiced a *dhāraṇī* like this: It can increase and [cause to] grow pure, white, and complete *dharmas*.	In the past, at the abodes of buddhas [numerous as] the grains of sand in the Ganges [River], I personally received and practiced this *dhāraṇī* that can [cause to] increase and grow all white *dharmas*.

15. Scriptures like the *Vimalakīrtinirdeśa-sūtra* tend to polarize the *śrāvaka* and bodhisattva ideals, arguing that the bodhisattva is far superior to the *śrāvaka*. However, recent scholarship has shown that this polarized representation is not characteristic of all early Mahāyāna texts. As mentioned above, the *Saddharmapuṇḍarīka-sūtra* espouses a more reconciliatory view. Another scripture in this vein is the *Ugraparipṛcchā*; see Nattier 2003a: 73–102. Also see Harrison 1987.

16. Akira Hirakawa (1963) has argued that early Mahāyāna arose in connection with *stūpa* worship inspired by lay participation in Buddhist cultivation and salvation. Within this framework, the bodhisattva doctrine was intended to replace the monastic renunciant ideal of early Buddhism. Studying Indian Buddhism, especially through epigraphy, Gregory Schopen refutes the basic assumption underlying Hirakawa's interpretation of the origin of Mahāyāna; instead Schopen argues that the *stūpa* cult did not originate in lay movements but had strong associations with the monastic communities (see Schopen 1985, 1989, 1991b). Moreover, Schopen has further challenged the proposition that the *stūpa* cult was integral to Mahāyāna development, proposing a link, instead, to the cult of the book; see Schopen 1975. In a similar vein, recent scholarship on early Mahāyāna is more inclined to emphasize its monastic, or rather renunciant, roots; see Williams 1989; Harrison 1987, 1995a, 1995b, 2000; Ray 1994; Silk 1994; Sasaki 1997; Gombrich 1998. Pagel (1995) has studied the ascetic tendencies in the bodhisattva discipline, while Nattier (2003a) has examined the strands of lay and monastic bodhisattvas in the *Ugraparipṛcchā*. It should be noted that older scholarship also treats the monastic bodhisattva; see Dutt 1930: 290–299; La Vallée Poussin 1930: 25, 32–33; Robinson 1965–1966: 25–56.

It can increase and [cause to] grow seeds, roots, stems, flowers, fruits, [all] kinds of medicines, and grains.	It can increase and [cause to] grow all seeds, roots, sprouts, stems, branches, leaves, flowers, fruits, medicines, grains, refined vapor, and savory taste.
It can increase and [cause to] grow clouds, rain, earth, water, fire, and wind.	It can increase [and cause] rain and marsh to grow and increase [and cause] beneficial earth, water, fire, and wind to grow.
It can increase and [cause to] grow fortune and happiness.	It can increase [and cause] joy and happiness to grow.
It can increase and [cause] property and material goods to grow.	It can increase [and cause] properties and treasures to grow.
It can increase and [cause to] grow boundless supreme retributions.	It can increase[and cause] supreme abilities to grow.
It can increase and [cause] rudimentary actions to grow.	It can increase [and cause] all useful resources and facilities to grow.
This *dhāraṇī* can beneficially eliminate all suffering, afflictions, and bondages.[17]	This *dhāraṇī* can bring about all wisdoms and thoroughly sever the bondage of mental afflictions.[18]

In esoteric Buddhism, which flourished in eighth-century China, the *dhāraṇī*, or spell, was highlighted as one of the standard accoutrements of the esoteric deity, used interchangeably with *mantra*, a string of mostly semantically senseless syllables regarded as spiritually potent sounds. *Dhāraṇī* (*tuoluoni* 陀羅尼) had already appeared in early Mahāyāna scriptures, and Central Asia witnessed a flourishing of scriptures from the fifth to the eighth centuries collectively referred to as *dhāraṇī* literature.[19] Scholars have proposed that *dhāraṇī* cults flourished as a transitional phase to esoteric Buddhism in China.[20] Use of *dhāraṇi*, like the practice of medicine, reflected broad religious concerns stemming from an abhorrence of death, poverty, ailments, natural catastrophe, and evil spirits, as well as a desire for a blessed life and a favorable rebirth.[21] The association of Dizang with the *dhāraṇī* in the *Scripture on the Ten Wheels* thus mirrors these larger Buddhist trends, and this early association provides a thread of continuity for subsequent Dizang developments.

17. *Da fangguang shilun jing*, T410:13.685b; cf. T410:13.685c.

18. *Dasheng daji Dizang shilun jing*, T411:13.726b; cf. T411:13.726c–727a.

19. *Dhāraṇī*s appear, for instance, in early Mahāyāna scriptures like the *Saddharmapuṇḍarīka-sūtra* and the *Suvarṇabhāsottama-sūtra*. On *dhāraṇī*s in early Mahāyāna scriptures, see Strickmann 2002: 103–109.

20. Waley 1931: xiii–xiv.

21. Schopen 1978: 271–275.

After the initial presentation, the Bodhisattva Dizang recedes and almost disappears from the text, appearing only briefly here and there in the role of questioner. It is Dizang who makes the following request resulting in the Buddha's preaching of the Ten Wheels:

Da fangguang shilun jing (T410)	*Dasheng daji Dizang shilun jing* (T411)
For thirteen *kalpa*s I have cultivated the fields of merits of the buddhas. I have eliminated all famine and disease for the sake of beings.	For thirteen *kalpa*s I have zealously cultivated ascetic practices. For the sake of all living beings I have eliminated the three catastrophes and the five turbulences.
To all the hundred thousand buddhas I have made inconceivable offerings. Today I witness the gathering of this great assembly to which pure beings have all come; Astutely wise and diligently zealous they have all come to this assembly. In an instant like the gathering of clouds all defilements do not exist.	At several *koṭi* of buddha-abodes I have made offerings without limit. I encounter and witness the gathering of this great assembly where beings with pure faith have come together; Astutely wise and diligently zealous all have come to the same assembly. I have never seen such a congregation [so] free of various delusions.
This degenerate world abounds in mockery and suspicion, engaging in evil that harms pure acts.	Why in this buddha-land do delusions and evil harm the pure and good?
Why do we not recognize well That distress destroys dignified demeanor?	[Why do living beings] remove [themselves] from what is wise And dwell together with those who engage in evil deeds?
That all are endowed with perversions and slander the correct Law?	Many commit the uninterrupted sins and slander the correct Law.[22]
They revile the holy saints and delusively attach [themselves] to nihilistic and eternalist views.	They harm the saints, engender negative views, and delusively expound nihilistic and eternalist theses.
They commit the ten unsalutary actions, not abhorring retributive suffering in future lives.	They have committed the ten unsalutary actions, not abhorring retributive suffering in future lives.

22. Uninterrupted sins (*wujian zui* 無間罪) are also known as the five heinous sins (*wu ni zui* 五逆罪). They are transgressions that incur rebirth in the *avīci* hell or *wujian diyu* 無間地獄 (uninterrupted hell) and include patricide, matricide, killing an arhat, wounding a buddha, and creating dissension in the *saṅgha*. See *Zengyi ahan jing,* T125:2.803a–804b.

They thwart the teaching of the
Three Vehicles, and flatteries drive
[them] toward the unfortunate
paths [of rebirth]. Ignorance
obscures their perception, and
they are greedy, envious, mostly
debauched, and hypocritical.
How [can one] turn the wheel of
teachings and release them from
all their flatteries?
Afflictions are like possessing the
vajra. How [can one] break them
and cause them to depart?
How [is one] able to maintain an
endurance that can gently
harmonize?
Never is there such an assembly
where I am able to meet the
General of this world.
A great congregation like this has
never taken place anywhere.
Complete with the practice of
dhūta, and having practiced for a
long time the way of awakening
(bodhi).
How [can one], in this place,
attain buddhahood and turn the
wheel of teachings?[23]

They are mostly distant from the
Three Vehicles, and odorous habits
drive [them] toward the unfortunate
paths [of rebirth]. Ignorance
obscures their perception, and they
are greedy, envious, mostly
debauched, and deceitful.
How [can one] turn the Buddha's
wheel and liberate these
living beings?
How [can one] break the continuity
[of their actions] when their
afflictions are like *vajra?*
How is one able to achieve
observances that result in such
endurance?
Today I encounter the Guiding
Teacher.
A great assembly [like this] is
exceedingly rare. Nowhere else
has one ever seen
Possession of such a collection of
merits. Endowed with numerous
merits diligently cultivating the
way of Awakening.
How, in a place of foolish beings,
is it possible to set into motion the
Buddha's wheel [of teachings]?[24]

This passage not only reinforces previous themes, but also introduces a new leitmotif: Dizang's emulation of the Buddha Śākyamuni. Dizang is thus scripted into the role of the Buddha's successor, who is to propagate Buddhist teachings in a spiritually degenerate world like ours. Whatever improvisations and modifications are introduced, Dizang remains a bodhisattva intimately related to this Sahā world.

The remaining text emphasizes the teaching of the Ten Wheels of Salutary Actions for the Three Vehicles, with individual sections elaborating the Ten Wheels of the Buddha (Tathāgata) (Chapters 3–4); those of the *śrāvaka*s (Chapter 8); and those of the bodhisattva (Chapter 9). The Ten Wheels are regarded as the teachings delivered by Buddha for living beings in this degenerate world; the wheels are compared to those of the *cakravartin*, or

23. *Da fangguang shilun jing*, T410:13.687a–b.
24. *Dasheng daji Dizang shilun jing*, T411:13.728b.

universal monarch.[25] The scripture enumerates the "ten unsalutary wheels" (*shi bushan lun* 十不善輪) along with sets of related moral infractions (Chapter 5) and condemns those *caṇḍāla* rulers who do not support the religion or the monastic institution, while assuring divine protection for true *kṣatriya* rulers who support Buddhism (Chapter 6).

The core text focuses on the socio-political undercurrents Buddhism faced in early medieval China. Its rhetoric is polemical and elevates the monastic vocation, arguing for monastic exemption from any form of state regulation. Some of its most persuasive arguments are presented as analogies or parables: The Buddhist monk is compared to "the *campaka* that even when withered surpasses all other flowers."[26] One tale relates how a group of hunters, disguised as monks, acquires the tusks of an elephant king who acquiesces to their request out of respect for the monastic habit.[27] In another story, a convict, about to be devoured by malignant *rakṣa*s, dresses himself as a monk. The *rakṣa*s, noticing his robes, not only leave him unharmed but also take refuge under him.[28] A startling argument declares that if somebody harbors ill intentions toward the monastic community, this is equivalent to plotting against the buddhas of the three times.[29] The image of a monk with a shaven head dressed in a *kāṣāya* robe underscores the entire text, driving home the point that the very appearance of a monk is meritorious in itself, regardless of whether he observes the precepts or not.[30] This preoccupation with the outward appearance of a monk readily connects to the representation of Dizang as a monk. Were the arguments for the privileges of a monk intentional? What circumstances prompted the set of concerns underscoring the text? This insistence on the supremacy of the monastic vocation recurs in the *Section on the Sumeru Treasury*.

The *Section on the Sumeru Treasury*

The Central Asian monk Narendrayaśas is said to have translated the *Section on the Sumeru Treasury* in 559 for the collection known as the *Mahāvaipulyasaṃnipāta-sūtra*, or *Da fangdeng daji jing* 大方等大集經 (The Great Extended Compendium of Scriptures).[31] Comprising four chapters, the *Section on the Sumeru Treasury* opens with exalting the bodhisattva's mastery of the perfection of concentration *(dhyānapāramitā)* and describes the vari-

25. *Da fangguang shilun jing*, T410:13.690b–692c.

26. Ibid.:13.694b.

27. Ibid.:13.697c–698a.

28. Ibid.:13.698b–699a.

29. Ibid.:13.703c.

30. Ibid.:13.705b: 剃頭著袈裟.

31. Because the *Section on the Sumeru Treasury* is mentioned in the Sui catalog *Lidai sanbao ji* 歷代三寶紀, authored in 597, we can assume that the text circulated in China from the second half of the sixth century. For further discussion on its date and authorship, see Appendix 2.

ous ways in which the bodhisattva benefits living beings while in states of meditation. Chapters 3 and 4 describe cosmic disorders and natural catastrophes, following which Buddhist deities preach their individual *dhāraṇīs* to ward off the calamities. Dizang Bodhisattva appears in Chapters 2, 3, and 4 in connection with *dhyānapāramitā* and *dhāraṇī* recitation.

In Chapter 2, Dizang is hailed as a bodhisattva mahāsattva (*pusa mohesa* 菩薩摩訶薩) known for his command of *dhyānapāramitā*—in particular a meditative state called the Samādhi in which all *dharmas* are found to be empty and beyond designation (*yiqiefa wu yuyan kong sanmei* 一切法無語言空三昧).[32] Except for this brief mention, the discourse in the first two chapters casts the bodhisattva as a generic figure in relation to the practice of *dhyānapāramitā*, which leads one to wonder whether or not this brief mention of Dizang could have been a later interpolation. Dizang is basically inserted into a long segment of discourse presenting the bodhisattva as a wonderworker.[33] The very attainment of *dhyānapāramitā* enables a bodhisattva, while in meditation, to roam freely from one buddha-land to the next, presenting offerings to the buddhas and performing supernormal feats of benefiting living beings. This thaumaturgical aspect is one of the standard functions attributed to the bodhisattva in early Mahāyāna literature. The image is also invoked in the *Scripture on the Ten Wheels*: Each dawn Dizang enters an array of meditative states during which he alleviates suffering and benefits living beings in many buddha-lands.[34] The *Section on the Sumeru Treasury* describes the event as follows:

> If the bodhisattva desires to enter into *samādhi* to mature living beings through the power of merits and wisdom, at that time, and for that reason, one must first utter this vow: "For the duration of time until I arise from *samādhi*, I wish to enable all living beings of this country, this realm, all under the four heavens, as well as in this buddha-world to possess the requisites of livelihood according to their necessities . . . food, clothing, bedding, necklaces, ornaments, gardens, forests, houses, dwellings, figures and forms, proportionate limbs, lovely sound, smell, taste, touch, and so forth, let them witness these things." At this time the bodhisattva will then enter this *samādhi*. After that, according to its duration, the living beings of this buddha-world and all under the four heavens will then procure the above requisites according to their needs.[35]

In Chapter 3, Dizang appears again. Śrī Devī (Gongde tian 功德天) first questions Dizang on how to convert living beings at a time when various classes of wrathful creatures are spreading havoc through unseasonal

32. *Xumizang fen*, T397:13.384a.

33. On the bodhisattva as wonder-worker, see Gómez 1977.

34. *Da fangguang shilung jing*, T410:13.683a–684a; *Dasheng daji Dizang shilun jing*, T411:13.723b–724b.

35. *Xumizang fen*, T397:13.384a.

winds and rains, destruction of agricultural crops, and pollution of the environment:

> Today, for my sake, you should arouse the great compassionate mind toward all under the four heavens and contemplate with your wisdom how to be able to bring about the subjugation of all venomous *nāga*s, *yakṣa*s, *rakṣa*s, *asura*s, *khumbāṇḍa*s, *preta*s, *piśācāḥ*s, *kaṭapūtana*s, and other malignant demons under the four heavens, so that winds and rains shall follow the seasons; moisture and dryness will be moderated; the falls will be substantive and sumptuous; the winters gentle and calm. By means of this causal condition, both the flavor of the earth and the fragrance of its smell shall multiply in strength.[36]

Dizang then advises Śrī Devī to ask the Buddha for a *dhāraṇī* to appease cosmic disturbances. After the Buddha has delivered his *dhāraṇī*, Dizang comes forward and preaches the Great Dhāraṇī for Sharpening Knives (*modao da tuoluoni* 磨刀大陀羅尼). This exchange again is reminiscent of the *Scripture on the Ten Wheels*, which says that Dizang possesses a *dhāraṇī* antidote for chaotic times. The author of the *Section on the Sumeru Treasury* may thus have been familiar with the *Scripture on the Ten Wheels* or vice versa.

Dizang reappears as a minor actor in Chapter 4. The discourse again focuses on ways to free the world from natural catastrophes, this time caused by vicious dragons (Ch. *long* 龍; Skt. *nāga*):

> [The dragons] frequently bring about unseasonal chills, heat, sinister clouds, stormy rains, droughts, and floods, which if not moderated will harm living brings as well as the five grains, sprouts, stems, branches, leaves, flowers, fruits, and medicinal grasses.[37]

The protagonist is Sumeru Treasury (Xumizang), also known as the Bodhisattva Mahāsattva Dragon Saint (Ch. Longxian 龍仙; Skt. Nāgarṣi), who had in the past aspired to convert all dragons.[38] The Buddha queries Sumeru Treasury for ways to eliminate the destructive actions of malevolent dragons and ensure the welfare of living beings. Sumeru Treasury replies that he will go to the dragons' palace and enter into meditative concentration, during which he will subdue all dragons so they will cease to inflict natural calamities on the world. Sumeru Treasury further promises to deliver from peril those who invoke his name or *dhāraṇī*.[39] Following his example, the dragon kings promise to protect those regions where the observance of precepts

---

36. Ibid.:13.386b.

37. Ibid.:13.388b. The dragon is an auspicious mythical animal associated especially with rain in China; its Indian equivalent, *nāga*, is usually translated as "serpent."

38. Ibid.:13.388b. The Sanskrit reconstruction would be "Nāga Rṣi Bodhisattva Mahāsattva." The Chinese generally used *xian* ("saint" or "immortal") as the translation for the Indian seer known in Sanskrit as *rṣi*.

39. Ibid.:13.388b–c.

flourishes and to destroy recalcitrant dragons who persist in causing calamities. The dragon kings then present their respective *dhāraṇī* teachings to the assembly.[40] Other Buddhist deities, including Dizang Bodhisattva, step forward to espouse *dhāraṇī* for the liberation of living beings:

> At that time the Bodhisattva Mahāsattva Dizang puts his palms together and prostrates to the Buddha, saying, "World-Honored One, I possess the liberating supermundane powers of all the meditation states *(samādhi)*. Today I too wish to preach the Dhāraṇī Method of the Banner and Staff (*chuangzhang tuoluoni fa* 幢杖陀羅尼法). If one hears with one's own ears this *dhāraṇī*, it can eliminate all ear diseases. Similarly all the maladies of greed, hatred, ignorance, and other afflictions [are eradicated]. Should they not be completely destroyed, they would be reduced or attenuated."[41]

In addition to Dizang, other bodhisattvas (Akṣayamati, Mañjuśrī, Maitreya, Avalokiteśvara) similarly preach their special *dhāraṇī*s to the assembly.

Chapter 4 is not important for its representation of Dizang, who is depicted in the standard rhetoric of bodhisattva literature; it is, however, important for its advocacy of themes reminiscent of the *Scripture on the Ten Wheels*. For example, a dragon king speaks on the supremacy of the monastic vocation and the need to foster ideal church-state relations. The text promises supernatural protection to benevolent rulers who observe Buddhist teachings and provide for the monastic community:

> Virtuous Bhagavān, in the country where the Buddha's disciples, *śrāvaka*s, bodhisattvas, and their communities of devotees and kin reside, all dragons and great dragons who are subservient to or dependent on me—be they born from the womb, egg, moisture, or through transformation—shall look upon [the Buddhists] with compassionate minds, without animosity or malice, and shall rest on a mind of peaceful equanimity. Moreover, we shall trust and protect the king of that country who dwells with a heart of pure faith in the Buddhist teachings, protects the Buddhist teachings, and does not, on account of the freedom of noble rank, become arrogant and destroy the Buddhist teachings. Neither should he distress monks, nuns, laymen, laywomen, or all those who follow the Buddha and renounce lay life, whether fitted to the task or not, and who shave off beard and hair, and don the *kāṣāya*. If in this country, there are other living beings who loathe the Buddhist teachings, the king should [accordingly] intervene and regulate. . . . This *kṣatriya* king protects well the land of his country. All disputes and disturbances in the country should be [treated] as stated previously. The other dragon kings and I will each decree to our relatives [our intention] not to procreate transformatory calamities.[42]

40. Ibid.:13.389a–391a.
41. Ibid.:13.391b.
42. Ibid.:13.389a–b.

The text then reiterates the supremacy of the monastic vocation and enumerates the wondrous attributes of the monastic garment:

> All the buddhas in the past have always empowered this dyed *kāṣāya* robe. This *kāṣāya* is then the seed of all bodhisattvas and the proper path that leads toward *nirvāṇa*. So, too, it is the steel knife that can cut off afflictions and is thus the seed of *nirvāṇa*. So, too, it is a luminous lamp for those who have strayed away from the path. It is also the medicine that will eliminate illness. It is like a fierce wind blowing at the clouds of ignorance. So it is a crutch for those desiring to travel on treacherous roads, a medication for nausea that can cause the poison of afflictions to be spit out. Then it is the adamantine (Ch. *jingang* 金剛; Skt. *vajra*) that crushes the animosity of *asuras*. Then it is the precious storehouse of salutary *dharmas*. It is like clear calm water that can wash away the stains of sins. Contemplating all *dharma* just like a bright mirror, it can focus dispersed thoughts like a net. It can hold *dhyāna* concentration just like a jeweled satchel. It is like the great earth that can produce the various [bodhisattva] perfections. It should be worn at the summit like a luminous pearl in the coiffure. It can hold forbearance just like a house. Then it is an undefiled vessel holding the practice of the ten stages *(bhūmi)*.[43] It obstructs the various heterodoxies like a city wall. And it is also an excellent remedy for the malady of afflictions. To all practitioners it is like Mount Sumeru. It eliminates the steam of afflictions just like the luminous moon. It eliminates the darkness of heterodox views just like the pure sun. It serves as a storehouse of wisdom like the vast sea. With regard to the factors of awakening, it is just like a garland of flowers. With regard to all knowledge, it is like a good vase. All buddhas protect it just like a wish-granting jewel. Moreover, all the buddhas protect this *kāṣāya*.[44]

The passage concludes with a prediction of widespread cosmic disorder in regions where wicked rulers destroy Buddhist teachings and intervene in the affairs of the Buddhist community by imposing taxation and other state regulations. The text insists that the evil ways of these rulers arouse the wrath of semimythical beings and supernatural spirits who will wreak havoc throughout the land. However, it is the wicked kings who are ultimately responsible for the rampant cosmic chaos. The long passage thus sets forth a paradigm for the ruling of a Buddhist country to receive divine sanction. Moreover, divine retribution is prophesied for cruel kings who do not observe proper relations with the Buddhist clergy. Such neglect will not only alienate the Buddhist deities, who will no longer protect the land of the evil ruler, but will also incur the rage of semimythical creatures and spirits. Again, the reader is left with no doubt that the mere appearance of a monk's shaven head and

43. *Bhūmi*, literally "ground," refers to the levels or stages of the bodhisattva path, usually presented as ten stages extending over millions of lifetimes.

44. *Xumizang fen*, T397:13.389b.

robe deserves respect, whether or not the monk himself remains true to his vocation.

It is interesting that both the *Section on the Sumeru Treasury* and the *Scripture on the Ten Wheels* juxtapose their depictions of Dizang with discussions on proper church and state relations. Such parallels may reveal something of the socio-political conditions surrounding this bodhisattva's appearance in sixth-century China.

The Intellectual and Socio-Political Climate

To comprehend the emphasis placed on the monastic vocation in both the *Scripture on the Ten Wheels* and *Section on the Sumeru Treasury*, it is imperative to locate the two scriptures within the Buddhist intellectual milieu of the fifth and sixth centuries. China was at that time politically divided: The north was ruled by non-Chinese autocrats, and the south by Chinese rulers and their courts. The two parted ways not only in socio-political matters, but also in Buddhist development. Broadly speaking, in contrast to the focus on *prajñā*, or wisdom philosophy, in the south, the north tended to concentrate on monastic discipline *(vinaya)*, meditation *(dhyāna)*, and thaumaturgic powers (Ch. *shentong* 神通; Skt. *ṛddhi*).[45] The similarities between the *Scripture on the Ten Wheels* and the *Section on the Sumeru Treasury* very likely mirrored Buddhist responses to socio-political conditions in sixth-century China that were continuous with earlier developments in Northern Liang Buddhism.

In the fifth century, Northern Liang rulers controlled the overland route through which Buddhism entered China. Their territory included Dunhuang, a strategic point where the northern and southern Central Asian routes crossed and a waystation for traveling missionaries and traders entering or leaving China. The Northern Liang then was at the fountainhead of the influx of new religious trends streaming into China from Central Asia. A pillar of Northern Liang Buddhism was the Central Asian translator Dharmakṣema (Tanwuchen 曇無讖, 385–433), who acted as royal advisor to the Northern Liang court during the reign of Juqu Mengxun 沮渠蒙遜 (r. 401–433).[46] Dharmakṣema played a salient role in introducing the teaching of the decline of Buddhism that culminated in the concept of *mofa* 末法

45. Because Chinese rulers and their courts were located in the south, it followed that concentrated in this region were learned elites and aristocrats, whose interest lay in the parallels between *prajñā* literature and Daoist writings. On the other hand, the foreign tribal leaders of the north were often attracted to charismatic monks from Central Asia who had entered China through the silk roads and whose spiritual powers could be enlisted to further the military and political agendas of their states. For Buddhism in the south and north, see Tang 1987: 730–734, 766–829.

46. On Northern Liang Buddhism, particularly translation activities, see Du 1995: 171–281, 1998. Also see Zhao 1989: 79–85.

(Final Dharma).[47] He is credited with translating two major works on the subject: the *Mahāparinivāṇa-sūtra* (*Da boniepan jing* 大般涅槃經) and the *Beihua jing* 悲華經 (The Scripture on the Compassionate Lotus Flower). These works, especially the *Scripture on the Compassionate Lotus Flower*, contain themes similar to those found in the *Scripture on the Ten Wheels*.

Scattered throughout the *Scripture on the Compassionate Lotus Flower* are references to the five turbulences—a concept discussed in the *Scripture on the Ten Wheels*—which contributed to the Chinese development of the decline tradition. As understood in the *Scripture on the Compassionate Lotus Flower*, the age of the five turbulences was precisely during Śākyamuni Buddha's lifetime.[48] This understanding is duplicated in Mahāyāna texts like the Amitābha Pure Land scriptures and the *Lotus Scripture*, which were translated around this time. In the *Scripture on the Ten Wheels*, the Bodhisattva Dizang helps living beings attain spiritual liberation during the vile age of the five turbulences.[49] Teachings on the decline of Buddhism are certainly discernible in early strata of Indian Buddhist literature.[50] Such portents not only intensified during the transmission from India via Central Asia, but also struck a profound chord in fifth- and sixth-century China—caught as it was in a prolonged period of political disunity and incessant warfare with considerable portions of its territories under foreign rule. Both the *Scripture on the Compassionate Lotus Flower* and the *Scripture on the Ten Wheels* thus reflect a time in Chinese Buddhist history before the core concepts of the decline tradition had been articulated and systematized by religious thinkers of the Sui period (581–618).

Like the *Scripture on the Ten Wheels*, the *Scripture on the Compassionate Lotus Flower* highlights the merits of the monk's *kāṣāya* robe.[51] The tendency to exalt the robe is found in Indian Buddhist literature, such as *vinaya* writings, the *āgama* texts, and early Mahāyāna scriptures.[52] In China, however, the su-

47. For the emergence of the teaching of the Final Dharma, see Nattier 1991; Hubbard 1996.

48. *Beihua jing*, T157:3.226b, 226b.

49. *Da fangguang shilun jing*, T410:13.681c, 683c.

50. Forebodings of the destruction of Buddhist teachings are already found in the *Nikāya*, or *Āgama*, scriptures; see Hubbard 1986: 15–24; cf. Chappell 1980: 124–127.

51. The *Beihua jing* lists five virtues of the monk's *kāṣāya* robe: (1) Despite committing serious infractions *(pārājika)* or falling into erroneous ways, the wearer will receive the prophecy of buddhahood *(vyākaraṇa)* according to the teachings of the Three Vehicles if he or she harbors even a single thought of respect for the Buddha and his monks; (2) Those who reverently make offerings, venerate, and exalt the robe will never backslide from the teachings of the Three Vehicles; (3) The poor and lower classes among humans, hungry ghosts, and lesser spirits who obtain but a small piece of the *kāṣāya* robe will procure abundant food and drink; (4) In the midst of conflict among living beings, thinking of the robe can give rise to the mind of compassion; (5) On the battlefield, if one takes a small piece of the robe and venerates it, one will be protected from all harm and definitely emerge victorious over others. See T157:3.220a–b.

52. For examples from the *āgama* literature, see *Za ahan jing* 雜阿含經, T99:2.303a; from the *Avadāna* literature, see *Xianyu jing* 賢愚經, T202:4.352c, 399a, 438b; from the *vinaya* writings, see *Sifen lü shanfan buque xingshi chao* 四分律刪繁補闕行事鈔, T1804:40.105a, 105b, 108a.

premacy of the monastic robe is related to a major controversy in Chinese Buddhist history concerning the establishment of proper church-state relations. A theme already present in the Indian Buddhist tradition, church-state relations took a critical turn in the early Chinese Buddhist context. Whereas the Indian tradition had always hypostatized the autonomy of the religious community and its exemption from state regulation, the power of the sovereign in China was regarded as deriving from a transcendental source of authority, referred to as "Heaven." The Chinese sovereign, in other words, possessed absolute power invested in him by an otherworldly source. The monastic institution's claim to autonomy would have posed a threat to the sovereign's absolute authority in all spheres of Chinese life. Not surprisingly, tensions in church-state relations surfaced at the outset of the transmission of Buddhism to China. In the south, with the support of court aristocrats, Chinese Buddhists were evidently able to debate openly the controversy over the *saṅgha*'s privileges. In this regard, an important document is the famous memorial titled *Shamen bujing wangzhe lun* 沙門不敬王者論 (Treatise on the Śramaṇa Not Having to Bow to the Ruler), composed in 404 by the southern Chinese aristocrat monk Huiyuan 慧遠 (344–416).[53] The text highlights the supremacy of monastic garments as part of the defense of monastic privileges.[54]

In the north, fourth-century Central Asian Buddhist missionaries such as Fotudeng 佛圖澄 (232–348) and Dharmakṣema of the Northern Liang were all directly employed in the service of the courts. Governed by autocratic non-Chinese tribal rulers, northern Chinese Buddhist proponents, unlike their southern counterparts, could not explicitly challenge the non-Chinese autocrat's authority by openly petitioning for the rights of the *saṅgha*. Although there were no open debates on the matter, several Buddhist scriptures circulating in the north voiced the necessity for monastic exemption from state regulation. Jan Nattier proposes that this kind of scriptural discourse was in fact a veiled argument for the *saṅgha*'s rights necessitated by political conditions in north China.[55] As one will recall, the *Scripture on the Ten Wheels* repeatedly voices stern admonitions against state

53. This treatise is important for understanding the early history of Chinese Buddhism; for a translation, see Hurvitz 1957: 2–36. For further discussion on church-state relations in this period, see Zürcher 1972: 231–239.

54. Huiyuan argues as follows:

> Furthermore, the *kāṣāya* robe is not apparel (one should wear) before an imperial audience, just as the *pātra* [should] not be used as a vessel in the palace. Soldiers and civilians [should] have different appearances; foreigners and Chinese should not mingle. If [the monastic rules of] people who shave their heads and mutilate their bodies become fused with the Rites of China, this is a sign of the mutual interference of difference species, which makes me feel uneasy. (*Hongming ji* 弘明集, T2102:52.84a)

55. Nattier 1991: 129.

intervention in *saṅgha* matters, contrasting the ideal rulership of the *cakravartin* with the despotism of the wicked *caṇḍāla* ruler.[56]

Before the appearance of the *Section on the Sumeru Treasury* in the mid-sixth century, anticipation of the demise of Buddhist teachings accelerated. The term *moshi* 末世 (final age) had entered Chinese Buddhist discourse as the translation for *paścimakala* (latter age), which refers to the period of spiritual decline after the Buddha's departure.[57] In early pre-Buddhist usage, *moshi* connoted an age of utmost evil and decadence, characteristically associated with the corrupt rule of wicked last descendants of legendary Chinese dynasties.[58] Not surprisingly, Chinese Buddhists attached political overtones to *moshi* that are absent from the Indian understanding of *paścimakala*. Imperial patronage of Buddhism triggered an ostentatious accumulation of material wealth in monasteries and generated widespread corruption in the *saṅgha*—particularly during the Northern Wei (386–534).[59] To the Chinese, the growing wealth and laxity of the *saṅgha* were sure indicators of the approaching demise of Buddhism.

On his arrival in 556 in the Northern Qi (550–577) capital of Ye 鄴 (in Henan), Narendrayaśas would have noted the widespread anticipation of Buddhism's demise in the region. Narendrayaśas himself had lived through the socio-political chaos of the Hephthalites' fifth-century invasion of northwest India and Kashmir.[60] His writings collected in the *Mahāvaipulya-saṃnipāta-sūtra*, a compendium of Mahāyāna scriptures attributed to several translators, were influenced by the political realities of his time. Moreover, he would personally witness the extensive devastation caused by the state proscription of Buddhism in 574 decreed by Emperor Wu 武 (560–578) of the Northern Zhou (557–581). In addition to widespread defrocking of monks and nuns, state curtailment of Buddhist activities resulted in the creation of a peculiar institution known as the *pusa seng* 菩薩僧 (bodhisattva monks). Comprised of lay clerics robed in court apparel, their heads unshaven, bodhisattva monks were given the task of overseeing religious institutions.[61] Although the reform lasted only two months, the monastic leadership must have been badly shaken by this turn of events. The harsh blows inflicted by the state had lasting repercussions on the Buddhist com-

56. *Da fangguang shilun jing*, T410:13.687a–b.

57. This use of *paścimakala* occurred in the work of Dharmarakṣa; see Nattier 1991: 117.

58. For examples of this pre-Buddhist usage, see the entry on *moshi* in Morohashi 1955–1960: 6:5736b, no. 14420.81.

59. The Chinese emperor most celebrated for his generous support of Buddhism was Emperor Wu 武 of the Liang (r. 502–549). One famous anecdote relates how this pious donor, unsatisfied with the material gifts he had bestowed on Buddhist monasteries, decided to present himself as a gift. Consequently, his ministers were forced to redeem the emperor using state funds. The first instance is said to have occurred in 528; the emperor renewed the practice in 546 and 547. On Emperor Wu's patronage of Buddhism, see Ch'en 1964: 124–128.

60. Nattier 1991: 114–116.

61. See Chen Jinhua 2002.

munity and further intensified the conviction that the dreaded epoch of Buddhism's collapse as prophesied in the scriptures had arrived.

The flourishing of the decline tradition certainly had an impact on Narendrayaśas's work. The *Sūryagarbha-sūtra* (*Rizang fen* 日藏分, Section on the Sun Treasury) and the *Candragarbha-sūtra* (*Yuezang fen* 月藏分, Section on the Moon Treasury), which he translated in 589, in the aftermath of the Northern Zhou persecution, deliver strong pronouncements on the decline of Buddhist teachings. He had translated the *Section on the Sumeru Treasury* in 559, shortly after his arrival in Northern Qi and prior to the Northern Zhou repression. The north was then still under non-Chinese rule, and Narendrayaśas, newly arrived, was probably not yet familiar with Chinese Buddhist developments. Perhaps for these reasons, the *Section on the Sumeru Treasury* expresses the imminent religious crisis largely in terms of collapse of the ecosystem and focuses on assaults of natural catastrophes unleashed by wrathful spirits on account of a king's action or lack of action—not unlike Central Asian scriptures such as the *Suvarṇabhāsottama-sūtra*, or the *Jin guangming jing* 金光明經 (Scripture on the Golden Light).[62] The *Section on the Sumeru Treasury* contains one passage that explicitly refers to the destruction of the religion and the Buddhist community through the enforcement of state regulations:

> Moreover, this *kāṣāya* robe is protected by all the buddhas. . . . For this reason, Bhagavān, should a cruel *kṣatriya* king destroy the Dharma, vex monks and nuns (including those fitted or unfitted to the task) who have followed the Buddha and renounced the lay life, or if he should regulate and punish their bodies, tax their properties, and [dare] even to take away their lives—for these reasons, the *deva*s, *yakṣa*s, *asura*s, *kumbhāṇḍa*s in that country will give rise to a wrathful mind toward all that belong to the *kṣatriya* king and will cause to arise in his country disputes; the peril of famine; epidemics; battles of weapons and soldiers; unseasonal wind, rain, drought, chill, and heat, ruining the five grains, seeds, sprouts, stems, branches, leaves, flowers, fruits, medicine, and smells. This is not the fault of the dragons. These

---

62. For example, the *Suvarṇabhāsottama-sūtra*, which dates to no later than the early fifth century, ascribes natural disorders to bad rulership in the following manner:

> The thirty-three gods are wrathful because its king permits evil deeds to go unpunished [and thus] ruins the country and the true teachings . . . enemies from other lands compete to invade and rob [his kingdom]. . . . Fiery winds stir up unexpectedly; evil rains falls constantly, unfavorable stars occur several times; the sun and moon lose their luminosity; all the five grains and fruits will not flourish. Because the king has abandoned righteousness and thus causes famine throughout his kingdom, the gods in the palace are grieved and angry. . . . On account of the gods' wrath, his kingdom will perish. . . . Epidemics and evil disease will accrue in his land. (*Jin guangming jing*, T663:16.347b)

The *Suvarṇabhāsottama-sūtra* makes no allusion to excessive state control over religion, and it does not elevate the status of the monastic vocation

> various dragons are themselves actually not guilty, [but they] unfortunately have acquired a bad reputation.[63]

This passage attributes universal chaos to a despotic rule that opposes the Buddhist religion and regulates *saṅgha* affairs. State intervention, in turn, enrages semimythical beings, who stir up social and natural upheavals throughout the kingdom. Like the *Scripture on the Ten Wheels*, the *Section on the Sumeru Treasury* elevates the monastic vocation, admonishes against state regulation of the monastic community, and eulogizes the *kāṣāya* robe through a series of similes. Scriptures translated by Narendrayaśas also reiterate the symbolic and soteriological significance of the *kāṣāya* robe. In this vein, the *Dabei jing* 大悲經 (Scripture on Great Compassion) states that even monks who violate their monastic livelihood will attain *nirvāṇa* under one of the future buddhas as long as they wear monastic garments.[64] The *Section on the Moon Treasury*, the Chinese version of the *Candragarbha-sūtra*, asserts that those who shave their heads and don the robes, even if they do not accept the precepts or violate them, bring great merit to their patrons.[65] It forewarns that whoever harasses, reviles, or beats those who shave their heads and don monastic garments will suffer punitive retribution far greater than that incurred for the heinous sin of drawing the Buddha's blood.[66] Insistence on the symbolic and soteriological significance of the monastic robes as an argument for the rights of the monastic community was already discernible in fifth-century Northern Liang Buddhism. However, it is very likely that between the fifth-century Northern Wei persecution of Buddhism and the Northern Zhou proscription in the late sixth century, northern Chinese Buddhists experienced an escalating sense of urgency to establish the rights of the monastic community and prevent the devastating effects of state regulation. Completed in the second half of the sixth century, Narendrayaśas' works reflect these larger religious and political concerns. The virtues of the monastic robe were vigorously upheld and further elaborated in the northern Chinese Buddhist context, perhaps in the hope of shielding the religious community from further prohibitive state measures against the religion.

The rhetoric in the *Section on the Sumeru Treasury* (and the other works mentioned above) was used to persuade rulers to support and protect the Buddhist religion—if not out of faith, then out of the desire to ward off supernatural beings and avert natural calamities. It can also be found in the fifth-century indigenous Chinese composition the *Renwang jing* 仁王經 (The Scripture on the Humane King), which promises protection to those kings who devoutly observe this scripture and predicts the withdrawal of

63. *Yuezang fen*, T397:13.389b–c.

64. *Dabei jing*, T380:12.958a. The supremacy of the monastic robe is mentioned elsewhere in this text; see T380:12.955b–c.

65. *Yuezang fen*, T397:13.354a–c.

66. Ibid.:13.356a–c. Drawing the Buddha's blood is listed as one of the five heinous sins (*wu ni zui*) that brings about rebirth in the *avīci* hell.

supernatural blessings for those who reject it.[67] Furthermore, both the *Section on the Sumeru Treasury* and the *Scripture on the Humane King* attribute the extinction of Buddhism to excessive state regulation of the monastic community.[68] According to Nattier, attributing the decline of Buddhism to excessive state regulation evolved in China.[69] Comparing various recensions of the *Candragarbha-sūtra*, Nattier notes that exhortations to rulers not to punish monks who fail to adhere to monastic rules are present only in the Chinese texts.[70] Hence, she concludes that excessive state control (taxation, ordination restrictions, corporal punishment) was a problem unique to Chinese Buddhism because Indian governments, whether they patronized Buddhism or not, "were hardly known for harassing the Buddhist communities by overregulation."[71] Concern with church-state relations was thus "added in a Chinese context, in response to Chinese circumstances."[72]

Both the *Scripture on the Ten Wheels* and the *Section on the Sumeru Treasury* thus reflect religious trends prevalent in northern China during the sociopolitical chaos of the period of disunity (317–589). Church-state relations,

67. Orzech 1998: 282–286.

68. This passage from the *Renwang jing* has obvious parallels with the previously cited excerpt from the *Xumizang fen*:

> After the five turbulent eras, *bhikṣu*, *bhikṣuṇī*, the four classes of disciples, the heavenly dragons and all of the eightfold spirit-kings, the kings of states, the great officers, the heirs apparent and princes will be haughty [and hold themselves in] great esteem and extinguish and smash my Teaching. Openly making laws to control my disciples—the *bhikṣu* and *bhikṣuṇī*—they will not permit people to leave the family to practice the Way, further they will not permit the making of Buddhist images or of Buddhist *stūpas*. They will establish superintendents [*tongguan*] to regulate the community and will set up registration of monks. *Bhikṣu* will stand on the ground while white-robed [laymen occupy] high seats. Soldiers and slaves will be made *bhikṣu* and receive preferential treatment while knowledgeable *bhikṣu* gather single-mindedly to befriend good *bhikṣu* and hold vegetarian meetings to seek blessings as in heterodox teachings. All of this is contrary to my Teaching. You should know at that time that it will not be long before the Correct Teaching [*zhengfa*] is about to be extinguished. (T245:8.833b; translated in Orzech 1998: 287)

Establishing superintendents and registering monks were the result of the political situation in fifth-century China. Note that, like the *Xumizang fen*, this passage also attributes the extinction of the Buddhist religion to an undue state regulation of the monastic community.

69. Nattier 1991: 129.

70. Ibid.: 185.

71. Ibid.: 129.

72. Ibid.: 185. It is perhaps tempting to make similar conclusions about the *Xumizang fen*. Unfortunately, in the case of this text, the dearth of variant versions rules out a comparative textual study. In light of its close relationship with the *Yuezang fen*, it is possible that the *Xumizang fen*'s exhortations against intervention in *saṅgha* affairs might also have been accreted during the translation process in fifth-century China. It is, however, equally important to note that the *Xumizang fen* reveals almost no other obvious Chinese interpolation except the repetitive use of the term "five grains" (*wugu* 五穀), which has a long history spanning back to early China. But because this term is fairly generic and frequently serves as the Chinese equivalent for cereals in general, it should not be counted as evidence of Chinese interpolation.

the status of the monk's robe, and references to the decline of the religion are all present in the *Scripture on the Ten Wheels.* In the *Section on the Sumeru Treasury* these themes are not only continued, but are often interwoven into a single rhetorical argument. They are explicitly connected to the image of Dizang Bodhisattva as a *śramaṇa,* which also appears in the *Scripture on the Ten Wheels.* Although the texts themselves do not mention Dizang directly in their discussion of church-state relations, presenting the bodhisattva-as-*śramaṇa* would have been very appealing to Buddhists in northern China, who would not have dared to submit publicly a memorial to non-Chinese autocrats concerning the privileges of the monastic community. Equating a *śramaṇa* with a bodhisattva would have helped secure monastic exemption from state regulation. Hailed as the savior of "the vile age of the five turbulences" in the *Scripture on the Ten Wheels,* the Bodhisattva Dizang has natural affinities with teachings of the decline of Buddhism.[73] In the seventh-century translation, Dizang is further characterized as the savior of "the evil age of five turbulences [in] the world without a buddha" (*wuzhuo e shi wufo shijie* 五濁惡時無佛世界).[74] This explicit equation of the era of five turbulences with the buddha-less world evolved as part of the teachings on the decline of Buddhism.

The chaos of the sixth century on the eve of the Sui unification of China offered fertile ground to nurture developments in the tradition of the Dharma's disappearance.[75] For early Chinese Buddhists, the collapse of socio-political and cosmic structures signaled the beginning of this unfortunate era of spiritual decadence as predicted in the scriptures. The Pure Land teacher Daochuo 道綽 (562–645) stated that the Chinese Buddhists of his time were living "in the evil age of five turbulences during the era without a buddha."[76] This notion of a buddha-less world rapidly circulated alongside the notion that Chinese Buddhists were living in the desolate interval after the demise of the Buddha Śākyamuni and prior to the advent of the future Buddha Maitreya. The phrase "in the interval of the two saints" (*er sheng zhi jian* 二聖之間) was coined about this time and appeared, for instance, in a sixth-century inscription from Shaanxi.[77] The buddha-less world is thus another strand in the teachings on the eventual extinction of Buddhism. The plight of living in a time without the guidance of holy saints also engendered a soteriologi-

73. *Da fangguang shilun jing,* T410:13.681c, 683c.

74. *Dasheng daji Dizang shilun jing,* T411:13.721c.

75. I have only summarized the Buddhist intellectual climate of sixth-century China, highlighting those aspects relevant to my discussion. For an excellent overview of this period, see Gimello 1976: 93–137.

76. *Anle ji* 安樂集, T1958:47.12b: 於五濁之世於無佛之時.

77. Tōdō Kyōshun points to the existence of this inscription at the base of a stone buddha image carved in 549 by a lay Buddhist society of Dingxiang 定襄 prefecture, Shaanxi. The inscription and others of similar purport are discussed in Tōdō 1962: 782–777 (Japanese pagination). For other similar inscriptions at Longmen, see the list compiled by Mizuno and Nagahiro (1941: 322–323). For a more recent study of fifth- and sixth-century inscriptions, see Hou 1998.

cal dilemma: What Buddhist practices should one undertake while living in a spiritually degenerate world and age, when the goal of salvation appeared unattainable? Some Mahāyāna texts espouse scripture and *dhāraṇī* recitation as one recourse. For example, in the *Section on the Sumeru Treasury*, Buddhist deities (including Dizang) preach their individual *dhāraṇī* to combat the maladies of a chaotic age. The *Scripture on the Humane King* advocates scripture recitation and depicts eight bodhisattvas preaching their respective *dhāraṇī*. By representing Dizang as the savior of the age of the five turbulences and a world without a buddha, the seventh-century *Scripture on the Ten Wheels* offers him as the answer to the soteriological crisis that Chinese Buddhists felt they were encountering.

It is in response to the same soteriological imperative that Chinese Buddhist thinkers formulated a range of soteriologies, especially crafted to suit the exigencies of that period. This formative milieu witnessed the inception of forms of Buddhist thought and practice such as Pure Land, Sanjie jiao, Tiantai 天台, and Huayan 華嚴, which came to be known as uniquely "Chinese Buddhist teachings" *insofar* as they had no counterparts in pre-Chinese developments. In particular, Pure Land and Sanjie jiao insisted that Chinese Buddhists were actually living in the abhorred era of the decline of *dharma*. As will be evident later, Dizang enjoyed a special relationship with these two movements in the seventh and eighth centuries. The Pure Land connection appears often in the history of Dizang worship. The soteriological implication of Dizang, the savior of "the evil age of five turbulences during the era without a buddha," resonated throughout the subsequent development of this bodhisattva in China.

CHAPTER 2
Cultic Beginnings Reconsidered

MODERN SCHOLARSHIP attributes the initial dissemination of the Dizang cult to the Teaching of Three Levels (Sanjie jiao) and cites Longmen sculptures and inscriptions as examples of Dizang worship in the seventh century. For example, the *Encyclopedia of Religion* says of the early history of Dizang:

> Knowledge of Kṣitigarbha [Dizang] was probably introduced to China around 400, but there is no evidence that [Dizang] became an object of widespread devotion there until much later. An important stimulus for the popularity of faith in [Dizang]'s vows seems to have come from the San-chieh Chiao [Sanjie jiao] . . . a group that believed that various of the teachings of the Buddha were designed to be beneficial to each of three historical ages. Hsin-hsing [Xinxing 信行] (540–594), the founder of the sect, promoted the worship of [Dizang] as appropriate to the present, the third and most evil of the three ages. Judging from the number and dates of images in the Buddhist caves at Lung-men [Longmen], worship of Dizang became popular among the aristocracy, in tandem with that of the Buddha Amitābha from 650–700.[1]

Two groundbreaking studies were responsible for calling attention to Sanjie jiao and Longmen for understanding early Dizang worship. In a seminal work published in 1927, Yabuki Keiki devotes a chapter to mapping the relationship between Sanjie jiao and Dizang worship.[2] Yabuki shows that Sanjie jiao regarded the *Scripture on the Ten Wheels* as a key scriptural authority for its teachings. He was convinced that the scripture fostered a connection between Dizang and Sanjie jiao and that the latter had promulgated Dizang worship as one of its practices.[3] In his study on Northern Wei Buddhism published in 1942, Tsukamoto Zenryū includes a monograph essay on Longmen art and inscriptions in which he makes use of statistical data to show that up until the sixth century, Śākyamuni and Maitreya were the most widespread objects of veneration at Longmen. Both were displaced, however, from the seventh century on by Amitābha and Guanyin.[4] About the same time, the

1. Levering 1987: 392.
2. Yabuki 1927: 638–658.
3. Ibid.: 642.
4. Tsukamoto 1942: 375–382.

number of Dizang images also increased.[5] As a result of the invaluable findings of Tsukamoto and Yabuki, scholars tacitly assumed that Sanjie jiao's promulgation of Dizang Bodhisattva lay behind the growing dissemination of Dizang worship documented at Longmen.

Archaeological and manuscript discoveries following the publication of these two classic studies have yielded a wealth of sources on Sanjie jiao and Dizang worship. It is thus necessary to revisit the Dizang cult's early history. Indeed, scholars have since uncovered a problem: If Sanjie jiao were in fact instrumental in the early dissemination of Dizang worship as witnessed at Longmen, why are there no references to Sanjie jiao patronage in the making of Dizang images at Longmen? Besides the possibility that critical evidence did not survive, there are two methodological problems with broaching the evidence in this fashion. First, there is the tendency to regard written texts as the "more substantive"; they provide authoritative interpretation while material artifacts are merely corroborative. Thus religious art is always regarded as derivative of texts. Devotional trends documented in art are marginalized as the by-products of doctrinal innovations outlined in texts. One ends up reading art and inscriptions in light of texts and teachings—hence the expectation that Longmen inscriptions should confirm the Sanjie jiao connection with Dizang worship. Rather than impose preconceptions derived from written and doctrinal sources, it is more helpful to ask: What do the art and inscriptions themselves tell us about Dizang worship? The second problem is an implicit assumption that cultic practices necessarily originate in the doctrinal formulations of some Buddhist thinker or movement. They are thus seen as the ripple effects of "more rudimentary" ideological innovations. Instead of presuming at the outset a one-way development in which doctrinal innovations always provide the rationale for cultic practice, it is more prudent to understand the relationship as a complex dialectical interaction.

Because of Tsukamoto's seminal findings, scholars have focused on Longmen for art-historical or inscriptional evidence of Sanjie jiao's connection to the Dizang cult. But in addition to Longmen, one also needs to investigate the art and inscriptions found at other Buddhist sites and to understand the Sanjie jiao connection and Longmen evidence in relation to them. This chapter introduces an array of sources connected to the beginnings of Dizang worship in the seventh century. It reexamines the Sanjie jiao documents and Longmen evidence and introduces less-studied textual and visual materials to amplify the picture of early Dizang worship. The thrust of my analysis is to allow both textual and visual sources to tell their stories independently before making conclusions about how they are related. What does the evi-

5. From his statistical studies, Tsukamoto concluded that no sculptural images of Dizang were constructed in the Northern Wei, but at least seven dated Dizang sculptures were from the early Tang (650–704). Tsukamoto counted a total of thirty-three dated and undated images of Dizang at Longmen; see Tsukamoto 1942: 375, 380. For another study of Dizang art and inscriptions at Longmen, see Chang 1990.

dence independently tell us about the circumstances that contributed to the spread of Dizang worship in the late seventh century? What practices were undertaken, who worshiped this bodhisattva, and why did they do so?

Buddhist Records of Dizang Worship

The earliest record of Dizang worship is found in a historical work authored by the *vinaya* master Daoxuan 道宣 (596–667). In the *Xu gaoseng zhuan* 續高僧傳 (Continued Biographies of Eminent Monks), which was completed in 645 and continuously updated until 665, Daoxuan recorded the efficacies of a Dizang image in Shan 陝 prefecture (in modern-day Henan):

> It was asked: Nowadays numinous *stūpas* are erected all over the various prefectures. Many auspicious omens have appeared in the two prefectures of Cao 曹 and Shan. To whom [are these omens] attributed? Reply: For Shan prefecture, it is the Tree Manifestation Dizang (Xianshu Dizang 現樹地藏); for Cao prefecture, it is the Luminous Flower Ākāśagarbha (Guanghua Xukong 光華虛空).[6]

Except for building *stūpas*, Daoxuan does not mention the practices of this local form of Dizang worship. State decrees were issued in 601, 603, and 604 to build numinous *stūpas* throughout the country. This trend was very likely prompted by the retelling of stories featuring miracles of *stūpa* and relic worship, especially the eighty-four thousand *stūpas* built by the Indian *cakravartin* Aśoka.[7] By the fifth century, Chinese narratives associated Aśoka's *stūpas* with the production of efficacious images with such frequency that *stūpa* and image worship became closely connected.[8] It is probable that the construction of *stūpas* also increased the production of images placed in the *stūpas* and venerated as part of the *stūpa* cult. Daoxuan seems to have blurred the distinction between *stūpa* and image worship when he cites Dizang and Ākāśagarbha as part of the cults of numinous *stūpas.* His pairing of Dizang with Ākāśagarbha is interesting, but the dearth of evidence makes it impossible to speculate on this relationship.[9] It should be noted that the Tree Mani-

---

6. *Xu gaoseng zhuan,* T2060:50.668b–c. The epithet is ambiguous and depending on the nature of the miracle, the name of the image could mean "The Dizang Who Manifested Trees," "The Dizang Who Manifested as a Tree," or "The Dizang Who Manifested from a Tree." The passage offers no clue on how to translate the phrase, and as far as I can determine, the epithet does not occur in other records.

7. See Daoxuan's records of the widespread building of *stūpas* in his *Guang hongming ji* 廣弘明集, T2103:52.213a–221a, and *Gantong lu* 感通錄 T2106:52.404a–412c. See Fan 1979: 107–109.

8. In his study of miraculous images, Koichi Shinohara (1998) demonstrated the relationship between the building of Aśoka *stūpas* and the stories about the efficacies of images related to Aśoka.

9. Ākāśagarbha very likely began as just another name in the bodhisattva directories, but he rapidly acquired a history and personality of his own. From a cluster of early Chinese trans-

festation Dizang is located in Shan prefecture, not far from Longmen Grottoes in the city of Luoyang 洛陽 (also in Henan).

Another work by Daoxuan, the *Shijia fangzhi* 釋迦方志 (A Gazetteer of Śākya), a record of Buddhist landmarks completed in 650, also mentions Dizang worship. After surveying Guanyin's miracles, Daoxuan concludes:

> Four hundred years have passed since the time when the country was divided into the sixteen [states of] Jin 晉, Song 宋, Liang 梁, Chen 陳, Wei 魏, Yan 燕, Qin 秦, and Zhao 趙. As for those who have obtained relief through the invocation and recitation of the names of Guanyin, Dizang, Maitreya, and Amitābha, it surpasses my ability to enumerate them. Thus the biographical and catalog records are limited.[10]

This passage suggests that Buddhist cults shared common practices such as intonation of the name (*chengming* 稱名), image recollection, and scriptural recitation (*niansong* 念誦). In the mid-seventh century, the term *nian* 念 referred to a broad range of practices from deep meditation of buddha-recollections to rote repetition of the name, both of which were adaptable to the nature and needs of the practitioner.[11] Because the intonation of the name is specified separately in the above passage, it is likely that *nian* here refers to a widespread form of devotional contemplation, which involves gazing piously at the image while engaging in some kind of recitation.

A similar reference to the worship of Guanyin, Dizang, Maitreya, and Amitābha—dating the practice to 536—appears in the *Fayuan zhulin* 法苑珠林 (The Pearl Forest of the Dharma Grove), an encyclopedic anthology of scriptural passages and miracle stories completed in 668 by Daoshi 道世 (d. 683).[12] In addition, *The Pearl Forest of the Dharma Grove* records the practice in 665 of copying a particularly efficacious painting of Dizang, which

---

lations of scriptures, the earliest of which is attributed to Dharmakṣema, one can conclude that the transformation happened in a pre-Chinese context; see, for instance, *Da fangdeng daji jing*, T397; *Xukongyun pusa jing* 虛空孕菩薩經, T408; *Guan Xukongzang pusa jing* 觀虛空藏菩薩經, T409. Moreover, the name Ākāśagarbha, unlike Kṣitigarbha, is obviously of Indian origin. Fifth in the Indian system of "great elements" *(mahābhūta)*, *ākāśa*, or "space," is not mentioned in the Chinese elaboration of elements. Although earth was one of the elements in the Indian system, it was referred to as *bhū*, not *kṣitī* or *dhāraṇī*, even though all these words can mean "earth." Significantly, Ākāśagarbha enjoys a close relationship with Dizang as the latter's complementary opposite, and the two bodhisattvas are frequently invoked together after the fashion of the Indian Vedic pairing of Dyaus (Sky) and Pṛthivī (Earth).

10. *Shijia fangzhi*, T2088:51.972b.

11. On the medieval Chinese use of *nianfo* 念佛, Andrews (1993: 18–19, 23–26) correlates the practices of buddha-invocation and buddha-contemplation, respectively, with the distinction between lay and monastic practitioners—a reductionist correlation deriving from his attempt to differentiate between lay and monastic forms of Pure Land devotion, which he equates with popular and elite practices. On continuities between lay and monastic practices, see Schopen 1985.

12. The *Fayuan zhulin* affirms that those who obtain relief by invoking and reciting the names of Guanyin, Dizang, Maitreya, and Amitābha surpass the written records. (T2122:

the artist Zhang Sengyou 張僧繇 (d.u.) originally executed in Yi 益 prefecture (modern-day Chengdu, Sichuan). The painting and all copies of it apparently emitted a mysterious light:

> The painting of Dizang Bodhisattva at the Monastery of Dharma Congregation (Faju si 法聚寺), located in the suburbs of Yi prefecture, shows him seated with legs pendant on a wickerwork couch. The height [of the image] is 0.8 or 0.9 feet. Zhang Sengyou painted the original icon. In the seventh month of 665, a monk in that monastery made a painted copy, which from time to time would emit a light like a ring of gold, exactly like the halo of the original. Thereafter copies were made and they all similarly emitted light. In the eighth month of that year, it was decreed that one [copy] be submitted to the imperial palace for worship. Nowadays, all the devotional paintings, which clerics and laity made inside and outside the capital, also emit light. One understands from this how immeasurable the Buddha's power is.[13]

Zhang's painting is the earliest recorded Dizang icon showing the deity alone and thus indicative of his growing cultic status. It is unclear why the painting was undertaken in the first place, but the local cult that formed around it was based largely on venerating and copying the image, which was done by both monks and laity. Because a copy of the painting was submitted to the imperial palace in 665, one may conclude that Dizang worship was practiced in the imperial precincts in the capital of Chang'an 長安 during the reign of Emperor Gaozong 高宗 (r. 649–683). According to Daoshi, the icon originated on China's southwestern border (Sichuan), but the earliest art-historical evidence (i.e., the sculptures at Longmen) locates Dizang's cult in north central China. Zhang's painting then is evidence of the transmission of a local strand of the Dizang cult. Through tales of its numinous efficacy and its duplication, the icon "traveled" from its birthplace in the southwest to the capital in central China.

Dizang worship must have been sufficiently widespread by the mid-seventh century to catch the eye of elite clerics engaged in documenting and perpetuating Chinese Buddhist history. It should be noted, however, that records do not link Dizang worship to Sanjie jiao. In his *Continued Biographies*, Daoxuan includes an account of Xinxing, the Sanjie jiao founder, which means he was aware of the movement and its activities.[14] Yet when speaking of cults, he does not connect Dizang Bodhisattva with this movement. Buddhist records place the dissemination of Dizang worship in a larger devotional milieu in which *stūpa* and image veneration were performed together. The Dizang cult seems to have spread through the usual

---

53.411c). A similar statement is found in a tenth-century non-Buddhist anthology titled the *Taiping guangji* 太平廣記, 111: 765.

13. *Fayuan zhulin*, T2122:53.392c. This story was subsequently collected in the tenth-century compilation of Dizang miracle tales the *Lingyan ji* (149: 354b).

14. *Xu gaoseng zhuan*, T2060:50.559c–560b.

channels—that is, through testaments of religious efficacy and their transmission. The records mostly mention Dizang in relation to other cults, which suggests that veneration of Dizang took shape in a cultic environment where variant forms of Buddhist piety flourished.

The Sanjie Jiao Connection

Sanjie jiao was one of several Buddhist movements that developed in the sixth century in response to the exigencies of living in the period of the decline of the Dharma. Like other Buddhist leaders of his time, its founder, Xinxing, was convinced that the dreaded epoch of Buddhism's demise had arrived and formulating a soteriology that would enable Buddhists to practice during such a period was essential.[15] The movement prospered briefly in the seventh and eighth centuries but eventually disappeared after the tenth century, following repeated persecution from ruling authorities. Because its texts were largely expunged from the canon, little was known about Sanjie jiao until some of its writings were recovered in the twentieth century from Dunhuang and Japanese archives.[16] Based on these manuscripts, Yabuki Keiki conclusively showed that Sanjie jiao proponents frequently looked to the *Scripture on the Ten Wheels* as one of their sources of scriptural authority. Xinxing composed two commentaries on the *Scripture on the Ten Wheels* and cited the fifth-century translation no less than 120 times in his early work, the four-scroll *Sanjie fofa* 三階佛法 (The Three Levels of Buddhist Teach-

15. Xinxing's biography is recorded in the *Xu gaoseng zhuan* (T2060:50.559c–560b) and stele inscriptions. Legend has it that Xinxing's mother dreamt he was given to her as a baby by a spirit. He was ordained as a monk at Fazang si 法藏寺 in Xiang 相 prefecture. He practiced asceticism, wore little, and often refrained from eating. When the Northern Qi (550–577) was destroyed by the Northern Zhou (557–589) and Buddhists were persecuted, Xinxing returned to lay life. But in 581, after Buddhism had been revived by the Sui (581–618), Xinxing was summoned to the capital, where a Sanjie cloister had been built inside Zhenji si 真寂寺. Here Xinxing and his disciples devoted themselves to promoting and composing Sanjie jiao works. Five other Sanjie cloisters were built in the capital: Huadu si 化度寺, Guangming si 光明寺, Cimen si 慈門寺, Huiri si 慧日寺, and Hongshan si 弘善寺. In accordance with his spirit of universal giving, upon his death in 594 his remains were sent to Mount Zhongnan and left for birds and animals. A pagoda with a stele inscription was erected at the foot of the mountain to house his relics. The site soon became a cemetery for his disciples, and Mount Zhongnan emerged as an important center associated with Sanjie jiao teachings. It was said that Xinxing had more than three hundred disciples, although the names of only a few are known. Among the most important were Benji 本濟 (562–632) and Sengyong 僧邕 (543–632).

16. Since the invaluable, pioneering study by Yabuki (1927), other important works on Sanjie jiao have been undertaken. Nishimoto Teruma's (1998) study of the movement, which introduces manuscript discoveries after Yabuki's publication, has become a classic. In the sphere of western scholarship, James Hubbard has researched and written on Sanjie jiao; see Hubbard 1986 for his unpublished dissertation and Hubbard 1991, 1996, and 2001 for his published work. Mark Lewis (1990) has also published an article that treats the suppression of Sanjie jiao.

ings).[17] In light of Sanjie jiao's promotion of the *Scripture on the Ten Wheels*, Yabuki believed that Sanjie jiao advocated Dizang worship and was instrumental in the initial spread of the cult.

To support his argument, Yabuki highlights the following passage in the second scroll of *The Three Levels of Buddhist Teachings* (S 2084):

> As for the realm of the One Vehicle, the living beings of the One Vehicle, during the time when a buddha resides in the world: It is the best of the benevolent worlds, benevolent times, and benevolent living beings. The teachings formulated are those of eternity, bliss, self, and purity. Various buddhas and bodhisattvas, led by Vairocana, Śākyamuni, and the Bodhisattva Mahāsattva Samantabhadra, have together practiced this [teaching]. This is based on the *Mahāvaipulya-avataṃsaka-sūtra* (the entire scrolls one and two), the *Laṅkāvatara-sūtra* (scroll one), and so forth.
>
> As for the realm of the five turbulences and various vices after the Buddha's quiescence, with living beings of nihilistic and eternalist views: It is the worst of vile worlds, vile times, and vile living beings. The teachings formulated are those of suffering, impermanence, lack of self, and defilement. Various buddhas and bodhisattvas, led by Śākyamuni and the Bodhisattva Mahāsattva Dizang, have together practiced this [teaching]. This is based on the *Scripture on the Ten Wheels*, the *Candragarbha Scripture*, the fourfold *āgama*, the *vinaya* of the various schools, the *Abhidharma* discourses, and so forth.[18]

This passage represents Dizang as the leading bodhisattva of this world of five turbulences—one who has mastered the third level of teaching that Sanjie jiao believed Chinese Buddhists should practice during the degenerate times in which they lived. But it does not conclusively show that Sanjie jiao promoted Dizang as a cultic object; Dizang is invoked only as a role model for practitioners of the third level of teachings. Moreover, because the above extract is missing from the Japanese manuscript copy of *The Three Levels of Buddhist Teachings*, it is possible that Xinxing's followers added this critical passage.

Facing the paucity of evidence in Sanjie jiao writings, Yabuki looked for corroboration outside of the Sanjie jiao corpus. He relied heavily on Pure Land polemical literature, specifically records of a debate among seventh- and eighth-century Buddhist intellectuals over the efficacies of the various

---

17. Yabuki 1927: 595. The commentaries are now extant only in partial quotations in other texts. The two commentaries ascribed to Xinxing are the *Shilun yi yi li ming* 十輪依義立名 and the *Shilun luechao* 十輪略抄.

18. *Sanjie fofa, Sanjie jiao can juan* 三階教殘卷, 23. Although this passage offers important confirmation of Dizang's possible role in Sanjie jiao's soteriology, it should be cautioned that it is not found in other versions of the *Sanjie fofa* and is missing, for instance, from the collated Japanese version in Yabuki's compilation. Using a set of partial manuscripts discovered in Japan, Yabuki provided a comparative edition of the entire text.

forms of Buddhist devotion. Pure Land exponents at the heart of this controversy attributed Dizang worship to Sanjie jiao and then contrasted it to the Pure Land practice of Amitābha worship. In his work, Kuiji 窺基 (632–682), a disciple of Xuanzang, describes adherents of Sanjie jiao as "ordinary fools of the inferior grade . . . suited to prostrate and confess before Dizang Bodhisattva."[19] Kuiji points out that if one were instead "to focus one's mind on invoking the [Amitābha] Buddha and aspiring to be reborn in the Pure Land," then upon death one would be reborn in the Pure Land. In such a circumstance, Kuiji argues, one is already eternally separated from the three evil paths of rebirth; there is no need to look to Dizang, whose vow was to relieve the suffering of living beings on the evil paths of rebirth.[20]

Another seventh-century Pure Land proponent, Huaigan 懷感 (d.u.), a disciple of Shandao 善導 (613–681), further argued that reciting Amitābha's name surpasses that of Dizang because the merits of a bodhisattva cannot equal those of a buddha:

> The *Scripture on the Ten Wheels* states: "If, for a hundred great *kalpa*s, a person single-mindedly recites [the name of] Guanyin Bodhisattva and so forth, it will not be comparable to recite momentarily once [the name of] Dizang Bodhisattva." If, for a hundred great *kalpa*s, one recites [the name of] Guanyin Bodhisattva, it will, as previously compared and calculated, definitely exceed making offerings to a thousand of a million countless names of bodhisattvas. If, for numerous *kalpa*s, one recites [the name of] the Bodhisattva Dizang, that is not comparable to just one utterance of single-minded recitation of [the name of] Amitābha Buddha. The merits will be countless and boundless. In this manner comparing the Buddha with Dizang Bodhisattva, and Dizang Bodhisattva with Guanyin Bodhisattva, and [then] Guanyin Bodhisattva with the other bodhisattvas numerous as the sixty-two *koṭi* of grains of sand in the Ganges River and so forth, one should then recite the [name of the] Buddha. The merits of a single utterance exceed [the merits] gained from reciting the names of as many bodhisattvas as the innumerable *kalpa*s of grains of sand in the Ganges River or from offering the four daily requisites to [this number of bodhisattvas].[21] In this manner, even a single instant of reciting [the name of the] Buddha will then exceed [the merits of] reciting [the names of] other bodhisattvas or [the merits] of one or two *kalpa*s of religious cultivation. How can one recite [the name of] the Buddha and yet have scarce merits? Through this comparative quantification, it should be known that the merits [from reciting the Buddha's name] are tremendous.[22]

19. *Xifang yaojue shiyi tonggui* 西方要決釋疑通規, T1964:47.108c.

20. Ibid.:47.109a.

21. The four daily requisites (*sishi gongyang* 四事供養) are usually listed as clothing, food or beverage, bedding or lodging, and medicine.

22. *Shi jingtu qunyi lun* 釋淨土群疑論, T1960:47.69b–c.

The controversy surfaces again in the work of Daojing 道鏡 (d.u.), who was either Huaigan's contemporary or must have lived shortly after.[23] In his *Nianfo jing* 念佛鏡 (Buddha-Recitation Mirror), Daojing also disputes Sanjie jiao's practice of Dizang worship:

> Question: Are the merits of the Sanjie jiao practice of reciting the name of Dizang Bodhisattva greater, lesser, or equal to those of reciting [the name of] Amitābha Buddha?
> Reply: The merits of reciting "Amitābha Buddha" exceed those of reciting "Dizang Bodhisattva" by a thousand million times. How does one know this? According to the *Guanyin jing* 觀音經 (The Avalokiteśvara Scripture), if a person makes offerings to bodhisattvas as numerous as the grains of sand in the sixty-two *koṭi* of the Ganges River, it will not be as good as venerating, prostrating, and making offerings just once to Guanyin Bodhisattva. The *Scripture on the Ten Wheels* states: "Reciting 'Guanyin' for one hundred aeons is not comparable to reciting once 'Dizang Bodhisattva.'" The *Qunyi lun* 群疑論 (Discourse on a Group of Doubts) states: "Reciting 'Dizang Bodhisattva' for one great *kalpa* is not comparable to reciting just once 'Amitābha Buddha.'" Why is this so? The Buddha is the King of the Dharma, [whereas] the bodhisattvas are the ministers of the Dharma. When the king is absent, the ministers inevitably become lax. . . . The Buddha is the perfectly realized being whose perfection of attainment surpasses all stages [of the path]. Hence the merits of those who increasingly recite [the Buddha's name] are the greatest, exceeding [those of reciting] Dizang['s name] a thousand million times. The bodhisattvas do not yet belong to the stage of buddhahood and their attainments have not yet been completely perfected. Therefore the merits [from reciting their names] are exceedingly scarce."[24]

For Yabuki, the Pure Land writings offer conclusive evidence that Sanjie jiao adopted Dizang as its patron saint—a natural development given the movement's preference for the *Scripture on the Ten Wheels*.[25]

Certainly Yabuki's contribution cannot be understated, but one should also be wary because his argument rests heavily on the presupposed validity of Pure Land polemical literature, which accentuates Dizang worship as a cardinal trait of Sanjie jiao practice in opposition to worship of Amitābha in Pure Land. The nature of apologetic literature raises questions as to the ac-

23. We know nothing about Daojing's life and work except for his composition of the *Nianfo jing*. The text is ascribed to both Daojing and Shandao; Shinkō Mochizuki (1975: 293–300) proposed that Daojing was probably Shandao's disciple, which would make him a contemporary of Huaigan. Julian Pas contends that no source on Shandao ever suggests his role in composing the *Nianfo jing*, and no sources list Daojing as Shandao's disciple; see Pas 1995: 112–115. Whether or not he was Shandao's disciple, Daojing was familiar with and cited Huaigan's work in the *Nianfo jing*.

24. *Nianfo jing*, T1966:47.127b–c. On Dao's writings, see Liu 2000: 425–432.

25. Yabuki 1927: 642.

curacy of its description by its opponents. Hence, one should exercise some caution when approaching polemical representations that may intentionally highlight doctrinal or practical distinctions to fortify an argument. After all, enforcing a strong contrast between their object of piety and that of Sanjie jiao was crucial for the Pure Land spokesmen because their main goal was to establish the supremacy of Amitābha over Dizang worship. Before adopting indiscriminately the Pure Land characterization, one needs to reexamine the association between Sanjie jiao and Dizang worship as represented in Sanjie jiao writings.

In this regard, a major contribution is Nishimoto Teruma's investigation of Sanjie jiao materials discovered after Yabuki's publication.[26] Mention of Dizang occurs in two Dunhuang texts edited by Nishimoto: the *Di san jie fofa guangshi* 第三階佛法廣釋 (The Extensive Explanation of the Third-Level Buddhist Teachings, S 6344) and the *Sanjie guanfa lueshi* 三階觀法略釋 (The Abbreviated Explanation of the Contemplation of Dharmas in the Three Levels, P 2268). Both texts were probably composed toward the end of the seventh century or even later.[27] A reference to Dizang occurs in *The Extensive Explanation* when the "Four Contemplations on Liberating Living Beings" (*Si zhong dusheng guan* 四種度生觀) are enumerated. In the fourth contemplation, "Liberation through Recitation," one is encouraged "to recite the separate names of Amitābha Buddha and Dizang."[28] Another example is the discussion of Sanjie jiao's teaching on non-dualism in *The Abbreviated Explanation*:

> From the causal perspective, there are no names for the living beings of the six paths nor are there forms of living beings of the six paths. From the perspective of effect, the separate names of Amitābha and Dizang do not exist nor do the separate forms of Amitābha and Dizang exist. This is the nameless, formless dharma.[29]

These passages hardly present Amitābha and Dizang as incompatible objects of worship belonging to disparate religious movements. A Sanjie jiao text, edited by Yabuki, explains the notion of universal nature through an analogy, likening the Buddhist deities to different parts of the body: In the analogy, Dizang is the body and Amitābha the heart.[30] Judging from these

---

26. Nishimoto 1998: 475–673.

27. As Nishimoto points out, because the *Di san jie fofa guangshi* quotes the *Miyan jing* 密嚴經, a work attributed to the Indian translator Divākara (Dipoheluo 地婆訶羅, 613–687), it should be dated toward the end of the seventh century or after. In the case of the *Sanjie guanfa lueshi*, he points to the obvious borrowing of language from the works of Xuanzang and the Huayan teacher Zhiyan 智儼 (602–668). Hence, he concludes that the work must be dated to the end of the seventh century or after; see Nishimoto 1998: 206, 212, 219.

28. The line reads: 稱阿彌陀佛地藏別名; see ibid.: 620.

29. Ibid.: 635.

30. *Xinxing kouji zhenrushi guan qi xu juan diyi* 信行口集真如實觀起序卷第一, *Sanjie jiao can juan*, 195.

references, Sanjie jiao members seem to have regarded Amitābha and Dizang as no different from each other in their fundamental nature, a suitable view given their emphasis on the Universal Buddha. Needless to say, this picture is contrary to Pure Land representations, which polemically contrast Dizang and Amitābha worship as two separate practices belonging respectively to Sanjie jiao and Pure Land.[31]

An archaeological excavation in 1981 uncovered a Sanjie jiao cave among the stone scripture grottoes at Golden Stream Bay (Jinchuan wan 金川灣), located in Chunhua 淳化, Shaanxi.[32] Inscriptions date the cave to 662–670. An image of Śākyamuni Buddha is sculpted at the back of the cave, and its walls are inscribed with no less than eight texts, among them the *Scripture on the Ten Wheels* and other compendia associated with Sanjie jiao.[33] The inscribed texts include a few that, until the discovery of the cave, were known only from their titles listed in the catalogs of Sanjie jiao works. The cave is thus a Sanjie jiao archive, the study of which will yield invaluable insights into the movement. Zhang Zong notes the lack of images in the cave—specifically those of Dizang. According to him, Sanjie jiao leaned toward iconoclasm, emphasizing buddhahood as a universal human ideal and rejecting the construction of images and pagodas. He concludes that Sanjie jiao's practice of Dizang worship did not necessarily involve the use of Dizang images and might have been confined largely to ritual prostration, recitation, and repentance. However, the Śākyamuni image on the back wall of the cave at Jinchuan wan disputes this. Moreover, one Sanjie jiao work, the *Dasheng fajie wujinzang fa shi* 大乘法界無盡藏法釋 (Explanation of the Inexhaustible Practices in the Dharma Realm of the Great Vehicle), exhorts the reader to undertake repairs of statues and temples as offerings made to the Buddha.[34] It would seem that Sanjie jiao's rejection of icons was a rhetorical strategy that stemmed from its teachings of universalism and non-dualism and did not necessarily translate into actual iconoclastic practices.[35] Therefore, although their writings frowned on the

31. One should note that the doctrinal teachings of Pure Land and Sanjie jiao were not as irrevocably polarized as the polemical literature would have us believe. Elsewhere Huaigan writes in a manner that actually seems to synchronize Pure Land and Sanjie jiao teachings; see *Shi jingtu qunyi lun*, T1960:47.44b. Also see Liu 2000: 336–337.

32. The discovery of the cave was first publicized in a newspaper article on archaeological finds; see Yao 1997. Chinese scholars are now studying this cave; for a report of initial findings, see Zhang and Wang 2003.

33. Zhang Zong 2003: 443. The image was originally made in the Tang period but was damaged during the Cultural Revolution and has since been restored.

34. *Dasheng fajie wujinzang fa shi* (S 721; Giles no. 5563), *Sanjie jiao can juan*, 174–175.

35. For instance, one of the key teachings of Sanjie jiao is the Universal Refuges, and the literature refers to the concepts of Universal Buddha, Universal Dharma, and Universal Saṅgha; see Hubbard 2001: 99–148. Reservations about the use of images to convey religious truth is found in early Buddhist history. It was expressed, for example, in early Mahāyāna texts such as the *Aṣṭasāhasrikā-prajñāpāramitā-sūtra*. The Chan Buddhist attitude toward images is encapsulated in the popular dictum "See the Buddha, kill the Buddha." Late Tang and Song Chan monks often railed against the use of language, images, ritual, and other

construction of massive temples and colossal statues, Sanjie jiao proponents were not necessarily iconoclasts. Zhang's assumption is questionable, but his argument is a useful reminder that the relationship between Sanjie jiao and Dizang worship needs to be reexamined.

From the above survey of the evidence, one can only conclude that Sanjie jiao promoted the *Scripture on the Ten Wheels* and viewed Dizang as the bodhisattva-savior of the defiled realm of the five turbulences. Sanjie jiao members certainly engaged in devotional practices involving Dizang Bodhisattva, but the literature does not indicate that the movement necessarily accepted this bodhisattva as its patron saint in the way Pure Land polemical writings suggest. Catalyzed by its adherence to the *Scripture on the Ten Wheels*, Sanjie jiao may have adopted practices of Dizang worship discernible in the religious environment surveyed by Daoxuan and Daoshi. Sanjie jiao did contribute to the spread of Dizang Bodhisattva veneration in the seventh century, but the evidence hardly suggests that Sanjie jiao was critical in the formation and spread of the Dizang cult.

The Work of the Translator and Exegete Sinbang

Who among the Sanjie jiao practitioners would be drawn to Dizang worship? What would such a person contribute to the spread of the Dizang cult? The seventh-century Korean translator and exegete Sinbang 神昉 (Ch. Shenfang, fl. 645–651) played an important role in fostering the connection among Sanjie jiao, the *Scripture on the Ten Wheels*, and Dizang Bodhisattva.[36] Sinbang originally resided at the Dharma Sea Monastery (Fahai si 法海寺) but soon joined Xuanzang at the Monastery for Propagating Merits (Hongfu si 弘福寺) as one of the eleven members of the first translation bureau, over which Xuanzang presided in 646.[37] Sinbang participated in Xuanzang's translation of the *Mahāvaibhāsa-śāstra* (*Da piposha lun* 大毘婆沙論) at the Great Compassionate Kindness Monastery (Da ci'en si 大慈恩寺) and also assisted in Xuanzang's final work, the translation of the *Mahāprajñāpāramitā-sūtra* (*Da bore jing* 大般若經, Scripture on Great Wisdom) at the Palace of Jade Flowers (Yuhua gong 玉華宮). Because Sinbang had worked with Xuanzang and his translation team, it is not surprising that among his works are Yogācāra writings. More relevant for our purposes, however, is Sinbang's participation in

forms of mediating between mundane reality and ultimate truth. But again, this rhetoric was never taken literally: Chan monasteries were connected with innovative expressions of iconic worship, including the mummification of awakened Chan teachers and the ritual use of portraits of Chan monks. On iconoclasm in Chinese Buddhist history, see Kieschnick 2003: 69–80. On iconic worship in Chan Buddhism, see Faure 1992; Foulk and Sharf 1993–1994. For Buddhist attitudes toward iconic worship, see Sharf 2001a.

36. The *Yuqie lun ji* 瑜伽論記 refers to Sinbang as the Silla master Bang (Xinluo Fang shi 新羅昉師); see T1828:42.682a. Yabuki called attention to Sinbang as an important link between Sanjie jiao, the *Scripture on the Ten Wheels*, and the cult of Dizang. Subsequent scholarship, including my treatment above, is very much indebted to Yabuki's work.

37. *Kaiyuan shijiao lu* 開元釋教錄, T2154:55.559a–b

Xuanzang's rendition of the *Scripture on the Ten Wheels.*[38] Sinbang was among the three copyists who wrote down the revised text, presumably as dictated by Xuanzang.[39]

In addition, Sinbang wrote a preface to the seventh-century translation and composed a commentary to the scripture, which explicitly aligns it and Dizang Bodhisattva with Sanjie jiao teachings.[40] He first introduces the concepts of the One Vehicle and the Three Vehicles and then associates the *Scripture on the Ten Wheels* with the period of the Final Dharma:

> The *Scripture on the Ten Wheels* is then the teaching of the Final Dharma for this world. How does one know this? The Buddha compared the corrupt roots [of those living] in the evil age of the Final Dharma, a time remote from the Buddha's departure from this world, to damaged vessels. Possessing nihilistic views is similar to being born blind. The deep intoxication in the five desires is likened to a rocky landscape where nothing will sprout. Indulgence in the ten unsalutary actions is like grimy dirt on a foul body. Therefore, this scripture can cleanse a foul body, open the eyes of the blind, mend a damaged vessel, and fertilize an arid land. The bodhisattva thus appears in the form of a monk *(śramaṇa).* The elephant king venerates the renunciate's robes. Using this symbolic appearance, [the bodhisattva] converts the shameless, shows protection and support of the two matters, and accomplishes the path and fruition of the Three Vehicles.[41]

Because the *Scripture on the Ten Wheels* does not mention the threefold division of times and teachings (One Vehicle, Three Vehicles, or Final Dharma), one may conclude that Sinbang was drawing from the Three Levels Teachings that flourished in Chang'an during his time. At the end of his preface, he bemoans the unfortunate circumstances of his day, decrying it as the interim period "when the previous buddha has gone and the next buddha has yet to come."[42] Sinbang's preface thus aligns the *Scripture on the Ten Wheels*

38. Françoise Wang-Toutain has questioned the attribution of the seventh-century translation of the *Scripture on the Ten Wheels* to Xuanzang. She argues that Xuanzang, with his erudition in Buddhist philosophy, could not have been associated with the scripture, which reflects popular Buddhist developments of the period. She proposes that it was more likely that his followers (perhaps someone like Sinbang) were behind the new translation, which was subsequently attributed to the famed Tang pilgrim-translator. In further support of her argument, she points to the connections that Xuanzang's followers like Sinbang must have had with Sanjie jiao, especially through common centers of religious activities like Zhongnan and Chang'an. See Wang-Toutain 1998: 116–117. Her argument presupposes a necessary separation of doctrinal evolution from so-called "popular religion." She implies that we should discredit Xuanzang's role as the translator of other "nonphilosophical" works such as the *Sukhāvatīvyūha-sūtra.*

39. *Dasheng daji Dizang shilun jing,* T411:13.728a.

40. The preface appears at the end of the new translation; see *Dasheng daji Dizang shilun jing,* T411:13.777a–c.

41. Ibid.:13.777a–b.

42. Ibid.:13.777c.

with contemporary teachings on the eventual extinction of Buddhism, specifically Sanjie jiao's interpretation of these teachings.

Although Sinbang's commentary, the *Shilun jing chao* 十輪經抄 (Writings on the Scripture on the Ten Wheels), is no longer extant, portions of his work are cited in a later Japanese text.[43] In Sinbang's commentary, he explains drawing from *The Three Levels of Teachings*:

> First are the living beings with the disposition for the One Vehicle: The teacher is Vairocana Buddha; the community is led by Samantabhadra Bodhisattva; [the scriptures are] the *Avataṃsaka-sūtra* and others of the same category. Second are the living beings with the disposition for the Three Vehicles: The teacher is Śākyamuni Buddha; the community is led by Dizang Bodhisattva; [and the scriptures are] this *Scripture on the Ten Wheels* and others of the same category. Just as living beings are classified into two ranks, the teachings are categorized into two methods, and the spheres are polarized into the purified and defiled realms. . . . There was a great spiritual friend, the Meditation Master Xinxing. Interacting with rare beings, consulting Sages of the Way, [he believed that we] must be dwelling in the confused and degenerate times of the Latter Dharma. . . . Therefore, among the Tripiṭaka teachings, he espoused only this [scripture] in the hope of making practice suitable to the disposition and making the teaching correspond to the maladies. He regarded the times to be the Latter Dharma, the disposition to be that of the Three Vehicles, and the main practice to be [the cultivation of] merits.[44]

The references to Xinxing and his teachings confirm that Sinbang was familiar with the Sanjie jiao movement. Xinxing certainly privileged the *Scripture on the Ten Wheels,* but it was by no means the only scripture associated with his movement. For Sinbang, the *Scripture on the Ten Wheels* was the paramount teaching for the defiled realm of the Sahā world during the demise of Buddhist teachings.

Sinbang's works reveal little about him besides his predilection for Yogācāra teachings and the *Scripture on the Ten Wheels.* A tenth-century description of Sinbang offers a glimpse into his daily religious practice:

> From an early age, the monk Sinbang of the Compassion Monastery (Cibei si 慈悲寺) had listened and studied the *Scripture on the Ten Wheels.* He zealously practiced asceticism, distinguishing himself from ordinary men. He wore discarded clothing, worshiped and repented six times a day, and begged for

43. Japanese catalogs of Buddhist scriptures attribute a *Shilun jing chao* in two or three fascicles to "The Mahāyāna Teacher Bang 昉." See *Hossō shū shōsho* 法相宗章疏, T2180:55.1139a; *Tōiki dentō mokuroku* 東域伝燈目録, T2183:55.1150b; *Chūshin hossō shū shōsho* 注進法相宗章疏, T2181:55.1141b.

44. Yabuki 1927: 639. The above passage was cited in a later Japanese Pure Land text, the *Gungi ron tanyō ki* 群疑論探要記 (Ch. *Qunyi lun tanyao ji*), attributed to an author named Dōshū 道忠.

> alms for his livelihood.[45] Every time he lectured on the *Scripture on the Ten Wheels*, he would always say that it was not fitting for the multitude to recite Mahāyāna scriptures and that those who recited [these scriptures] would descend into hell. Finally, when his last hour arrived, his body was burnt alive by the fire of hell. Black smoke covered his physical [remains]. The monk Sijian 思簡 [d.u.] from the Monastery of Teachings to Relieve [the World] (Jifa si 濟法寺) personally witnessed this incident and was convinced that those who discontinued the study of wisdom will inevitably incur inauspicious omens. The sight of the body [burning alive] was a testament.[46]

Because Xinxing and his followers were known to beg for alms, perform austerities, and conduct repentance during the six daily intervals, the above passage suggests that Sinbang carried out Sanjie jiao practices and was, therefore, a follower of the movement.[47] Sinbang was attacked for the "heretical piety" he displayed toward the *Scripture on the Ten Wheels* and for his denunciation of Mahāyāna scriptures. Evidently, he preached the *Scripture on the Ten Wheels* often and may even have advocated its recitation over other Buddhist texts.[48] Religious activities of monks like Sinbang probably facilitated the widespread dissemination of the *Scripture on the Ten Wheels* in medieval China.

Archaeological findings confirm that the *Scripture on the Ten Wheels* was widely circulated from the seventh century on. Several stone-scripture sites like the previously mentioned Jinchuan wan, the Sleeping Buddha Cloister (Wofo yuan 臥佛院) in Anyue 安岳 (Sichuan), and the Stone Scriptures Hill (Shijing shan 石經山) in Fangshan 房山 (Beijing), all contain engravings of the *Scripture on the Ten Wheels*.[49] These inscribed stone scriptures were under-

45. In India the six periods are defined as sunset, early night, midnight, dawn, morning, and noon. This temporal division was the basis for liturgical worship and confession in the sixth and seventh centuries. For a study of the six periods of worship in relation to Pure Land ritual, see Pas 1986–1987: 49–82.

46. *Shimen zijing lu* 釋門自鏡錄 by Huaixin 懷信 (fl. 843), T2083:51.806b. This condemnation of Sinbang's misplaced piety occurs immediately after a passage criticizing Xinxing.

47. Daoxuan describes Xinxing's religious activities as follows:

> Furthermore, at the capital, Master [Xinxing] established five monasteries. The five monasteries are the Huadu si 化度寺, Guangming si 光明寺, Cimen si 慈門寺, Huiri si 慧日寺, and Hongshan si 弘善寺. Since that time, all these temples have exalted and continued his regulations. All made offerings, circumambulated six times daily, and begged for alms for their livelihood. Such sincere and pure piety cannot be surpassed! (*Xu gaoseng zhuan*, T2060:50.560a)

48. The above record does not exactly tell us that Sinbang recited the *Scripture on the Ten Wheels*, but we know from the *Continued Biographies* that the monk Sirui 思睿 (d.u.) recited the scripture regularly; see *Xu gaoseng zhuan*, T2061:50.863a–b.

49. For a preliminary study of the inscribed scriptures at Jingchuan wan, see Zhang and Wang 2003: 71, figs. 11, 12. Wofo yuan houses 139 niches, 15 of which contain cliff inscriptions of Buddhist texts executed in the Tang period. The *Scripture on the Ten Wheels* is one of the scriptures inscribed at Wofo yuan, dated to ca. 728; see Wang 1989: 91–92. A seventh-century trans-

taken from the eighth century and after. Dedicatory inscriptions reveal that inscribing scriptures on the rocks was frequently undertaken as an offering.[50] Visual representations of the scripture were also executed. For example, the *Lidai minghua ji* 歷代名畫記 (A Chronological Record of Famous Painters), dating to 847, records the painting of the *Scripture on the Ten Wheels* on the walls of the Monastery of Reverence and Love (Jing'ai si 敬愛寺) in Chang'an.[51] A reexamination of wall paintings of grottoes 74 and 321 at Dunhuang Mogao has led the Chinese art historian Wang Huimin to identify these paintings as the opening scenes of the *Scripture on the Ten Wheels*—that is, the section that eulogizes the Bodhisattva Dizang.[52] If Wang's identification proves accurate, then these Dunhuang murals constitute the sole surviving illustrations of this scripture.

At Dunhuang, several copies of the *Scripture on the Ten Wheels* were discovered among the manuscripts recovered from a hidden library in cave 16.[53] Wang-Toutain has ascertained that Dunhuang copies of this scripture were properties of monasteries rather than individuals, and she argues that the cult of the *Scripture on the Ten Wheels* may have been confined largely to monastic circles.[54] Copies of the scripture and commentaries existed in Japanese collections as early as the middle of the eighth century.[55] *Dhāraṇī* writings relating to the *Scripture on the Ten Wheels*, probably used in a liturgical context, were also recovered from Dunhuang. Among these are the *Dizang pusa tuoluoni* 地藏菩薩陀羅尼 (Dhāraṇī of Dizang Bodhisattva, S 4543) and the *Dizang pusa hushen tuoluoni* 地藏菩薩護身陀羅尼 (Dizang Bodhisattva Dhāraṇī for Bodily Protection, S 431). Both of these consist of *dhāraṇī* formulae. There also exists a modern edition of the *Foshuo da fangguang shilun jing tuoluoni zhou* 佛說大方廣十輪經陀羅尼咒 (The Mantra Dhāraṇī in the Scripture on the Great Extended Ten Wheels Spoken by the Buddha), evidently derived from the anonymous edition of the *Scripture on the Ten Wheels*.[56] A text presenting itself as a "*dhāraṇī* scripture" is the *Dizang pusa tuoluoni jing* 地藏菩薩陀羅尼經 (Scripture on the Dhāraṇī of Dizang

---

lation of the *Scripture on the Ten Wheels* is inscribed in grottoes 1, 2, 3, and 6 of Shijing shan at the eastern peak of Yunju si 雲居寺; see Lü 1999: 94–95. Evidently, the scriptures were first inscribed in the Tang period but were subsequently restored in the Liao (907–1124); see Lü 1999: 136. On the rock-cut scriptures at Fangshan, also see Lancaster 1989.

50. See Lü 1999: 2, 244–245.

51. Cited by Acker 1954: 321; cf. Mair 1986: 30.

52. Mogao grotto 321 is usually dated to the end of the seventh century, whereas grotto 74 is dated to sometime around 755. The murals were originally identified as paintings of the *Baoyu jing* 寶雨經 (T660); see Wang 2004, 2005.

53. The majority of the Dunhuang manuscript copies are based on the *Da fangguang shilun jing*. For a listing of Dunhuang copies of the two translations of the *Scripture on the Ten Wheels*, see Wang-Toutain 1998: 307–308.

54. Ibid.: 66.

55. Manabe 1960: 81.

56. Zhang Zong 2003: 31. He mentions a work, the *Dizang san jing jikan* 地藏三經集刊, published by Shanghai guji chubanshe, which added two *dhāraṇīs*, one of which is the *Foshuo da fangguang shilun jing tuoluoni zhou*. Unfortunately, I do not have access to this publication.

Bodhisattva), reprinted from a Japanese manuscript copy kept in the Temple of Eastern Esoterism (Tōmitsu-ji 東密寺).[57] On scrutiny, this *dhāraṇī* scripture turns out to be the opening chapter of the anonymous edition of the *Scripture on the Ten Wheels* with a new passage added at the end.[58] Strictly speaking, the *Scripture on the Dhāraṇī of Dizang Bodhisattva* is thus not a *dhāraṇī*. Why was the first chapter of the anonymous edition of the *Scripture on the Ten Wheels* circulated independently in the guise of a *dhāraṇī* text? It was not unusual for a chapter from a longer work to circulate independently as the scriptural focus for another Buddhist cult. A well-known example is Chapter 25 of the *Lotus Scripture*, which circulated under the title *Guanyin jing* 觀音經 (Guanyin Scripture), the key scripture for Guanyin worship.[59]

The concluding passage added to the *Scripture on the Dhāraṇī of Dizang Bodhisattva* provides a set of ritual instructions. After listing the various titles of the scripture, the Buddha explains the different ways of observing it: prostrating to Dizang, intoning his name, reciting the *dhāraṇī* scripture, repenting of wrongdoing, professing vows (*fayuan* 發願), keeping the five precepts, and abstaining from meat and the five pungent roots (*wu xin* 五辛).[60] The practitioner is to uphold the bodhisattva precepts and take refuge in the Three Jewels. The text further states that if a monk, nun, layman, or laywoman observes this *dhāraṇī* and sets up a sanctuary—a place where paintings, banners, and canopies are hung, the ground is plastered with fragrant mud, and incense is burnt and flowers scattered—then he or she will avoid retribution for transgressions committed unless they include lack of faith in Dizang or stealing from a monastery or its religious community. It concludes by enumerating the benefits that will accrue from observing this *dhāraṇī*.

57. *Dizang pusa tuoluoni jing*, T1159B:20.655b–660a; also found in *Kokuyaku issai kyō* 国訳一切経 *daishū bu* 大集部 5: 273–283.

58. For the passage appended at the end, see T1159B:20.659c–660a.

59. This is the chapter known as "Pumen pin" 普門品 (Chapter on the Universal Gate), which exalts the efficacies of Guanyin worship. For the religious significance of the *Guanyin jing* in China, see Campany 1993a. A substantive collection of Chinese paintings of this chapter, including Dunhuang illustrations, confirm the widespread dissemination of the *Guanyin jing;* for a study of these paintings, see Murase 1971.

60. The five pungent roots are usually identified as garlic, onion, scallion, leek, and chive, all of which belong to the family of lily bulbs. In certain Mahāyāna treatments, they are referred to as the five *paevayaya* and their consumption is a violation of precepts known as *duskṛta*; the transgressor must confess the violation to another monastic; see Tso 1982: 114. It is believed that if consumed raw, these pungent roots cause irritability, and if cooked they act as an aphrodisiac. It should be noted that their prohibition is found also in non-Buddhist diets. A common Indian classification details three categories of food: (1) *sattvic* (grains and vegetables), which increase life and purity; (2) *tamasic* (meat, fish, egg, and intoxicants), which increase impurity; and (3) *rajasic* (anything excessively spicy, bitter, or sour, including the five pungent roots), which over stimulate the body and mind and destroy the balance necessary for happiness. In the *Brahmājala-sūtra* (Ch. *Fanwang jing* 梵網經) consuming the five pungent roots is one of the forty-eight secondary transgressions; see T1484: 24.1005b.

The new conclusion thus transforms the first chapter of the anonymous edition of the *Scripture on the Ten Wheels* into a ritual focus for the Dizang cult.

Dunhuang manuscript remains have yielded another example of a liturgical composition inspired by the *Scripture on the Ten Wheels*. Presented as a repentance rite, the *Zanli Dizang pusa chanhui fayuan fa* 讚禮地藏菩薩懺悔發願法 (Procedure for Repentance and Profession of Vows Involving Praise and Veneration of Dizang Bodhisattva) comprises in part a verse summary of the opening chapter of the Tang *Scripture on the Ten Wheels*. The *Procedure for Repentance and Profession of Vows*, now kept in the Beijing Library as manuscript *zhong* 重 22, or *bei* 北 8422, was likely composed from the ninth to the tenth centuries and constitutes the earliest repentance manual for the Dizang cult.[61] For Wang-Toutain this text should be a Sanjie jiao composition because the Dunhuang manuscript in which it was written includes copies of Sanjie jiao liturgical works.[62] She thus ignores the possibility that the donor or scribe may have strung together the sequence of liturgies in *zhong* 22 in an ad hoc fashion. The selection may thus serve more as a barometer of the widespread dissemination of these ritual texts than an indication that their practice necessarily belonged to a specific religious group.[63] Moreover, the *Procedure for Repentance and Profession of Vows* is a relatively late text, dating to the period of Sanjie jiao's decline in the late ninth or tenth century, so it may have circulated independently of Sanjie jiao. Regardless of its origin, the *Procedure for Repentance and Profession of Vows* further confirms that the *Scripture on the Ten Wheels* was developing a cultic presence in association with Dizang worship.

Even after Sanjie jiao's decline and the censorship of its writings, the *Scripture on the Ten Wheels* continued to be copied, recited, and illustrated, especially in connection with Dizang veneration in the tenth century.[64] A miracle tale collected in *A Record of Numinous Verifications*, for instance, describes

61. Wang 1999: 200. The text has been published in a modern edition of Dunhuang Buddhist ritual texts; see Wang 1995: 118–119.

62. Wang-Toutain 1998: 198–199. On the same Dunhuang manuscript are copied: (1) an untitled piece identified as the *Qijie foming jing* 七階佛名經; (2) *Zhouye liushi fayuan fa* 晝夜六時發願法; and (3) *Renji lu yi zhu dashengjing zhong lue fayuan fa* 人集錄依諸大乘經中略發願法. The first two are recognized as Sanjie jiao compositions. The *Renji lu yi zhu dashengjing zhong lue fayuan fa* and the *Zanli Dizang pusa chanhui fayuan fa* have been published in Wang 1995: 114–117, 118–119.

63. The *Zhouye liushi fayuan fa* references the Sanjie jiao practice of ritual repentance and homage during the six periods of the day. Another manuscript copy of the *Zhouye liushi fayuan fa* (S 2574), found in a British collection of Dunhuang manuscripts, is indubitably a Sanjie jiao dedicatory text because it cites Xinxing in both the subtitle and conclusion. It is very plausible that the *Zhouye liushi fayuan fa* in Dunhuang manuscript *zhong* 22 was part of the Sanjie jiao liturgical materials. However, liturgies similar to the *Zhouye liushi fayuan fa* were evidently used in Tiantai and Pure Land circles at about the same time: for Pure Land, see Pas 1986–1987; for Tiantai, see Stevenson 1986: 68–72. For a study of repentance liturgies in medieval China, including a discussion of the *Zhouye liushi* rite, see Wang 1998.

64. State proscription of Sanjie jiao activities occurred in 600 under Emperor Wen 文 (581–604), in 694 and 699 under Empress Wu, and in 721 and 725 under Emperor Xuan-

a tenth-century village monastery in Liao City whose community daily recited the *Scripture on the Ten Wheels* and the *Guanyin Scripture*.[65]

Icons of Dizang and the Six Paths in Shaanxi Art

As previously mentioned, scholars have been puzzled by the fact that the Dizang images and inscriptions at Longmen contain no indication of Sanjie jiao patronage. Because it is plausible, however, that Dizang worship did not originate with Sanjie jiao, it is not surprising that early Longmen art and inscriptions do not document a connection. Perhaps one needs to look elsewhere for visual and inscriptional evidence. If one considers Sanjie jiao geography, Shaanxi immediately comes to mind. The Tang capital of Chang'an (present-day Xi'an) and the Zhongnan 終南 mountains, where Xinxing and his Sanjie jiao communities resided, are located in Shaanxi. The area has also yielded a substantive collection of Dizang images that has not been as widely studied as the Longmen examples. It is Dizang art from Shaanxi that hints at Sanjie jiao's interpretation and promulgation of the *Scripture on the Ten Wheels.*

The most intriguing piece among the examples from Shaanxi can be found in niche 8 of Medicine King Mountain (Yaowang shan 藥王山) in Yao 耀 county (see Figure 4). Art historians refer to it as the Niche of Dizang and the Six Paths (Dizang liudao kan 地藏六道龕).[66] Measuring 68 cm high, the niche features a relief carving of a figure sitting with one leg pendant and the six paths of rebirth emanating from his body. Although the head was added at a later date, the lines of a buddha's top knot (Ch. *rouji* 肉髻; Skt. *uṣṇīṣa*) derive from the original carving, which dates to the Tang period.[67] At the Monastery of the Great Buddha (Dafo si 大佛寺) in Bin 彬 county, art historian Chang Qing classifies one-leg-pendant figures as either bodhisattvas or buddhas; inscriptions conclusively identify two of the buddhas at the monastery as Dizang. Chang argues that, based on stylistic resemblances alone, the one-leg-pendant buddhas at Dafo si must be Dizang.[68] It follows then that the figure in Yaowang shan niche 8 could very well be a one-leg-pendant Buddha Dizang—with the addition of the six paths of rebirth. If so, this intriguing iconography most likely was inspired by the *Scripture on the Ten Wheels.*

The visual imagery of Dizang, Lord of the Six Paths, offers a distinctive iconography that was critical for his transformation into a major focus of Buddhist worship in China. The motif of the six paths of rebirth is discernible in Dizang iconography at Longmen. Although the majority of Dizang

zong 玄宗 (r. 712–756). For accounts of these suppressions, see Yabuki 1927: 133–135; Lewis 1990: 207–238; Hubbard 2001: 189–201.

65. *Lingyan ji,* 366a. See Chapter 5 for discussion of the *Lingyan ji.*

66. For use of the phrase *Dizang liudao kan,* see Li 1999: 106. Also see Chang 1998: 251, pl. 167; Han, Chen, et al. 2001: 32, pl. 32; Li 1999: 108; Zhang and Wang 1994: 10, pl. 4.

67. Chang 1998: 250.

68. Local art historians label the statues Q19 and Q32; see ibid.: 234.

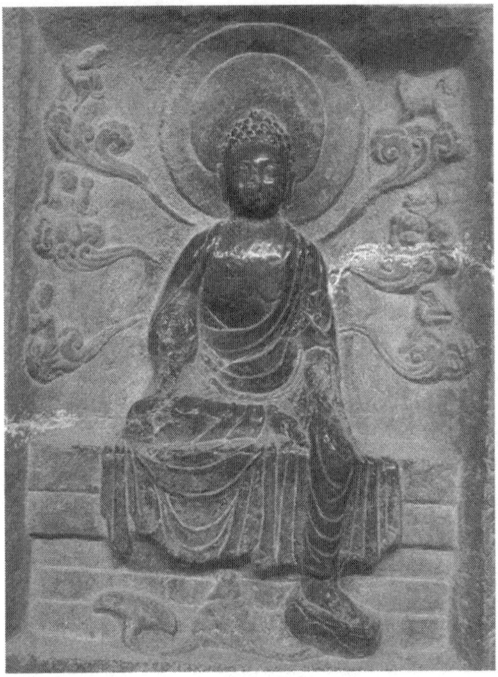

FIGURE 4. Dizang and the six paths. Yaowang shan niche 8, Shaanxi.

statues at Longmen are dressed in the traditional princely garb of the bodhisattva, four images depict Dizang as a monk, either seated with one leg pendant and holding a jewel or standing with the six paths of rebirth emanating from a raised hand.[69] Shaanxi has also yielded a significant number of Dizang images portraying the bodhisattva with the six paths of rebirth. Besides Yaowang shan niche 8, another set of six Dizang images was sculpted in niche 32 at the Cave of Thousand Buddhas (Qianfo dong 千佛洞) at the Dafo si (see Figure 5). The six images represent Dizang's manifestations in the six paths of rebirth according to the *Scripture on the Ten Wheels.* Each morning Dizang assumes various manifestations during states of meditative absorption. Today the statues are partially damaged; only the lower halves of the bodies have survived. The six images can be divided into three complementary pairs, each pair consisting of one statue with its left leg pendant and one with its right leg pendant. The presence of three separate inscriptions suggests that a different donor commissioned each pair of images. The inscriptions date the Dizang statues to 695 and identify the three donors as military officers.[70]

Another set of Tang examples depicting Dizang and the six paths of rebirth, also from Shaanxi, consists of tile images, each measuring 6 or 7 cm high. The images were unearthed during archaeological excavations conducted on the grounds of Buddhist monasteries in the vicinity of Chang'an

69. For line drawings of Dizang images at Longmen, see Chang 1990: pls. III, IV, V.
70. For the inscription text, see Chang 1998: 119.

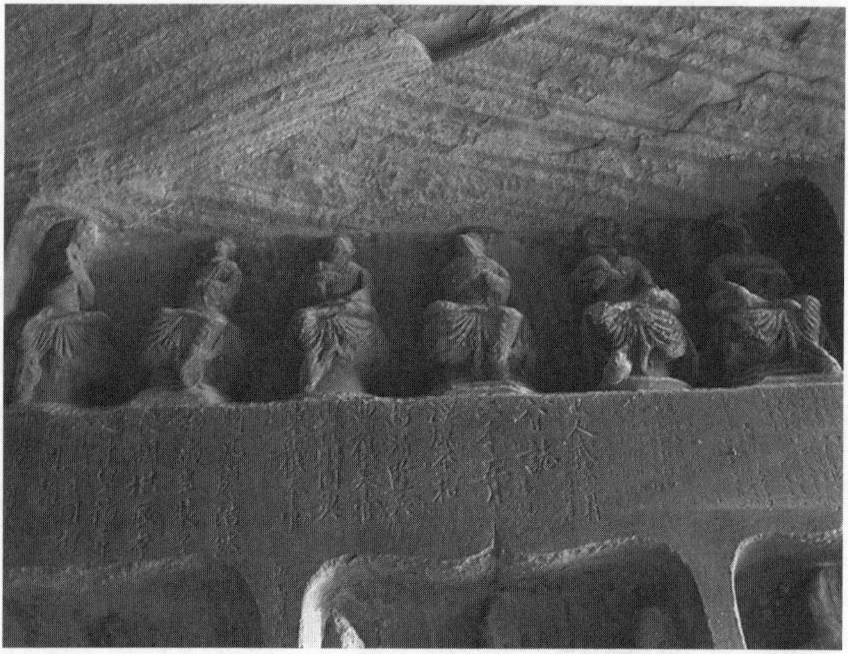

FIGURE 5. Six Dizang images. Qianfo dong niche 32, Shaanxi.

(modern-day Xi'an). They form a sizeable collection of molded clay icons ranging from 4 to 11 cm in height. Comparable to the *tsa-tsa* in Tibetan Buddhism, these icons are referred to as images made of "excellent karmic clay" (*shanye ni zaoxiang* 善業泥造像).[71] The clay was mixed with the ashes of eminent monks before being poured into a mold and fired. The images are stylistically similar: They show Dizang as a one-leg-pendant monk, his right hand grasping a wish-granting jewel from which stream the six realms lined up at his side. An exquisite piece, now kept in the Beijing National Palace Museum, was unearthed in 1956 near Tumen 土門 village on the western boundary of Xi'an.[72] Another less well-preserved tile image of Dizang and the six realms was excavated in 1983 on the grounds of the Font of Rites Monastery (Liquan si 禮泉寺), also in Xi'an.[73] In his early overview of Chinese Buddhist art, Ōmura Seigai reproduced photographs of these images, including one of a monk and the six realms, which resembles the piece recovered at the Liquan si.[74] The various

71. The phrase *shanye ni zaoxiang* occurs on one fragmented tile image of a buddha triad; see He 1957: 87. He's report is dated 1956; however, Yao (2002) cites 1953 as the date of this archaeological find. For a discussion on the collection of tile images, see Jin 2004: 155–165.

72. For a photo reproduction, see He 1957: 87.

73. For a photo reproduction, see Yao 2002: 310, pl. 5.

74. Ōmura 1922: 359, pl. 835. Ōmura mistakenly identifies the tile as an *arhat* image. Because Ōmura's classic work was published prior to the 1956 and 1983 archaeological exca-

examples all document the circulation in Shaanxi of a roughly common iconography showing Dizang with the six paths of rebirth.

The Dizang and Six Paths icon resonated with the teaching of the Final Dharma that dominated the intellectual and religious ethos of sixth- and seventh-century Buddhist China. Because the *Scripture on the Ten Wheels* was widely circulated by proponents of Sanjie jiao, the icon's visual imagery would have been quite familiar to its intended audience. The *Scripture on the Ten Wheels* presents Dizang as heir to the Buddha Śākyamuni, who had been entrusted by the Buddha to transform the living beings in the defiled realm of the Sahā world—a task the Buddha himself had carried out while he was alive. The six paths of rebirth furnishes apt visual imagery for the defiled world, which the *Scripture on the Ten Wheels* designates as the domain of Dizang Bodhisattva's salvific activities. Unlike the Pure Land, which contains no suffering states of existence, defiled lands like the Sahā world encompass all six paths of rebirth. This iconography represents an earlier phase of Dizang art. Later, as Dizang was increasingly looked upon as the bodhisattva savior of the infernal regions, the jewel and staff became the salient features of his iconography; however, the six paths of rebirth continued to appear, sometimes with a special focus on underworld imagery.[75]

Another key element in this religious ethos was the anxiety Buddhists felt at the coming of the future Buddha Maitreya. Medieval Buddhists feared they would not live to witness this highly anticipated moment, when the spiritual wasteland in which they were living would come to an end. To avert the possibility of not being able to encounter Maitreya in this world, they prayed to be reborn in Tuṣita heaven; here they could meet the future Buddha in his bodhisattva form and descend with him to Jambudvīpa.[76] Fifth- and sixth-

vations, we can assume there was another similar tile image of Dizang and the six paths of rebirth that Ōmura had access to, although its current whereabouts are unknown. Another interesting image from Ōmura's collection of tile pieces portrays a standing buddha figure with a top knot holding a staff and a jewel, which Ōmura identifies as Dizang; see Ōmura 1922: 359, pl. 834. Whether this image is in fact Dizang remains controversial.

75. Some examples dated to the tenth or early eleventh century are Mogao grottoes 6, 176, and 456, which portray Dizang presiding over the Ten Kings of purgatory and the six paths of rebirth. The jewel and staff combination is not found at Longmen and is less common in the north central plains. However, it is typical of Dunhuang and Sichuan Dizang art, particularly after the ninth century. A stone engraving of Dizang and the six paths, located at Ziyan si 資延寺, Ciyun ling 慈雲嶺, in Hangzhou, has an inscription dating its commission to 942 by the Wuyue 吳越 king Qian Hongzuo 錢弘佐 (r. 941–947). For a photo reproduction of this Dizang image and a discussion of Ciyun ling, see Chang 1995.

76. Chinese worship of Maitreya is usually traced to the monk Daoan 道安 (312–385). He was said to have gathered eight of his disciples before an image of Maitreya, where he vowed to be reborn in Tuṣita Heaven and accompany Maitreya during the latter's descent to earth; see *Gaoseng zhuan* 高僧傳, T2059:50.353b. The proliferation of Maitreya images at Yungang 雲崗 and Longmen indicates that the Maitreya cult enjoyed state patronage. Numerous smaller engravings also show that this bodhisattva was a dominant expression of Buddhist devotion for all segments of early Chinese Buddhist society; see Tsukamoto 1942: 228–233, 368–369, 375–376, 377–382, 513. For Maitreya statues from the Northern Dynasties (386–577), see Wong 2001, 1998–1999. The Longmen caves represent the high point of

century inscriptions frequently reiterate themes connected to the Maitreya mythology: the aspiration to be reborn in Tuṣita Heaven; the hope to encounter the future buddha; and the rare opportunity to be present at the three preaching assemblies presided over by Maitreya under the Nāgapuṣpa tree (*longhua sanhui* 龍華三會).[77] Shaanxi inscriptions from this period indicate a strong presence of Maitreya worship in the region. One Shaanxi inscription dated to 569 expresses the donor's hope "to be reborn in Tuṣita, to see Maitreya face to face, and to forever listen to the True Teachings."[78] Another inscription, dated to 568 and dedicated by one Xie Sizu 謝思祖 and his wife, states: "May (the deceased) be reborn in the Land of Miaoluo 妙洛 in the west and eternally be in the buddha-assemblies under the dragon-flower tree."[79] In a dedication dated to 549 and inscribed at the base of a stone buddha commissioned by a lay Buddhist society in Shaanxi's Dingxiang 定襄 prefecture, one reads about "the interval between the two sages," a phrase invoking sentiments similar to a "world without a buddha" mentioned in the seventh-century edition of the *Scripture on the Ten Wheels.*[80]

A visual artifact that further elucidates the religious ethos of seventh-century Shaanxi is a limestone stele engraving commissioned by one Cui Shande 崔善德 in 670.[81] Housed in Paris in the early twentieth century, the stele, measuring 56 cm high, has since disappeared and its whereabouts are presently unknown.[82] A triad of Maitreya Bodhisattva, who sits with two legs pendant in Tuṣita, awaits his descent to earth.[83] On the reverse side is an exquisite engraving of Dizang, dressed as a monk and sitting with one leg pendant, each hand holding a wish-granting jewel from which stream the three

---

Maitreya worship in northern China, but it should also be noted that Maitreya art flourished at Dunhuang from the fifth century onward.

77. For a discussion of Maitreya worship in fifth- and sixth-century inscriptions, see Hou 1998: 190–204. For the myths on the ascent to Maitreya's paradise and the descent with Maitreya to earth, see Nattier 1988.

78. For the inscription text, see Hou 1998: 203.

79. Ibid.: 202.

80. Tōdō 1962: 787–777 (Japanese pagination); cf. *Dasheng daji dizang shilun jing,* T411:13.721c: 五濁惡時無佛世界; *Anle ji,* T1958:47.12b: 於五濁之世於無佛之時.

81. For studies of the limestone carving, see Chavannes 1914: 34–37, pls. L–LII; Mikami 1967: 42–46.

82. Li 1995: 217.

83. The engraving portrays a seated Maitreya Bodhisattva flanked by attendant bodhisattvas and world protectors *(lokapāla).* A pagoda is chiseled above the niche, thus rendering the scene as one of Maitreya waiting in Tuṣita with his entourage. By the fifth and sixth centuries, the Maitreya cult was flourishing in China; this is evident in the proliferation of gigantic statues and numerous smaller carvings of Maitreya at major Buddhist sites like Yungang, Longmen, and Dunhuang. At this time, Maitreya iconography became established in China: Standing images of Maitreya usually show him preaching in Ketumati, the Pure Land he would realize on earth; when seated either in the "crossed-ankle pose" or with two legs pendant, he is shown waiting to make his descent from Tuṣita. Both styles are closely juxtaposed in the art of the Northern Dynasties, indicating that these two aspects of the Maitreya cult were interrelated in early medieval China; see Lee Yu-Min 1983, 1984.

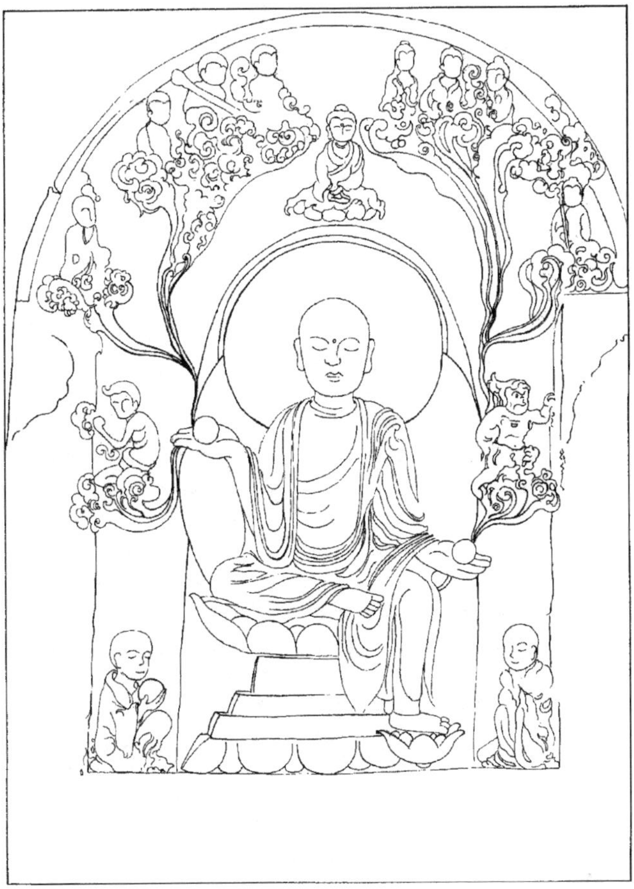

FIGURE 6. Cui's stele engraving of Dizang. Author's line drawing based on a photograph from Mikami 1967.

paths of rebirth (see Figure 6).[84] Stylistically, this image is comparable to other Shaanxi images of Dizang and the Six Paths from the seventh century, especially the engraving in niche 8 of Yaowang shan. Art historians, therefore, believe that Cui's stele originated in or around Shaanxi. Its images and inscription provide important information about the largely forgotten relationship between Dizang and Maitreya worship. Elsewhere I have traced the Maitreya connection in Dizang development from the seventh to the tenth centuries in art, epigraphy, and popular narratives.[85] Suffice it to say that because Dizang and Maitreya were both connected in separate scriptural mythologies to the plight of living in the Sahā world in an age without the Buddha, medieval Chinese naturally associated the two deities in their cultic practices as they sought a surrogate buddha for this world. As the future

84. On either side of Dizang's feet kneels a small monk making offerings. Above the halo encircling Dizang's head sits a miniature meditating buddha.

85. See Zhiru 2005.

Buddha, Maitreya Bodhisattva is naturally the heir to the historical Buddha. So too is Dizang Bodhisattva, whom the *Scripture on the Ten Wheels* casts as the appointed successor who seeks to emulate Śākyamuni Buddha's activities in the defiled sphere of the Sahā world. In Cui's stele engraving, a little buddha hovers over Dizang, who is surrounded by the six paths—perhaps a visual reminder that Dizang Bodhisattva aspired to emulate Śākyamuni Buddha by keeping vigil over this defiled world in the absence of the Buddha. One may recall that this is what attracted Sanjie jiao supporters like Sinbang to Dizang. Although Sanjie jiao may not have been directly responsible for the visual imagery of Dizang presiding over the six paths of rebirth, its emphasis on the *Scripture on the Ten Wheels* and understanding of Dizang's function certainly contributed to the production of this distinctive iconography for Dizang. Its emergence coincided with the broad dissemination of Dizang worship in north central China from the seventh century on. The tile images described previously were manufactured from clay molding, which means that the icons were produced in substantive quantities. Portrayals of Dizang as a lone figure—as in niche 8 of the Yaowang shan and Cui's stele engraving—imply that he had become a cultic focus for Buddhists.

Representations of Dizang as a one-leg-pendant buddha most likely evolved as part of a quest for an iconography that would communicate Dizang's role as understood by seventh- and eighth-century Buddhists in north central China. The buddha imagery offers a critical look at medieval perceptions of Dizang's role in the religious and intellectual climate of the teaching of the Final Dharma, particularly as expressed in the *Scripture on the Ten Wheels* and by Sanjie jiao. Dizang's appearance as a one-leg-pendant buddha is not surprising given the widespread longing for a buddha to appear in this world. In the absence of the Buddha—both in the sense of the historical Buddha Śākyamuni, who departed from this world, and the future Buddha Maitreya, who is yet to come into this world—medieval Buddhists viewed Dizang as a savior and surrogate for the Buddha who would relieve their anxieties of living in degenerate times and in a degenerate world. One may recall that in the *Scripture on the Ten Wheels*, Dizang expresses his admiration for the Buddha Śākyamuni's salvific activities in the challenging conditions of the defiled world and further announces his intention to emulate Śākyamuni by working for the salvation of those living in the defiled realm.[86] Medieval Chinese seemed to have seized upon the idea, not fully articulated in the scripture, that Dizang was the appointed heir to Śākyamuni Buddha in this defiled realm.

The one-leg-pendant position may further reveal the dynamic underlying Dizang's iconography. In East Asian Buddhist art, this sitting posture is identified with the contemplating bodhisattva (*siwei pusa* 思惟菩薩), and its iconography was discerned in China as early as the late fifth century. The

86. *Da fangguan shilun jing,* T410:13.687a–b; cf. *Dasheng daji Dizang shilun jing,* T411:13.728b. The passages are translated in Chapter 1.

earliest examples of this image are commonly identified as Prince Siddhārtha; he sits with one leg pendant, often with his head slightly lowered and his finger touching his chin or with a hand resting on his forehead, brooding over the miseries of living beings.[87] Over time this iconography came to be associated with Maitreya Bodhisattva, and the contemplating Maitreya gained widespread popularity, especially in Japan and Korea.[88] According to Chang Qing, Dizang iconography at Longmen and the Dafo si largely shows him in the one-leg-pendant pose.[89] Other one-leg-pendant bodhisattvas are found in Shaanxi, some identified by inscriptions as Guanyin. The iconography of one leg pendant is thus always associated with bodhisattvas or buddhas-to-be like Prince Siddhārtha and Maitreya Bodhisattva. Stylistically, the one-leg-pendant posture links Dizang to the bodhisattva careers of the present Buddha Śākyamuni and the future Buddha Maitreya.

Most of the Shaanxi pieces link Dizang worship to the *Scripture on the Ten Wheels*, but one example may provide evidence of a Sanjie jiao connection. Amy McNair has identified a stele engraving of a one-leg-pendant crowned bodhisattva, now preserved at the Shaanxi Provincial Museum in Xi'an, as Dizang in princely guise.[90] On the reverse side of the stele is an epigraph—now effaced except for the title, inscribed in early Tang regular script: Stele for the Three Levels Bhadanta Meditation Master of August Tang. The image is reminiscent of those of Dizang at Longmen dating to the second half of the seventh century and after. If McNair's identification is accurate, this stele then provides a rare record of Sanjie jiao's worship of Dizang.[91]

Rethinking the Early Dissemination of Dizang Worship

In view of the above reevaluation of the beginnings of Dizang worship, one must be wary of attributing the rise of the Dizang cult *solely* to Sanjie jiao activities. Buddhist authors like Daoxuan and Daoshi situated the dissemination of Dizang worship in a broader devotional milieu, among the growing cults of *stūpa* building and image-making. Initiated by state decrees,

87. On the contemplating bodhisattva in art, see Sasaguchi 1975; Lee Jung-hee 1984. For photo reproductions of late fifth- and early sixth-century sculptures of Prince Siddhārtha in the posture of the contemplating bodhisattva, see Alphen 2001: 100, pls. 2–4. Based on textual descriptions of the pose, especially in Indian *vinaya* literature, Gregory Schopen (1996) has argued that the finger on the chin or the hand on the forehead are indicative of fretting or a brooding state of mind. Siddhārtha in this pose then is brooding over the difficulty of preaching to the living beings of this defiled world.

88. Especially fine is the famed statue of Miroku Bosatsu (Maitreya Bodhisattva) in the Chūgū ji 中宮寺 in Ikaruga-cho, Nara prefecture. Made of camphor wood and measuring about 123 cm high, the piece shows the bodhisattva dressed in princely garments, his hand lightly touching his chin, and sitting with one leg pendant. The imperial family commissioned the statue during the Asuka period (550–710).

89. See Chang 1998: 235.

90. The original location of this stele engraving is unknown.

91. McNair 1996: 325–392.

large-scale construction of *stūpa*s in various counties and districts surely contributed to the spread of Buddhist cults. In early medieval China, the *stūpa* cult, centered on the relics of the Buddha, attracted the attention of rulers who sought to emulate or rival Aśoka's massive constructions. The *stūpa* cult quickly incorporated the production and veneration of images.[92] In time the cultic trends expanded beyond relics and images of the historical Buddha to include other Buddhist deities. Thus, in his *Continued Biographies,* Daoxuan discusses the efficacies of the Tree Manifestation Dizang and the Luminous Flower Ākāśagarbha while addressing the topic of numinous *stūpa*s (*ling ta* 靈塔).

Another factor in the spread of Dizang worship was the practice of building cave temple complexes, which began at Clouded Ridge (Yungang 雲崗) and Longmen in the fifth century and spread across the central plains (e.g., Xiangtang shan 響堂山 between Hebei and Henan, Xumi shan 須彌山 in southern Ningxia, the sculptural sites in Shaanxi) to the border regions (e.g., Dunhuang Mogao ku, the Sichuan sites).[93] Construction of Buddhist sites led to the making of images on a large scale, increasing the proliferation of Buddhist cults in medieval China. As Tsukamoto has shown in his study of Longmen, the early foci of devotion were the Buddha Śākyamuni and the future Buddha Maitreya, but as time passed patterns of devotion diversified and other deities arrived on the scene. The rapid ascendancy of Guanyin and Amitābha was certainly a product of this vibrant blossoming of cultic expressions.[94] Dizang was also gaining considerable notice as an object of worship.[95] Although anticipation of Buddhism's decline played an important role in the rise of savior buddhas and bodhisattvas in the sixth and seventh centuries, it should be remembered that merit-making for oneself and one's loved ones was an equally important impetus behind all the vigorous building and sculpturing.[96] Image-making and veneration were bound to the practices of merit-making and merit transference, especially for the dead. Merit transference enabled the making and veneration of Buddhist images to be aligned

---

92. As previously mentioned, this development is already evident in early medieval Chinese stories that combine the legends of Aśoka and his building of *stūpa*s with accounts of his production and worship of images; see Shinohara 1998.

93. The early Buddhist cave temples of Yungang and Longmen have attracted significant attention, especially from Japanese scholars. Besides Tsukamoto's important publication, see the classic studies by Mizuno and Nagahiro 1941, 1951.

94. On the emergence of the Guanyin cult, see Makita 1970; Satō 1982: 17–38; Campany 1996b; Yü 2001.

95. According to Tsukamoto's statistics, no sculpture of Dizang seems to have been constructed at Longmen in the Northern Wei, but at least seven of the extant Dizang sculptures are from the early Tang period. Tsukamoto counted a total of thirty-three dated and undated images of Dizang at Longmen; see Tsukamoto 1942: 375, 380.

96. For instance, the rapid rise of the Amitābha cult was linked to the development of Pure Land, which took shape as one of several responses to the apocalyptic forebodings of the eventual extinction of Buddhism. In Chinese Buddhist history, the beginnings of Amitābha worship can be traced to Huiyuan of Lu shan 廬山; *Gaoseng zhuan,* T2059: 50.358c.

with Chinese practices such as ancestor worship that address anxiety over the welfare of deceased family members and fear of the destructive otherworldly forces that death may unleash. In the next chapter, we will examine the *Scripture on the Past Vows*, a late medieval Chinese text that emphasizes making and venerating images as a way for daughters and sons to free their deceased parents from damnation in hell and secure their salvation.

The works of Daoxuan, Daoshi, and other seventh-century Buddhist authors indicate that Buddhist cults, especially those that involved the veneration of images, were conspicuous elements in medieval religion. Worship of Buddhist deities involved recollecting and intoning the deity's name, making and venerating images, and reciting key scriptures associated with the deity. Examining medieval attitudes to resonances, or *ganying* 感應 (literally, "simulating response"), Koichi Shinohara concluded that Chinese Buddhists like Daoxuan regarded records of numinous experiences as verifications of the religious efficacy of an image, relic, or saint.[97] They believed a miracle to be the natural result of a devotee's worship of an image or relic or a virtuous life as lived by a saint. The extent to which Buddhist intellectuals discussed cultic practices suggests that not only did they not marginalize Buddhist devotion, but they also considered cultic elements to be integral to Buddhist doctrine and practice.

Given the kaleidoscope of cultic expressions, sometimes in competition with and sometimes complementing one another, it is probable that Dizang piety existed in the seventh century as one of several growing modes of Buddhist devotion prior to its association with Sanjie jiao. As I will show in the next chapter, the *Zhancha jing*, composed in China in the sixth century, presents Dizang Bodhisattva as the patron saint of repentance and divinatory rites. The scripture has no connection with Sanjie jiao or its teachings. The *Scripture on Divination*, with its confessional, divinatory, and meditative rites, may better reflect practices of Dizang worship in the broader religious milieu. The early indisputable connection between Sanjie jiao and the *Scripture on the Ten Wheels* certainly contributed to the diffusion of Dizang worship, but it is questionable whether the movement explicitly adopted or promoted Dizang as its patron deity. Unlike Pure Land polemicists, who pitted Dizang worship against Amitābha worship, Sanjie jiao writers actually invoked the two deities simultaneously, side by side, without any perceptible incongruity. To be sure, Pure Land writings, which were intended to bolster the worship of Amitābha as the supreme form of Buddhist devotion, cannot provide an impartial account of the historical relationship between Dizang worship and Sanjie jiao. Part 2 of this study will endeavor to investigate three sets of sources (religious writings, art and epigraphy, and narratives) so as to elucidate developments other than Sanjie jiao that contributed to shaping Dizang worship from the sixth to the tenth centuries.

97. Shinohara 1991: 213.

PART 2

Multiple Images

This World, Hell, and Pure Land

CHAPTER 3
Indigenous and Accretionary Scriptures

BETWEEN THE SIXTH and tenth centuries, a small corpus of scriptures foregrounding the Bodhisattva Dizang appeared in China. To a greater or lesser extent, this set of "Dizang scriptures" reflects broader patterns of religious and cultural amalgamation that existed at the time.[1] Each scripture connects Dizang to varied aspects of Chinese religion that cannot be reduced to any singular theme. If not the focus of the scripture, Dizang appears frequently and the text endeavors to integrate Dizang worship with its main subject. According to this definition, those scriptures that mention Dizang's name but do not treat the bodhisattva substantively will not be included within the purview of Dizang scriptures.[2] The scriptures discussed in this chapter are:

1. *Zhancha shan'e yebao jing* 占察善惡業報經 (Scripture on Divining the Retribution of Skillful and Negative Actions; henceforth, *Scripture on Divination*), ascribed to Putideng 菩提燈 (Bodhidīpa?, d.u.). T839:17.901c–910c.
2. *Dizang dadao xin quce fa* 峷㠓大道心驅策法 (The Exorcism Method of Dizang's Aspiration Toward Great Awakening; henceforth, *The Exorcism Method*).[3] T1159A:20.652c–655a.
3. *Dizang pusa yigui* 地藏菩薩儀軌 (A Ritual Manual on the Bodhisattva

1. Note that my usage of "Dizang scriptures" is specific to the definition I have given above. I am not employing the phrase as it is used in modern Chinese Buddhism, where *Dizang jing* 地藏經 often functions as a designation for the three key scriptures of the Dizang cult: *Shilun jing*, *Zhancha jing*, and *Benyuan jing*. *Dizang jing* may also serve as the abbreviated title for the *Benyuan jing* (e.g., Zhengyan 2003).

2. Another Chinese text recovered from Dunhuang known sometimes by the title *Dizang pusa shizhai ri* 地藏菩薩十齋日 (S 2568, transcribed in T2850:85.1300a–b) is also frequently discussed in relation to Dizang literature. Because its title mentions Dizang, it is commonly assumed that this text deals with Dizang worship. However, Dizang's name did not appear in earlier versions; it was added later, most likely in response to the mention of the observance of the Ten Feast Days (*shizhai ri* 十齋日) in the *Benyuan jing*. Because the *Dizang pusa shizhai ri* did not develop as part of Dizang literature and its contents moreover do not particularly discuss the role of Dizang, it will not be examined in this chapter.

3. *Dizang** indicates a phonetic reconstruction of two anomalous characters. I have transliterated them as "Dizang," following a convention set by premodern and contemporary Buddhist scholarship.

Dizang; henceforth, *A Ritual Manual*), ascribed to Śubhakarasiṃha or more commonly Śubhakara (Ch. Shupojialuo 輸婆迦羅, also known as Shanwuwei 善無畏, 637–735). T1158:20.652a–c.

4. *Foshuo Dizang pusa jing* 佛說地藏菩薩經 (Scripture on the Bodhisattva Dizang). Dunhuang manuscript S 6257 *DHBZ* 3:484, transcribed in T2909:85.1455b–c.
5. *Dizang pusa benyuan jing* 地藏菩薩本願經 (Scripture on the Past Vows of Dizang Bodhisattva; henceforth, *Scripture on the Past Vows*), ascribed to Śikṣānanda (Shicha'nantuo 實叉難陀, 652–710). T412:13.777c–790a.

As the title of this chapter indicates, these Dizang scriptures can be classified into indigenous and accretionary works. "Indigenous scripture" is used here as an equivalent to the more commonplace "apocrypha." As a category of religious literature, "apocrypha" has strong overtones of the western Judaeo-Christian tradition for which the term was coined.[4] To avoid western connotations, I employ "indigenous scripture" instead. Calling attention to this neglected genre of Buddhist literature, Erik Zürcher defined Chinese Buddhist apocrypha as "works produced in China by (obviously anonymous) Chinese" that pretend to be "translations" of non-Chinese texts. Zürcher described them as generally short texts "written in a primitive and rather incoherent language, with little doctrinal sophistication, and full of references to ideas and beliefs that are not of Buddhist origin but are part and parcel of the Chinese indigenous tradition."[5] Although some of these works have made their way into the transmitted Buddhist canons, many were considered heretical, unorthodox, morally subversive, and even politically dangerous. Since Zürcher there has been considerable progress in the study of indigenous Chinese Buddhist scriptures, and their relevance for understanding Chinese Buddhist history has been acknowledged.[6]

The *Scripture on Divination* is a "canonical" indigenous composition; the *Scripture on the Bodhisattva Dizang* is a text recovered from Dunhuang manuscripts. Scholarly consensus regards both titles as indigenous scriptures composed in China.[7] *The Exorcism Method* and *A Ritual Manual* were retrieved from Japanese archival copies and reprinted in modern editions of the Chi-

4. On the problems of the use of "apocrypha" in the study of Buddhism, see Buswell 1990: 3–7.

5. Zürcher 1982a: 168. Prior to Zürcher, Japanese scholars have already begun to study indigenous Buddhist scriptures in East Asia, most notably Makita (1975).

6. Heeding Zürcher's call, western scholars have begun to study indigenous Chinese Buddhist scriptures; see Buswell 1990.

7. Kokyo Tokuno (1994: 25–27) classfies the extant corpus of indigenous Chinese scriptures according to their whereabouts:

1. Dunhuang manuscripts;
2. Texts in the *Xuzangjing* 續藏經 (J. *Zokuzōkyō*, Supplement to the Canon);
3. Nanatsu-dera manuscripts;
4. "Canonical" apocrypha—that is, either those texts that were once suspected of

nese Buddhist canon. They were in all likelihood composed in Tang China. The textual history of *A Ritual Manual* is particularly problematic (its authenticity has been debated since the Kamakura, 1185–1333); here we may well be dealing with a "twice apocryphal" text in the sense that it is a Chinese composition that was either reimagined or added to in Japan. The *Scripture on the Past Vows* poses similar problems: The site of its original composition remains ambiguous; the scripture could have been composed in either Central Asia or China.[8] If defined as works composed outside of the original geographical sphere of the religion, indigenous scriptures theoretically should exclude those texts with problematic origins that suggest multiple geographical and cultural colorings. Scriptures containing patently Chinese ideas or themes were not necessarily composed in China; these elements could also have been assimilated during the transmission, translation, and redaction of the text. Similarly, Japanese editions of scriptures authored in China could have accrued extraneous elements in the new cultural setting. Hence categorizing scriptures as "genuine" or "apocryphal" ultimately limits our understanding of them. The bifurcation simplifies the complexities underlying the production of scriptures and ultimately freezes them into stagnant entities rather than acknowledging their constantly shifting realities. The classification "indigenous scripture" does not exhaust the range of scriptural writings that accommodated complex processes of religio-cultural appropriation and helped to mold Chinese Buddhism.

In his study of the textual recensions of the *Amitāyurdhyāna-sūtra* (*Guan wuliangshou fo jing* 觀無量壽佛經, Scripture on the Visualization of the Buddha of Immeasurable Life; henceforth, *Visualization Scripture*), Jonathan Silk proposes an "accretionary" model that investigates texts through a process of philological archaeology.[9] Using this approach, Silk shows that accretionary layers of religio-cultural adaptation are formed through protracted processes of critical edition, translation, and transmission that result in variant recensions and versions of a single text. The *Scripture on the Past Vows* contains an intriguing amalgamation of literary motifs and themes derived from more than one culture. In view of its multiple layers of cultural motifs, the *Scripture on the Past Vows* is best understood as an example of "accretionary composition." However, unlike the *Visualization Scripture*, no *complete* variant textual recension of the *Scripture on the Past Vows* exists other than the Chinese version.[10] Hence, it is impossible, at least for now, to submit the text to

being apocryphal but were later accorded canonical status, or those texts from the canon that modern scholarship has established as apocryphal; and

5. Lost indigenous texts that survive only in quotations in Chinese commentaries and treatises.

8. Elverskog 1997: 54.

9. Silk 1997: 181–256.

10. Manuscript fragments of the *Benyuan jing* in other languages have been discovered at archaeological sites; see subsequent discussion in this chapter.

critical comparative philology in the hope of reconstructing its textual history. Until more information is uncovered, it is perhaps more helpful to bear in mind the model of "accretionary composition" rather than an "authentic Indian" or "indigenous Chinese" designation when discussing the *Scripture on the Past Vows.* Similarly, *A Ritual Manual* may be viewed as an accretionary scripture in the reverse direction given the fact that the core of its text was most likely composed in China.

The *Scripture on Divination*: From Karmic Divination to Philosophical Meditation

Currently scholars agree that the *Scripture on Divination* was composed in China sometime in the sixth century. Chinese Buddhist catalogues confirm that from its inception the scripture's "authenticity" was in question.[11] The *Zhongjing mulu* 眾經目錄 (Catalog of All Scriptures), compiled in 594 by Fajing 法經 (fl. 594) and others, was the first catalog to list the text under the category of "dubious" works.[12] A few years later, the *Lidai sanbao ji* 歷代三寶紀 (Chronological Record of the Three Jewels), compiled in 597 by Fei Changfang 費長房 (d.u.), ascribed it to an obscure translator named Putideng. (Fei also recorded his doubts concerning the scripture's authenticity.)[13] It is the *Dazhou kanding zhongjing mulu* 大周刊定眾經目錄 (The Authoritative Catalog of All Scriptures in the Era of Dazhou), dated 695 and sponsored by Empress Wu, that affirmed the authenticity of the *Scripture on Divination.*[14] Subsequently, the *Kaiyuan shijiao lu* 開元釋教錄 (Records of Śākya's Teachings in the Era of Kaiyuan), compiled in 730, officially admitted it into the Buddhist canon.[15]

The *Scripture on Divination* begins with the Buddha calling on the bodhisattva Dizang to elaborate on the method of salvation for those living in the critical interval between the time of the Semblance Dharma (*xiangfa* 像法) and the Final Age. The first fascicle presents Dizang preaching a divinatory method for the spiritually inferior, which requires the use of three sets of wooden divinatory wheels.[16] The first set of ten wheels discloses the

---

11. For an overview of evaluations of the *Zhancha jing* in various scriptural catalogues, see Makita 1975: 108–109.

12. In his listing of dubious scriptures, Fajing states:

> [As for] the twenty-one preceding scriptures, the explanation of the title can be found in numerous catalogues. The style is complicated and it has not yet been determined whether they were false or real scriptures. This will require more research. This is why they are catalogued among dubious scriptures. (*Zhongjing mulu*, T2146:55.126b–c)

13. See *Lidai sanbao ji*, T2034:49.106c.

14. See *Dazhou kanding zhongjing mulu*, T2153:55.379a, 442b.

15. See *Kaiyuan shijiao lu*, T2154:55.551a.

16. Both Whalen Lai (1990: 179) and Michel Strickmann (2005: 80) read the wheel to be some kind of spinning top. However, Kuo (1994b) follows the Ming Buddhist reformer

ten skillful and ten unsalutary actions one has committed in the past; the second set of three wheels (signifying physical, verbal, and mental actions) reveals the strength of one's *karma* (distant or imminent, strong or weak); the third set of six wheels divulges past, present, and future retributions, yielding a possible range of 189 prognostications.[17] Prior to the divination, the adept must perform preliminary rites of worship and repentance, in particular invoking Dizang to ensure the success of the divination. Should the first two divinations reveal bad *karma*, the adept must then observe ritual purification through confession and repentance. Only when the divination results indicate that body, speech, and mind have been purified can the penitent assume that the bad *karma* has been eradicated. As further verification, the penitent should experience auspicious omens in the form of unusual lights, aromatic scents, or celestial visitations in a dream before the third set of divinations can be performed to prognosticate his or her level of spiritual attainment or on matters pertaining to daily life.

In the second fascicle, Dizang preaches a twofold meditation technique as an expedient means to enter the teachings of the Great Vehicle. First, during the contemplation of mind- or consciousness-only (*weixinshi guan* 唯心識觀), one should trace the arising of all physical, verbal, and mental actions in the mind. Next, during the contemplation of the reality of true thusness (*zhenrushi guan* 真如實觀), one should examine the undefiled nature of the mind, unproduced, indestructible, and free from all discrimination. Through either contemplation, one achieves particular states of *samādhi* (Ch. *sanmei* 三昧) before cultivating *śamatha-vipaśyanā*, or calm and insight meditation, to generate intuitive insight and deep conviction in the Mahāyāna. Should karmic obstruction or lack of faith hinder the contemplation, the adept is to invoke Dizang's name at all times and in all places until mental concentration is achieved. One should then contemplate Dizang's *dharma* form as identical in nature not only to the bodies of all the buddhas, but also to one's own.

Mochizuki Shinkō inaugurated the study of the *Scripture on Divination* and highlighted its patterns of acculturation in relation to another important sixth-century Chinese indigenous text, the *Dasheng qixin lun* 大乘起信論 (Treatise on the Mahāyāna Awakening of Faith).[18] Mochizuki was especially interested in how the philosophical views of the *Scripture on Divination* synchronized Yogācāra and Tathāgathagarbha teachings on the nature

Zhixu 智旭 (1599–1655) and likens the wheel to dice. The contemporary Chinese preacher Mengcan has written a manual outlining the Dizang method of divination. The manual comes with a packet of nineteen divination wheels, each in the shape of a hexagon.

17. The text includes detailed instructions on divining and the exact measurements of the wheels.

18. Mochizuki 1946: 485–493. The *Dasheng qixin lun* was ascribed to the second-century Indian monk Aśvaghoṣa (Maming 馬鳴), but scholarly consensus has since declared it to be an indigenous Chinese composition. Two versions of the text exist today: T1666:32.575a–583b, attributed to the Central Asian translator Paramārtha (Zhendi 真諦, 499–569), and T1667:32.583b–591c, attributed to Śikṣānanda.

of the mind. For Makita Tairyō, the *Scripture on Divination* is an example of "plebeian scripture" (*shomin kyōten* 庶民経典), which deliberately incorporates the perennial Chinese pursuit for "this-worldly benefits" (*gensei riyaku* 現世利益).[19] Whalen Lai argues that the text's sophisticated amalgamation of religious elements refutes reductionist characterizations of magic as "folk" practices and philosophical speculation as "elite" religion.[20] Finally, Kuo Li-ying explores the scripture as an instance of "reciprocal adaptation" between Buddhism and the local culture of China, again emphasizing its fusion of philosophy and praxis.[21]

The *Scripture on Divination* presents a Chinese Buddhist method of divination. Early Buddhism issued formal scriptural strictures warning against the practice of the mantic arts.[22] Wheel divination does, however, have certain affinities with practices found in Indian Buddhist literature: One story relates how a person should keep track of every good or evil intention with white and black stones and how to purify the mind by reversing the ratio of the colors.[23] The issue is not so much whether divination is Indian or Chinese in origin, but rather that the *Scripture on Divination* is important precisely because it attests to the ways in which Chinese Buddhists apprehended and practiced the doctrine of *karma* in terms of the mechanical predictability of a divination formula that had a long history in China and a special appeal to a Chinese audience. In Chinese society, divination existed as part of a larger network of practices—including astrology, exorcism, and medicine—to comprehend and manipulate natural and seemingly "extrahuman" forces.[24] Ancient Chinese cosmology insists on the presence of regulating patterns of correlation across the biological, ecological, moral, political, and social planes; the malfunction of any element in this multi-

19. Makita 1975: 108–114. Makita is certainly right to identify the pursuit of worldly benefits as perennial in Chinese religion. However, his approach may reflect the classification of religion in Japanese scholarship. In the study of Japanese religions, *gensei riyaku* is regarded as a theme underscoring "new" religions in Japan. See Reader and Tanabe (2004), who studied *gensei riyaku* (which they translate as "practically religious") from historical and contemporary perspectives as an important expression of Japanese religion.

20. Lai 1990.

21. See Kuo 1994b. Michel Strickmann (2005: 80) also treated the *Scripture on Divination* when discussing Chinese Buddhist oracles and divination.

22. For instance, see the *Brahmājāla-sūtra* of the *Dīrghāgama*, translated from the Pāli by T. W. Rhys Davids (1899: 16). Similar prohibitions are voiced in the Chinese version of the *Brahmājāla-sūtra* (*Fandong jing* 梵動經); see *Chang ahan jing* 長阿含經, T1:1.89b–c. Also see *Fanwang jing* 梵網經, T1484:24.1007a, 1007b; *Shami shijie bing weiyi* 沙彌十戒并威儀, T1471: 24.927a.

23. Cited in Lai 1990: 184.

24. Divination in China can be traced back to the use of oracle bones during the Shang period (1500–1100 BCE); see Chang 1983: 44–55. For the Chinese use of divinatory bamboo slips, see Li Ling 1990. For divination during the Warring States and Qin, see Harper 1999a, 1999b; during the Han, see Loewe 1994; Poo 1998: 41–68. For divination and fortune-telling in premodern China, see Smith 1991. For a recent work on written oracles and related divinatory practices in China, see Strickmann 2005.

layered system reverberates throughout the other levels.[25] This in turn triggers a causative process of breakdown throughout the entire socio-eco system, which can be repaired only by reinstating the "original" cosmic harmony. Divination exists in this worldview as a means to apprehend not only the causes of, but also the remedies to, disharmony in a multilayered cosmic system.

On the other hand, the Buddhist doctrine of *karma* was a principle of moral causation, which stipulated that any intended physical, verbal, or mental action will incur karmic retribution. In the *Scripture on Divination*, wheel divination essentially seeks to unravel patterns of past, present, and future karmic retributions in the hope of improving one's lot in present and future existences or to solicit guidance for spiritual development. Thus divination is no longer a way of comprehending cosmic patterns of correlative causation but a tool for investigating the workings of moral causation, which would otherwise have appeared to the Chinese as unpredictable. Chinese Buddhists, therefore, concretized the principle of *karma* into a procedure of religious praxis, a combination of ritual divination and repentance, which could be pragmatically enacted to avert karmic consequences and lay the foundation for spiritual practice.[26] Both Buddhism and religious Daoism were prone to appropriate the array of mantic arts that flourished in medieval China. The priests of Heavenly Master Daoism (Tianshi dao 天師道) were known for engaging in mantic consultation to diagnose causes of maladies before performing Daoist curative rites.[27]

Curiously, most scholarship on the *Scripture on Divination* has paid little attention to Dizang. The bodhisattva is cast in the familiar role of savior in the degenerate times of the five turbulences, but it becomes an avenue for religio-cultural amalgamation. Seemingly discordant religious elements are interwoven into an overarching soteriology configured so as to direct the practitioner from the secular realm to the transcendental goal of awakening. On the lower end of the soteriological spectrum are the repentance rites and the karmic divinatory method prescribed for the spiritually inferior; at the more advanced level, the technicalities of Buddhist meditation and abstruse doctrines on the nature of the mind are extolled as Mahāyāna prac-

25. On early Chinese cosmology, see Hart 1983; Schwartz 1985: 350–382.

26. There is another sense in which wheel divination departs from Chinese divinatory procedures—namely its use of the wheel metaphor. This metaphor is derived from the ten wheels of *cakravartin*s, buddhas, and bodhisattvas described in the *Shilun jing*. The wheel has strong connotations in the Indian tradition, where it is one of the attributes of the ideal ruler. In Indian Buddhism, the metaphor of the Buddha turning the wheel of the Dharma was deliberately used in contrast to the *cakravartin*'s wheel. Appropriately, the *Zhancha jing* employs the wheel to emphasize its Buddhist connection as opposed to the shell and milfoil of Chinese divination. Previous scholarship on the *Zhancha jing* has noted its symbolic use of the wheel metaphor; see Lai 1990: 183–184; Kuo 1994b: 151.

27. An important work on Heavenly Master Daoism, a ritual compilation titled *Chi songzi zhangli* 赤松子章曆 includes examples of petitions attesting to the use of divination before curative rites; see Nickerson 1996a: 492–536.

tices. Dizang fits into this schema as the patron of divination to whom sincere homage is paid to ensure the success of the forecast on the one hand and on the other as the object of ritual repentance and worship for those performing self-purification during the divination procedure. In Fascicle 2, Dizang is also the object of meditative contemplation that will ultimately lead the practitioner to states of calm and insight otherwise achieved by meditating on the nature of the mind. In short, ritual efficacy, meditative techniques, and doctrinal exegesis all coexist in this soteriological vision, thus refuting any tendency to polarize practice against doctrine.[28] Through his multivalent role, Dizang brings together ritual actions, Buddhist meditation techniques, and abstruse philosophical speculation.

By the sixth century, when the *Scripture on Divination* was composed, through his role as a savior in degenerate times, Dizang had emerged as an important symbol for medieval Chinese as they reimagined Buddhist doctrines and practices to fit their circumstances. That Dizang was a lesser-known and fairly obscure figure—as compared to the other major bodhisattvas—perhaps provided the necessary flexibility to accommodate the religious experimentation of the period. In the *Scripture on Divination* Dizang takes on new roles: He becomes the patron of divination and the object of meditation, but he retains the classic characteristics of the bodhisattva paradigm. However, it is uncertain whether the *Scripture on Divination* necessarily led to the widespread dissemination of Dizang Bodhisattva in the sixth century. The *Chronological Record of the Three Jewels* describes a method of penitence inspired by the *Scripture on Divination*:

> There was in Guang 廣 prefecture a monk who practiced a method of penitence based on the *stūpa* (*ta chanfa* 塔懺法). He had fabricated two small plaques from leather and written the characters "good" on one and "bad" on the other. He encouraged people to throw [the plaques]. Those who got the plaque on which the character "good" was written were [deemed to be] virtuous, while those who got the other were [considered] unvirtuous. He further practiced the method that involved "throwing oneself on the floor" (*zipu fa* 自撲法) as a means of eradicating wrongdoings. Men and women were [permitted] to mix together [during the practice]. In Qing 青 prefecture [in Henan], a learned man similarly practiced these methods. In the thirteenth year of the *kaihuang* 開皇 era [593], a person reported these bizzare facts to the military prefect of Guang prefecture.[29]

The mention of *zipu fa*, a confession rite practiced in Daoist circles, indicates that the *Scripture on Divination* was most likely formulated in a milieu where Buddhist and Daoist practices coexisted and were fairly interchange-

28. On the nuanced relationships between practice and theory, see Bielefeldt 2005.

29. *Lidai sanbao ji*, T2034:49.106c. Fei Changfang, the author of the *Chronological Records of the Three Jewels*, concludes the entry by questioning the authenticity of the *Scripture on Divination*.

able.[30] This record makes no reference to Dizang worship. Although this may well be an accidental omission, it may also indicate that in the sixth century Dizang was not quite the cultic object he was to become in the seventh and eighth centuries. Apparently, Chinp'yo (b. 718) introduced the *Scripture on Divination* to Korea in 740, and its divination technique was used at Mount Hiei during the Edo period (1603–1867).[31] By the seventeenth century, when the Buddhist reforms of the monk Zhixu were introduced, the *Scripture on Divination* also flourished as part of a revitalization of Dizang worship.[32]

The Exorcism Method: A Buddho-Daoist Formula for Demonology

Recovered from Japanese archival collections, *The Exorcism Method* locates the bodhisattva at the heart of a complicated religious amalgamation involving an array of Buddhist and Daoist elements.[33] The date of its composition is uncertain. The colophon appended to the extant version indicates that by 1087 the text was already circulating in Japan and a copy was kept at the Śūraṅgama Cloister (Shuryōgon-in 首楞嚴院).[34] Ōmura Seigai identified the first two anomalous characters in the title as belonging to a set of invented characters implemented during the reign of Empress Wu; he concluded that they were another way of writing Dizang's name but cautioned that the text had not necessarily been composed in that era.[35] The *Sanbao ganying yaolue lu* 三寶感應要略錄 (A Summarized Record of the Responsive Manifestations of the Three Jewels), which was compiled during the Liao (907–1125) by the Buddhist monk Feizhuo 非濁 (d. 1063), includes a narrative that is extracted, as Feizhuo himself acknowledges, "from the *Dizang dadao xin quce fa*" (出地藏大道心驅策法).[36] The text also reveals patently Daoist elements. Hence scholars agree that it is an indigenous composition belonging to the mid-Tang

30. The early practice of formal confession and breast-beating as a form of self-punitive action can be traced to the *Taiping jing* 太平經; see Tsuchiya 2002. For a comparative study of Buddhist and Daoist repentance rites, see Yamada 1994.

31. See Lai 1990: 196.

32. Zhixu composed four commentaries on the *Zhancha jing*. On his revitalization of Dizang worship, see Shengyan 1975: 186–192.

33. As previously mentioned, I have transliterated the two characters for "Dizang" according to the convention set by ancient and modern Buddhist scholarship. They are not found in normal Chinese usage. *The Exorcism Method* is translated in Appendix 3.

34. *Dizang dadao xin quce fa*, T1159A:20.652a.

35. 不詳譯時譯者，然題名地藏二字，以則天文字記之，蓋當時之作歟頗可疑焉。
(The dates of translation and translator are uncertain. However, in the title the two words "Dizang" are recorded using the [new] characters [from the period of Empress Wu] for "Zetian." It is indeed uncertain whether this is actually a work of that period!) Ōmura 1918: 348. For a study of the new characters introduced during the empress's reign, see Tokiwa 1943.

36. Part 3, Story 35, titled *Dizang pusa jiu Qiaoti zhangzhe jia e'gui nan ganying* 地藏菩薩救喬提長者家惡鬼難感應, in *Sanbao gunying yaolue lu*, T2084:51.855a–b. Note the changes in the title: from 埊閩 to 地藏; from 高提 to 喬提. On Feizhuo's works, see Chen 1979.

period, although the exact date is uncertain.[37] Heeding Ōmura's cautionary note, Manabe Kōsai dated the text to sometime *after* the Wuzhou period, whereas Osabe Kazuo argued, on the grounds of its distinctive Buddho-Daoist synthesis, that the scripture was part of the religious trends *during* the empress's reign, most likely belonging to an important but little-studied phase of esoteric Buddhism on the eve of Amoghavajra's (705–774) formulations.[38]

In terms of literary style, *The Exorcism Method* consists of a narrative and a prescriptive discourse delineating the demonological techniques taught by the Bodhisattva Dizang. The text begins by plunging the reader into the world of Buddhist mythology: On Mount Gṛdhrakūṭa, the *axis mundi*, the Buddha presides in silence over an assembly of esoteric adepts. Almost immediately the text shifts from this silent center to the world of action, where the bodhisattva roams the universe to relieve the suffering of living beings. Having established this Buddhist setting, the work next introduces the kernel story of Elder Gaoti 高提 and his household, who were deprived of their vital vapor (*jingqi* 精氣) by malevolent ghosts (*e'gui* 惡鬼).[39] This story of demons afflicting humans and depriving them of health and longevity strikes a chord in both Chinese and Indian cultures.

In the Chinese conception, the distinction between demons (*mo* 魔) and ghosts is blurred, so *gui* is the more common term used to mean both the disembodied dead as well as sinister demons or spirits.[40] Such beings are frequently conceived of as malicious forces that suck the vital vapor from the living, causing ailments, disease, or death. In pre-Buddhist Chinese society, illness and disease were frequently explained as demon possession.[41] Religious Daoism appropriated concerns with exorcism and the subjugation of menacing demons and troubling ghosts, integrating these early Chinese themes with the path and goal of salvation promised by the Dao.[42] Similarly, the early Indian Vedic world attributed disease and illness to the invasion of

37. Manabe 1960: 115.

38. Ibid.: 116; Osabe 1982: 9–14. "Buddho-Daoist" is used here for descriptive purposes; I am not implying a "corrupt" mixture of "pure" breeds of Buddhism and Daoism.

39. As early the fourth century BCE, *qi* and blood were considered the essential components of human life. Donald Harper translates *qi* as "vapor" to avoid the popular associations of the term in modern Chinese and English usage. Note that this understanding of *qi* is not equated with the harmful emanations of the internal organs associated with the old western medical understanding of "vapor"; see Harper 1998: 77–78.

40. For ghosts in early China, see Poo 2004; in medieval China, see Poo 1997.

41. See Volume 5 of De Groot 1892–1910 for a survey of Chinese demonology with relevant citations from pre-Han and Han (202 BCE–220 CE) sources. As early as the Shang dynasty, the Chinese regarded illnesses and other disorders as omens sent by ancestral spirits; see Unschuld 1985: 19–28. Bibliographic records indicate that demonological literature circulated among the elite of the Warring States, Qin, and Han, but none of it survives today in the transmitted traditions. However, tomb excavations have yielded an important corpus of this otherwise lost genre of "magico-religious" literature. For studies on demonology in the Warring States period, see Harper 1985, 1996.

42. For a close investigation of the role of demonology in the mortuary rites and afterlife beliefs of early religious Daoism, see Nickerson 1996a: 83–165.

the body by evil spirits and demons, variously known as *piśāca, rakṣa, yakṣa,* and so forth.[43] Vedic ritual texts offer an array of healing rites, including the use of charms and incantations to avert, destroy, or subdue demons.[44] Although the earliest strata of Buddhist literature, which includes the *Nikāya* and *Āgama* scriptures, regularly condemns such Vedic-Brahmanic practices, meditators were known to incant *dhāraṇī* or *paritta* to ward off snakes and other dangers in the forest.[45] The Vedic view linking physical ailments to demonic attacks resurfaces in Indian Mahāyāna scriptures. Passages from these texts mention fear of spirits and demons stealing one's vital warmth *(ojaḥ),* thus causing physical ailments and even death.[46] This anxiety was widespread in the genre of scriptures known as *dhāraṇī* literature, which were especially popular in Central Asia and China and frequently offered a spectrum of incantation spells for an array of secular benefits—not least for curative purposes in the event of demonic afflictions and ailments.[47] It would have taken

---

43. Zysk 1989: 123–143.

44. The *Arthaveda* refers to spells for exorcising, "speaking away" *(apa-vaktri),* warding off, or averting supernatural pests and their leaders, as well as rites against demons (5.15–16). Elsewhere in the text charms are recommended for the expulsion of adversaries, rivals, wizards, and assorted demons (2.18); see Gonda 1980: 305.

45. For examples of the prohibition against reciting spells as a means of livelihood, see *Chang ahan jing,* T1:1.84b; *Sifen lü* 四分律, T1428:22.960c. In early Buddhism, monks were usually taught the meditation of loving kindness *(metta bhavana)* to combat the dangers of the forest such as wild animals or poisonous reptiles. Occasionally, the use of spells was also recommended. For example, in the *Āgama,* after a *bhikṣu* had been bitten by a poisonous snake, the Buddha taught the method of incantation (*zhoushu* 咒術) to avert forest dangers; see *Za ahan jing* 雜阿含經, T99:2.60c–61b.

46. The *Bhaiṣajyaguru-sūtra,* for instance, lists one kind of untimely death for "those who are excessively careless, dwelling in carelessness" that occurs when "non-human beings steal away their vital warmth" *teṣām amānuṣā ojam apaharanti* (Schopen 1978: 262). Schopen also highlights other similar passages in the *Bhaiṣajyaguru-sūtra*: For instance, if an expectant mother performs a particular *pūjā* to Bhaiṣajyaguru, she will give birth to a son for whom "it will not be possible for his vital warmth to be snatched away by non-human beings *(na tasya śakyam amānuṣena ojo grahītum).*" Similar references occur in other Mahāyāna scriptures like the *Saddharmapuṇḍarīka-sūtra,* the *Ratnaketuparivarta-sūtra,* and the *Gilgit Prajñāpāramitā-sūtra* (Schopen 1978: 263–264).

47. The Sanskrit word *dhāraṇī,* usually translated as "spell," is typically regarded as an extended *mantra,* the recitation of which is said to bestow extraordinary powers on the speaker. Exalted as potent condensations of *sūtra,* these incantation formulae often occur toward the end of the text. Scriptures centered around the use of spells figure conspicuously in the lists of works translated into Chinese as early as the second century. The daunting number of *dhāraṇī* scriptures baffled scholars for some time, and they tended to regard *dhāraṇī* as a unique phenomenon; see Waley 1931: xiii–xiv. *Dhāraṇī* scriptures were previously regarded as heralding "tantric" (esoteric) Buddhism; they were thought to belong to a "proto-tantra" phase; see Osabe 1982: 9–14; Strickmann 2002: 89–122. However, *dhāraṇī* had already appeared in early Mahāyāna literature (e.g., *Saddharmapuṇḍarīka-sūtra*) and, although they grew in significance and quantity over time, they were not really associated with explicitly "tantric" soteriologies. Instead they largely addressed concerns about death, rebirth, and averting misfortunes—all themes that are consistent with Mahāyāna literature. Hence scholars now agree that *dhāraṇī* should be more accurately viewed as a Mahāyāna development; see Schopen 2005: 337.

no leap of imagination to connect the Indian notion of *ojaḥ* with the indigenous Chinese concept of "vital vapor." Apprehending the parallels, Chinese translators used the latter term to render the former idea, so that the pre-Buddhist Chinese paranoia of renegade spirits sucking out one's vital vapor rapidly melded with the Buddhist conception.[48]

The motif of a household suffocated by malevolent ghosts, resonant as it is in both Chinese and Indian cultures, produces a fluid narrative that expedites Buddho-Daoist amalgamation in *The Exorcism Method.* Within this narrative, another is embedded, one reminiscent of the Indian *avadāna* (genesis story) highlighting the classic bodhisattva career in Mahāyāna Buddhism. The prototypical *avadāna* is based on the past lives of the Buddha Śākyamuni: his arousing the mind of awakening, the utterance of his vows, and the prediction of his buddhahood through aeons of bodhisattva practice.[49] In *The Exorcism Method,* the plight of the Elder Gaoti and his household becomes the occasion for Dizang to recall his bodhisattva career. The story begins like a standard *avadāna,* stretching back to the mythical time of the Buddha King of Sun Radiance. However, it quickly introduces a twist to the standard *avadāna* plot: After the Buddha King of Sun Radiance enters *nirvāṇa,* Dizang, commiserating with the plight of those possessed by malevolent ghosts, aspires to study the art of quelling ghosts from a saint (*xian* 仙) living on Mount Kuṭṭāra who has mastered the magical arts (*daoshu* 道術). Through this ingenious twist, the art of quelling ghosts was integrated into the classic paradigm of the bodhisattva career, becoming part of the bodhisattva's practice of compassion. In Chinese *Āgama* literature, *xian* is often used to translate the Indian *ṛṣi,* or "seer"; it also refers to the Daoist adept who has achieved the goal of immortality. These dual connotations of the term are thus pivotal to the Buddho-Daoist amalgamation underscoring the entire text.

The exorcism technique espoused in the text can be broken down into three ritual steps: (1) the rite of summoning ghosts (*zhao gui* 召鬼); (2) the rite of fearlessness in confronting ghosts (*jiangui wuwei* 見鬼無畏); and (3) the rite of dispatching the ghosts in one's service (*shicu gui* 使促鬼). This configuration of summoning, encountering, and dispatching ghosts assimilates elements from early medieval Daoist liturgy that have roots in pre-Han and Han therapeutic demonology and funerary practices.[50] Study of tomb artifacts and documents unearthed from pre-Han and Han burial sites in recent decades has resulted in a new appreciation of the prehistory of Daoism. It is now common knowledge that the roots of early religious Daoism lie in the

---

48. This practice is already evident in Chinese translations of *Āgama* texts though not with the same frequency as in Mahāyāna literature.

49. The past lives of the historical Buddha are recounted in *jātaka* and *avadāna* tales. The beginning of his bodhisattva career is usually traced to his previous existence as the brahmin ascetic Sumati, known as Sumedha in Pāli literature, or Megha in the *Mahāvastu.*

50. For the purposes of this book, no sharp distinction is made between *mantra* and *dhāraṇī.* They are used interchangeably and translated as "incantation spell."

grave-quelling writs and the magico-religion recorded in tomb manuscripts and artifacts.[51] In particular, Angelika Cedzich has argued that early Heavenly Master Daoist liturgy derives from pre-Han grave-quelling beliefs and practices.[52] Although the grave-quelling religion aimed only to banish the dead forever from the human realm, Daoist rituals not only protected descendants from visitations of ancestral sins, but also redeemed the dead and opened the way for them to be reintegrated and promoted into otherworldly hierarchies.

A Sichuan stele inscription mentions a "demon-soldier of the heavenly troop" (*tianzu guibing* 天卒鬼兵) named Hujiu 胡九 who attained the Dao and signed a contract with six Daoist libationers, promising henceforth to spread the law of the Way of the Heavenly Master. "Demon-soldier" probably refers to the lowest rank conferred on the dead upon their entering otherworldly service.[53] They would be listed together with the hundreds of other spirits in registers (*lu* 籙) detailing the authority and rank of both laymembers and priests in the Heavenly Master organization. The beginning of religious Daoism is closely associated with the shift from shamanistic sacrificial appeasement of demons and spirits to a new, fearless attitude that sought to "resolutely and overpoweringly coerce the divinities into submitting to the human adept."[54] Hence, the Daoist priest claimed to possess powers that included the ability to exorcise, subjugate, and employ ghosts using an array of ritual paraphernalia (spells, registers of spirits' names, seals, talismans). Several of these ritual methods can be traced to pre-Han and Han therapeutic demonology documented in the medical manuscripts unearthed from the Mawangdui 馬王堆 tombs.[55] The widespread use of ritual practices to summon and conjure ghosts has a long history dating back to pre-Han soul-summoning rites such as those recorded in the *Chuci* 楚辭 (Songs of the South).[56]

The configuration of rites (summoning, confronting, subjugating, and dispatching ghosts) in *The Exorcism Method* deliberately invokes the Daoist liturgy. The practitioner of Dizang's exorcism method is in a sense no different

51. For grave-quelling writs, see Seidel 1982, 1987b, 1987c, 1997. For pre-Han and Han magico-religious traditions, see Harper 1985, 1996, 1998, 1999a, 1999b, 2004.

52. Cedzich 1993: 23–35.

53. Ibid.: 32–33. Demons in the service of the Dao are mentioned, for example, in the late fourth- or fifth-century Daoist texts *Nüqing guilü* 女青鬼律 and *Dongyuan shenzhou jing* 洞淵神咒經; see Nickerson 1996a: 556–561.

54. Maeda 1995: 62; cf. Nickerson 1996a: 556–561.

55. For a study and translation of Mawangdui medical manuscripts, see Harper 1998.

56. The *Chuci* is an anthology of compositions dating from the late fourth century BCE to the second century CE. As it exists today, the anthology is traditionally attributed to a scholar named Wang Yi 王逸 (ca. 89–158). It contains two soul summons titled *Zhaohun* 召魂 and *Dazhao* 大召. According to early scholarship, shamans used these to threaten or coax a spirit into returning to its body before ascertaining that a person was really dead; see, for example, Hawkes 1959: 101. Stephen Bokenkamp questioned this interpretation, arguing for the more likely scenario that the soul was summoned to rejoin its body not in life but for a continued existence in the grave (1989: 10). For medieval Daoism, see Nickerson 1996a: 625–631; 2002.

from a Daoist adept. Following in Dizang's footsteps, he is expected to master magical incantation, ritual spitting, "teeth clapping" (*kouchi* 叩齒), and talismanic writing, all of which appear regularly in Daoist ritual. As early as the second or third centuries BCE, magical incantations and ritual spitting were associated with breath magic, which concentrated the vapor as it was ejected from the mouth, thus serving as a means to access the spirit world and cure demonic ailments. These actions, if executed by a person possessing potent breath, protected one against renegade ghosts and demonic affliction. The *Recipes for Fifty-two Ailments* (*Wushi'er bingfang* 五十二病方), a Mawangdui text, invokes demon-quelling spirits known as "spouters" (*penzhe* 噴者) and prescribes ritual spitting before incanting magical utterances to dispel ghosts.[57] A Fangmatan 放馬灘 tomb document dating to the Warring States warns against spitting when performing sacrifices at tombs, lest it should frighten the ghost into leaving.[58] In Daoist texts, spitting is often practiced with incantation sequentially as part of ritual therapy.[59] An early example of teeth clapping is found in the *Baopuzi neipian* 抱朴子内篇 (One Who Embraces Simplicity, Inner Chapter), a Daoist text that instructs the ritualist to hit the upper and lower rows of his teeth against each other. This accords with a practice described in the *Zhengao* 真誥 (Declarations of the Perfected), which states that the sounds of clapping teeth and magical utterances strike fear in malignant ghosts and spirits.[60] The talisman relies on the written word to communicate with the other world. Prepared like an official document, it was issued at the command of an official high in the divine hierarchy to lowly spirits responsible for human misfortunes.[61] *The Exorcism Method* provides instructions for preparing and handling talismans reminiscent of those given in Daoist practice: Written with vermilion sand and then imprinted three times with a seal (*yin* 印), nine slips of paper are swallowed or carried on the body.[62] Ritual spitting, teeth clapping, and the use of talis-

57. See Harper 1998: 163–165.

58. See Harper 1994: 14.

59. See Strickmann 2002: 29–31.

60. *Baopuzi neipian*, HY 50211, 15: 12a; *Zhengao*, HY 71294, 15: 10a–b.

61. Talismans were already in use during the feudal Zhou period, when it was customary for a prince who had assigned a task to one of his subjects to break in two an inscribed piece of wood or jade and retain one of the pieces for himself. The remaining half was then presented to the person delegated with the task to serve as proof of the official nature of his mission (Unschuld 1985: 40). Talismans were "messages of command" intended to be read by spirits, not ordinary mortals, and they were written in a familiar script "just enough to allow their recognition as a form of written language (as opposed to random marks) but not enough to permit the uninitiated to make any sense of them" (Campany 2002: 61).

62. Ingesting talismans is a regular component in Daoist curative and exorcistic rites. For example, the *Lu xiansheng daomen ke lue* 陸先生道門科略, composed by Lu Xiujing 陸修靜 (406–477), declares: "The ill were not to take medicine or use the acupuncture needle or moxa. They were only to ingest talismans, drink water [into which the ashes of the burnt talismans had been mixed], and confess all their sins from their first year of life" (translated in Nickerson 1996b: 352). On Daoist talismans and written documents, see Campany 2002: 61–

mans or seals are also discerned in Buddhist *dhāraṇī* scriptures, particularly those recovered from Dunhuang manuscripts.[63]

It would, however, be a mistake to emphasize the Daoist character of *The Exorcism Method* over its Buddhist aspects. By the eighth century, *dhāraṇī* incantation, ritual hand gestures (*mudrās*), and name recitation were discernible elements in both Buddhist and Daoist soteriology.[64] In Tang China, Buddhist *dhāraṇī* and *mantras* blended so inextricably with incantations used in indigenous magical practices that it is difficult to differentiate between the two. Moreover, the Daoist use of hand gestures (*shoujue* 手訣), which evolved from the Buddhist *mudrā* (*shouyin* 手印), had already occurred in the Six Dynasties (222–589) in a range of ritual settings—from subjugating ghosts to healing ailments. It did not take long before Daoists also dabbled in creating hand signs of their own, so that in the Tang milieu there was a highly fluid situation where both Buddhists and Daoists expanded their repertory of ritual hand gestures through mutual borrowing and self-modification.

Ultimately, the remarkable achievement of *The Exorcism Method* lies in its seamless blending of Daoist and Buddhist voices. The conversion of a ghost in *The Exorcism Method*, for example, cannot be characterized simply as either Buddhist or Daoist. Initially, the text employs Buddhist terminology and appeals to Mahāyāna soteriology: The ghost claims that the ritualist's prowess has freed him from retributive evil ways and caused him to aspire to awakening, explicitly invoking the bodhisattva ideal. The ghost then requests Buddhist teachings to annihilate his sins completely and transform his malevolent form. To achieve conversion and salvation, the ritualist addresses the ghost as follows:

> "You and I will always be good spiritual friends who will together liberate living beings. You and I will together bestow on living beings whatever they take delight in." Again say, "Wherever there are living beings requesting various kinds of knowledge or magical arts, we will go there together to teach them. Whatever they entreat for, all shall be satisfied. If there are living beings afflicted with various forms of bodily suffering and distress; or if there are living beings undergoing capital punishment ordered by kings or officials; or if there are living beings caught in flood and fire calamities; or if there are menacing birds, beasts, poisonous serpents, vengeful enemies, thieves, and bandits; for all of these circumstances, we shall go together to relieve [these beings] and bring about their deliverance. Whatever material

69. For comparisons between Daoist and Buddhist usages, see Strickmann 2002: 123–193; Xiao 1993a.

63. See Xiao 1993b: 185–194, 241–249; Strickmann 2002: 29–31.

64. *The Exorcism Method* refers to three types of hand gestures: the all-encompassing sign (*doushe yin* 都攝印), the sign that saves and encompasses according to one's desires (*suixin jiushe yin* 隨心救攝印), and the sign of fearlessness (*wuwei yin* 無畏印). For a description of Buddhist *mudrās*, see Saunders 1960. On the Daoist use of hand gestures, see Mitamura 2002.

requisites they need, we will rejoice in granting them and enabling them to be peaceful and joyous."[65]

Clearly, the ghost has been converted and delivered from his evil ways as well as recruited into the pantheon of protective deities. Once the perpetrator of ills and harm to humans, the ghost has now become a benign spiritual friend intent on securing the happiness and welfare of living beings. Prior to the coming of Buddhism, Heavenly Master Daoism also held out the vision of salvation to demons its priests had subjugated and recruited into their service. By Tang China, the twofold aspiration of attaining the Dao and saving living beings underscored Daoist writings and was integrated into the daily liturgical structures of Daoist monasticism not only through rituals addressed to the deities, but also in daily recitations accompanying routine acts of hygiene.[66]

Religious amalgamation, moreover, occurs in the explication of the efficacies of talismans. Of the forty talismans, the first twenty promote secular benefits like the avoidance of calamities and ailments and the resurrection of the dead, whereas the remaining twenty allow the actualization of transcendental goals, including the Buddhist attainment of the four unobstructed wisdoms (*wuai zhi* 無礙智), the transcendence of life and death, and the protection of buddhas and bodhisattvas.[67] The description of the adept integrates Daoist conceptions of sainthood: On account of the practitioner's prowess, his relatives will secure the Buddhist tolerance of the birthlessness of all phenomena (*wusheng faren* 無生法忍), thereupon "each will spread out his body and fly away."[68] After wearing talismans for up to fifty days, the practitioner's "last finger will then emit a radiance and his body will naturally be lucid and transparent both inside and outside just like pristine glass."[69] The image of a numinous and immaculate body spread out in flight is reminiscent of the Daoist adept who, through various cultivation techniques, sheds

65. *Dizang dadao xin quce fa*, T1159A:20.653c–654a.

66. This sentiment is expressed in the following verse to be chanted when cleaning one's teeth:

Washing with ashes to remove the dirt,
Using the ashes as a primary means,
May foulness go and perfection arise.
Cleansing the heart and cleansing the mouth,
Realizing the Dao and saving others,
Heaven is great and Earth everlasting!
Swiftly, swiftly, in accord with the statutes and ordinances!

(*Shishi weiyi* 十事威儀, 8b, translated in Kohn 2003: 117)

67. *Wuai zhi* is known in Sanskrit as *pratisaṃvid*. They are the bodhisattva's powers of reasoning in (1) *dharma* (*fa* 法); (2) *artha* (*yi* 義), or the meaning (of the *dharma*); (3) *nirukti* (*ci* 辭), or any language or form of expression; and (4) *pratibhāna* (*leshuo* 樂說), or eloquent speaking and argument.

68. *Dizang dadao xin quce fa*, T1159A:20.655a: 各騰身而去.

69. Ibid.: 20.655a: 小指並放光明其身自然如淨琉璃內外明徹.

his mortal body and achieves an immortal body in union with the entire cosmos.[70] The Tang audience was certainly familiar with the Buddho-Daoist formulations in Lingbao 靈寶 Daoist literature, which conspicuously appropriated and assimilated Buddhist teachings and practices.[71]

The Exorcism Method introduces the startling image of Dizang as the exorcistic healer, an adept in a range of magico-therapeutic techniques to relieve ailments (particularly those associated with demons), extend the life span, and bring spiritual salvation. In some sense, this image is the logical culmination of trends in early scriptural representations of Dizang. After all, both the *Scripture on the Ten Wheels* and the *Section on Sumeru Treasury* associate Dizang with *dhāraṇī* incantation and the subjugation of malevolent forces that cause widespread cosmic disorders. Besides revealing a hitherto-neglected aspect of Dizang's character in Chinese Buddhism, *The Exorcism Method* also offers one of the first *scriptural* sources for an image that will be repeatedly invoked in connection with his role as savior of the damned. In *The Exorcism Method*, when Dizang recites his *dhāraṇī*, hell beings are freed from their retributive afflictions and, seated on lotuses, they attain temporary respite from the torments of hell. This image of Dizang transforming hell recurs in literary descriptions of his place in the underworld. Its passing mention in *The Exorcism Method* may indicate that Dizang's underworld function originated in a set of larger concerns with subjugating malevolent ghosts and relieving the suffering of living beings.

A Ritual Manual on the Bodhisattva Dizang: Dizang in Esoteric Rites

Recovered from Japanese archival collections and reprinted in twentieth-century editions of the Chinese Buddhist canon, *A Ritual Manual on the Bodhisattva Dizang* is attributed to Śubhakara, one of the Indian monks who propagated esoteric Buddhism under the Tang court's sponsorship.[72] However, *A Ritual Manual*'s authorship and textual history were questioned as early as the Kamakura period, when Kakuzen 覚禅 (b. 1143) expressed skepticism over its origins.[73] Adopting the traditional Buddhist stance, modern Japanese scholarship for some time regarded the text as a Japanese composition.[74] More recently, Japanese scholars have revisited the issue and admitted that the contents and language should place it among Tang Buddhist esoteric texts. Osabe Kazuo sees parallels between *A Ritual*

70. For Daoist conceptions of the body, see Schipper 1978. On the early Daoist pursuit of the immortal body, particularly in terms of the concept of *shijie* 尸解 (release from the corpse), see Campany 2002: 52–60; Cedzich 2001; Seidel 1987c.

71. On Lingbao Daoism, see Bokenkamp 1983, 1989, 1990.

72. *Dizang pusa yigui*, T1158.20:652a–c. Four manuscript copies of *A Ritual Manual* are preserved in Japanese archival collections; see Hoshino 1961: 106. For further discussion on the Taishō edition, see the introductory note to the translation of the text in Appendix 3.

73. See Hoshino 1961: 105–107.

74. Manabe 1960: 114; Osabe 1982: 11–13.

Manual and *The Exorcism Method* and concludes that *A Ritual Manual* was based on some original text composed under the sway of esoteric Buddhism at its height in the Tang court.[75]

According to Ōmura Seigai, because the terminology in the text's *mudrā* description is derived from the *Sarvatattvasaṃgraha-sūtra*, *A Ritual Manual* should be more accurately dated to the period after the *sūtra* was introduced to China in 720.[76] For Ōmura, *A Ritual Manual* most likely dates to the second half of the Tang era but was posthumously ascribed to Śubhakara. Moreover, its title classifies the text as a ritual manual, or *yigui* 儀軌, the Chinese counterpart of the *sādhana*, a class of ritual texts outlining deity worship and visualization in esoteric Buddhism. Besides its title, the text's contents, which presuppose the fairly extensive training of esoteric masters under the sponsorship of the Tang court, also link it to the corpus of short esoteric manuals on deity worship composed in the late Tang period.[77] Finally, *A Ritual Manual* prescribes an unusual iconography for Dizang, showing him crowned with an ornate headpiece, an image atypical of illustrations of the monk preserved in Japanese esoteric writings.

In terms of style, *A Ritual Manual* can be divided into narrative and prescriptive discourse. The text opens with the Buddha Śākyamuni preaching at Mount Kharādīya. Dizang steps out from among the congregation and requests permission to preach numinous *mantra*s to benefit living beings. On receiving the Buddha's approbation, Dizang immediately recites three *mantra*s of varying length:

> At that time, Dizang Bodhisattva ascended into the air, gave praise to, and took refuge in the World-Honored One. He also exhibited countless supernormal powers in the air and uttered a *mantra* through his sacred mouth: *An anmota anmoer jubi jubi sanmanduo suopohe* 唵闇摩他巕摩爾 俱苾 俱苾 三曼多娑婆賀. Then he uttered the middle mantra: *An yanmantazhe suopohe* 唵 炎曼他啫 娑婆賀. Then he uttered the short mantra twice: *An shisi* 唵磃 呬.[78]

The image of the Buddhist saint as a wonder-worker flying into the sky and performing magical feats in midair, as well as the sacred incantation, is certainly common in early Buddhist and Mahāyāna literature.[79] However, *A Ritual Manual*'s description of the sacred incantation employs the esoteric classification of long (*da zhou* 大咒), medium (*zhong zhou* 中咒 or *xin zhou* 心咒), and short (*xiao zhou* 小咒 or *xin zhong xin zhou* 心中心咒). Each *mantra* strings together Chinese characters that possess little semantic sense because they were selected to simulate the sounds of Indian syllables. The brief

75. Osabe 1982: 13.

76. Ōmura 1918: 443.

77. Manabe 1960: 114.

78. *Dizang pusa yigui*, T1158:20.652a.

79. On the bodhisattva as wonder-worker, see Gómez 1977. On monks as wonder-workers, see Kieschnick 1997: 67–111.

description of Dizang "uttering [the *mantras*] though his divine mouth" (*yi shenkou shuo* 以神口說) suggests the sacralizing of speech, one of the three mysteries (*san mi* 三密) in esoteric teaching.[80] The power of Dizang's *mantras* is evident by their enormous impact on the audience:

> On his recitation of these *mantras*, the great bodhisattvas of the tenth stage and so forth lost their original aspiration and became confused. The *devas*, *nāgas*, and others of the eight classes, *yakṣas*, demons, and spirits fled in great apprehension and collapsed to the ground. The sun, moon, and stars lost their luminosity and darkness pervaded the sky. Showers of precious flowers rained down. Even if one were to discourse on the power of the *mantras* for an entire aeon, one cannot exhaust [this subject].[81]

The ritual efficacy of sacred incantation surpasses even the bodhisattva path; even the most advanced tenth-stage bodhisattvas are frightened into abandoning their original aspiration to achieve awakening. In a sense the narrative deftly transforms Dizang Bodhisattva into an all-powerful esoteric saint beyond the tenth-stage bodhisattva. Continuities with earlier themes in the making of Dizang's history are obvious: Dizang's association with *dhāraṇī* and his role as interlocutor requesting (or invited) to preach a method in chaotic times. But the foregrounding of sacred incantation and the subordination of tenth-stage bodhisattvas herald subtle shifts.

At this juncture, the text abruptly adopts a prescriptive tone and begins outlining the esoteric ritual in which Dizang presides as the deity receiving veneration. This discourse intentionally aligns the text with esoteric ritual manuals on making images for worship and visualization. The text prescribes the making of the deity's image, the enumeration of the deity's specialized *mudrās* and *mantras*, and finally the practice of ritual offerings (Ch. *humo* 護摩; Skt. *homa*) to bring about a broad range of worldly benefits. Two forms of Dizang iconography are outlined: the first depicts Dizang as a *śrāvaka* dressed in a *kāṣāya* robe; his right shoulder is bared, his left hand holds a blooming flower, and his right hand makes the gesture for granting fearlessness (Ch. *shiwuwei yin* 施無畏印; Skt. *abhayamudrā*).[82] The second form resembles the first except that Dizang wears a celestial coiffure (*tianguan* 天冠), sits on a lotus throne, and manifests himself as the Great Being (Ch. *dashi* 大士; Skt. *mahāsattva*). These two iconographies follow the *Scripture on the Ten Wheels* in presenting Dizang Bodhisattva clothed in the *kāṣāya* robe. However, in the second set of instructions, the monk Dizang acquires princely regalia (the ornate headpiece, the lotus seat), which are probably not so much intended as royal insignia, but to visually "deify" the bodhisattva and perhaps mark his integration into the pantheon of esoteric deities. As we will see in the

80. The three mysteries are those of the body, speech, and mind.

81. *Dizang pusa yigui*, T1158:20.652a.

82. In the *abhayamudrā*, the right hand is raised and the palm faces front; see Saunders 1960: 55–65.

next chapter, until the tenth century there was no sign of the five-buddha crown now common in Dizang iconography.

The manual next outlines a set of four *mudrās* and *mantras* associated with Dizang Bodhisattva that the practitioner should master and enact in ritual performance. The practitioner is instructed to make a sequence of four gestures beginning with a type of *añjali,* or palms together, on to a *mudrā* of universal offerings (*pu gongyang yin* 普供養印), a third general *mudrā* (*zong yin* 總印), and finally, the *mudrā* for inviting and praising [the deity] (*qingzan yin* 請讚印). The text explains the gestures through a code of hand symbolism used in Buddhist esoteric rites which correlates the two palms to merits (*fu* 福) and wisdom (*zhi* 智), and the fingers to the ten perfections (*pāramitā*) on the bodhisattva path. The text characterizes the making of *mudrās* as the meditation of hand visualization (*guan shou chan* 觀手禪), which alludes to the ritual logic inherent in visualizing the deity in esoteric practice.[83]

Finally, *A Ritual Manual* provides a protracted list of seventeen ritual offerings *(homa)*, differentiated by the herb or plant used and the occasion for the ritual. Based on his or her needs, the practitioner is instructed to perform a relevant offering on the eighth, fourteenth, or fifteenth day of the month to secure ritual success, or *de chengjiu* 得成就, which is the usual translation of the esoteric Sanskrit term *siddhi.* This terminology, coupled with the *mudrās* and *mantras* mentioned above, point to the existence of an esoteric soteriology within the text. The remaining ritual benefits are for the most part worldly: an abundant harvest, wealth and reputation, health, harmonious friendship, and conjugal bliss. They are really no different from those derived from Mahāyāna cultic practices except for the use of terms like *homa* and *siddhi.* As Osabe observed, the offerings bring to mind the list of religio-magical curative "recipes" in Buddho-Daoist or *dhāraṇī* literature (e.g., *The Exorcism Method*) that have deep roots in early Chinese medical practice.[84]

Among the Dizang scriptures, *A Ritual Manual* records the Tang idea of Dizang Bodhisattva as a patron deity of esoteric ritual. In terms of content and structure, the text belongs to the outpouring of ritual texts from the eighth to the tenth centuries, the bulk of which reflect the deliberate recruitment of deities into the Buddhist pantheon as a result of so-called esoteric developments. These texts normally set up a deity as a patron saint for discrete veneration, the singular focus of a self-contained cult; esoteric exegesis addresses these deities as *bie zun* 別尊—as opposed to to *zhu zun* 主尊, a central figure presiding in a configuration of deities. Not only were new deities created, but familiar figures in the Mahāyāna pantheon were reconfigured to align with the paradigmatic representation of deities in esoteric Buddhism. Ritual texts normally prescribed for each deity a repertory of iconic representations, accoutrements and regalia, *dhāraṇī* or *mantras*, *mudrās* and

83. For ritual visualizations of Zhunti, see Gimello 2004.

84. Osabe 1982: 13. For another list of curative recipes using plants and herbs, see *Qianshou qianyan Guanshiyin pusa zhibing heyao jing* 千手千眼觀世音菩薩治病合藥經, T1059:20.103c–105c, translated in Unschuld 1985: 314–321.

body postures.[85] In *A Ritual Manual*, Dizang, a member of the bodhisattva pantheon, was reconceived in light of esoteric teachings in Tang China. Dizang Bodhisattva as the patron deity of esoteric ritual still retains marked continuities with earlier texts, notably his appearance as a monk in the *Scripture on the Ten Wheels.* Moreover, the use of ritual efficacy—especially sacred incantation and hand gestures to subjugate malevolent spirits, reverse malignant curses, and bestow this-worldly benefits—is neither "new" nor uniquely esoteric. To a greater or lesser extent, these functions and techniques already appeared in the *Scripture on the Ten Wheels*, the *Section on the Sumeru Treasury*, and *The Exorcism Method.* What makes the text "esoteric" is its rearticulation of these functions and techniques, mostly continuous with Mahāyāna, through linguistic and soteriological configurations that were increasingly identified as "esoteric" in East Asian Buddhism.

The *Scripture on the Bodhisattva Dizang*: From Hell to Pure Land

Recovered from Dunhuang, this indigenous Chinese composition is transcribed in Volume 85 of the Taishō edition of the Chinese Buddhist canon. A total of twenty-two copies of this *sūtra* are preserved in Dunhuang manuscript collections around the world.[86] These copies mostly date from the twelfth century, but DX 2636 from the Leningrad collection and *sheng* 25 from the Beijing collection contain information pointing to the year 976.[87] Based on this evidence, Françoise Wang-Toutain proposed that this scripture was written toward the end of the ninth century or the beginning of the tenth. The Dunhuang manuscripts contain variant versions of the scripture but, broadly speaking, there exists a short version, T2909 (a transcription of S 6257), and a long version, S 431.[88] Its title, the *Scripture on the Bodhisattva Dizang*, in late medieval China, was used to designate both the *Scripture on the Ten Wheels* and the *Scripture on Divination.*[89] The author possibly adopted it to lend credibility to his text.

The *Scripture on the Bodhisattva Dizang* situates Dizang in the context of medieval Chinese afterlife beliefs, particularly the passage from hell to paradise. The scripture opens with the bodhisattva contemplating living

85. Zhunti was one of the new deities created in connection with Buddhist esoteric development; see Gimello 2004: 225.

86. Wang-Toutain 1998: 145. In the appendix, Wang-Toutain lists the following manuscripts: P 2289, P 2873, P 3932, P 3748 from the Bibliothèque Nationale de France; S 431, S 4489, S 5531, S 5618, S 5672, S 5677, S 6257 from the British Library; *sheng* 25, *zhi* 64, from the Beijing collection; Dx 2025, Dx 2636 from the Leningrad collection. Also see Wang-Toutain 1998: 309–310. I have translated this scripture in Appendix 3.

87. Wang-Toutain 1998: 145–146.

88. An annotation to the Taishō edition states that the text was based on S 197. Wang-Toutain, however, identifies this as an error, stating that the manuscript used was actually S 6257; see Wang-Toutain 1998: 146, n. 581.

89. Wang-Toutain 1998: 145, n. 580.

beings as they suffer in hell; the tortures they endure are depicted in gruesome detail. Unable to bear the painful sights, Dizang leaves his Lapis Lazuli World in the south to preside over hell together with King Yama.[90] Toward its conclusion, the text assures readers that venerating Dizang will bring about rebirth in the Land of Bliss (Sukhāvatī) and promises that Dizang himself will welcome dying devotees, who will henceforth reside forever in the same place as the bodhisattva.

The *Scripture on the Bodhisattva Dizang* significantly heralds the underworld connection that will emerge as Dizang's most celebrated characterization in East Asian Buddhism. It is a genesis account of Dizang's role as savior of the damned and relates how he came to share the rule of the underworld, a task traditionally assigned solely to King Yama. The text gives four reasons for Dizang's "migration" from his land in the south to the infernal realm:

> First, he feared that King Yama's judgment of crimes would be unreliable; second, he feared that the written documents could have been confused; third, he was concerned for those who had died in an untimely fashion; fourth, he [desired that] those who had received their punishments would be able to leave the riverbanks of hell.[91]

The scripture presumes the Chinese conception of the underworld as a bureaucracy responsible for maintaining records of the living and the dead. Traces of an underworld bureaucracy already appear in Chinese tomb documents dating as far back as the fourth century BCE.[92] By the time Buddhism made its way into Chinese territories in the Han period, Mount Tai 泰 (in modern Shandong) was established as the administrative seat of the dead, where the registers of life and death were kept and the spirits of the deceased reported.[93] Although the bureaucratization of the underworld exists in other cultures, it emerged especially early in China, has persisted in every elaboration of the underworld, and is undeniably one of its distinctive characteristics.[94] It also introduced the threat of premature death

90. One will recall that in the *Scripture on the Ten Wheels*, Dizang Bodhisattva also arrives from the south to grace the Buddha's assembly; see *Da fangguang shilun jing*, T410:13.681a–b; cf. *Dasheng daji Dizang shilun jing*, T411:13.723b.

91. *Foshuo Dizang pusa jing*, T2909:85.1455c.

92. On the bureaucratization of the underworld, see Harper 1994.

93. On Mount Tai and its place in early Chinese conceptions of the afterlife, see Chavannes 1910 and Sakai 1937.

94. This prominent characteristic of the Chinese underworld is in part a reflection of the political structure of Chinese society, which developed a form of centralized bureaucracy as early as the Warring States. On the relationship between the development of the underworld bureaucracy and the political structure of Chinese society in the Warring States, see Harper 1994. Bureaucratization was an important component in the reimagination of ritual structure that produced what is now known as religious Daoism. For an excellent study of bureaucracy in religious Daoism, see Nickerson 1996a. On the impact of bureaucracy on the structure of Chinese society, see Balazs 1964: 13–27, 129–149.

resulting from confused identities due to similar names or a misreading of names in the registers.[95]

The Chinese concept of hell underwent significant changes after the introduction of Buddhism; in particular, the doctrine of *karma* and rebirth and the structuralization of hells left indelible imprints.[96] Medieval China witnessed several modifications to afterlife practices, culminating in the purgatorial visions of the *Scripture on the Ten Kings* (*Shiwang jing* 十王經).[97] By the time of the *Scripture on the Bodhisattva Dizang*, that is, in the ninth or early tenth century, Indian and Chinese themes had sufficiently coalesced to engender visions of the underworld that cannot be justifiably characterized as either Chinese or Buddhist. In this scripture, karmic retribution has largely become part of a judicial and administrative system prone to errors and oversight. If the *Scripture on Divination* transformed the abstract principle of *karma* into a divinatory system, the *Scripture on the Bodhisattva Dizang* concretized the principle through a bureaucractic and judiciary system.

Moreover, the *Scripture on the Bodhisattva Dizang* offers a rare glimpse of Dizang's association with another afterlife expression, the Pure Land. It points to an intriguing relationship not documented in the transmitted corpus of Buddhist scriptures preserved in the Chinese canon, although vestiges of such a link can be traced to other forms of evidence.[98] The Pure Land connection is established in the concluding paragraph of the text. The relevant portion of the text from the long and short versions is translated below:

T2909 (based on S 6257)	S 431
If there is a good man or woman who has carved images of the bodhisattva, copied the *Scripture on the Bodhisattva Dizang*, and recited the name of the Bodhisattva Dizang, he or she	If there is a good man or woman who has carved images of the bodhisattva, copied the *Scripture on the Bodhisattva Dizang*, and recited the name of the Bodhisattva Dizang, he or she will surely attain rebirth

95. Mistaken identity as the cause of premature death has ancient origins in China, occurring in the Fangmatan manuscript studied in Harper 1994. It continued throughout the development of Chinese hells and was the main theme of the half-comic, half-tragic accounts of the underworld journey collected under the genre *zhiguai*; see Campany 1990, 1995; Pas 1989.

96. A number of studies on the historical development of Chinese hells have been attempted. The classic treatment is Sawada 1968; also see Sakamoto 1990. Taiwanese scholarship has recently shown a great deal of interest in the development of Chinese hells and purgatory; see Xiao 1989, 1996. In English no book-length study of the historical development of Chinese hells has been attempted (except for the now dated Thompson 1989), although Teiser's works (1988b, 1994) are important contributions.

97. Several studies can be found in Japanese and Chinese scholarship. For a study in English, see Teiser 1994.

98. These include artistic representations and literary writings such as eulogies and dedications, which are discussed in the Conclusion.

will surely attain rebirth in the Land of Supreme Bliss in the west.	in the Land of Supreme Bliss in the west.
	He or she will manifest through transformation on a lotus in front of Amitābha Buddha. It will be inconceivable. He or she will possess completely the six supernormal powers and they will extend in the ten directions.[99]
[He or she will travel] from one buddha-land to another buddha-land, from one heaven to another heaven.	[He or she will travel] from one buddha-land to another buddha-land, from one heaven to another heaven.
If there is a good man or woman who has carved images of the bodhisattva, copied the *Scripture on the Bodhisattva Dizang*, and recited the name of Dizang Bodhisattva, he or she will surely attain rebirth in the Land of Supreme Bliss in the west.	Because in the past he or she has carved images of Dizang and recited the *Scripture on the Bodhisattva Dizang*,
On the day when this person dies, the Bodhisattva Dizang himself will come to welcome him or her, and he or she shall always be in the same place as the Bodhisattva Dizang.[100]	on the day when this person dies, the Bodhisattva Dizang himself will come to welcome him or her, and he or she shall always be in the same place as the Bodhisattva Dizang.[101]

In recompense for devotion to the Bodhisattva Dizang, one will attain rebirth in the western Land of Supreme Bliss (*jile shijie* 極樂世界), or Sukhā-

99. *Ṣaḍ abhijñāḥ* is the most common list of paranormal powers in Buddhist literature. They are usually described as follows: (1) *shenzutong* 神足通 *(ṛiddhi-pāda)*, or supernormal physical powers that appear or take any form at will in any place without hindrance; (2) *tianertong* 天耳通 *(divya-śrotra)*, or the ability to perceive sounds at any distance and understand all languages in the realms of form; (3) *taxintong* 他心通 *(paracitta-jñāna)*, or the ability to penetrate one's thoughts or intuitive knowledge of the minds of all beings; (4) *sumingtong* 宿命通 *(pūrva-nivāsānusmṛti)*, or recollection of prior lives and knowing their states and antecedents; (5) *tianyantong* 天眼通 *(divya-cakṣus)*, regularly associated with the supernormal vision of *devas*, who can see to any distance as well as the destiny of all beings in future rebirths; (6) *loujintong* 漏盡通 *(āsrava-kṣaya-jñāna)*, or recognition that one has been purged of spiritual defilements, also known as the state of having "no outflows." The six powers are closely associated with the cultivation of the four *dhyāna*s. Accounts of these four basic states of meditation are often followed by the claim that, once the contemplative has mastered the *dhyāna*s, he or she can apply the power of concentration to the cultivation of five or six supernormal powers.

100. *Foshuo dizang pusa jing*, T2909:85.145c. The complete text is translated in Appendix 3.

101. *Foshuo dizang pusa jing* 佛說地藏菩薩經, S 431, *DHBZ* 3: 484.

vatī, the land of Amitābha Buddha. T2909 makes no specific reference to Amitābha, but S 431 explicitly invokes the image of rebirth on a lotus before Amitābha.

The deity invoked in this text is Dizang Bodhisattva rather than the Buddha Amitābha, whom one typically associates with the Land of Supreme Bliss. Even in the case of the long S 431 version, which preserves the Amitābha connection, the Buddha Amitābha only figures in the background, and the Bodhisattva Dizang is the protagonist of the text. The practices associated with the Dizang cult are all exalted as soteriological techniques that enable devotees to gain rebirth in the Pure Land. Moreover, both versions of the scripture state that it is Dizang who will lead dying devotees to the Pure Land. According to Fujita Kōtatsu, the role of welcoming the deceased at their deathbeds originated as a function of Amitābha Buddha but subsequently became so widespread in Mahāyāna literature that it was eventually ascribed to other Buddhist deities like the thousand buddhas and the eight attendant bodhisattvas of the Bhaiṣajyaguru Buddha.[102] In the *Scripture on the Bodhisattva Dizang*, it is Dizang who functions as the spiritual guide escorting the deceased to an afterlife paradise. Although not recorded in other scriptures, this form of Dizang appears elsewhere in East Asia, particularly in Japan, where Dizang, in the guise of Jizō, assumes a kaleidoscopic array of manifestations. An important form is the Indō Jizō, who figures in *raigō* 来迎 (welcoming descent) scenes from the tenth century on.[103]

The *Scripture on the Bodhisattva Dizang* is obviously not part of the scholarly systematization of Pure Land Teaching (Jingtu jiao 淨土教), which took shape in later Chinese Buddhist history.[104] Instead, it recalls the generaliza-

102. Fujita 1970: 574, 580, 566–585. Mention of Amitābha Buddha appearing to lead dying devotees to the Pure Land occurs in the *Larger Sukhāvatīvyūha-sūtra*. In a past life as the monk Dharmākara, Amitābha Buddha aspired: "May I not achieve perfect awakening if, at the instant that I attain buddhahood, any among the throng of living beings in the ten directions of the universe who has resolved to seek awakening, has cultivated all the virtues, and has single-mindedly aspired to be reborn in my land, and if, *when they approached the moment of their death, I did not appear before them, surrounded by a great assembly*" (translated in Gómez 1996: 166; my italics). The *Saddharmapuṇḍarīka-sūtra* states that the thousand buddhas (Ch. *qianfo* 千佛; Skt. *buddhasahasra*) will appear to the dying to lead them to be reborn in Tuṣita, the heavenly abode of the future Buddha, Maitreya; see *Miaofa lianhua jing* 妙法蓮華經, T262:9.61c. The *Bhaiṣajyaguru-sūtra* speaks of the eight bodhisattvas welcoming the dying; see *Yaoshi liuliguang rulai benyuan gongde jing* 藥師琉璃光如來本願功德經, T450:14.406b. The phenomenon of Buddhist deities arriving at the deathbed to welcome the dying to paradisal lands is known as *linzhong laiying* 臨終來迎.

103. On the Japanese manifestation known as the Indō Jizō, see de Visser 1914: 121–133. Beautiful illustrations of *raigō* art, including the Indō Jizō, are reproduced and published in Matsushima 1986, pls. 49, 73, 82, 108–111. Also see Jōji 1977: 158–163.

104. For standard textbook surveys of Chinese Pure Land based on the perspective of Pure Land orthodoxy, see Ch'en 1964: 338–350; Michihata 1985b. A recent study by the mainland Chinese scholar Liu Changdong (2000) delineates the development of Amitābha Pure Land largely through the sequence of the patriarchate mapped out by the so-called Pure Land orthodoxy. This approach has recently been critiqued on several counts. Scholars have pointed to the problem of designating Pure Land as a discrete school. Furthermore,

tion of Pure Land that Gregory Schopen has outlined for Indian Buddhism. Schopen argues that as early as the second century Sukhāvatī was disassociated from the specific cult of Amitābha Buddha so veneration of Amitābha and other buddhas like Śākyamuni and Bhaiṣajyaguru could expedite rebirth in Sukhāvatī.[105] The *Scripture on the Bodhisattva Dizang* presents an analogous tendency in which Amitābha recedes into the background so the newcomer in Pure Land, Dizang Bodhisattva, can assume center stage. Apparently, the generalization process that occurred in early Indian Pure Land continued in medieval China.[106] Chinese texts like the *Scripture on the Ten Kings* and the *Xuming jing* 續命經 (Scripture on Prolonging the Life Span) not only invoke a range of deities other than Amitābha to facilitate rebirth in the Pure Land, but also envisage rebirth in an array of Pure Lands that extend beyond those associated exclusively with Amitābha.[107]

In the *Scripture on the Bodhisattva Dizang*, we are given glimpses of both hell and the paradisal world of Sukhāvatī, and in Dizang we have the instrument through which the two strands are synchronized. Dizang is at once the deliverer from the grisly torments of hell and the guide who leads the dead to the Land of Bliss. Some indication concerning the role of the text in the actual religious praxis of medieval China can be deduced from the dedicatory colophon attached to the text in manuscript Dx 2636:

> Xing Pozhao 幸婆趙 copied this scripture on the twenty-first day of the fifth month of the ninth year, the *bingzi* 丙子 year of the *kaibao* 開寶 era [976], for

---

the notion of a Pure Land orthodoxy in part reflects an uncritical adoption of the sectarian biases of Japanese Buddhism, which ultimately distorts the complexity of medieval Chinese developments. Studies of Song Buddhism have shown that the accepted genealogies and patrairchates were largely constructed in the Song period and do not always mirror historical realities. For a comprehensive discussion on the various problematic assumptions underlying previous scholarship on the Pure Land school, see Sharf 2002b: 282–301. A notable exception to such approaches in the study of Pure Land has been provided by Kenneth Tanaka (1990), who examines the contribution of Jingying Huiyuan 淨影慧遠 (523–592), a figure generally not included in the Pure Land orthodox lineage.

105. Schopen 1977: 204. Also see Nattier 2000. Jan Nattier proposes that the Land of Akṣobhya most likely preceded Amitābha and his Land of Bliss. See Nattier 2003b for further comparisons of Akṣobhya and Amitābha in relation to the emergence of Pure Land belief in Indian Buddhism.

106. Fujita Kōtatsu has demonstrated that *jingtu* as a nominal phrase is essentially a Chinese convention with no exact Sanskrit equivalent. It was originally a verbal noun phrase used to translate the Sanskrit for "purifying the land" but subsequently evolved to become a specific technical term in its own right that was incorporated into Chinese Buddhist terminology. See Fujita 1970: 506–511; 1996a: 33–36; 1996b: 20.

107. For the *Scripture on the Ten Kings*, see the translation in Teiser 1994: 204. Also see *Xuming jing*, T2889:85.1405a. The generalization of Pure Land in medieval China has been explored through other approaches. For Tang examples of Pure Land funerary rites in the Chan monastery, see Cole 1996. For a study of Dizang's role in Pure Land as documented in art, epigraphy, and narrative literature, see Zhiru 2001–2002. On the connection between Maitreya and Dizang worship, see Zhiru 2005.

> the benefit of her deceased husband, Mr. Zhang, Chief Commissioner of the Bursary, in the hope that he may be reborn in the Pure Land.[108]

This colophon confirms that copying the *Scripture on the Bodhisattva Dizang* was undertaken as part of afterlife and mortuary practices. Evidently, medieval Chinese heeded the injunction to copy the scripture if they wished to see their deceased loved ones reborn in the Pure Land.

The *Scripture on the Past Vows*: A Canonization of Filial Piety and Afterlife Practices

In Chinese religion today, the best-known Dizang scripture is surely the *Scripture on the Past Vows.*[109] Attributed to the seventh-century Khotanese monk Śikṣānanda, it may have been composed in either Khotan or China.[110] The scripture was incorporated into the Chinese Buddhist canon only during the Ming period (1368–1644)—probably in the aftermath of a resurgence in Dizang worship inspired by seventeenth-century Buddhist reformers like the monk Zhixu, who also promoted the *Scripture on Divination.*[111] However, a stele engraving, dated to 932 and currently preserved at the Museum of History in Beijing, mentions the *Scripture on the Past Vows.*[112] Moreover, the compiler of *A Record of Numinous Verifications*, a compilation of Dizang miracle stories completed in 988, also refers to the *Scripture on the Past Vows* in his preface.[113] Hence the *Scripture on the Past Vows* was already circulating in China by the early tenth century. Several copies of it, too many to enumerate here, are found in Dunhuang manuscripts, thus attesting to its spread especially in western China.

Recent scholarship has pointed to the existence of fragments of the scripture in other languages. Peter Zieme has identified parts of it among Üighur manuscripts from Bäzäklik, which are now kept in the Turfansammlung.[114] Fragments in the Tangut language have also been discovered; a set forms part of the Pelliot collection in the Bibliothèque Nationale de France.[115] Moreover, recent excavations of the northern section of the Mogao Grottoes

108. Based on the French translation by Wang-Toutain (1998: 145). Unfortunately, I did not have access to the manuscript copy.

109. The Sanskrit title has been reconstructed as *Kṣitigarbha-bodhisattva-praṇidhāna-sūtra.*

110. Elverskog 1997: 54; Zhang Zong 2003: 8.

111. Manabe 1960: 84; Zhang Zong 2003: 8. Manabe further mentions that the *Benyuan jing* was cited in the second scroll of the *Daming sanzang shengjiao mulu* 大明三藏聖教目錄. On the role of Dizang worship in Zhixu's life and thought, see Shengyan 1975: 186–192.

112. This information is derived from Wang-Toutain who, in turn, learned about it from the current curator of the Beijing Museum. The stele engraving in Beijing contains the inscribed text of the *Foding zunsheng tuoloni jing* 佛頂尊勝陀羅尼經 *(Buddhoṣṇīṣnavijaya-dhāraṇī-sūtra)*, but the title of the *Scripture on the Past Vows* is invoked; see Wang-Toutain 1998: 78–79.

113. See discussion of this relationship in the *Lingyan ji* in the Conclusion.

114. Zieme 1990: 379–384, facsimiles: pls. I–II. Also see Yang 1995: 28.

115. Manabe 1960: 86–87.

have uncovered a stack of printed leaflets in Tangut from the *Scripture on the Past Vows*.[116] Preliminary study of these indicates that they come from an edition that was either different from the Taishō one or similar but with interpolations. Because translation of Buddhist texts into the Üighur and Tangut languages took place only after the tenth century—that is, after the Chinese text was already known—the existence of these manuscript fragments in other languages has little import for dating the text.[117]

Although the possibility of Khotanese origins cannot be completely ruled out, the contents of the *Scripture on the Past Vows* suggests that, even if the text was not composed in China itself, accretionary layers must have been added in a Chinese setting. Among the motifs are distinctly Chinese conventions such as the names of spirit and ghost kings—in particular the use of *wangliang* 魍魎 for "mountain spirits." The text also refers to Chinese otherworldly functionaries like Lord of the Life Span and displays a strong preoccupation with the cult of the dead, especially the need to take care of deceased ancestors. But this is not to say that the *Scripture on the Past Vows* was solely Chinese in its religious orientation; it is important to note that the scriptural narrative also highlights a visibly Buddhist conceptual framework. The overview of Dizang's bodhisattva career is conspicuously construed after the classic bodhisattva paradigm set forth in early Mahāyāna literature, and it is precisely this paradigm that allows "byways" to be introduced so that various religio-cultural threads are tightly interwoven into a single fabric.

Consisting of thirteen chapters, the *Scripture on the Past Vows* offers a more complete overview of Dizang's bodhisattva career than any of the scriptures discussed thus far. It opens with a preaching assembly in Trāyastriṃśa heaven, where Mañjuśrī asks Śākyamuni Buddha to explain how Dizang came to be such a great bodhisattva.[118] The stage is thus set for elaborating Dizang's religious history. To sketch out Dizang's character, the scripture relies on the narrative structure of Indian Buddhist literature, particularly the *avadāna* or *jātaka* narratives and the closely related genre of literature on the past vows (Ch. *benyuan* 本願; Skt. *pūrvapraṇidhāna*). Relaying the heroic past lives of the Buddha, the *avadāna* narratives delineate the classic paradigm of the bodhisattva career—from the arising of the *bodhicitta*, the utterance of bodhisattva vows before a previous buddha, and the prediction of the initiate's future buddhahood, to the numerous lives during which the bodhisattva must perfect his training. In the fashion of *avadāna* tales, the *Scripture on the Past Vows* describes four of Dizang's past lives to account for his present accomplishment as a bodhisattva at the tenth (and final) stage of the path. In the story of his first past life, Dizang is the son of an elder who pronounces the bodhisattva vow before a past *tathāgata*.[119] In the second life, Dizang is re-

116. Zhang Zong 2003: 101–107.

117. On the earliest phase of the translation of Buddhist texts into Üighur, see Elverskog 1997: 9. On the translation of the Buddhist canon into Tangut, see Dunnell 1996: 27.

118. *Benyuan jing*, T412:13.778b.

119. Ibid.

born as a young Brāhman woman who, with the help of one of the past buddhas, descends into hell to relieve the sufferings of her deceased mother and subsequently vows to liberate beings undergoing suffering for their wicked deeds.[120] In the third life, Dizang is a king who vows not to become a buddha until he has liberated all beings who are suffering on account of previous offenses.[121] Finally, in the fourth life, Dizang is another filial daughter named Luminous Eyes (Guangmu 光目); with an arhat's help, she saves her deceased mother from the sufferings of hell and subsequently aspires to relieve all beings in the unfortunate realms.[122]

These past-life stories deliberately interweave Chinese motifs into a narrative structure derived from *avadāna* literature. Although traces of filial piety are evident in Indian Buddhist materials, the stories focusing on filial daughters parallel the tale of Mulian 目蓮 (Skt. Maudgalyāyana), the monk-disciple of the Buddha who descends into hell to save his mother from retribution for her previous wicked deeds.[123] The Mulian myth is itself the product of religio-cultural assimilation in medieval China, and it flourished in the Tang as the foundation myth of the Ghost Festival. Standard motifs found in indigenous Chinese mortuary practices are evident in this subgenre of Chinese Buddhist literature that promulgated some form of Buddhist filial piety. Most prominent perhaps is the preoccupation with the afterlife fate of one's parents and the belief that descendants had to ensure the continued welfare of deceased ancestors. The Chinese Buddhist emphasis on filial piety has already been reiterated in modern scholarship: in older works by Michihata Ryōshū and Kenneth Ch'en and more recently by Stephen Teiser and Alan Cole.[124] Especially pertinent here is Cole's provocative argument that medieval Chinese Buddhists deliberately crafted an alternate model of filial piety that highlighted the mother-son relation than the father-son paradigm at the core of traditional (Confucian) formulations of filial piety.[125] Although Cole's argument is controversial, he does call attention to alternate threads of filial piety operating in medieval Chinese society.

The *Scripture on the Past Vows* provides a vignette of medieval filial piety practices that highlight the mother-daughter relation.[126] By representing Dizang as a filial daughter in two of his past lives, the scripture harmonizes two

120. Ibid.:13.778b–779a.

121. Ibid.:13.780c.

122. Ibid.:13.780c–781b.

123. On filial piety in Indian Buddhism, see Schopen 1984; Strong 1983. For an English translation of the Mulian legend, see Mair 1983: 87–121.

124. Michihata 1985a; Ch'en 1968; Teiser 1988b; Cole 1998.

125. As I argue later in the Conclusion, Cole's representation polemically reduces the complexity of Confucian expressions of filial piety. For a more nuanced study of Confucian practices of filial piety from the second to the sixth centuries, see Knapp 2005.

126. However, it is equally significant to observe that the mother-daughter relation did not appear solely in Chinese Buddhist formulations of filial piety but had been introduced in the Han classic the *Biographies of Virtuous Women* (*Lienü zhuan* 列女傳). For female observances of filial piety in early medieval China, see Knapp 2005: 164–186.

paradigms circulating in medieval Chinese society: the bodhisattva and the filial child. In other words, if the tale of Mulian places the Buddhist monk at the core of Chinese practices of filial piety, then the *Scripture on the Past Vows* locates the bodhisattva ideal at the heart of the cult of filial piety, especially in relation to afterlife practices. Therefore, it is not incidental that, like the Mulian story, the *Scripture on the Past Vows* exhibits a strong concern with the fate of rebirth in hell and the plight of ancestors undergoing hell torments. One chapter is devoted to enumerating and describing the range of Buddhist hells and their grisly tortures.[127] Despite the space devoted to the elaboration of hells, the scripture does not go so far as to hail Dizang as the savior of the damned.

In addition to *avadāna* narratives, the *Scripture on the Past Vows* adopts another classic Indian paradigm of the bodhisattva career, the Mahāyāna systematization of the bodhisattva path into the tenfold schema known as the ten stages (Ch. *shidi* 十地; Skt. *daśabhūmi*).[128] The allusion to Dizang as a tenth-stage bodhisattva places him within this schema of the bodhisattva path.[129] The consecration of Dizang and the prediction of his buddhahood occur early in the scripture:

> At that time the World-Honored One extended his golden-colored arm and rubbed the [bare] heads of all the reduplicated bodies of the great Bodhisattva Dizang from incalculable and inconceivable worlds. He spoke these words: "I teach and convert [living beings] in the five degenerate evil eras. . . . If they should fall into the evil paths of great suffering, you should recall that in the Palace of Trāyastriṃśa Heaven, I have painstakingly entrusted you to assist all living beings from the Sahā world until the advent of Maitreya to be freed and eternally separated from all suffering, to encounter the Buddha, and to receive prophecies [from the Buddha]."
>
> At that time the reduplicated bodies of Dizang Bodhisattva from all the worlds together became a single form again, which then wept and commiser-

127. This chapter has significant implications for studying the development of Buddhist hells in medieval China—an issue that is not an immediate concern of this study.

128. In the *Daśabhūmika-sūtra* (*Shidi jing* 十地經), the ten stages of the bodhisattva path are: (1) *huanxi* 歡喜 *(pramuditā),* or joy at having overcome former difficulties and to be entering on the path to Buddhahood; (2) *ligou* 離垢 *(vimalā),* or emancipation from all defilements; (3) *faguang* 發光 *(prabhākarī),* or splendor; (4) *yanhui* 焰慧 *(arciṣmatī),* or flaming wisdom; (5) *ji'nansheng* 極難勝 *(sudurjayā),* or mastery of utmost or final difficulties; (6) *xianqian* 現前 *(abhimukhī),* or the open way of wisdom transcending all conceptions of impurity and purity; (7) *yuanxing* 遠行 *(dūraṃgamā),* or transcending notions of self to save others; (8) *budong* 不動 *(acalā),* or irreversibility; (9) *shanhui* 善慧 *(sādhumatī),* or attaining of the finest discriminatory wisdom, knowing where and how to save, and possessing the ten powers; (10) *fayun* 法雲 *(dharmameghā),* or attaining the cloud of teachings. The ten stages correspond to the ten *pāramitās,* the cultivation of which extends over millions of lifetimes. See the annotated translation of the *Daśabhūmika-sūtra* by Honda Megumu (1968).

129. *Benyuan jing,* T412:13.778b: "It has been more than a thousandfold the above analogy [of time] since Dizang Bodhisattva attained the fruit of the tenth-stage [bodhisattva]. And all the more so when Dizang Bodhisattva was at the stages of *śrāvaka* and *pratyekabuddha!*"

> ated, saying to the Buddha, "From remote distant aeons I have received the Buddha's guidance, which has caused me to acquire inconceivable numinous powers and great wisdom. My reduplicated bodies pervade worlds as numerous as the grains of sand in the Ganges River. In each of those worlds, I transform into countless numerous bodies; each of the bodies liberates an incalculable [number of] people and causes [them] to take refuge and venerate the Three Jewels and to be eternally removed from birth and death until [they attain] the joy of *nirvāṇa*. However, through the good deeds that they have done within the Buddhist teachings, [even though they are as little] as a feather, a drop, a speck of sand or dust, or tiny hairs, I will eventually rescue and liberate them and enable them to procure great benefit. I only wish that the World-Honored One will not fret over those living beings with bad *karma* in the future ages." In this manner, [Dizang] repeated three times to the Buddha: "World-Honored One, do not fret over living beings with bad *karma* in future ages."
>
> At that time the Buddha praised Dizang Bodhisattva saying, "Excellent, excellent, I shall gladly assist you. You are capable of accomplishing the great and vast vows, which you made long ago in distant aeons. Once you have completed the liberation of [living beings], you will instantly attain awakening."[130]

In this passage we see Dizang charged with saving the Sahā world during the vile age of the five turbulences, the period from the quiescence of the Buddha Śākyamuni to the coming of the Buddha Maitreya—a task entrusted to him by Śākyamuni himself. This harks back to trends in the sixth and seventh centuries that centered around the *Scripture on the Ten Wheels* and the climate of doom and anxiety generated by the conviction that the end of Buddhism had arrived. The *Scripture on the Past Vows* explicitly states that Dizang is the savior of this world *until the coming of the future Buddha Maitreya.*

Besides unfolding Dizang's bodhisattva career, the *Scripture on the Past Vows* significantly functions as the scriptural basis for funerary and afterlife rites centered on the Dizang cult, just as the Mulian story served as the scriptural foundation for the afterlife rite of the Ghost Festival in medieval China. It exhorts the reader to recite the scripture during death rites to relieve the suffering of those dying and procure for them a better rebirth:

> If, in future, men and women are bedridden with a long illness and despite their wishes are unable either to get well or to die; or in the night they dream of evil ghosts, of family and relatives, or of wandering on dangerous paths; in numerous nightmares they roam with ghosts and spirits . . . one should recite the scripture in a loud voice before the images of all buddhas and bodhisattvas and take the possessions loved by the sick one, such as clothing, jewels, gardens, or houses, saying in a loud voice in front of the sick one, "On behalf

130. Ibid.:13.779b–c.

> of this sick one, I so-and-so present all such things before the images and scriptures." Or [one should] make offerings to images and scriptures, or commission images of the buddhas and bodhisattvas, or build *stūpa*s and temples, or light oil lamps and present gifts to the *saṅgha.*
>
> One should speak in this manner three times, so that the sick person hears and understands. If his or her consciousnesses are separated and departed and his breath exhausted, then for one, two, three, four, and on through seven days, one should only recite aloud in a clear voice this scripture. After that person's life ends, he eternally attains liberation from the retributions of past lives and from serious sins, even the five uninterrupted sins. Wherever one is born, one will always know one's past lives. Moreover, if a good man or woman himself or herself copies this scripture or teaches others to copy it, or if one carves or draws images [of Dizang] or teaches others to carve or draw them, the causal effect and retribution one receives should bring great benefit.[131]

Scripture recitation is also recommended as a means for descendants to alleviate the sufferings of ancestors reborn in unfortunate paths of rebirth:

> If all living beings and so forth in the future in their dreams or sleep see various ghosts, spirits, and other forms mourning, weeping, sad, lamenting, fearful, or terrifying, [you should know that] all of them are your past fathers, mothers, sons, daughters, brothers, sisters, husbands, wives, and relatives, from a single, ten, hundred, or a thousand lives ago, who have been reborn on the evil paths and are unable to be liberated. They have no source of hope for the power of blessings to rescue them, so they must relate to their flesh-and-bone [descendents] of their former lives and prompt their descendents to establish the expedient wish to free them from the evil paths. Universally Expansive, you should deploy your supernormal power and dispatch all these families, so that they should themselves recite this scripture resolutely before the images of all the buddhas and bodhisattvas or request others to recite it [on their behalf], either three or seven times. After the scripture has been thus recited for that number of times, relatives on the evil paths should attain liberation and [the living] will never again see [dead relatives] in their dreams or sleep.[132]

Whether or not this passage is a Chinese interpolation, it describes attitudes toward death and the afterlife in medieval society. The fear of being haunted by the disembodied spirits of deceased kin—as well as the duty of the descendant to ensure the afterlife welfare and salvation of roaming ancestral spirits—has a long history in China. In the larger milieu, sacrificial rites in the form of offering meat and wine to wandering spirits were per-

131. Ibid.:13.783a–b.
132. Ibid.:13.783b.

formed frequently in the hope of averting ailments and misfortunes. (Unlike "proper" deities, who partake of only vegetarian offerings, "blood-eating ghosts" must be propitiated with blood [that is, meat] sacrifices.)[133] Although it inherited concerns from early Chinese mortuary practices, religious Daoism openly condemned the popular use of sacrificial rites and instead developed a soteriological vision of salvation for the deceased revolving around an array of ritual therapeutic techniques including penitential rites.[134] A similar vision developed in medieval Chinese Buddhism and, as conceived in the Tang rite of the Ghost Festival, ancestral spirits reborn in unhappy realms could be relieved of their suffering through the ritual practice of making offerings to the monastic establishment.

In the *Scripture on the Past Vows*, one finds what might be another Chinese Buddhist example of this central preoccupation. The scripture critiques the common Chinese practice of conducting sacrificial rites on behalf of the dying:

> I [Dizang] exhort the living beings of Jambudvīpa, on the day when they are dying, to abstain cautiously from killing, harming, or committing negative causal deeds; praying and sacrificing to demonic spirits; worshiping ghosts and spirits; or seeking various spirits *(wangliang)*. Why? Because all those you kill and harm or venerate and sacrifice do not possess even a little power to benefit the dying person. Instead such actions will cause offensive conditions to worsen and become deeper and heavier. If [the deceased] has obtained the saintly merits to be reborn in the human or heavenly [realm], whether in a future or present life, [but] on account of the evil causes committed by various family and relatives at the time of his or her dying, these will also cause the dying person's accumulation of misfortune to be disputed [and hence] delay his or her rebirth in a good place. Moreover, if the dying person possesses not even a mote of virtue when alive, he or she will undergo the evil realms in accordance with his or her own *karma*. It is unbearable that the family and relatives should add more negative deeds on him or her. It is as if a person coming from a distant place is cut off from provisions for three days and carries a burden of more than a hundred catties; he or she suddenly meets a neighbor who further increases his or her original load with a few more things so that [his or her load] becomes heavier and more distressing.[135]

The scripture promulgates a set of Buddhist rites to replace the widespread sacrifices performed as part of mortuary or funerary rites. Besides chanting Buddhist scriptures and making offerings before images of Buddhist deities, the scripture advocates preparing and hosting vegetarian feasts to accrue merit on behalf of the deceased:

---

133. On the practice of blood sacrifice and prohibitions against it, see Kleeman 1994.

134. Cedzich 1993: 23–35; cf. Maeda 1995: 54–68. For a discussion of Daoist preparation of offerings, see Kleeman 2005. For Buddhist vegetarianism, see Kieschnick 2005.

135. *Benyuan jing*, T412:13.784a.

> Moreover, elder, when living beings of such bad *karma* die, their family, relatives, flesh-and-bone [descendents] may cultivate preparatory vegetarian feast to assist them on their karmic path. [In doing this] vegetable leaves or water from washing the rice should not be scattered on the earth when the feast has not concluded or during the preparation of the feast; and all the food should be eaten only after they have been offered to the Buddha and the Saṅgha. If the dietary taboos are violated or not rigorously enforced, the deceased will not receive empowerment [from the offering]. If purity is rigorously maintained when making offerings to the Buddha and the Saṅgha, the deceased will receive one seventh [of the merit]. Therefore, elder, if the living beings of Jambudvīpa are able to make vegetarian offerings after the death of their fathers, mothers, families, and relatives, with determination and supplication on their behalf, such persons will benefit the living and the dead.[136]

The *Scripture on the Past Vows* outlines the events one faces upon death, drawing on the doctrine of *karma* and rebirth as well as the popular conception that the dead must report to an otherworldly bureaucracy to receive judgment:

> When the great ghost of impermanence makes an untimely arrival, the spirit roams in the dark [region], not knowing yet its offenses and merits for forty-nine days, as if one were ignorant and deaf or as if all the officials were arguing over the karmic retribution. Once judgment has been determined, one is reborn according to one's *karma*. During the interval before [the rebirth], there are thousands of ten thousands of desolate forms of suffering. What more is it to fall into the various evil paths and so forth! Although this deceased has yet to undergo rebirth, one would hope that for every successive thought in the forty-nine days, all of one's flesh-and-bone descendents, family, and relatives would rescue one through the power of merits they perform [on one's behalf]. After those [forty-nine] days, one will receive retribution according to his *karma*. If one is an offender, one passes through a hundred thousand years without a day of liberation; if [the offenses are] the five uninterrupted sins, [one] falls into the great hell where one undergoes various sufferings for thousands of ten thousands of *kalpa*s.[137]

The passage stipulates an interval of forty-nine days between death and the next rebirth, a kind of limbo existence. During this interval, the immediate kin of the deceased should intervene by performing meritorious actions on the behalf of the deceased. Present here are embryonic concepts of penance and purgation that will be fully articulated in the afterlife vision of the *Scripture on the Ten Kings*.

136. Ibid.:13.784b.
137. Ibid.

The *Scripture on the Past Vows* provides us with a model of Buddhist afterlife and death rites in late medieval China. It cannot be conclusively determined whether the scripture sought to canonize afterlife practices widespread in the larger milieu or whether it was an orchestrated venture on the part of the Buddhist establishment to disseminate the Dizang cult by forging links that enabled the cult to penetrate the core of daily religious life in medieval Chinese society. The scripture was apparently well known by the tenth century and emerged as a core text in the Dizang cult. For example, in the tenth-century canonical collection of Dizang miracle tales, the compiler invokes scenes from the *Scripture on the Past Vows* in his preface, and several stories in the compilation are fashioned after the *Scripture on the Past Vows*.[138] Through its subtle maneuverings of narrative plot and motifs, the *Scripture on the Past Vows* was able to shape Dizang's personality in such a manner that he remained true to the classic bodhisattva ideal while evincing distinctive traits and functions that aligned him with filial piety and indigenous afterlife cults.

New Scriptures, New Images of Dizang

The earliest images of Dizang circulating in sixth-century China were based on the *Scripture on the Ten Wheels,* which supplied the mythological foundation for subsequent localized permutations. The flowering of Dizang scriptures from the sixth to the tenth centuries produced a range of new images as Dizang the savior in an era of spiritual degeneration became a conduit for religious innovation and experimentation. The new scriptures introduced soteriologies that effectively produced a series of fascinating and, at times startling, images of Dizang.

Like the *Scripture on the Ten Wheels* and the *Section on the Sumeru Treasury,* the sixth-century *Scripture on Divination* invokes a mood of eschatological anticipation. By this time, the spiritual doomsday, conceived in fairly generalized terms in earlier texts, had become a well-defined event in Buddhist history as expressed in the Semblance Dharma and the Final Dharma.[139] Reshaped by the new soteriology espoused in this text, Dizang took on additional roles: Besides being an object of ritual confession, he became a patron deity of a form of karmic divination and an expedient object of meditative contemplation. As a patron deity of divination, Dizang represents yet another example of Buddhist efforts to integrate practices from the mantic arts that flourished as part of the grassroots religion in China.

The soteriological vision of *The Exorcism Method* also draws on Dizang's connection to apocalyptic eschatology and his role as savior during the time

138. For the *Benyuan jing*'s influence on the *Dizang pusa xiang lingyan ji,* see Chapter 5.

139. However, the references to Semblance Dharma and Final Dharma do not necessarily indicate the presence of the Chinese tripartite temporal formulation (True Dharma, Semblance Dharma, Final Dharma). See the discussion on how the *Zhancha jing* fits into the development of the periodization of the decline of the Dharma in Nattier 1991. 98–99.

of the Buddha's absence. Like the *Scripture on the Ten Wheels* and the *Section on Sumeru Treasury, The Exorcism Method* ascribes a *dhāraṇī* to Dizang that he supposedly acquired in his previous bodhisattva career. However, rather than receiving the *dhāraṇī* from the Buddha as in the *Scripture on the Ten Wheels*, here Dizang learns it from a saint living in the mountains. This shift opens the way for a Buddho-Daoist amalgamation that runs through the entire text. Again the text's soteriological concerns cast the bodhisattva in a new, different light: Dizang emerges as a shamanic ritualist skilled in exorcism—not unlike the liturgical priest of religious Daoism, adept at subjugating demonic spirits and recruiting their services. Two paradigms, the bodhisattva-savior and the priest-exorcist, coalesce and engender a new hybrid ideal whereby the bodhisattva-savior employs the use of talismans, ritual magic, and even a cavalry of netherworldly spirits to benefit and liberate living beings.

The world of ritual continues in *A Ritual Manual*, which has Dizang Bodhisattva presiding over esoteric rites as the deity receiving veneration. If *The Exorcism Method* casts Dizang as the priest with the ritual keys to appease unknown and dark forces, then *A Ritual Manual* enthrones Dizang as an all-powerful esoteric deity, an object of worship and visualization, at once an embodiment of Buddhist salvation and the promise of worldly benefits. The practitioner visualizes himself as the deity while ritually enacting incantations and hand gestures attributed to Dizang. As the deity to whom an array of ritual offerings is presented, Dizang confers a broad range of worldly benefits. In his esoteric guise, Dizang's personality is further concretized: His speech patterns (sacred incantation) and physical actions (bodily posture and hand gestures) are spelled out through ritual instructions.

In the *Scripture on the Bodhisattva Dizang*, chaotic times are no longer specific to an era of spiritual degeneration but are the general plight of those reborn in hell. Dizang retains his classical bodhisattva character but is exalted as the savior specializing in afterlife matters. He takes on several afterlife functions: He is the judge who, along with King Yama, pronounces judgment on the dead in the underworld; he is the afterlife savior who brings temporary respite to tormented hell beings; he is the otherworldly guide directing dying devotees to the Land of Bliss; he is a member of the pantheon of Pure Land deities, the worship of which can ensure rebirth in the Land of Bliss.

Finally, the *Scripture on the Past Vows* maps the past lives in Dizang's career as a bodhisattva and fully develops his personality by filling in evident gaps. It creates a more distinctive mythology for Dizang, one that goes beyond the generalized bodhisattva lore offered in the *Scripture on the Ten Wheels*. It became necessary to endow Dizang with a religious history and personality that would distinguish him from other bodhisattvas before his cult could lodge itself permanently in the sinitic religious landscape. As its title suggests, the *Scripture on the Past Vows* was consciously framed as part of the literature on the past vows of buddhas and bodhisattvas, a genre that effectively connects Dizang with the classic bodhisattva ideal as outlined in Indian Mahāyāna literature. Through its narrative plot and motifs, the *Scripture on the Past Vows* endows Dizang with traits and functions aligning him with filial piety and afterlife cults in medieval China. New images of Dizang appear through the subtle interlacing of variegated themes: Dizang as a filial daughter (a motif that links him to Tang religious trends embodied in the Mulian myth) and Dizang as the patron deity of death and afterlife rituals. At the same time, he is the bodhisattva-savior entrusted with looking after living beings in the Sahā world during the interval between Śākyamuni Buddha and Maitreya Buddha.

Perhaps because of his relatively indistinct personality in the pre-Chinese Buddhist tradition, Dizang Bodhisattva's image was especially malleable and invited religious experimentation and innovation. Whatever new image or function Dizang assumed, he never lost his original identification with the bodhisattva ideal in Indian Mahāyāna. His new roles were always subsumed under and introduced through the bodhisattva ideal of liberating and relieving living beings.

CHAPTER 4

Art and Epigraphy

WRITTEN TEXTS ARE not the sole medium in which religious negotiations and innovations take place. Visual and material objects document devotional practices that written records often overlook, especially forms of religious piety that take shape outside so-called orthodoxy and are thus marginalized by the elite clerics responsible for writing religious history. As discussed in Part 1, Shaanxi iconography proved to be critical for elucidating seventh-century Chinese Buddhists' visualizations of Dizang Bodhisattva inspired by the *Scripture on the Ten Wheels.* In this chapter, a wider range of art and inscriptions will be considered to amplify our knowledge of Dizang. Viewed through these extracanonical material artifacts, this bodhisattva reveals commonly overlooked interrelationships with other Buddhist deities, forged through cultic rivalry, religious adaptation, and the complicated dialectics between "elite" and "popular" interpretations. The Dizang examples suggest that religious art does not necessarily mirror textual formulae; it often constitutes a vibrant forum for religious negotiation and improvisation that has the power to reshape religious history.

The main sites for Dizang art from the sixth to the tenth centuries are located in Henan, Hebei, Ningxia, and Shaanxi (north central China); Gansu (northwest China); and Sichuan (southwest China). Among the cave temples, Longmen Grottoes, located in Luoyang (Henan), houses the oldest images of Dizang (the earliest dating to 650–655), depicted mostly in princely attire.[1] Numerous images of Dizang were apparently made at Longmen during the reigns of Gaozong 高宗 (r. 649–683) and Wu Zetian 武則天 (r. 684–705).[2] Dizang art then spread across various sites in the north central plains. Images dating from 695 to 716 have been found at Mount Hall of Echoes (Xiangtang shan), located between Hebei and Henan.[3] To the northwest in southern

1. The statue of Dizang standing at Binyang nan dong 賓陽南洞 has been dated to 650–655 on the basis of iconographic style. Dizang is dressed in princely garb, adorned with jewels, and holds a vase in one hand. For a line drawing of this standing Dizang, see Chang 1990: 29, fig. 2. According to Chang Qing, this statue is stylistically comparable to those of Amitābha and a standing bodhisattva at Longmen; accompanying inscriptions date the statues to the *zhenguan* 貞觀 era. However, on the basis of extant inscriptional dating, the earliest Longmen representation of Dizang would be the sculpture in the niche outside Yaofang dong 藥方洞, dated to 664; see Chang 1990: 29. Few pictures of the Longmen Dizang statues have been published; Chang's article includes only a handful of line drawings. For a rare color reproduction of a damaged statue, see the exhibition catalog by Alphen (2001: 124–125, n. 23).

2. Chang 1990: 30.

3. Mizuno and Nagahiro 1937: 119–146.

Ningxia, Mount Sumeru (Xumi shan) also contains several statues. At both Xiangtang shan and Xumi shan, Dizang is usually shown as a monk; he sometimes appears singly on cave pillars or in niches. As mentioned earlier, Shaanxi has yielded miniature tile images and full-size single sculptures, usually surrounded by the six paths of rebirth. These signal Dizang's ascendancy as an independent focus of cultic piety.[4]

On the northwest border, the Grottoes of Unsurpassed Height (Mogao ku 莫高窟) at Dunhuang are known for their large collection of scroll paintings and cave murals. Dizang appears at Dunhuang by the late eighth century, often as a monk holding a wish-granting jewel and clothed in ornate robes. Beginning in the tenth century, pictures of Dizang in the company of the Ten Kings of purgatory and their court retinues fill the ceilings of passageways opening onto the main chambers of several grottoes. On Sichuan's southwest border, Northern Mountain (Beishan 北山) in Dazu 大足 county posesses a series of small niches containing pairings of Dizang with Guanyin or single images of Dizang commissioned from the ninth century on.[5] Relatively unstudied until recently, Sichuan sites house an extensive collection of Dizang images, especially significant because the art reflects less studied cultic patterns in Tang China.

The geographical shift from central China to the western borders in part reflects larger trends in Buddhist art that were prompted by political conditions. Under the auspices of the Northern Wei rulers from the late fifth century, Buddhist cave art was initiated on a gigantic scale at two sites: Yungang near the old capital (Datong 大同, Shanxi) and later at Longmen outside the new capital, Luoyang (Henan). This explosion of Buddhist art in central China continued into the eighth century. In the wake of the Northern Wei sites, other cave temples like Xiangtang shan and Xumi shan were built in north central China, beginning in the sixth century. Meanwhile construction of cave-temple complexes began in Gansu and Sichuan, although the epitome of Buddhist art was not reached in the western region until the Tang period. The Dunhuang and Sichuan sites were begun primarily by local elites in contrast to the state sponsorship of cave sites in the central plains. Nonetheless, state authorities also contributed to the flowering of Buddhist art on the western borders, especially in Sichuan, which maintained close relations with the Tang court.[6] Wu Zetian's ascendancy, for instance, coincided with the es-

4. See previous discussion in Chapter 2.

5. Baoding shan 寶頂山, also in Dazu, contains a monumental cliff sculpture of Dizang and the Ten Kings presiding over scenes of hell torture.

6. The treasures unearthed at Sichuan Buddhist sites have recently attracted the attention of art historians. In western scholarship, Angela Howard was among the first to call attention to Sichuan art, and she has produced a set of important studies on Sichuan (1988, 1989, 1990, 1998, 2001). Henrik Sørenson (1989a, 1989b, 1991, 1995a, 1995b, 1997, 1998) has published several articles and field reports on Sichuan Buddhist art. Two important dissertations have been written on two major sites in Sichuan Dazu: For a comprehensive study of Beishan 北山 with a complete catalog of the niches and translations of the inscriptions, see Suchan 2003; for Baoding shan, see Kucera 2002. In the arena of Chinese scholarship, the efforts of

tablishment of major Buddhist sites at Guangyuan 廣元 (northeast Sichuan), Wu's birthplace.[7] Moreover, when Emperor Xuanzong 玄宗 (r. 712–756) fled to Sichuan seeking refuge from political chaos, the attending court retinue included monks and artisans who were instrumental in promoting religious activities like the construction of Buddhist sites in Sichuan from the eighth century on. The rapid breakdown of centralized powers, which followed on the heels of the An Lushan 安祿山 (703–757) revolt in 755, heralded a radical shift in the foci of Buddhist cave art from the central plains to the outskirt regions of Dunhuang and Sichuan. The geographical displacement witnessed in Dizang art, from north central China to the western boundaries, thus mirrored these larger patterns in the history of Chinese Buddhist art.

In what follows, I examine only those examples of Dizang art and epigraphy that are most relevant to the thematic issue under discussion. Given the extensiveness of Dizang art, it is expedient for a study of this nature to reiterate the perspective of religious history over that of art history, leaving such scrutiny of Dizang images to the trained eyes of art historians.[8]

A Princely Householder or Monk Bodhisattva?

An important aspect of the Bodhisattva Dizang, as he is known in East Asia today, is his role as a *śramaṇa*. As previously mentioned, the earliest recorded

the Sichuan Chinese Academy are reflected in the continuous output of research published in the journal *Sichuan wenwu*. Members of the academy have also published important book-length surveys: Liu, Hu, and Li 1985; Li Fangyin 1990; Guo Xiangying 1993; Hu 1994. For a critical edition of Dazu inscriptions that compares the inscriptions in situ with literary records of the inscriptions, see Guo 1999a. Art books reproducing Sichuan sculpture have also been published. For an overview of Sichuan sculpture, see Zhongguo meishu quanji bianji weiyuanhui 1988. For Anyue, see Liu Changjiu 1997; for Dazu, see the four-volume compilation Guo 1999b; Liu 1999.

7. Besides Huangze si 皇澤寺, which was named after Wu herself, another important Buddhist site in Guangyuan is the Qianfo ya 千佛崖. For a discussion of Qianfo ya, see Ma and Ding 1990.

8. Dizang art in Dunhuang has attracted the most attention from art historians. In particular, the beautiful paintings of Dizang and the Ten Kings, as well as the "hooded Dizang," have been the subject of quite a few Japanese studies; see Matsumoto 1922, 1933, 1937; Kawahara 1974: 99–123. In recent years, Chinese art historians have also published essays on Dunhuang Dizang art, specifically its connection with the Ten Kings; see Luo 1993; Luo Shiping 1998; Pan 1998. For Dizang art in Longmen, see Chang 1990. Dizang art in Sichuan has attracted a growing body of scholarship. Moroto Fumio (1986) offers an early study of the hooded Dizang in Dazu Beishan. Hu and Jiang (1997) provide a preliminary overview. Both Chen Mingguang (2002) and Kucera (1995) have undertaken studies of the monumental sculpture of hell in the cave at Baoding shan in Dazu. In addition to Dazu, other sites in Sichuan have attracted attention. For pairings of Dizang and Guanyin in Sichuan, see Hu 1994: 226–230. Yao (2002) has studied the Dizang art in Guangyuan, focusing on the folklorization of his underworld aspect. For Dizang and the six paths of rebirth in cave 25 of Nan kan 南龕 at Bazhong 巴中, see Ju 1999. Dizang art in other parts of East Asia has been more substantively studied. Pak Young-Sook's dissertation explores Kṣitigarbha art in Korea during the Koryŏ (918–1392) dynasty. (I regret that I did not have access to this work.) Pak has published some of her findings (1977, 1995, 1998) and is currently completing a book on Chijang art in Korea. Many studies examine Jizō art in Japan: e.g., Kawakatsu 1974; Kajitani 1974; Nakano 1974.

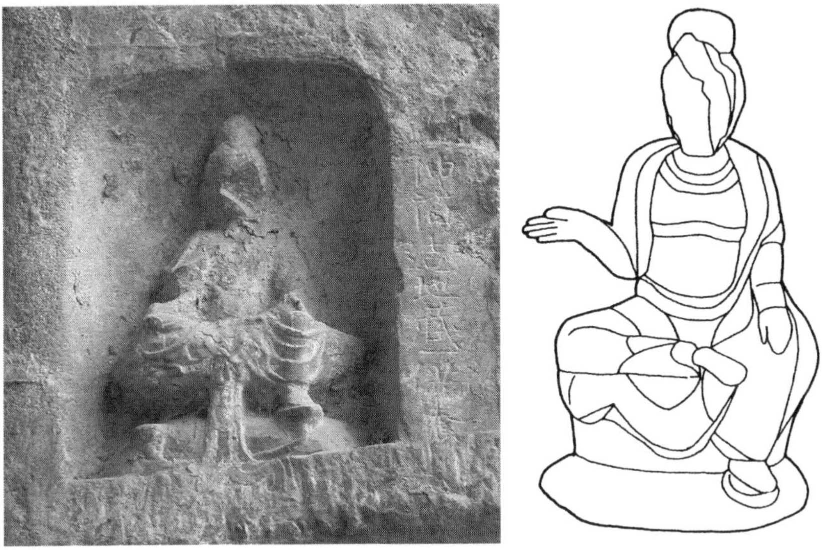

FIGURE 7. (l) Seated Dizang. Southern wall outside Wanfo dong, Longmen, Henan. (r) Seated Dizang, Binyang dong, Longmen. Drawing courtesy of Chang Qing.

image of Dizang, a wall illustration at Faju si (in modern-day Chengdu) by Zhang Sengyou, portrays the bodhisattva as a monk, seated with one leg pendant on a couch.[9] However, this seventh-century painting is no longer extant. The early Longmen examples of Dizang often show him in the guise of a traditional bodhisattva, usually seated in the "pose of royal ease" *(lalitāsana)*—one leg pendant and the other folded on the seat—a stylistic detail that art historians consider characteristic of Dizang art at Longmen (see Figure 7).[10]

In contrast to the numerous princely bodhisattva representations, Longmen only possesses four images of Dizang as a *śramaṇa*, dating to the second half of the seventh century.[11] Three of the figures, two at Wang Yuangui's Cave (Wang Yuangui dong 王元軌洞) and the third at the Cave of the Officer of the Eight Crafts (Bazuo si dong 八作司洞), are seated in the *lalitāsana* pose with the right hand holding a jewel.[12] The fourth image,

9. Daoshi recorded and dated this image to 665; see *Fayuan zhulin*, T2122:53.392c. Also see previous discussion of this miraculous image in Chapter 2.

10. See Chang 1990: 27–29, figs. 1, 2. On the basis of stylistic consistency, it has been proposed that several other bodhisattva sculptures in similar *lalitāsana* postures situated along the northern and middle sections of the western hill at Longmen should be regarded as Dizang images. These date from the reigns of Emperor Gaozong to Empress Wu, or roughly from the mid-sixth to the early seventh centuries; see Chang 1990: 29–30; cf. McNair 1996: 333.

11. Chang 1990: 31. Note that none of the images can be dated through inscriptions.

12. *Bazuo si* is an official title; the eight crafts are: plastering (*ni* 泥), painting (*chibai* 赤白), varnishing (*tongyou* 銅油), stonework (*shi* 石), tilework (*wa* 瓦), bamboo work (*zhu* 竹), masonry (*zhuan* 磚), and well work (*jing* 井). The cave is most likely named after its sponsor, who held the

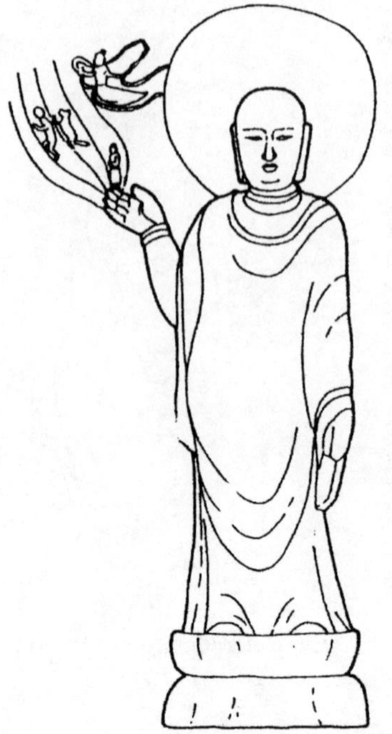

FIGURE 8. Dizang and the paths of rebirth, Binyang dong, Longmen, Henan. Drawing courtesy of Chang Qing.

at the Middle Cave of the Setting Sun (Binyang zhong dong 賓陽中洞), portrays Dizang with the paths of rebirth streaming out from his raised palm (see Figure 8).[13]

Given the number and earlier date of the images dressed in royal garb, one may speculate that Chinese artisans first sculpted Dizang using the iconography of bodhisattvas known to them—that is, in the guise of a princely householder.[14] Drawing inspiration probably from the *Scripture on the Ten Wheels*, artisans created the alternative *śramaṇa* iconography, in the process of which they might have faced the dilemma of how to differentiate Dizang Bodhisattva from an ordinary monk disciple. The *Scripture on the Ten Wheels* furnishes the motifs of the precious gem and the six paths of rebirth.[15] Both

office of the eight crafts. There are two Dizang images, one at each extreme end, in the Wang Yuangui dong. Each statue portrays Dizang with a shaven head and dressed in monastic robes, seated on a lotus pedestal with one leg pendant. He carries a jewel in one hand while the other hand rests on his knee. An inscription preserved inside the cave mentions the year 687; see Chang 1990: 30, figs. 4, 5. In the lower section of the Bazuo si dong is an image of a monk measuring 0.92 m high. He wears a robe with folds flowing down from the shoulders and across the chest and is seated in the *lalitāsana* pose, holding a jewel in his raised right hand; see Chang 1990: 31, fig. 6. The style of Dizang's robe differs somewhat in these two caves.

13. See Chang 1990: 30, fig. 3.

14. Note that among Longmen sculptures of Dizang in princely attire are the two earliest extant carvings of him, those located at Yaofang dong and Binyang nan dong.

15. In the *Da fangguang shilun jing*, T410:13.681a–b, it is said that when Dizang arrived at the buddha assembly, astonishing transformations occurred. The audience found them-

images remained distinctive of Dizang iconography, although over time other motifs were introduced as Dizang's functions expanded. At Dafo si, Dizang is shown as both a princely householder and a monk seated in the *lalitāsana* pose.[16] A stele carving preserved at the Shaanxi Provincial Museum in Xi'an, which Amy McNair identifies as Dizang, shows a one-leg-pendant seated bodhisattva dressed like a prince and crowned with a diadem.[17] In Xiangtang shan and Xumi shan, the majority of the images depict Dizang as a one-leg-pendant seated monk. An inscription toward the southern end of Xiangtang shan (niches 3–39), dated 695, characterizes Dizang as a *śramaṇa*: "in veneration constructed [ ] statue(s) of the *śramaṇa* Bodhisattva Dizang" 敬造沙門地藏菩/□□鋪.[18]

By the eighth century, the *śramaṇa* iconography was widely accepted as the norm for representing Dizang. Dunhuang and Sichuan contain so many images of Dizang as a monk that it is unnecessary to enumerate them all. Two attributes, the hood and the staff (Ch. *xizhang* 錫杖; Skt. *khakkara*), probably of Central Asian origin, merit special note. At Dunhuang and Sichuan, Dizang frequently wears a piece of cloth wrapped around his head that cascades onto his shoulders or is sometimes knotted around each ear.[19] Matsumoto dubbed this image the "hooded Dizang" (*hibō jizō* 被帽地藏).[20] Central Asian travelers protected their heads from the harsh climate with a cape, which was widely adopted—although not always sanctioned—in the Indian *vinaya* as part of the monastic habit in the region.[21] The hooded Dizang (Kor. Chijang) was transmitted from the Chinese borders to Korea and appears frequently in paintings and sculptures from the Koryŏ and Chosŏn (1392–1910) periods.[22] The staff is immensely popular in both Dunhuang

---

selves miraculously adorned, each hand grasping a luminous wish-granting gem, which exuded rays of light illumining all the buddha-lands. They also found themselves experiencing miraculous acts of healing, allaying suffering, and so forth. Also cf. *Dasheng daji dizang shilun jing*, T411:13.721a–b.

16. Chang 1998: 235.

17. For a reproduction of this stele carving, see McNair 1996: 379, fig. 10.

18. Lee 1992: 12.

19. In Dunhuang, the hooded Dizang is frequently depicted on the ceilings of archways leading into the principal cave shrine. He also appears in scroll paintings preserved in museums outside of China. Matsumoto Eiichi was among the first scholars to highlight the hooded Dizang in Dunhuang art. Dazu Beishan in Sichuan has several instances of the hooded Dizang; see Figures 23 and 24 for examples from niches 279 and 281. The hooded Dizang also appears, albeit with less frequency, elsewhere in Sichuan: For example, Anyue Yuanjue dong 安岳圓覺洞 niche 60; see Figure 29. Two instances are also found in niche 62 of Bazhong nan kan; for line drawings, see Ding 1990: 48. For a study of the hooded Dizang iconography in Sichuan Dazu, see Moroto 1986: 34–37.

20. Matsumoto 1937: 368.

21. The hooded Dizang continued to flourish in Chinese Buddhist art. It is found for instance in a thirteenth-century hanging scroll painting of Dizang with the monk Daoming 道明 and the Demon King No-Poison (*wudu wang* 無毒王), now preserved in Engaku-ji 圓覚寺 in Japan. For a photo reproduction of this painting, see Little 2003: 56, fig. 3.

22. For Koryŏ examples of the hooded Chijang, see Little 2003: 52–56. An eminent Chosŏn example is found in Muwi-sa 無為寺 in Kangjin, Chonnam province. This temple

and Sichuan art. Like the hood, the staff may have become part of Dizang's iconography because of its widespread adoption as one of the requisites of a Buddhist monk.[23] Monks are encouraged to sound the staff to either frighten off harmful reptiles while walking on forest paths or signal their presence at the doorsteps of almsgivers.[24] The staff also functions as a crutch for elderly monks. Dizang's staff is usually shown with a large ring at the top through which are threaded smaller rings—generally six to symbolize the six paths of rebirth. It is important to note that although the staff came to be adopted in Dizang iconography because it was part of a monk's paraphernalia, its symbolism expanded with the "underworld Dizang," who is said to use a staff to smash open hell's gates.[25]

Yet another element of Dizang's iconography is the decorative jewelry prominent in ninth- and tenth-century Dunhuang art. Among those Dunhuang paintings recovered by Stein (e.g., Stein 125, 118 in the British Museum) and Pelliot (e.g., EO 1186, MG 17768, EO 1398, MG 22798, EO 1168, EO 1180, MG 17779, MG 17658 in the Musée Guimet) are several banners that portray Dizang standing, head completely shaven, dressed in fine robes and ornamented with earrings, a necklace, and wrist or arm bracelets.[26] In certain portraits, the hooded Dizang also wears a jeweled necklace (Stein 19, 23; MG 17664, 17793, 17795, 17662, 17794; EO 3644, 1173, 3580).[27] Several examples of Dizang are painted on the ceilings in the passageways or on walls located in situ at Dunhuang (e.g., caves 116, 390, 384) and in the neighboring Elms Grove Grottoes (Yulin ku 榆林窟), south of Anxi 安西 county (e.g., caves 12, 33).[28] This jewelry motif is found not only in Dunhuang, but

---

possesses a mural painting, dated to 1476 and designated a national treasure, of an Amitābha triad with Chijang and Kwanum (Guanyin) as attendant bodhisattvas. A gilded sculpture of the trio stands in front of the wall painting. Dizang wears a hood in both the painting and sculpture; see Moon 1984, pl. 27.

23. For studies on the *khakkara*, see Amanō 1988: 285–291; 1989: 69–78; Gao 1993: 9–19.

24. This is necessary because monks do not have the right to knock on doors.

25. In the narrative versions of the Mulian story, the foundation myth of the Ghost Festival, the Buddha gave his own staff to Mulian, who used it to open the gates of hell. In the Dunhuang version of this narrative, the Buddha says:

> Quickly I take my metal-ringed staff and give it to you,
> It can repel the eight difficulties and the three disasters;
> If only you remember diligently to recite my name,
> The hells will certainly open up their doors for you. (translated in Mair 1983: 104; cf. 107)

26. For reproductions, see Whitfield 1982–1985: 1, pls. 44, 45; Giès 1995: 2, pls. 51–59.

27. For reproductions of Stein 19, 23, see Whitfield 1982–1985: 2, pls. 22, 24. For reproductions of MG 17664, 17793, 17795, 17662, 17794, see Giès 1995: 2, pls. 60–67.

28. On the ceiling of the Mogao cave 390 passageway is Dizang, head shaven and holding the staff and the jewel. One can discern the six paths of rebirth streaming from his nimbus, while the courts of the Ten Kings are depicted along the two sides and directly below him; see the reproduction published in Duan 1990b: 111, fig. 107. On the ceiling of the Mogao ku cave

also in Sichuan. Dazu Beishan niche 253 shows a standing Dizang with a shaven head, attired as a monk and decorated with earrings and necklaces. The jewelry operates as a visual reminder of Dizang's status as a bodhisattva and differentiates him from other disciple monks (see Figures 9 and 10).

As we saw earlier, *A Ritual Manual* prescribes a form of Dizang icon that portrays the bodhisattva in monastic robes with a deity's crown upon his head. Another work dating to the ninth century, the *Huanhun ji* 還魂記 (Record of a Returned Soul), a narrative recovered from Dunhuang (S 3092), relates the underworld sojourn of a monk called Daoming 道明.[29] In this story, Daoming initially fails to recognize Dizang in the underworld because of discrepancies in his iconography. Daoming explains that Dizang the bodhisattva is usually shown as a monk with his head exposed; the "real" Dizang before him is a monk wearing some kind of jeweled and floral headgear. Upon hearing this, an indignant Dizang instructs Daoming, on his return to the living realm, to make known the bodhisattva's true appearance as a monk bedecked with a jeweled coiffure and attended by a lion. It is clear from this tale that Dizang's iconography was still controversial in late medieval China.

Although *śramaṇa* iconography was eventually established as the norm, Dizang as the princely householder did not vanish altogether but was perpetuated especially in esoteric art, which I will discuss later. The *śramaṇa* with the shaven head has never lost its appeal and persists alongside the sovereign imagery of the five-buddha crown in modern Dizang iconography.

Dizang and Guanyin as Saviors of This World

Françoise Wang-Toutain and Yü Chün-fang, who studied Dizang and Guanyin independently, have both called attention to possible medieval connections between these two Buddhist deities.[30] Indeed visual, inscriptional, and narrative materials suggest that Dizang and Guanyin were frequently venerated together in medieval China. No scriptural source, at least not in the re-

384 passageway is a hooded Dizang, the fingers of his right hand forming a *mudrā* and his left hand holding the *cintāmaṇi*. One can make out the paths of rebirth streaming from his nimbus, while the courts of the Ten Kings are depicted along the two sides and directly below him; for a reproduction, see Duan 1990a: fig. 18. Above the doorway of the western wall in Yulin cave 12 is a hooded Dizang wearing a necklace and holding a *khakkara* and a *cintāmaṇi*; for a reproduction see Duan 1990b: 113, fig. 108. Above the doorway of the eastern wall in Yulin cave 33 is Dizang as a monk with a shaven head, surrounded by the six realms of existence. He wears a necklace and holds in his hands a *khakkara* and a *cintāmaṇi*. The cave is dated to the tenth century. For reproductions of this painting, see Dunhuang yanjiuyuan 1997, fig. 77; Duan 1990b: 140, 148, fig. 140.

29. For a discussion and translation, see Teiser 1988a: 447–450. I discuss the narrative in greater detail in Chapter 5.

30. Wang-Toutain 1998: 292; Yü 2001: 323. In fact the portrayal of Dizang's attributes and salvific activities in the *Scripture on the Ten Wheels* closely resembles those of Guanyin in the *Lotus Scripture*. The parallels are so striking that scholars have argued that the introduction of Dizang in the *Scripture on the Ten Wheels* was a later addition and modeled after Chapter 25 of the *Lotus Scripture*, a chapter devoted to exalting Guanyin worship; see Soper 1959: 210–211.

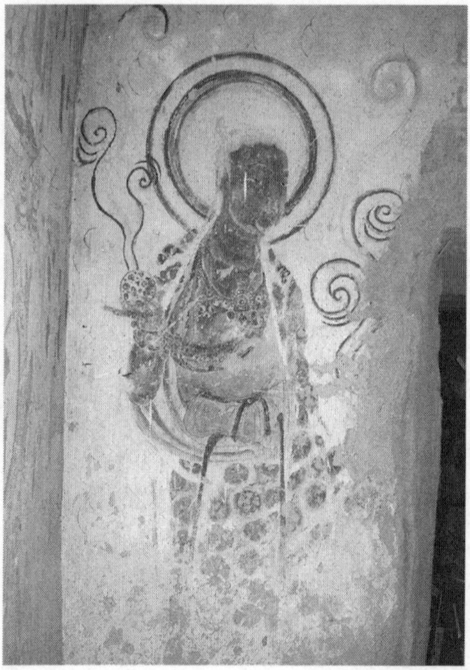

FIGURE 9. Dizang with jeweled necklace. Mogao grotto 16, Dunhuang, Gansu. Photograph courtesy of Wang Huimin.

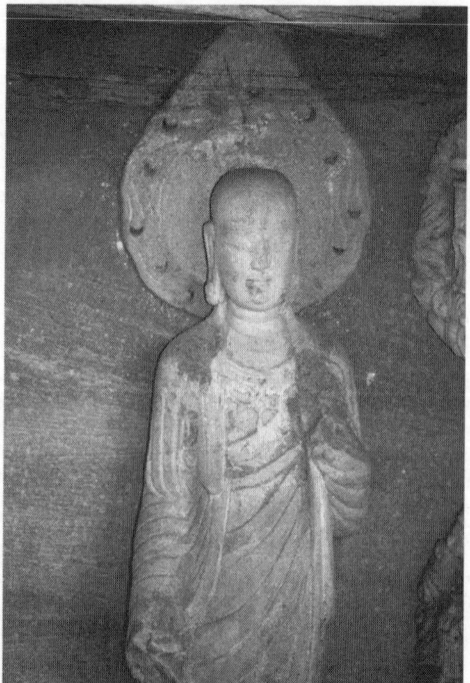

FIGURE 10. Dizang wearing jewelry. Beishan Fowan niche 253, Dazu, Sichuan.

ceived archives we have today, details the relationship between Dizang and Guanyin in medieval China.[31] Although the literature affords parallels between the two bodhisattvas, the pairing of Dizang and Guanyin as a focus of veneration is concretized mostly through visual imagery, an indication that the association probably took shape in the broader religious milieu.

Unlike Dizang, the Indian counterpart of Guanyin, Avalokiteśvara, is a fairly well-defined personage in Indian literature. From the third century on, scriptures on Guanyin were translated into Chinese, and collections of miracle tales on the efficacies of this bodhisattva multiplied.[32] There was a sharp increase in the production of Guanyin images at Longmen.[33] Scholars have pointed out that some portrayals of Dizang possess attributes or accessories typical of Guanyin iconography. For example, in Longmen and Dunhuang art, Dizang sometimes holds a sprinkler vase, an object more commonly associated with Guanyin.[34] Three Dunhuang paintings of Dizang are styled after the so-called "Water-moon Guanyin" (Shuiyue Guanyin 水月觀音).[35] In light of these stylistic resemblances, Françoise Wang-Toutain concluded that early on artisans deployed Guanyin iconography as a model.[36] But it is critical to acknowledge the fluidity of iconography, especially in the early phase of religious history, and to exercise caution when imposing what we now accept as definitive attributes of deities at a time when Buddhist iconography was less defined.[37] For instance, until the seventh or eighth cen-

31. Scholars sometimes cite the *Scripture on the Past Vows* as the scriptural source for associating Dizang with Guanyin for two reasons: (1) the presence of Guanyin as an interlocutor in Chapter 12; and (2) the comparison of the merits of venerating Dizang and Guanyin in Chapter 11. However, neither instance really spells out any special connection with Guanyin. Upon scrutinizing the relevant passage in Chapter 11, it turns out that Dizang worship is compared not only to that of Guanyin, but also Maitreya, Mañjuśrī, and Samantabhadra; see *Dizang pusa benyuan jing*, T412:13787a. Moreover, the date of the *Scripture on the Past Vows* is uncertain, and we can only ascertain that the text circulated in China by the tenth century. Because the trend of pairing Dizang with Guanyin is present in Longmen and other sites in north central China dating as early as the interval between the seventh and eighth centuries, the iconography most likely preceded the introduction of the scripture.

32. For the dating of these texts, see Campany 1996b. For a study of Guanyin miracle tales, see Makita 1970.

33. Guanyin is a well-investigated topic in art history; the studies are too numerous to enumerate here. For a recent overview of Guanyin art, see Karetzky 2004.

34. For a line drawing of Dizang with a sprinkler vase (Binyang nan dong niche 16), see Chang 1990: 29, fig. 2. Stein painting 118, dated to the ninth century, is a Dunhuang example showing Dizang holding this vase; see Whitfield 1982–1985, pl. 45. A cartouche in the right corner identifies the bodhisattva.

35. Wang-Toutain 1998: 292. Wang-Toutain lists two paintings from the Musée Guimet collection (MG 17659 and MG 17794) and a third painting located in the Chinese collection. The Water-moon Guanyin typically sits in the midst of water on a rock promontory that symbolizes Potala, her head encircled by a nimbus against a background landscape usually containing some kind of vegetation. For studies on the Water-moon Guanyin, see Chan 1996; Rösch 2006.

36. See Wang-Toutain 1998: 292–293.

37. This is not to say that modern religious iconography is "frozen"; novel interpretations continue to emerge, but they are now negotiated against a background of well-defined Buddhist iconography.

tury, the vase was a fairly common accessory for Buddhist deities; it is seen in the iconography of not only Dizang and Guanyin, but Maitreya as well.[38] Whatever the original inspiration behind the association, the two bodhisattvas Dizang and Guanyin were inextricably linked in the medieval imagination.[39]

The pairing of deities is certainly not confined to Dizang and Guanyin; the practice can be traced to the duplicating of bodhisattvas that emerged early in Chinese Buddhist art.[40] This swiftly gave way to placing together two different bodhisattvas; in time Dizang-Guanyin became the most common pair. Early pairings of the two are found at Longmen and appeared soon afterward in other north central sites like Xiangtang shan. They occur frequently on the western borders of Sichuan and Gansu, and were especially widespread in Beishan during the late ninth and tenth centuries.[41] At Beishan Fowan 佛灣 (Buddha Bend), a total of forty niches (twenty percent of the total number) contain different combinations of bodhisattva pairs, the most recurrent of which is Dizang-Guanyin.[42]

Why were Guanyin and Dizang linked in the medieval imagination? Thomas Suchan has pointed to a piece of visual evidence that could elucidate the mindset of tenth-century Chinese who venerated these two bodhisattvas together: Niche 1 at the Monastery of the Winding Steppe (Pantuo si 盤陀寺) in Qionglai 邛崍 contains a statue of Amitābha Buddha dated by inscription to 820; immediately outside the main niche is a smaller one housing two bodhisattvas seated on separate lotus pedestals, both with one leg

38. For example, Gandharan art depicts Maitreya with a vase in his hand.

39. Early Tang sites in central China contain inscriptions and sculptures pairing the two bodhisattvas. At Longmen, six inscriptions refer to this pairing; see inscription texts 11, 20, 21, 26, 30, and 32 listed in Chang 1990: 32. Of these, text 32 mentions an eleven-faced Guanyin. I have located three relevant inscriptions from southern Xiangtang shan:

1. Inscription dating to 701–704 found in niche 1: 為亡妻陳造觀音地藏菩薩像記 (text 9 in Mizuno and Nagahiro 1937: 123, and pl. 10B);
2. Inscription dating to 712 found in niche 2: 荊□□等造地藏觀音像記 (text 31 in ibid: 127, and pl. 15A); and
3. Inscription dating to 705 found in niche 2: 荊義[振]等造地藏觀音像記 (text 42 in ibid: 130, and pl. 15A).

40. For reproductions of Tang examples of the bodhisattvas duplicated in a single niche, see Han 2001: 19, 25.

41. On the pairing of Dizang and Guanyin in Sichuan, see Hu 1994: 228–229.

42. Other iconographies pair Candraprabha (Yueguang 月光) with Sūryagarbha (Riguang 日光), Mañjuśrī (Wenshu) with Samantabhadra (Puxian), and Guanyin with Mahāsthāmaprāpta (Dashizhi). Dizang and Guanyin pairings are located in Beishan Fowan niches 17, 29, 58, 82, 117, 121, 170, 171, 172, 187, 191, 193, 196, 221, 228, 241, 244, 248, 249, 253, 257, 275, and 277. The majority of these niches, however, lack inscriptions and the images have been identified through iconographical attributes. Pairings of Dizang and Guanyin occur in other Sichuan sites: for example, niche 38 at Feixian ge 飛仙閣 (Pavilion of Flying Celestials) in Pujiang 浦江, and niche 119 at Qianfo ya in Jiajiang 夾江, both dated to the middle of the late Tang.

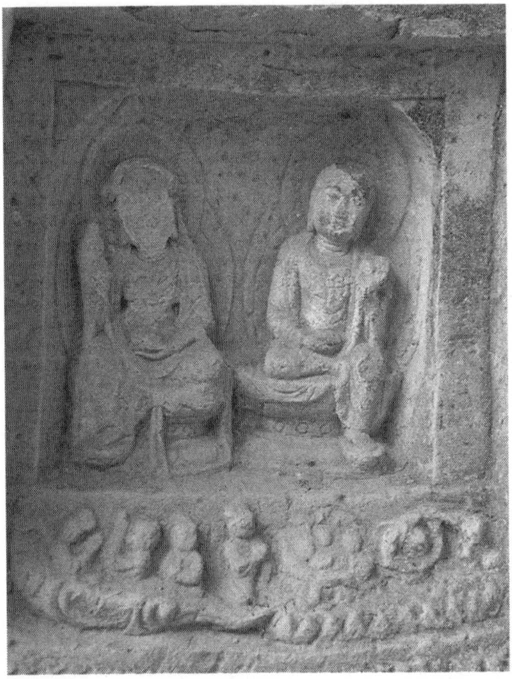

FIGURE 11. Dizang and Guanyin, Pantuo si niche 1, Qionglai, Sichuan. Photograph courtesy of Thomas Suchan.

pendant (see Figure 11).[43] One of them, a monk with a shaven head, wears a necklace, while the other is draped in princely robes and long flowing scarves. Immediately below the monk is a vignette of hell retribution; wretched sinners are submerged in a boiling cauldron over which two wardens keep vigil and all are surrounded by flames. Below the other image swirling tides well up to sweep away four figures. (This scene points to the *Lotus Scripture*'s injunction to incant Guanyin's name when facing danger at sea.)[44]

Although no inscription accompanies this sculpture, the imagery identifies the two bodhisattvas as Dizang and Guanyin. Through scenes of hell and peril at sea, the artist upholds Dizang as the promise of otherworldly mitigation in hell and Guanyin as the rescuer of those caught in the exigencies of living in this world. From the perspective of Buddhist cosmology, hells are located within the cosmography of our Sahā world, a defiled realm encompassing all six paths of rebirth. In other words, both Dizang and Guanyin are deities invariably tied to the fortunes of this world. However, one should reiterate that medieval Chinese essentially viewed the universe as three-tiered: the heavens above (*tian* 天); the human (*ren* 人) world; and the world beneath the earth (*di* 地).[45] The main niche, which houses the large Amitābha image,

43. See Suchan 2005.

44. *Miaofa lianhua jing*, T262:9.56c.

45. This three-tiered stratification is discernible as far back as the Shang. The Chinese character for king, *wang* 王, is explained as a logograph that renders the king, especially in Shang shamanism, as the religio-political mediator who bridges heaven, humans, and earth.

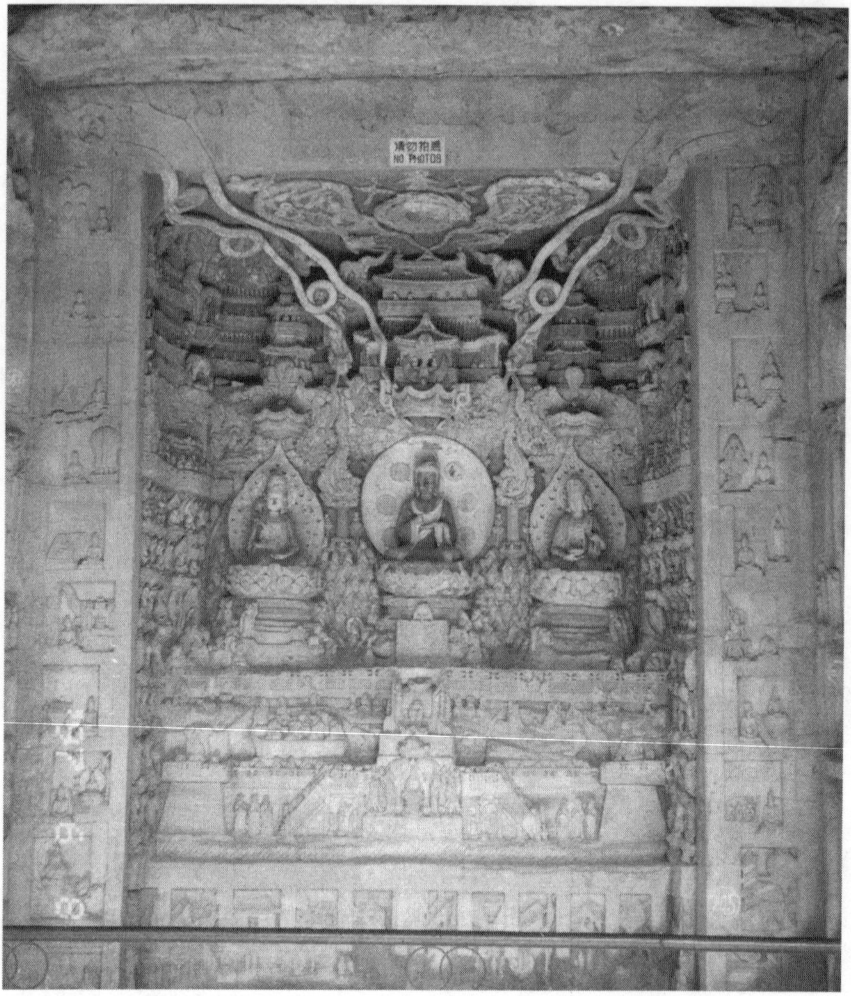

FIGURE 12. Pure Land transformation tableaux. Beishan niche 245, Dazu, Sichuan.

corresponds to the heavens, while the smaller niche and its engravings invoke the realms of the living and the underworld. Dizang and Guanyin, on account of their geographical associations, were more readily integrated into the spatial categories of Chinese cosmography. Whatever its origin, cultic practice addressed to a Dizang-Guanyin pairing probably spread in connection with their identities as this-worldly saviors. We cannot be sure when the smaller exterior niche was carved, but given its contents, it was in all likelihood a later addition, no earlier than the ninth century.

Three further points should be made regarding the pairing of Dizang with Guanyin: first, its connection with Pure Land worship; second, its

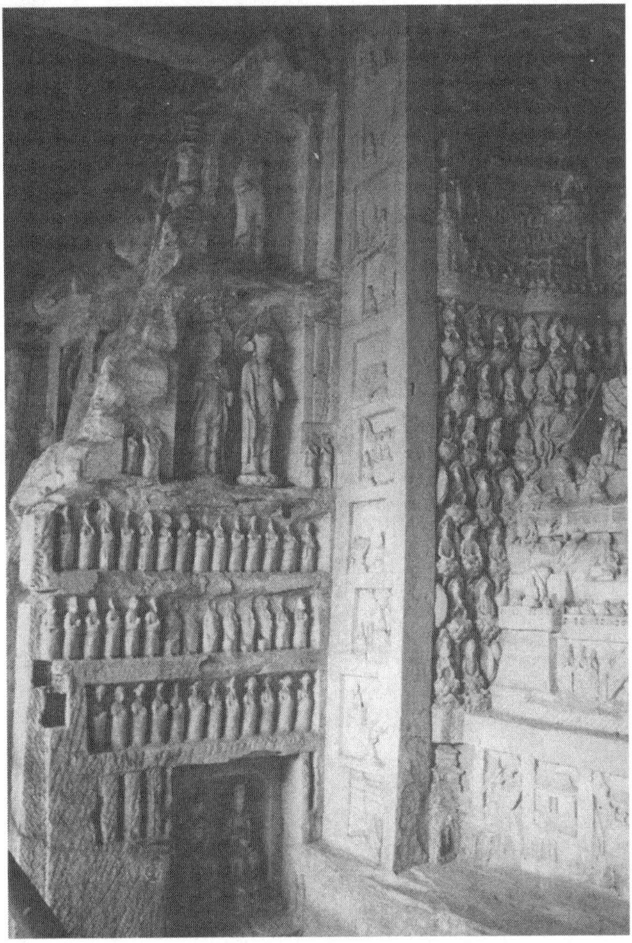

FIGURE 13. Promontory lateral wall facing south. Outside Beishan niche 245, Dazu, Sichuan.

broader connection with the cult of the multiple buddhas; and finally, its association with the Ten Kings. As we will see later in this chapter, Dizang and Guanyin sometimes flank Amitābha or Bhaiṣajyaguru Buddha to form a triadic icon, although it is unclear as to which configuration, the triad or the pairing, came first or how they are related to one another. Particularly important is Beishan Fowan niche 245 and its large, intricate carving of the Buddha Amitābha's realm, the Western Land of Bliss, surrounded on three sides by scenes from the *Visualization Scripture*, including the sixteen visualizations for rebirth in the Western Paradise (see Figure 12). An inscription indicates that this carving existed by the beginning of the tenth century.[46]

Significantly, two walls of small niches (numbered 237–244, 246–249)

46. For the inscription text, see Guo 1999a: 17. This partially effaced inscription mentions the *jimao* 己卯 year, which Guo reconstructs as the year 919.

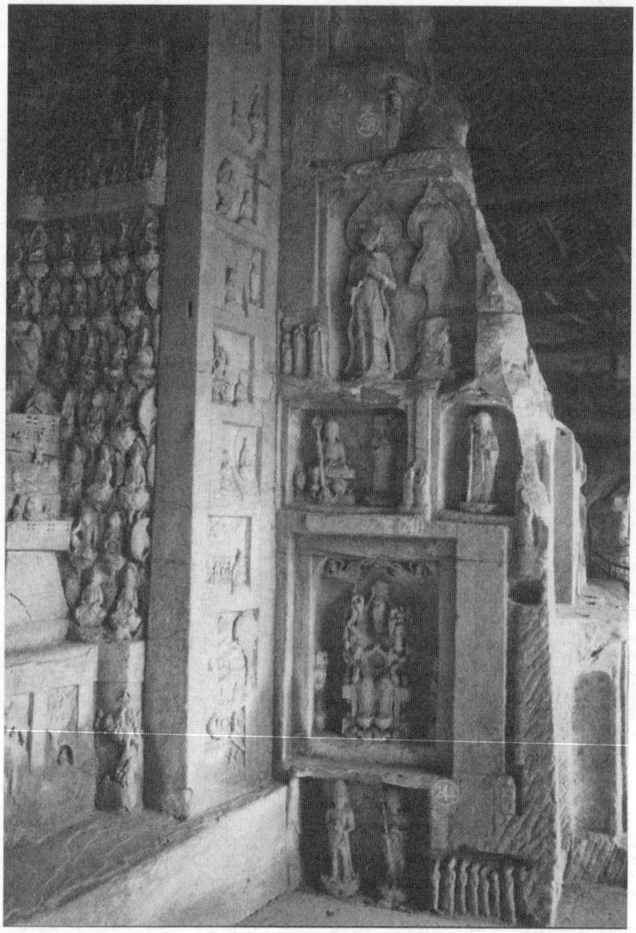

FIGURE 14. Promontory lateral wall facing north. Outside Beishan niche 245, Dazu, Sichuan.

containing miniature images of Dizang or Guanyin or the two together were attached to either side of the central niche, forming flanking protrusions (see Figures 13 and 14). From the spatial arrangement, one could conclude that these smaller niches were added after the large relief engraving was finished.[47] The additions to the main relief carving of the Western Pure Land may suggest cultic contestation that pitted the divine efficacies of the Buddha against those of the bodhisattva.[48] The spatial arrangement at niche 245 thus represents a local response to this cultic dilemma in which venerating Dizang and Guanyin was viewed as an appropriate extension of Amitābha Buddha worship. The distance to the seemingly remote

47. Not all the smaller niches have inscriptions, but the few with dates suggest that they were made in the latter half of the tenth century.

48. This controversy over the efficacy of reciting the Buddha's name versus the bodhisattva's is recorded in Tang Pure Land polemical literature; for relevant passages, see the previous discussion in Chapter 2.

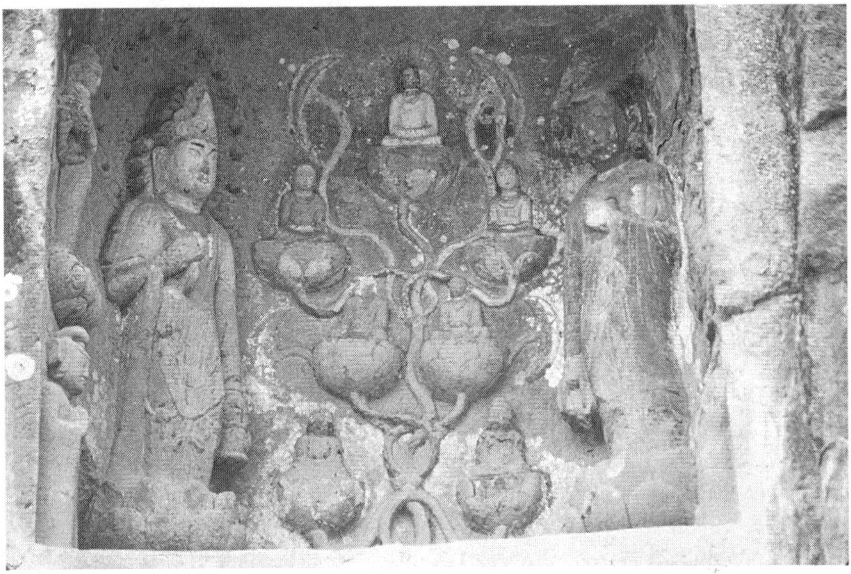

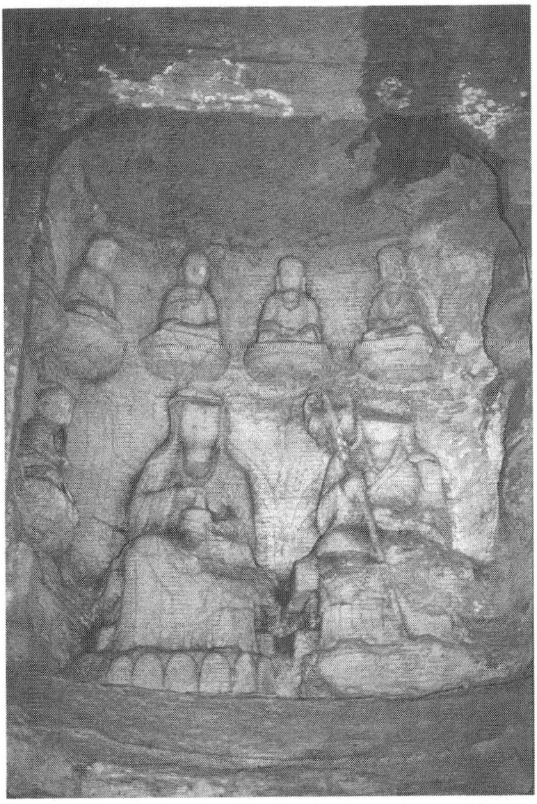

FIGURE 15 (above). Dizang and Guanyin with seven buddhas. Qianfo ya niche 125, Jiajiang, Sichuan.

FIGURE 16 (left). Dizang and Guanyin with six buddhas. Beishan niche 172, Dazu, Sichuan.

paradise of Amitābha would then be bridged by the two bodhisattvas, Dizang and Guanyin, to whom family members must pray to ensure that the dead do not fall into evil destinies.

Other iconography surfaces in Sichuan art: small meditation buddhas, varying in number and seated on lotuses with intertwining stems, juxtaposed against larger statues of Dizang and Guanyin. The earliest examples of the two bodhisattvas with smaller buddhas are in niches 162 and 125 at the Cliff of Thousand Buddhas (Qianfo ya 千佛崖) in Jiajiang 夾江, both dating to the middle of late Tang (see Figure 15). Three later examples, all dating to the Song period, are found in Beishan Fowan: niche 191 (probably dating to the tenth century) portrays ten buddhas on lotuses arising from a vessel placed between a seated Guanyin and a hooded Dizang; niche 187, a duplication of niche 191; and niche 172, which features six buddhas together with the two bodhisattvas (see Figure 16).[49] Originating in Indian sources, the seven buddhas of the past and the buddhas of the ten directions invoke strong temporal and spatial connotations. In these visual imaginings, Dizang and Guanyin are probably perceived as acting in this world on behalf of all the buddhas through all ages and in all worlds. In other words, Dizang and Guanyin are the divine intercessors par excellence who bridge this world and other realms.

The pairing of Dizang with Guanyin also occurs regularly in Dunhuang art from the early Tang period. Dunhuang yields several examples dated to the tenth century or after in which these two bodhisattvas appear together with the Ten Kings. Over the ceiling of the passageway in cave 6 are painted two panels: one portrays a water-moon Guanyin and the other Dizang presiding over the court of the Ten Kings.[50] Similar iconographies are found in tenth-century paintings now kept at the Musée Guimet: For example, EO 3644, a silk painting, shows an eleven-headed Guanyin with a hooded Dizang and the courts of the Ten Kings below.[51] EO 1173, a painting on hemp cloth, portrays a thousand-armed, thousand-eyed Guanyin as the main deity with Dizang and the Ten Kings pictured in one corner.[52] At the British Museum, illustrated in separate panels on the frontispiece of a mutilated scroll of the *Scripture of the Ten Kings* are Dizang and a six-armed Guanyin attended by the Ten Kings, also dated to the tenth century.[53] In contrast to Dunhuang, configurations of Guanyin, Dizang, and the Ten Kings are rare in Sichuan except for one prominent example, Fowan niche 253 in Beishan. Judging from the frequent pairing of Dizang with Guanyin, one may conclude that the two bodhisattvas were linked as powerful saviors in the medieval imagination.

49. For discussion and a photograph of niche 187, see Howard 1990: 56–57, and fig. 13.

50. For a catalog description of EO 3644, see Dunhuang yanjiuyuan 1996: 6.

51. More accurately, the main head is depicted with a crown from which spring eleven smaller heads; see Giès 1995: 2, pl. 64.

52. Ibid.: pl. 65.

53. Whitfield 1982–1985: pl. 64.

From Amitābha Triads to Rebirth in the Pure Land

Dizang art visually documents the Pure Land connection articulated in the *Scripture on the Bodhisattva Dizang*. On the one hand, art and epigraphy from Longmen and Sichuan attest to the reconfiguration of Dizang into Amitābha triads. In the *Larger Sukhāvatīvyūha-sūtra*, an early Mahāyāna scripture repeatedly translated into Chinese from the third century, Avalokiteśvara (Guanyin) and Mahāsthāmaprāpta (Dashizhi) are the two attendant bodhisattvas assisting Amitābha Buddha in his buddha-land, Sukhāvatī.[54] The triad of Amitābha Buddha, Avalokiteśvara, and Mahāsthāmaprāpta occurs early in the history of Buddhist art; together they are known today as the Three Saints of the West (*xifang sansheng* 西方三聖), an epithet in use probably from the Song.[55] Not so commonly studied are the Amitābha triads in which Dizang replaces Mahāsthāmaprāpta as an attendant bodhisattva. For instance, Longmen contains five inscriptional records of Dizang in Amitābha triads:[56]

1. Inscription dating to 675, located outside the Universally Tranquil Cave (Putai dong 普泰洞):
   On the sixth day of the second month in the second year of *shangyuan* 上元 [675], disciple [ ] [ ] [ ], mother Qiao 喬 [ ] [ ], here below the wife [ ] [ ] zang 藏, and so forth today [reverently] construct an image of the venerated Amitābha, [ ] one [image] of Guanyin Bodhisattva Who Relieves Suffering (Jiuku Guanshiyin 救苦觀世音), [ ] one [image] of Dizang Bodhisattva. Today they have been completed. By this merit, may all beings everywhere share this meritorious fruit.[57]
2. Inscription dating to 693 from a niche in the Lotus Cave (Lianhua dong 蓮華洞):

54. This configuration occurs repeatedly in the *Visualization Scripture*; see *Foshuo guan wu liangshou fo jing* 佛說觀無量壽佛經, T365:12.342c, 345a. The two bodhisattvas are also mentioned in the *Larger Sukhāvatīvyūha-sūtra*; see *Foshuo wuliangshou jing* 佛說無量壽經, T360:12.273b, attributed to the Sogdian monk Saṅghavarman (Sengqiebamo 僧伽跋摩; also known as Kang Sengkai 康僧鎧, ca. 252). The configuration is further cited in the *Guanshiyin pusa shouji jing* 觀世音菩薩授記經, T371:12.353c.

55. A preliminary survey suggests that the "Three Saints of the West" first appeared in the *Fozu tongji* 佛祖統紀, compiled by the Song monk Zhipan 志磐 (fl. 1258–1269 CE); T2035:49.209b, 218c, 225c, 261c, 276c, 279a, 279b. We can preliminarily conclude that it was not used in the Tang era, although further investigation should be conducted to determine when the phrase actually gained wide currency. In modern Chinese Buddhism, the epithet is frequently employed as a shorthand reference to the three Pure Land deities. The triadic icon is common in Chinese Buddhist art: for example, the Huayan (Avataṃsaka) triad (*huayan sansheng* 華嚴三聖), comprising Vairocana Buddha and the two bodhisattvas Mañjuśrī and Samantabhadra. For a study of the Huayan triad, see Gimello 1996.

56. Inscription texts 5, 9, 12, 14, and 25 in Chang 1993: 28–29.

57. Ibid.: 28, inscription text 5. There is a character missing after *fu*, or "merit." From the context, the missing character is likely to be *de* 德, thus making the compound *fude* 福德, or "meritorious virtue."

On the twenty-third day of the fourth month in the second year of *changshou* 長壽 [693], Ren Zhiman 任智滿 made images of Amitābha, Dizang Bodhisattva, and Guanyin Bodhisattva for the sake of my deceased mother. May my deceased mother be reborn in the Western Land.[58]

3. Undated inscription from a niche in the Old Dragon Cave (Laolong dong 老龍洞):

   . . . mother . . . Amitābha Buddha . . . Dizang . . . one [image and] one [image of] Guanyin. All for the sake of teachers, *saṅgha*, parents, and all living beings [that they may] always procure peace and bliss.[59]

4. Undated inscription from a niche in the Twin Caves (Shuang yao 雙窯):

   [ ] [ ] the first month of the fourth year, [ ] [ ] [ ] day, Li Qutai 李去泰, a disciple of the Buddha, reverently constructs [an image of] Amitābha; an [image of] Guanyin Bodhisattva, who relieves suffering; and Dizang Bodhisattva, so that his teachers, *saṅgha*, parents, and all the living beings in the Dharma Realm, as well as living family members and relatives, may soon achieve awakening.[60]

5. Undated inscription from a niche in the Old Woman Cai Cave (Cai Laoniang dong 蔡老娘洞):

   Bhikṣunī Jiu Niang 九娘 (Ninth Daughter) of the Great Happiness Monastery (Jinfu si 景福寺), [on behalf of] her deceased mother, reverently constructs an image of Amitābha for [the purpose of] veneration . . . reverently constructs an image each of Guanyin and Dizang for [the purpose of] veneration.[61]

The inscriptions suggest that the incorporation of Dizang into Amitābha triads occurred as early as 675 in Longmen. They do not mention the goal of rebirth in the Pure Land with the exception of Ren Zhiman, who hopes that his deceased mother may be "reborn in the Western Land." The other four inscriptions transfer the merit of constructing the triad to goals ranging from spiritual achievement to secular benefits like the welfare and happiness of loved ones.

Sichuan sites also contain several instances of Amitābha triads in which Dizang appears as an attendant bodhisattva. Early examples are a cluster of niches (151, 152, 153, and 154) located at the Qianfo ya in Jiajiang (see Figures 17 and 18). Niches 151, 153, and 154 all have an inscriptional dating of 739, whereas niche 152 is dated to 712.[62]

Other examples of this kind of Amitābha triad are located at Beishan,

58. Ibid.: 28, inscription text 9.

59. Ibid.: 28, inscription text 12.

60. Ibid.: 28, inscription text 14.

61. Ibid.: 29, inscription text 25.

62. Unfortunately, I do not have access to these inscriptions; my information is based on Hu Wenhe's research. According to Hu, the inscription for niche 152 is missing characters, so the date is not certain. However, on the basis of stylistic resemblances with niches 151, 153, and 154, Chinese art historians believe niche 152 should date to 712. See Hu 1994: 33.

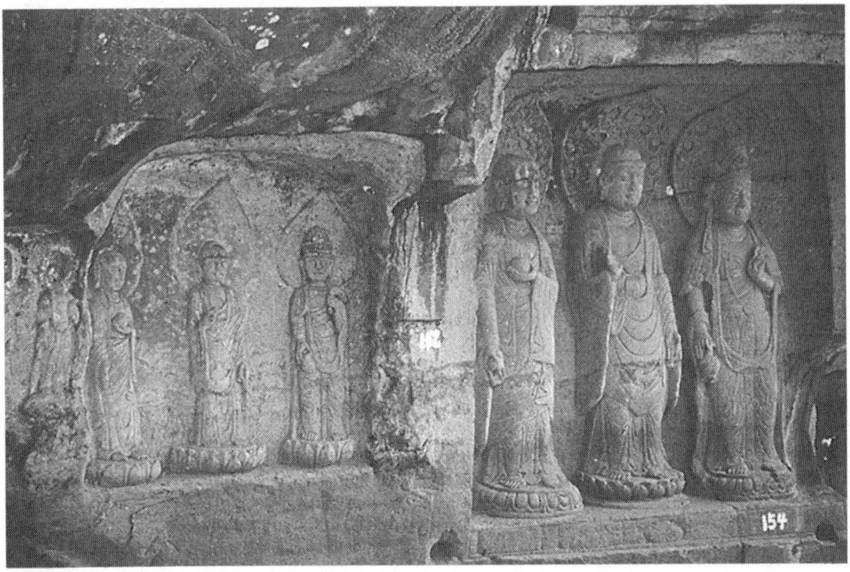

FIGURE 17. Amitābha, Dizang, and Guanyin. Qianfo ya niches 152 and 154, Jiajiang, Sichuan.

a site dating no earlier than 892. Here Dizang figures in Amitābha triads in a total of five niches (40, 52, 53, 57, and 73).[63] Only niches 52 and 53 are accompanied by inscriptional dating; scholars of the Sichuan Academy date the remaining niches to the Five Dynasties (907–960).[64] Constructed in 897, niche 52's inscription identifies the images:

> The female disciple née Li 黎, in honor of her deceased husband, Liu 劉 [ ], respectfully forged one image of Dizang Bodhisattva; one image of Amitābha; one [image] of Guanyin Bodhisattva Who Relieves Suffering. After [the images] were respectfully constructed, a vegetarian feast was hosted and hymns recited on the twenty-third day of the first month of the fourth year of *qianning* 乾寧 reign era (897).[65] [ ] my deceased husband [ ]

63. Identification of the sculptures is given in the catalogue of Dazu caves in Liu, Hu, and Li 1985: 364–575.

64. This dating of the Beishan niche is from the catalogue by Liu, Hu, and Li (1985). Note that Li and Wang (1988) classify Beishan sculptures according to three phases (late Tang, Five Dynasties, and after). They place niches 40 and 52 in the same period (late Tang).

65. The inscription refers to *biao zan* 表贊, translated as "reciting a hymn." The Indian *gāthā* is translated as *zan*, or "hymn," in Chinese Buddhism. The use of hymns was common in both Daoist and Buddhist rites. Typically, a formal declaration of the rite's intent is recited at the close of the opening phrase in which incense is offered to the Three Jewels. The deities are then invoked sequentially in the altar space and a short verse of praise (probably composed for the deities invoked) is recited by the chief celebrant or sponsor. In the case of installing images or making niches, a hymn addressing the deity represented was probably recited. I should

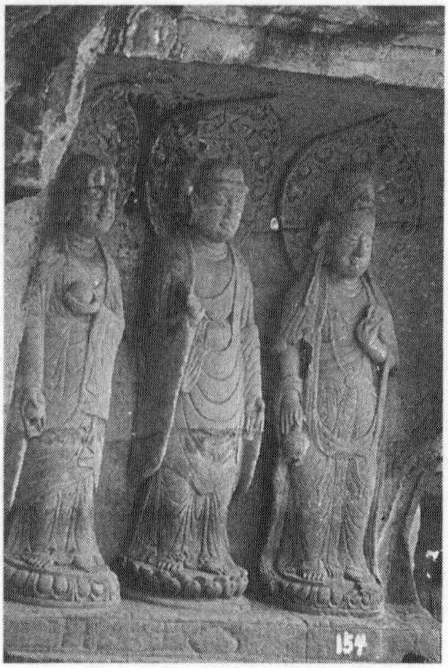

FIGURE 18. Amitābha, Dizang, and Guanyin. Qianfo ya niche 154, Jiajiang, Sichuan.

[ ] the [ ] [ ] of Chang[zhou], General [ ] [ ] and [Acting] Censor-in-Chief to be [ ] [ ] for making offerings.[66]

Niche 53, dating to 915, has the following pair of inscriptions on the left and right sides of the niche, respectively:

> Respectfully, the Officer on the Left and General of the Number Three Military Superior Prefecture, Zhong Shenneng 種審能, made an [image of] Dizang Bodhisattva. He made the above piece for his deceased son Xiyan 希言, who was wounded and vanquished by bandits, in the hope that the merit of making the above [image] will enable [the deceased] to be reborn in the Western Paradise, meet the Buddha, and listen to the teachings. On the fourth day of the fourth month in the fifth year of the *yongping* 永平 reign era (915), the seven [vegetarian] feasts had been set up and hymns recited to conclude [the merit]. [The image is to] receive everlasting offerings.
>
> [An image of] Guanyin Bodhisattva has been respectfully made so that Yanyan 鄢鹽 may enjoy everlasting peace and freedom from calamities.[67] It is also tranquilly made for our son's teacher, Qi Chouhu 乞丑胡 [?]. [An image of]

thank Daniel Stevenson for sharing his insights on the ritual procedure. For hymns to the dead, see Teiser 1992.

66. Guo 1999a: 14, inscription text 6.

67. From the context, Yanyan is most likely located somewhere in Sichuan, but I have not been able to identify its exact location. Beishan was originally the site of a fortress, so it is likely the son was killed in a battle against rebels. The inscription refers to "brigands," but it should be remembered that rebels were often called "brigands." More significantly, in the widespread political chaos of the Five Dynasties (907–960), China saw the rise of those from the lowest strata of society to military and political power. Wang Qian, a former brigand who

> Amitābha Buddha is also respectfully forged. May the fourth month from the beginning to the end be prosperous and this disciple, Zhong Shenneng, receive blessings.[68] On the sixth day of the seventh month of the fifth year of *yongping*, a vegetarian feast was hosted and hymns recited to conclude [the merit].[69]

This dedicatory inscription utilizes Pure Land motifs that also occur in the longer version of the *Scripture on the Bodhisattva Dizang*: transformatory rebirth (on a lotus), meeting the Buddha Amitābha, and listening to his preaching.[70] Evidently, its exhortation to venerate Dizang as a means to achieve rebirth in the Pure Land was heeded in medieval religious practice. The inscription attests to the common understanding of Pure Land as a generic goal for rebirth in Tang China, and the veneration of deities other than Amitābha as a viable means of securing that goal.[71] Moreover, Beishan Fowan's inscriptions, especially those dating to the tenth century, suggest that sponsors of Buddhist images often liturgically concluded the merit of making images by hosting vegetarian feasts and reciting hymns. It may also be discerned from other Sichuan sites that these practices mirror broader patterns of ritual observed in conjunction with building cave temple sculpture. A close study on image-making and associated rituals in late medieval China must be conducted separately. But from the above comparison of Longmen and Fowan inscriptions, it seems that ritual abstinence from eating meat (i.e., vegetarian feasts) was practiced regularly with image-making only in the late medieval period. This was perhaps in part catalyzed by the rapid ascendancy of the cult of the Ten Kings, which I will discuss later.

The Pure Land connection is also evident in Dunhuang paintings and dedicatory inscriptions. Especially interesting is the dedication of one Dunhuang donor by the name of Kang Qingnu 康清奴, who commissioned a silk painting of a hooded Dizang presiding over the paths of rebirth (Stein painting 9):

> The commissioner of the painting was the disciple of pure faith Kang Qingnu. His body resides in the house of fire and he is apprehensive about falling into the five paths [of rebirth]. Disaster and fortune are inconstant; his heart yearns toward emancipation [from *saṃsāra*]. . . . On account of the merit may [Dizang's] golden staff quake until lotuses manifest in hell, and may [Dizang's] radiant gem illuminate the paths of delusion until they resemble the Pure Land. Also may his relations by marriage and immediate family both rest in

---

gained power while in the military, carved out a kingdom for himself in Sichuan. The Wang brothers who were to reign in Fujian 福建 (southeast China) were former Henan bandits.

68. The inscription reads *si yue* 四月, which I have translated as "fourth month." It is unclear from the inscription why the donor should call attention to this month.

69. Guo 1999a: 17, inscription text 18.

70. For previous discussion on this topic, see Chapter 4.

71. This phenomenon was already evident in the fifth and sixth centuries, especially in inscriptional records; see Hou 1998: 150–248.

> health and peace, and may his brothers and cousins together partake of the portion of merits. This inscription was written on the twenty-second day of the fifth month, the fourth year of the *jianlong* 建隆 reign era (963).[72]

The motif of lotus buds spontaneously springing up in hell, as well as the transformation of hell into Pure Land, is strongly reminiscent of the *Scripture on the Bodhisattva Dizang*, which explains the genesis of Dizang's role in hell and elaborates his ties with the Pure Land.

The last example for discussion is another tenth-century Dunhuang painting on hemp cloth (EO 3580) portraying Amitābha and Dizang.[73] The upper portion of the painting shows a wooden balustraded platform built over a pool and presided over by a buddha (probably Amitābha) and a number of his retinue, including heavenly musicians. In the lower section, a hooded Dizang sits, one leg pendant and the six paths of rebirth emanating from his nimbus. He is attended by his retinue and the Ten Kings of purgatory. A bridge spans the pool, thereby linking these scenes of paradise and the underworld. Again this Dunhuang painting visually renders the striking polarity between the two afterlife destinies highlighted in the *Scripture on the Bodhisattva Dizang*. In the medieval religious imagination, Dizang was recognized as the passport in the afterlife passage from hell to Pure Land.

Among the materials considered, the two Dunhuang pieces, which reflect themes from the *Scripture on the Bodhisattva Dizang*, are both dated to the tenth century, whereas the integration of Dizang into the Amitābha triad is an earlier iconography from the seventh century. The relationship between Dizang and Pure Land may be traced to cultic practice in which Dizang was venerated alongside Amitābha, Guanyin, and, to a lesser extent, Mahāsthāmaprāpta, all of whom were by then regarded as core members of the Pure Land pantheon. Inscriptions and art reflect a range of permutations through which Dizang was incorporated into Pure Land iconography. For instance, it was common practice to displace Mahāsthāmaprāpta with Dizang, probably because the latter was more widely venerated and was already evolving a more distinctive personality and iconography. Other representations portray him as an addition to the Amitābha triad. An inscription located between niches 15 and 17 at Yaowang shan in Shaanxi records the carving of a quartet during the late Tang in which Dizang was added to the triad of Amitābha, Guanyin, and Mahāsthāmaprāpta.[74] Such permutations of deities indicate the amorphous nature and lack of rigorous stratification in medieval Pure Land. Moreover, dedicatory inscriptions suggest that the worship of Dizang was then regarded as one way to ensure rebirth in the Pure Land

72. For the inscription text, see Waley 1931: 33; Whitfield 1982–1985: 2.318.

73. See Giès 1995: 2, pl. 66.

74. An inscription outside niches 15–17 has been dated to the late Tang period (Zhang and Wang 1994: 16). It reads: 阿彌陀像一區，大勢至菩薩、觀世音菩薩／京兆府□□孫□□地藏，造阿彌陀佛一鋪。

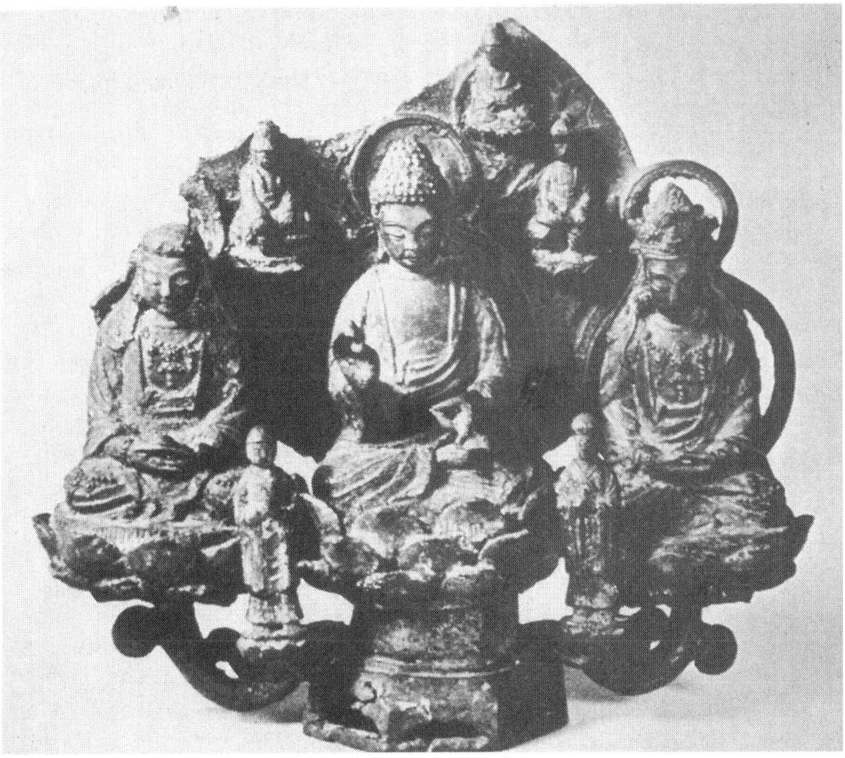

FIGURE 19. Gilded bronze sculpture. Dongkuk University Museum Collection, Seoul, Korea. Photograph courtesy of Jaejung Lee.

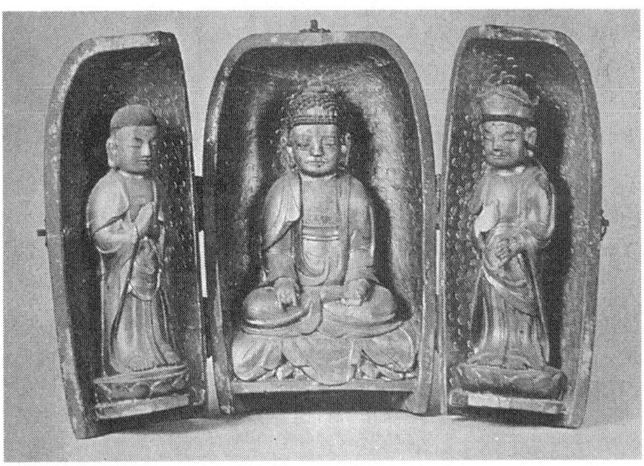

FIGURE 20. Portable wooden shrine. Dongkuk University Museum Collection, Seoul, Korea. Photograph courtesy of Jaejung Lee.

and incorporate imagery like the concept of transformational rebirth, meeting the Buddha, and hearing the Dharma in the Pure Land.

The inclusion of Dizang in Amitābha triads, an iconography evident at Longmen from the late seventh century, persisted into the tenth century. This triadic configuration appears elsewhere in East Asia. In a study of Jizō art, Matsushima Gen calls attention to several Kamakura paintings and sculptures of Amitābha flanked by Jizō (Dizang) and Kannon (Guanyin).[75] Examples are found in Korea, usually dating to the Chosŏn era (1392–1910) but sometimes as early as the Koryŏ period (918–1392). A Koryŏ color silk painting, now preserved in the Hoam Art Museum in Yong'in-gun, Kyŏnggi province, highlights an Amitābha triad (Amitābha, Kṣitigarbha, and Avalokiteśvara) in the act of welcoming a dying devotee.[76] Moreover, the art historian Pak Young-sook argues that another Koryŏ painting of Amitābha and Chijang (Dizang) in the New York Metropolitan Museum of Art may originally have been part of a three-panel screen that included Avalokiteśvara.[77] Sculptural representations of Amitābha with Chijang, largely from the Chosŏn period, have been preserved, including an exquisite bronze sculpture now in the Cleveland Museum of Art.[78] In Seoul, the Dongkuk University Museum contains two Chosŏn examples of triads: a gilded bronze sculpture and a three-panel portable wooden shrine (see Figures 19 and 20).[79] Most interesting of all is perhaps a mural painting of the triad, dated to 1476, in the Paradise Hall in the Monastery of Non-Action (Muwi-sa 無為寺) in Kangjin, Chonnam Province.[80] Evidently, this form of Amitābha triad circulated as a cross-cultural strand of religious devotion in Buddhist East Asia.

Glimpses of a Bhaiṣajyaguru Connection?

Dizang and Bhaiṣajyaguru (Yaoshi fo 藥師佛, the Healing Buddha) are also represented together in art and epigraphy, but their association is not mentioned in Buddhist literature. It has largely been neglected because of limited textual and visual evidence. The problem is further complicated by the paucity of collaborating inscriptions.[81] Although an examination of the ma-

75. Matsushima 1986: 33, pl. 49.

76. For a photo reproduction, see Ahn 1986: 48, pl. 9.

77. Pak 1998: 402–449. It has been discovered that Amitābha and Chijang were on separate pieces of silk that were later mounted together. According to Pak, the two might have been "originally part of a set of three hanging scrolls, along with a now lost representation of Avalokiteśvara [Guanyin] flanking Amitābha on the other side." Pak argues that, whatever the original configuration of the paintings, devotees in the Koryŏ period would have immediately understood the intrinsic iconological significance of portraying Dizang with Amitābha.

78. Cleveland Museum of Art, slide order no. 18.501.

79. Thanks are due to Jaejung Lee for generously sharing his collection of pictures with me.

80. A gilded sculpture of the triad sits before the painting. See Moon 1984, pl. 27.

81. On the possible relationship between the two cults, see Wang-Toutain 1998: 303–305. Wang-Toutain's survey was limited to what was available in other publications, and she omits discussing the Bhaiṣajyaguru tableaux of Beishan, niches 279 and 281.

terial often results in more questions than answers, a relationship did in fact exist between the medieval cults of Dizang and Bhaiṣajyaguru.

If identification by the Dunhuang Research Academy is accurate, the earliest vestiges of the connection between these two Buddhist deities are the Tang murals at the Mogao Grottoes. According to the Academy, grottoes 166, 176, 205, and 444 contain evidence of Dizang and Bhaiṣajyaguru.[82] In grotto 166, Dizang and Bhaiṣajyaguru complement each other. To the north of the eastern doorway of the same cave is a painting that brings together Dizang, Amitābha Buddha, Bhaiṣajyaguru Buddha, Prabhūtaratna Buddha, and fourteen other buddhas.[83] On the northern wall of grotto 176, Bhaiṣajyaguru is flanked by either Dizang or Guanyin with the thousand buddhas in the background.[84] A similar triad appears on the southern wall of grotto 205, immediately beneath a larger mural of Amitābha's Land of Bliss.[85] In grotto 205, Bhaiṣajyaguru holds a staff and alms bowl while Dizang is portrayed as a monk and Guanyin is dressed in princely robes (see Figures 21 and 22). Finally, above the western doorway of cave 444 is a partially damaged mural pairing Dizang with Bhaiṣajyaguru.[86]

Executed primarily during the mid-Tang period, this small assortment of Dunhuang paintings indicates that Dizang and Bhaiṣajyaguru were shown together usually to enhance an important scene—just as miniature buddhas were often employed to augment Dunhuang murals. (Dizang and Bhaiṣajyaguru frequently appear together with multiple buddhas.) The other iconography assigns Dizang and Guanyin as chief attendant bodhisattvas to Bhaiṣajyaguru, patterned after the Amitābha triads previously discussed. No textual source exists for Bhaiṣajyaguru triads in which Dizang is highlighted as one of the attendant bodhisattvas, but grotto 205 may hold a clue to this triad. The Bhaiṣajyaguru triad in this cave, as already pointed out, is immediately below a larger rendition of the Amitābha entourage. In early Indian Mahāyāna, the Bhaiṣajyaguru cult was one of several expressions of Pure Land—not only because Bhaiṣajyaguru presides over a Pure Land, the Lapis Lazuli Realm (*liuli shijie* 琉璃世界) in the east, but also, according to the *Bhaiṣajyaguru-sūtra* (*Yaoshi jing* 藥師經, Scripture on the Healing Buddha), adherents to Bhaiṣajyaguru worship could aspire to rebirth in Amitābha's land, Sukhāvatī.[87] Given the Pure Land overtones of the Bhaiṣajyaguru cult and

82. The identifications are given in Dunhuang yanjiuyuan 1996.

83. Ibid.: 66.

84. Ibid.: 70.

85. Ibid.: 82. For a photo reproduction of this triad, see Duan 1990b: 17, fig. 50.

86. Dunhuang yanjiuyuan 1996: 183.

87. Several Chinese translations of the *Scripture on the Healing Buddha* exist; for a study with English translations, see Birnbaum 1979. The *Yaoshi liuliguang rulai benyuan gongde jing* 藥師琉璃光如來本願功德經, translated by Xuanzang in 650, states: "As for those desiring to be reborn in Amitābha Tathāgata's abode, the Western Land of Supreme Bliss, on account of hearing the name of this World-Honored Healing Teacher, the Lapis Lazuli Radiance Tathāgata's name, at the time of dying, the eight bodhisattvas will ascend into the sky to show the way, so that they will be spontaneously reborn in multicolored jeweled flowers in

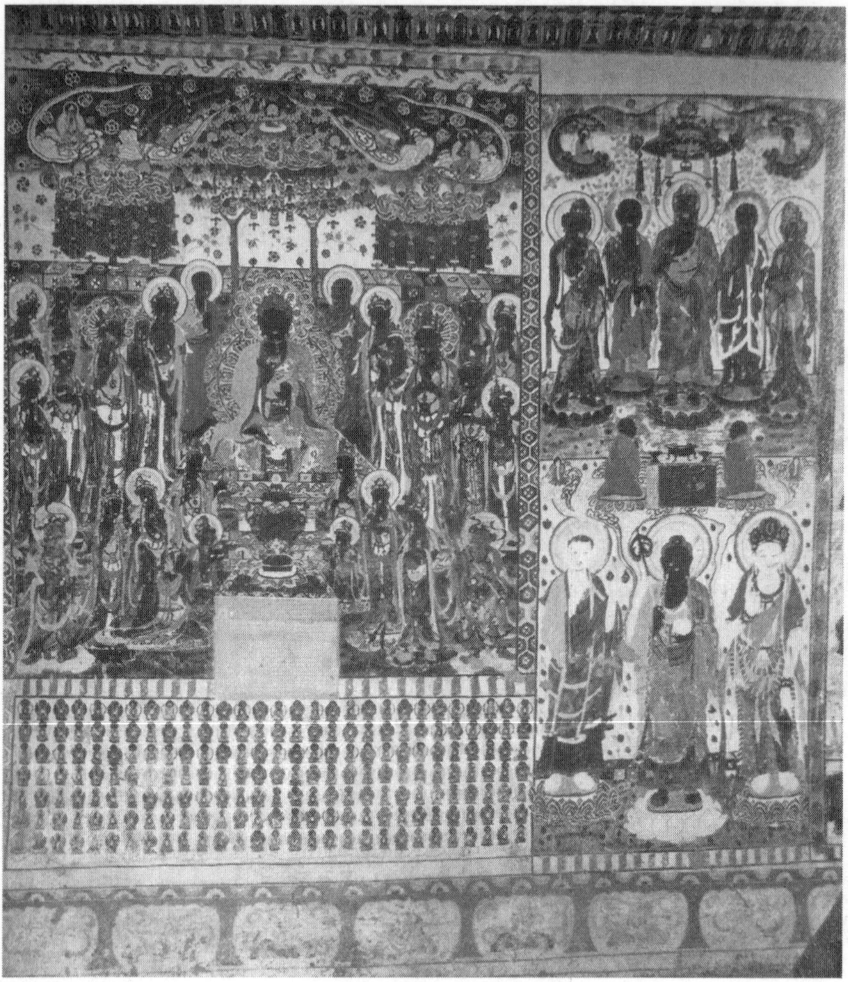

FIGURE 21. Bhaiṣajyaguru, Dizang, and Guanyin. Southern wall, Mogao grotto 205, Dunhuang, Gansu. Photograph courtesy of Wang Huimin.

the popularity of Dizang and Guanyin, artisans may have seen fit to modify the Bhaiṣajyaguru's entourage by replacing his attendant bodhisattvas—usually designated in texts as Candraprabha (Yueguang 月光, Moonlight) and Sūryagarbha (Riguang 日光, Sunlight)—with the more widely known Dizang and Guanyin, after the fashion of the Amitābha triads.[88] Chinese art histori-

---

the [Western Paradise]" (T450:14.406b). Cf. *Foshuo Yaoshi rulai benyuan jing* 佛說藥師如來本願經, T449:14.402c; *Yaoshi liuliguang qifo benyuan gongde jing* 藥師琉璃光七佛本願功德經, T451:14.414b. This promise of rebirth in the Western Paradise is also found in the Gilgit manuscripts of the scripture; see Schopen 1977: 177–210.

88. The *Scripture on the Healing Buddha* designates Candraprabha and Sūryagarbha as Bhaiṣajyaguru's chief attendant bodhisattvas; see, for example, *Foshuo Yaoshi rulai benyuan*

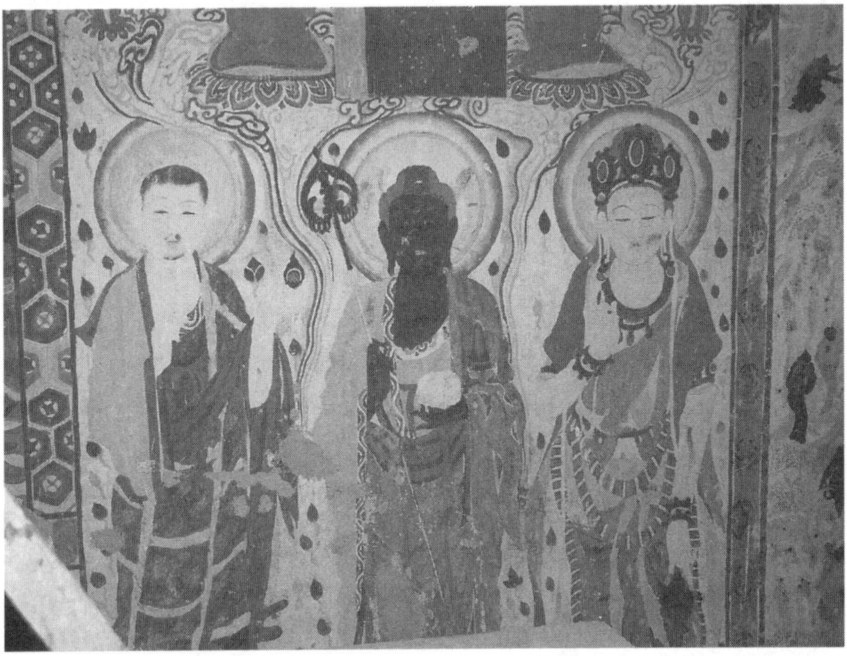

FIGURE 22. Bhaiṣajyaguru, Dizang, and Guanyin, close-up. Southern wall, Mogao grotto 205, Dunhuang, Gansu. Photograph courtesy of Wang Huimin.

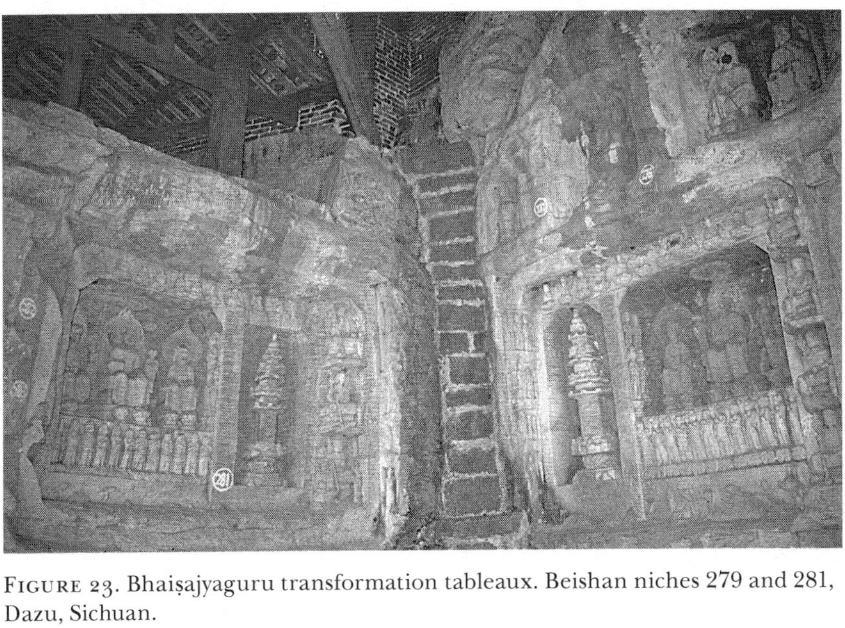

FIGURE 23. Bhaiṣajyaguru transformation tableaux. Beishan niches 279 and 281, Dazu, Sichuan.

ans of the Sichuan Academy discovered this form of Bhaiṣajyaguru triad at Sichuan sites but, like the Dunhuang paintings, these examples are problematic because they lack corroborating inscriptions to confirm identities.[89]

However, Beishan Fowan has yielded two salient examples (niches 279 and 281) with inscriptions that link Bhaiṣajyaguru and Dizang, as well as Amitābha, in local cultic practices.[90] Built in consecutive years during the mid-tenth century, the two niches mirror each to the point that it is evident they were intentionally conceptualized as a pair (see Figure 23).[91]

Niche 281, the earlier of the two dating to 954, contains the following dedicatory inscription:

> Reverently [we have commissioned] the sculpting of the Buddha of Healing and Lapis Lazuli Radiance (Yaoshi liuliguang fo 藥師琉璃光佛), the eight bodhisattvas, a group of twelve spirit kings (*shen wang* 神王), as well as the seven buddhas, the buddhas of the three times, Amitābha Buddha, a pillar of the *Buddhoṣṇīṣa-vijaya-dhāraṇī* (Buddha's Topknot Victorious Dhāraṇī), and also three figurines of Dizang Bodhisattva, all [placed] in a single niche. The honorable disciple and Township-Chief Administer on the Right Liu Gong 劉恭 and his aunt née Ren, sons and daughters, first and second wives, and

---

jing, T449:14.402a; *Yaoshi liuliguang rulai benyuan gongde jing*, T450:14.405c; *Yaoshi liuliguang qifo benyuan gongde jing*, T451:14.413c. For triads of Yakushi (Bhaiṣajyaguru) flanked by Jizō and Kannon in Japan, see Fowler 2000–2001. On the emergence of Candraprabha and his messianic implications, see Zürcher 1981, 1982b.

89. According to the Sichuan Academy, one of the numerous niches at Guangyuan Qianfo ya is said to contain a triad consisting of an image of Bhaiṣajyaguru Buddha holding a staff, flanked by Dizang in monastic robes and Guanyin holding a vase and staff; see Liu, Hu, and Li 1985: 385–386. Chinese scholars have identified at least two other sculptures from Dazu in which Dizang, with Guanyin, is portrayed as a member of Bhaiṣajyaguru's entourage. One example is from Beishan Fowan, niche 110 (no date), and the other is from Shimen shan 石門山, niche 1, in Dazu county, dated by inscription to 1151. In both cases, the main deity is Bhaiṣajyaguru; his retinue, the twelve *yakṣa* generals, is present somewhere in the representation. The Bhaiṣajyaguru statue is flanked by a mendicant carrying a staff (identified as Dizang) and another bodhisattva said to be Guanyin. However, the accompanying inscriptions lack names for the attendant bodhisattvas. For instance, the inscription at Shimen shan, niche 1, records:

> Having set up this single niche of the Healing Buddha, I pray and beg for peace and happiness in this very existence and to be reborn in a heavenly world. Life after life, may the retributions of my merits be inexhaustible. It is the twentieth day of the eleventh month in the *xinwei* year of the *shaoxin* reign era. [The image is] carved by the sculptor Jian Zhongjin and [the dedication is] written by the abbot Wen Daosheng. (Liu, Hu, and Li 1985: 541)

Obviously the inscription does not identify either Dizang or Guanyin.

90. Françoise Wang-Toutain, one of the first to call attention to this forgotten connection between Bhaiṣajyaguru and Dizang, overlooked these sources in her account (1998: 303–305).

91. See also Figures 23 and 24 of this study. Both of these photographs of Dazu Beishan niches 279 and 281 were taken in the summer of 1997 during a field trip to Sichuan. For an early picture of niche 279, see Bai 1985, pl. 37. Detailed descriptions of the two niches are given in Liu, Hu, and Li 1985: 425–427; cf. Hu 1994: 264–265.

> sons Renshou 仁壽, Renfu 仁福, and Renlu 仁祿, together have aspired to forge the aforementioned images for merits. Today, moreover we form a circle to prostrate and pray that our bodies be at ease, we may have longevity and prosperity, our family may have health, peace, high offices, and prosperous ranks, and our deceased distant ancestors may have mutual benefits and goodness. On the seventeenth year of the *guangzheng* 廣政 reign era (954), the fifty-first day of Jupiter's second month, the eleventh day of the forty-third new moon, we have completed hosting a vegetarian feast and reciting a hymn. May [the images] forever be looked on with reverence![92]

Niche 281's iconography is distributed vertically into three registers: the first register to the right is an octagonal pillar intricately engraved and inscribed with the *Dhāraṇī-sūtra* (*Tuoluoni jing chuang* 陀羅尼經幢).[93] The middle register is the main niche, which portrays a partially damaged Buddha Bhaiṣajyaguru, sitting with legs pendant, accompanied on either side by an attending bodhisattva with the eight great bodhisattvas on the niche's walls and the twelve *yakṣa* generals grouped on the wall just below the niche.[94] These deities are all prominent members of the Bhaiṣajyaguru assembly in the *Scripture on the Healing Buddha*, so one can assume that this scripture inspired and shaped niche 281. The third register to the left comprises a column of three Dizang statues, all seated with one leg pendant, flanked by a standing attendant at each side. Each Dizang wears a hood and holds in his hands a staff and a wish-granting jewel.[95] The *Scripture on the Healing Buddha* cannot account for Dizang's presence in this sculpture. Miniature buddha images line the top of the niche: The buddhas of the three times are above the pillar column, the seven buddhas are above the Bhaiṣajyaguru tableau, and Amitābha Buddha is sculpted between the two subsets of multiple buddha cults (see Figure 24).

A year later, in 955, a local official named Wang Chengxiu 王承秀 and his wife sponsored another engraving (niche 279) on the adjacent cliff wall. It was deliberately modeled after niche 281, so the two visibly form a pair.[96] A partially effaced inscription tells of the circumstances under which the niche was built:

---

92. Guo 1999a: 20, inscription text 25.1.

93. The niche contains an inscription recording the pillar's refurbishing in 1005; see Guo 1999a: 73, text inscription 4. Pillars inscribed with the *Dhāraṇī-sūtra* were widespread in Sichuan during the late Tang and Five Dynasties periods. See Hu 1994: 264; Liu Shu-fen 1996, 1997.

94. As previously noted, in the *Scripture on the Healing Buddha*, the eight bodhisattvas are the otherworldly guides who come to welcome the dying devotee who has venerated Bhaiṣajyaguru to the Western Paradise. The twelve *yakṣa* generals are protective spirits who assist those who worship Bhaiṣajyaguru. They may be related to the twelve astrological houses and the twelve time periods (two hours each) that make up the day as understood in China and Japan; see Birnbaum 1979: 82.

95. It appears that the jewels have eroded completely over the years; see Figure 24.

96. Niche 279's pillar column and Bhaiṣajyaguru tableau are on different sides of niche 281; it also contains four Dizang images, one more than the number found in niche 281.

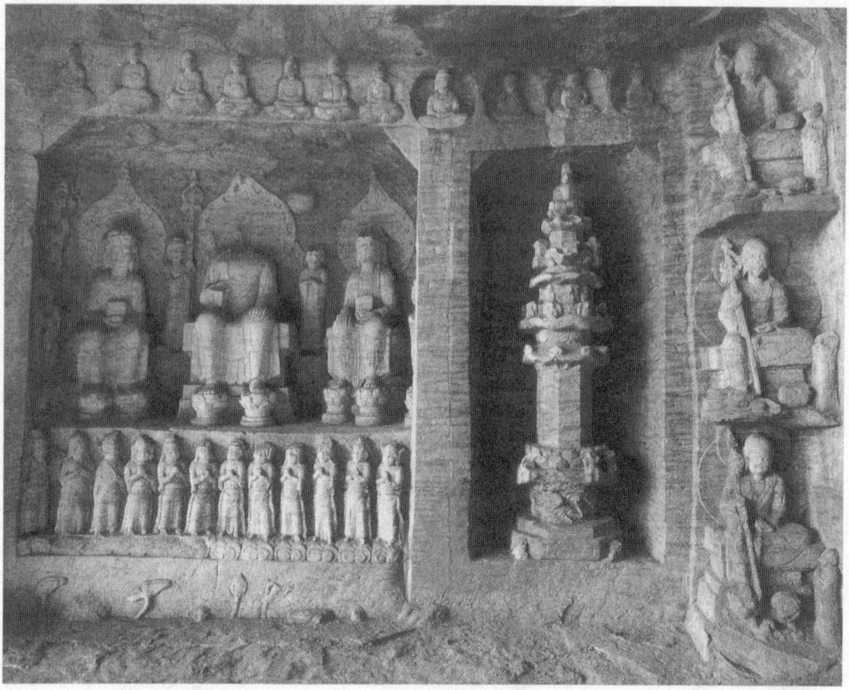

FIGURE 24. Bhaiṣajyaguru transformation tableaux and three Dizangs. Beishan niche 281, Dazu, Sichuan.

> Seeking liberation, the disciple and Official of the Reception Office and Column Leader Wang Chengxiu and his wife, the female disciple Zhang 張, [have commissioned the statues] of [Bhaiṣajyaguru Buddha's] entourage, the buddhas of the ten directions, Amitābha Buddha, a pillar of the *Buddha's Topknot Victorious Dhāraṇī*, and four Dizang Bodhisattva images, all together in one buddha niche.[97] Née Bao 保 has aspired to recite the one-scroll *Scripture on the Healing Buddha* and has further donated money to adorn this niche together with née Shao 劭, who has aspired to forge the above images [ ] [ ] it is now accomplished. We pray for wealth and longevity and for the family to avert difficulties and obstacles [ ] [ ] to have integrity and fortune in public and private [life]. On the twenty-fourth day of the second month of the eighteenth year of the *guangzheng* reign era (995), a vegetarian feast was hosted and the merit [dedication] recited, with the wish that the Bao family flourish and prosper.[98] May Mrs. Bao have good health, her sons be wealthy, [ ] [ ] [ ] [ ] wife [ ] [ ] née Li 李 and née Zhou 周, the second and fourth daughters [ ] [ ] [ ] [ ] and son-in-law, Yu Cheng-

97. Another inscription in the pillar niche states that the pillar was decorated in 999; see Guo 1999a: 72, text inscription 2.

98. The inscription reads *biao de* 表德, which refers to the reciting of a formal dedication of the images at the time the niche was ritually consecrated.

> jiang 于承江, and his sons, Wuxiang 五香, Erxiang 二香, and Sanxiang 三香, and daughter, Xiaoxiu 肖休, be free from disasters. On the eighteenth day of the fourth month of the fourth year of the *xianping* 咸平 reign era (1001), banners were suspended, a vegetarian feast was hosted, and a formal declaration made.[99] Recorded by Official of the Reception Office and Column Leader Wang Chengxiu.[100]

The relationships among the donors are unclear, but it can be assumed that niche 279 belonged to a family, perhaps an extended family given the varying last names. From the inscription, it appears that at least one female donor addressed cultic practices to Bhaiṣajyaguru in her daily life. Although it is unclear why this tenth-century woman chose this scripture as her devotional focus, one can conclude that for née Bao and other local donors, Bhaiṣajyaguru worship had naturally merged with and subsumed an array of cults like those of the multiple buddhas, Amitābha Buddha, Dizang, and the *Buddhoṣṇīṣa Dhāraṇī*. The niche's contents prompt us to ask: Why was a column of Dizang images installed on the right side? What relationship does Dizang Bodhisattva have with the cultic practice inspired by the *Scripture on the Healing Buddha?*

If one relies solely on the scripture to understand the niche's visual imagery, Dizang's presence here would seem baffling. But clues to this local cultic practice lie in the two deities' iconographies and functions. As a buddha, Bhaiṣajyaguru dons a monk's robes as does Dizang, and although Bhaiṣajyaguru is usually depicted carrying an alms bowl, he sometimes carries the staff and wish-granting jewel more commonly associated with Dizang.[101] Although the two figures are easily confused, they can usually be distinguished by the absence or presence of a protuberance on the head (Ch. *rouji* 肉髻; Skt. *uṣṇīṣa*), which, respectively, signifies bodhisattva or buddha status. The connection between these two figures, moreover, extends to religious function. The *Scripture on the Healing Buddha* associates Bhaiṣajyaguru with averting untimely death, curing life-threatening ailments, extending the life span, and preparing for death—functions usually associated with savior bodhisattvas like Guanyin and Dizang. (In particular, the *Scripture on the Healing Buddha*'s rites for curing fatal illness

---

99. Evidently, six years after making the niches, the donor family sponsored another vegetarian banquet in connection with the performance of a ritual confession at the site; the reason for this event is not recorded.

100. Guo 1999a: 21, text inscription 27.1.

101. An example of Bhaiṣajyaguru with a staff is in Beishan Fowan niche 147, which contains a seated buddha flanked by bodhisattvas holding either a sun or a moon disc. One of the two standing attendants holds the Buddha's staff. On the wall beneath the niche are sculpted the twelve *yakṣa* generals; see Guo 1999b: vol. 1, 147, pl. 158. Although there is no inscription, the imagery is clearly derived from the *Scripture on the Healing Buddha*, which leads one to conclude that the buddha is Bhaiṣajyaguru. Another example is at Shuining si 水寧寺 in Bazhong, where the center buddha holds a staff and jewel in his hands; for a photo reproduction, see Liu 1999b: 154.

and preparing for a good death and a paradisal afterlife resonate with the *Scripture on the Past Vows.*) From the inscriptions we know that local officials constructed both tableaux for the welfare of immediate and extended family members in this life and the one to come. The dedicatory prayers state their hopes for success and prosperity, blessings and peace, health and longevity, and, according to niche 281's inscription, a good rebirth for dead ancestors. In light of the iconographic and functional parallels, it is not surprising that the local community at Beishan seems to have linked Dizang and Bhaiṣajyaguru in their cultic behavior. Perhaps the significance of these two niches lies not so much in their aligning Dizang with Bhaiṣajyaguru, but in their incorporating local cultic expressions that resisted convenient categorization into discrete sects circumscribed by a deity's identity, function, even iconography. The tenth-century Buddhists at Beishan seem to have regarded the *dhāraṇī*, Bhaiṣajyaguru, Dizang, and Pure Land cults as sources of religious techniques that complemented one another to form a single cultic expression to combat the exigencies of life, particularly sickness, demon troubles, and calamities, while conferring blessings for a good life on this earth and expediting the dead to a paradisal afterlife. The multiple buddhas lining the top of the niches would then serve to communicate the desire for such an afterlife—a visual counterpart to verbalizing the desire for rebirth in the Pure Land, understood in a general manner as "happy destination" or "paradise."

A Ray of Light in the Ten Kings' Dark Courts

In tenth-century China, it was commonly held that the deceased would be brought for judgment to the courts of the Ten Kings before proceeding to the next life. Cultic practices associated with the Ten Kings included a set of preparatory and memorial rites such as abstaining from eating meat, which the family performed on behalf of the deceased.[102] As Stephen Teiser has suggested, in Chinese religious history the Ten Kings function as the equivalent to the western concept of purgatory, serving as a composite vehicle for ritual confession and penance on the one hand and bureaucratic negotiation on the other. The late medieval amalgamation of Dizang and the Ten Kings constituted a lasting cardinal change that would dominate East Asian imaginings of the passage from death to rebirth for the next thousand

102. On the cult to the Ten Kings in China, see Teiser 1994; Du 1995; Ledderose 2000. The ten memorial rites associated with the Ten Kings evolved from the widespread observance of the seven-seven rites (*qiqi* 七七). These were originally formulated to coincide with the forty-nine-day interval during which the dead waited before being reborn. It was believed that at this time merits accrued on behalf of the deceased could significantly improve his or her chances for a good rebirth. The weekly rites included abstaining from eating meat, known as seven-seven feasts (*qiqi zhai* 七七齋). These feasts were actually communal vegetarian banquets sponsored by a donor in memory of the deceased and to procure merit on his or her behalf.

years.[103] Scriptural sources furnish little documentation on the connection between the two cults, but there is substantial evidence of this in Buddhist art from areas on China's western borders.[104] The numerous illustrations of Dizang and the Ten Kings found in Dunhuang art, mostly dated to no earlier than the tenth century, are well known to modern scholars.[105] Recently, Sichuan sites have yielded important examples of Dizang and the Ten Kings, which often capture themes absent in the Dunhuang material.[106]

Early vestiges of Dizang attended by the Ten Kings are present in Sichuan art and epigraphy. Niche 85 at Zizhong 資中 may be the earliest datable representation.[107] An inscription confirms the Ten Kings' identity and dates the restoration of the niche to 898–901.

> After completing the vegetarian feast and [recitation of] the celebratory eulogy that were performed to repay kindnesses, the head sponsor of the vegetarian feast, the disciple Liu 劉 [ ] [ ] [prays]: May the merit of [making] the above image universally benefit the four [objects] of gratitude and the three directions, as well as the living beings of the dharma realm, and may all together partake of this blessing.[108] During the [ ] year of *guanghua* 光化 (899–901) [ ] [ ] Yundeng 雲登 and other donors of Zhongsheng 忠勝 village repaired and installed the Ten Kings images right in this cloister and hosted a vegetarian feast to repay kindnesses.[109]

Again epigraphy records the hosting of vegetarian feasts to conclude the making of images.

Another example of Dizang and the Ten Kings is located in Guangyuan: In the south wall of the Grottoes of Numerous Treasures (Duobao ku 多寶窟) on the Qianfo ya, there is a Dizang sculpture, clad in a *kāṣāya* robe and sitting with one leg pendant, flanked by five miniature figurines standing on auspicious clouds. The figurines have been identified as the Ten Kings, and the niche has been dated to the Tang.[110] More intricate motifs were gradually woven into the Sichuan iconography. Dated to the tenth century, Beishan

103. Sørenson 1996: 118. In Korean Buddhist art, Dizang is frequently represented in the company of the Ten Kings; see Pak 1977, 1995.

104. The *Scripture on the Ten Kings* contains only sporadic reference to Dizang. In Stephen Teiser's translation of the scripture, based on tenth-century manuscripts, Dizang appears only once, as a member of an entourage of six bodhisattvas who arrive at an assembly to praise the Buddha; see Teiser 1994: 204–205.

105. For studies on Dizang and the Ten Kings in Dunhuang art, see Luo 1993; Luo Shiping 1998; Kawahara 1974; Matsumoto 1922; Pan 1998.

106. For studies on Dizang and the Ten Kings in Sichuan art, see Chen Mingguang 2002; Kucera 1995.

107. The niche is located on the western cliff; see Ding 1988: 53.

108. The four objects of gratitude are the Buddha (*fo en* 佛恩), parents (*fumu en* 父母恩), teachers (*shi en* 師恩), and the nation (*guo en* 國恩).

109. For the text inscription, see Ding 1988: 53.

110. Ma and Ding 1990: 15 and pl. 2. Also see Yao 2002.

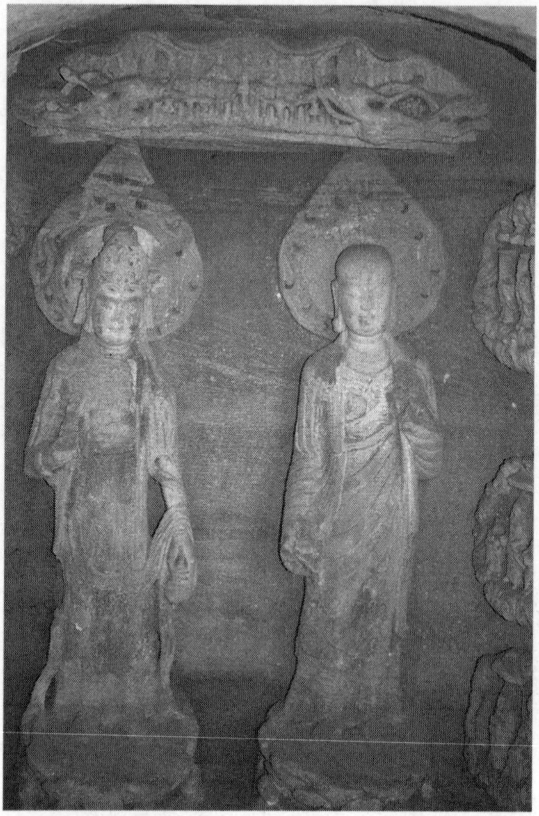

FIGURE 25. Dizang and Guanyin. Beishan niche 253, Dazu, Sichuan.

niche 253 preserves an elegant engraving of Dizang and Guanyin with pairs of small figures in various postures (praying, horse-riding, standing) chiseled on the side walls. These figures have been identified as the Ten Kings and their messenger officials.[111] An inscription outside the niche records the donors hosting a vegetarian feast in 1001 (see Figures 25, 26, and 27). This Sichuan iconography differs conspicuously from other tenth-century representations that have survived at Dunhuang, where the Ten Kings appear comparable in size and detail to the other figures.

In another depiction dated prior to 1096 and located in niche 9 of the Stone Seal Mountain (Shizhuan shan 石篆山) in Dazu, Dizang is accompanied by the Ten Kings, five on each side with seven attendants behind them (see Figure 28).[112] It is at Anyue that sculptural representation of Dizang and the Ten Kings incorporates portrayals of hell. In a pair of niches, numbers 60 (84) and 56 (80) in the Grottoes of Perfected Awakening (Yuanjue dong 圓覺洞) (see Figure 29), dated no later than 934–965, new elements

111. Liu, Hu, and Li 1985: 421.

112. No exact date is available. My estimate is based on the inscriptional data in ibid.: 421. Also see Hu and Chen 1998a: 46–47 and fig. 9.

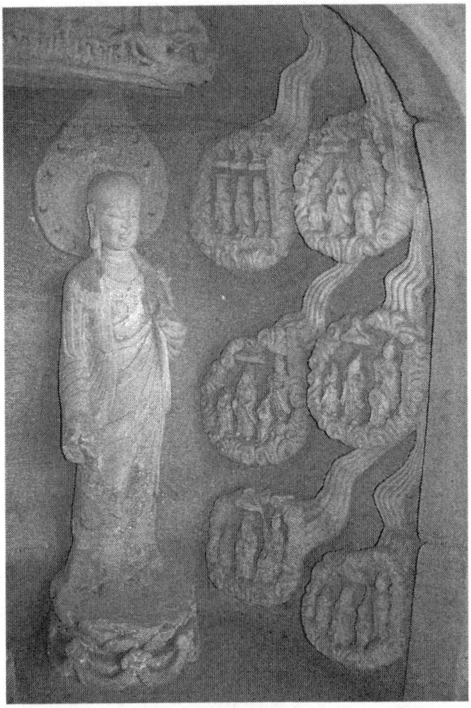

FIGURE 26. Dizang. Beishan niche 253, Dazu, Sichuan.

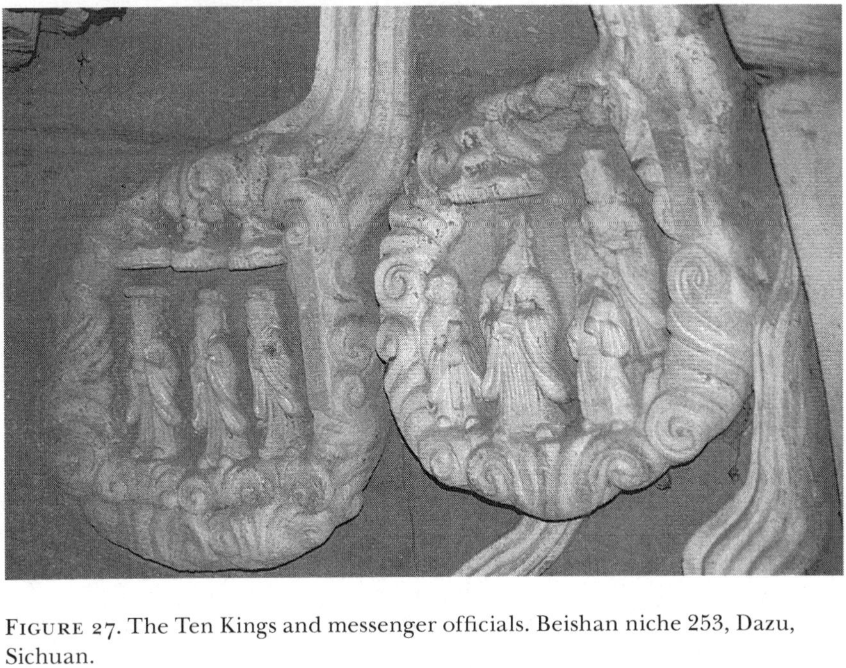

FIGURE 27. The Ten Kings and messenger officials. Beishan niche 253, Dazu, Sichuan.

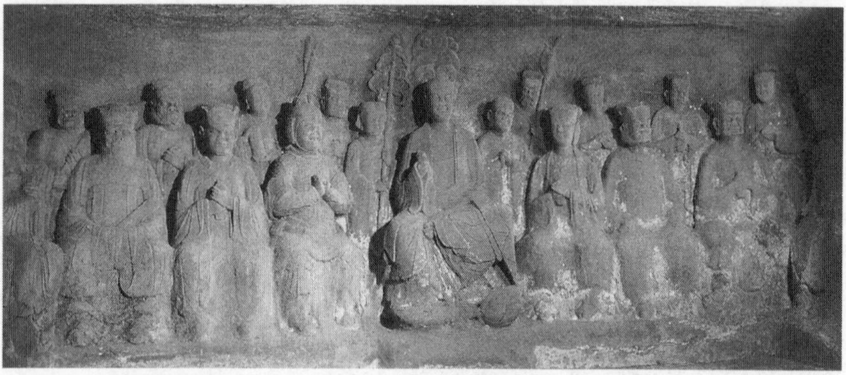

FIGURE 28. Dizang and the Ten Kings. Shizhuan shan niche 9, Dazu, Sichuan.

were added to the basic iconography of Dizang and the Ten Kings.[113] In niche 60, the better preserved of the two, a hooded figure seated in the center holds a staff and a wish-granting jewel. At his feet lies a hybrid animal, and he is flanked by registers displaying the Ten Kings, three above and two below on each side, all dressed as Chinese bureaucrats (see Figure 29.) Behind the kings are several attendants also clad in Chinese costume. Immediately beneath the central hooded figure are hell reliefs, one of which shows a warden dragging a woman by the hair before a *karma* mirror (*yejing* 業鏡) (see Figure 30).

Chinese art historians have proposed that the woman represents the mother of Mulian, the Buddha's great disciple, who was renowned for his supernormal powers and is said to have descended into hell to rescue his wicked mother.[114] In some versions of the legend, the mother is reborn as a dog, which may account for the animal at the feet of the hooded figure in the carving. Following this reading, some art historians suggest that the central character should be Mulian rather than Dizang, arguing that Mulian is a monk and that in folktales he was given a staff to smash open the gates of hell.[115] However, because the iconography is identical for hooded Dizang images of the same period from Sichuan, it seems equally, if not more, plausible that the figure is Dizang. The monk holds in his hand a wish-granting jewel, an important symbol in Dizang's iconography that is rarely associated with Mulian. Furthermore, in depictions of the underworld, Dizang Bodhisattva is frequently accompanied by a lion.

If Mulian motifs are present, they were probably added as part of an effort

113. The variation in the numbering of the niches reflects two different categorizations used by scholars at Sichuan Academy. For the rationale behind the dating, see Hu 1994: 303.

114. Liu Changjiu (1997: 71) identifies the central figure as Mulian with an iconography similar to Dizang's.

115. In the Dunhuang version of the transformative text on Mulian, the Buddha is said to have given Mulian a staff with twelve metal rings to open the gates of hell; see the translation in Mair 1983: 104, 107.

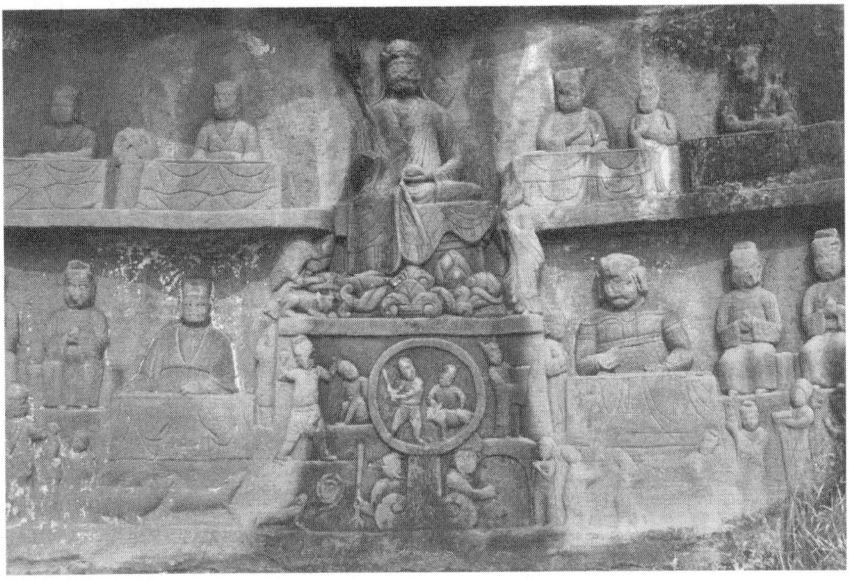

FIGURE 29. Dizang and the Ten Kings. Yuanjue dong niche 60 (84), Anyue, Sichuan. Photograph courtesy of Hu Wenhe.

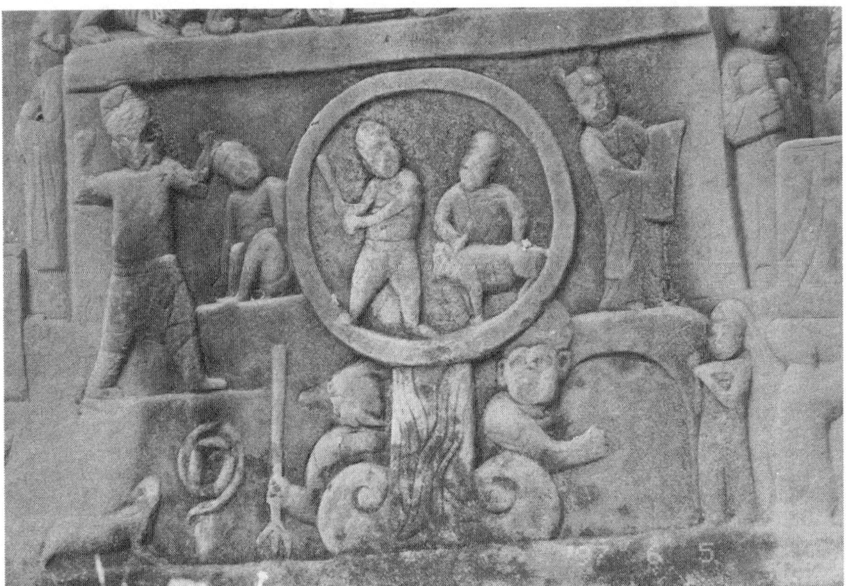

FIGURE 30. Karma mirror. Yuanjue dong niche 60 (84), Anyue, Sichuan.

to embellish and concretize the image of hell in the minds of medieval Chinese. In a widely circulated narrative version of the Mulian story, dated to around 800 and preserved in a Dunhuang transformatory text (*bianwen* 變文), Dizang appears briefly as one of several people whom Mulian encounters on his underworld journey.[116] Mulian's descent into hell constitutes a key chapter in medieval imaginings of the underworld, one in which the Chinese bureaucratic metaphor was imposed on punitive and grisly Buddhist hells.[117] Moreover, in Tang society, Dunhuang transformatory texts were circulated through storytelling and were often accompanied by illustrations, so that the Mulian story would have been extremely familiar to medieval Chinese.[118] It is thus hardly surprising that motifs from this story were internalized in the hell scenes in the Yuanjue dong. Whether the central character was originally meant to be Mulian or Dizang, there is no mistaking the similarities in their iconography, mythology, and religious function. Anyue's sculptural reliefs thus encapsulate the growing amalgamation of afterlife elements in a larger religious setting.

From the tenth century on, Dunhuang produced several syntheses of afterlife concepts involving Dizang. The Dunhuang examples generally do not highlight the gruesome details of suffering in hell but focus more on the legal and bureaucratic aspects of postmortem judgment. But cave 33 in the neighboring Anxi Yulin Grottoes contains a tenth-century wall painting featuring a Dizang with a shaven head and the six paths of rebirth emanating from his body.[119] He presides over scenes in which menacing guards hunt down half-dressed hell dwellers amidst a boiling cauldron and a *karma* mirror. Also in attendance are the two acolytes of good and evil and the General of the Five Paths (Wudao jiangjun 五道將軍; also known as the Spirit of the Five Paths, or Wudao shen 五道神), members of the growing pantheon of underworld deities in late medieval China. In charge of maintaining records of the actions of living beings, the two acolytes have distinct origins in pre-Han religion, which stipulated that life span registers be maintained at Mount Tai, the seat of otherworldly administration.[120] The General of the Five Paths is closely affiliated with the afterlife—and the underworld in particular—in early Chinese religion; he serves as the precursor to the last member of the Ten Kings, the King Who Turns the Wheel of the Five Paths (Wudao zhuanlun wang 五道轉輪王).[121]

---

116. In the Dunhuang narrative, Dizang appears briefly to notify Mulian of his deceased mother's whereabouts; see the translation in Mair 1983: 95.

117. Teiser 1988b: 168–195.

118. For a study of *bianwen* in Tang China, see Mair 1989; for Indian and Central Asian precedents for Chinese pictorial storytelling, see Mair 1988: 1–53.

119. For a photo reproduction, see Dunhuang yanjiuyuan 1997: pl. 77.

120. The acolytes of good and evil are said to accompany a person through life, recording his or her actions. Their records would be submitted to the courts of the Ten Kings at the time of one's death. On the two acolytes and their iconographies, see Soymié 1966: 45–78; 1967: 141–170. On the quantification of fate or life span, see Kohn 1998. A pair of acolytes was also assigned to Guanyin; see Idema 2000.

121. On the General of the Five Paths in Tang and pre-Tang China, see Dudbridge 1996–1997: 85–98; Oda 1976: 14–29; Sawada 1968: 90–92.

The paintings in situ at Dunhuang (Mogao grottoes 6, 176, 202, 314, 379, 380, 384, 390, and 456) mostly show a one-leg-pendant Dizang in the center, frequently wearing a hood and carrying the staff and wish-granting jewel. The six paths of rebirth emanate from his body and the courts of the Ten Kings appear laterally or directly below. Pairs of beings are often added to the retinue, usually in the lower portion of the painting. In addition to the pair of good and evil acolytes, another recurring duo is the monk attendant Daoming and the hybrid animal resembling a lion-dog, both from the *Record of a Returned Soul*. The Ten Kings and their courts are depicted with Dizang in several scroll paintings preserved in museum collections outside Dunhuang, dating from the tenth century or later.[122] Similar paintings have been found at Yulin ku. Illustrations accompanying manuscripts of the *Scripture of the Ten Kings* recovered from Dunhuang and Turfan feature Dizang in the frontispiece and elsewhere, although he does not play a conspicuous role in the text.[123]

The physical location of the relevant paintings in situ at the Mogao ku in Dunhuang may be of consideration. Except for caves 314 and 456, all examples of Dizang and the Ten Kings occur over the ceiling of a passageway between the antechamber and the principal chamber of the cave. This architectural schema most likely follows the deceased's passage to the intermediate state between death and the next rebirth, during which judgment is administered.[124] Dunhuang cave architecture may thus have stimulated more than an aesthetic response; by painting Dizang and the Ten Kings over the passageway artists created ritual and spatial symbolism. Visitors to the caves were able to enact the afterlife sojourn, which began in the passageway with judgment in the courts of the Ten Kings. Dizang's presence in this court reassured them of compassionate intervention. For the pious, the ordeal ended favorably with immediate rebirth in the paradisal realm of the celestial buddhas and bodhisattvas in the main chamber. Dizang thus represented a gateway, the promise of salvation, a bridge between judgment and an idyllic life in the next world.[125]

Judging from the number of visual representations and the growing

122. For a listing and description of Dunhuang scroll paintings, see Teiser 1994: 230–232.

123. For discussions on the Üighur manuscript illustrations to the *Scripture on the Ten Kings*, see Gabian 1973: 47–71, 1977: 25–35. Paintings of the Ten Kings produced in Ningbo (eastern China) were evidently exported to Japan, where some pieces have survived and are preserved at the Sekaidō Library; see Kwon 1999.

124. Wang-Toutain 1998: 290. The use of architecture to express religious or cosmological concepts is, of course, not new to the study of the history of religions. The Chinese imbued architecture with cosmological meaning as far back as pre-Buddhist times with concepts like the halls of light (*mingtang* 明堂). For a study on the *mingtang* and Buddhist utopias in relation to the history of the astronomical clock in Chinese civilization, see Forte 1988. The famous *vinaya* monk Daoxuan wrote an illustrated text on Jetavana (T1899:45.882c–895c), the famed Indian monastery, that correlates monastic architecture with religious concepts and functions. For studies of this text, see Ho 1995; Zhihui 2002.

125. This layout is reminiscent of one Dunhuang painting's (EO 3580) depiction of Amitābha's paradise, which appears immediately above a scene of Dizang in the courts of the Ten Kings.

complexity of the iconography, the merging of Dizang and the Ten Kings may have crystallized just before the tenth century. It is only with the tenth-century depictions from Anyue, Dazu, and Dunhuang that the visual imagery expands and the Ten Kings are transformed from miniature to full-sized figures, an indication of their growing importance in Buddhist cultic practice. To communicate and reinforce the bureaucratization of the underworld, the Ten Kings are shown dressed as Chinese officials, surrounded by a retinue of court attendants and scribes and tables strewn with writing instruments and documents.

Guiding the Way in the Afterlife: The Bodhisattva Yinlu

Another deity who crosses paths with Dizang in the underworld is the Bodhisattva Yinlu 引路 (Leading the Way), who appears in Buddhist art of the ninth and tenth centuries. The Buddhist equivalent to the psycho pomp of shamanistic religions, Yinlu leads the souls of the deceased to their destinations in the afterlife.[126] Usually depicted as a female deity, she holds a flying banner while standing on clouds, her face turned toward a miniature figure representing the deceased. First noticed among the Pelliot and Stein collections of Dunhuang paintings, this deity was for some time confused with Dizang, and the phrase "Yinlu pusa" was treated as a label for one of Dizang's functions.[127] Tsukamoto Zenryū was the first to distinguish between these two bodhisattvas, introducing evidence outside of Dunhuang, where the two are illustrated together and identified separately in inscriptions.[128] The relationship between Dizang and Yinlu is undeniable and helps illumine another dimension of Dizang's role in medieval imaginings of the afterlife.

Dated to 983, the Dunhuang silk painting MG 17662 features a hooded Dizang encircled by the Ten Kings and other members of Dizang's retinue.[129] In the left corner of the bottom register, a smaller deity, identified by a cartouche as Yinlu Bodhisattva, descends from a cloud, carrying a banner and looking backward to guide the deceased, who is shown in the right corner. This depiction of Dizang and Yinlu together might be dismissed as incidental were it not for similar pairings found outside Dunhuang. Among the representations to which Tsukamoto has called attention was a stele engraving dated to 932 showing Yinlu, in the company of Dizang, with an inscribed

126. Derived from the Greek, "psycho pomp" is the technical term for one who guides the dead in the afterlife. It was first used in the field of anthropology in relation to afterlife beliefs and practices in shamanic religions.

127. Tsukamoto 1931: 130–182. Among the collections of Dunhuang paintings are several pieces depicting Yinlu Bodhisattva (EO 1133, EO 1398, MG 17657, MG 17697, and MG 17662 from the Pelliot collection; Stein 47 from the British Museum). For reproductions, see Giès 1995: 2, pls. 63, 68, 69, 72, 73.

128. See Tsukamoto 1931: 138–158.

129. For a reproduction of MG 17662, see Giès 1995: 2, pl. 63.

text of the *Scripture on the Buddha's Topknot Supremely Victorious Dhāraṇī.*[130] Moreover, niche 1 at the Guanyin Slope (Guanyin po 觀音坡) in Dazu, dated to 1154, contains two badly damaged images, one holding a staff and the other a banner, named in the inscriptions respectively as Dizang and Yinlu.[131] On the right wall of niche 2 at the same site, dating to the Song, is a seated image grasping a staff; next to it stands a figure on partially damaged clouds, holding a banner—perhaps yet another pairing of Dizang and Yinlu.[132]

What then is the significance of the pairing of these two figures? The key lies in the origin of Yinlu Bodhisattva, whom Chinese Buddhists created in the late medieval period. Buddhist literature details guiding the deceased in the afterlife, but *yinlu* is not used. The Pure Land concept of *laiyin* 來引 (more commonly known in Japanese as *raigō*) is undoubtedly a Buddhist precursor to the concept of Yinlu Bodhisattva. However, indigenous ideas certainly contributed to the formation of this new Buddhist deity. The function of a psycho pomp was already anticipated in early Chinese mortuary practices. In Chinese shamanic rites the terrifying geography of hell persuades the dead to return to their bodies. Tomb excavations have yielded artifacts that illustrate the afterlife journey undertaken by the deceased.[133] Although a psycho pomp may not actually figure in either context, a desire for guidance in the world beyond the grave is evident in early indigenous practices. With the subsequent introduction of Buddhist ideas and practices, especially the Pure Land concept of welcoming the deceased, the stage was set for the birth of a Buddhist deity who specialized in directing the dead on their sojourn.

The term *yinlu* was probably first coined to describe a generic function performed by bodhisattvas. In fact, in one of the Stein paintings, Guanyin herself leads the deceased.[134] The task of guiding souls was eventually assumed by a new deity in the Chinese Buddhist pantheon; this change was one of several that occurred in the rapidly expanding conceptions of the afterlife in late medieval China. Dizang's connection with death and the afterlife developed over this period as did the purgatorial concept of the Ten Kings. It is thus not surprising that a Buddhist psycho pomp like Yinlu Bodhisattva should surface during the ninth and the tenth centuries. The thought of appearing before the courts of the Ten Kings struck fear in the hearts of sinners, whose guilt seemed all the more fixed when faced with the dreadful prospect of inescapable judgment; procuring help in the af-

130. Tsukamoto 1931: 138–141.

131. See Guo 1999a: 35, text inscription 48. The date is recorded in the inscription.

132. Liu, Hu, and Li 1985: 452. Chinese scholars have identified the figure holding the staff as Dizang and have suggested that the other figure could be either Daoming or Yinlu. Given the banner and clouds, the figure is more likely the Bodhisattva Yinlu.

133. A prominent example is the banner painting found in Mawangdui tomb 1. For a discussion of the afterlife motifs depicted in the banner, see Loewe 1979: 17–59. Loewe believes that the painting functions like a talisman, guiding the soul of the deceased in the afterlife.

134. For a reproduction of this painting, see Whitfield 1982–1985: 2, pl. 10.

terlife became a matter of urgency. Dizang answered the need for a savior who would temper justice with mercy, while Yinlu offered benevolent guidance through the dark courts of the Ten Kings. In Guanyin po niche 1, an inscription addresses the two deities as "The Bodhisattva King Dizang" (Dizang wang pusa 地藏王菩薩) and "The Bodhisattva King Yinlu" (Yinlu wang pusa 引路王菩薩).[135] This is one of the first inscriptions that identifies Dizang as ruler of the underworld. No doubt the metamorphosis from bodhisattva to sovereign was influenced by the image of the Ten Kings reigning over the courts in the underworld. Unfortunately, because the statues are badly eroded, it is impossible to determine if this linguistic consecration also resulted in the replacement of the jeweled coiffure with the five-buddha crown, which characterizes Dizang in late imperial and modern Chinese iconography.

After the tenth century, Dizang's association with the Ten Kings and judgment after death became a key element in the Chinese vision of the afterlife—so much so that Dizang quickly gained prominence as the patron saint in Buddhist death rites, while Yinlu Bodhisattva gradually faded from the religious landscape. In the Ming paintings used for the Repentance Rites of the Water and Land Creatures (*shuilu chan* 水陸懺), the Bodhisattva King Yinlu appears as a member of the pantheon of Buddhist deities but having no special connection to Dizang, who is also included in these paintings as one of the major bodhisattvas.[136]

Images of Dizang in Esoteric Buddhist Practices

A Ritual Manual, as mentioned previously, includes two sets of instructions for making Dizang images used in esoteric rites addressed to the bodhisattva. In the version that exists today, *A Ritual Manual* contains no illustrations of these images. However, Japanese illustrated texts of esoteric deities have been collated and published as appendices to the Taishō edition of the Chinese Buddhist canon in volumes 86–97, under the series "Illustrated Images" (*Tuxiang bu* 圖像部). In the Japanese texts, Dizang is represented either as a disciple draped in monastic robes or as a householder bodhisattva dressed as an Indian prince, replete with jewels and ornate coiffure—never as a monk wearing a celestial coiffure as *A Ritual Manual* describes. I will not discuss here the Dizang images in the Taishō canon derived from Japanese editions; they merely reflect usages in Japanese esoteric Buddhism, despite the fact that they claim to be of Chinese origin.

Visual sources place Dizang in the Maṇḍala of the Eight Great Bodhisattvas (Ch. *Ba da pusa mantuluo* 八大菩薩曼荼羅; Skt. *Aṣṭamahābodhisattva-*

135. Liu, Hu, and Li 1985: 451.

136. A cartouche identifies the Bodhisattva King Yinlu, who is clothed in colorful householder's robes and jewelry, one hand holding a bell and the other an incense holder, in the company of two female attendants. See the photo reproduction in Shanxi sheng bowuguang 1988, pls. 87–88; for Dizang Bodhisattva, see pl. 13.

maṇḍala). The earliest evidence of Kṣitigarbha, the Indian counterpart to Dizang, is among representations of the eight bodhisattvas in the cave temples of Ajanta and Ellora from the eighth century. Tracing the cult's history, Phyllis Granoff has shown that the eight great bodhisattvas originated in Mahāyāna cultic practice and were subsequently adapted to esoteric practice.[137] Listings of the deities in early Chinese Buddhist texts were not standardized, but the same set of eight bodhisattvas began appearing from the eighth century—although in varying permutations and with some disparities in appellation or attribute.[138] In esoteric art and texts, a central buddha was added to the eight bodhisattvas to form a *maṇḍala*, an important esoteric concept. Several texts include the Maṇḍala of the Eight Great Bodhisattvas, the earliest of which are Chinese works dating to the eighth century.[139]

Stein painting 50 from Dunhuang, now preserved in the British Museum, shows a central buddha, hands in a gesture of meditation and surrounded on either side by four bodhisattvas.[140] Inscriptions in Tibetan identify four of these bodhisattvas as Sarvanivaraṇaviṣkambhin (Chugaizhang 除蓋障), Samantabhadra, Dizang, and Mañjuśrī. Together with Avalokiteśvara, Maitreya, Ākāśagarbha, and Vajrapāṇi (Jinggang shou 金剛手), they constitute the eight great bodhisattvas enumerated in the *Ba da pusa mantuluo jing* 八大菩薩曼荼羅經 (*Aṣṭamahābodhisattvamaṇḍala-sūtra*; Scripture on the Maṇḍala of the Eight Great Bodhisattvas), attributed to the eighth-century esoteric master Amoghavajra.[141] However, the iconography in the Stein painting does not coincide with the scripture. In the painting, Dizang grasps a flaming jewel in his left hand, whereas the *Scripture on the Maṇḍala of the Eight Great Bodhisattvas* describes Dizang as follows:

> His head embellished with a jeweled coiffure and his face expressing tranquil peace, he is compassionately mindful of all living beings. His left hand rests beneath his navel and grasps an alms bowl; the palm of his right hand is inverted and turned downward, with the thumb and index finger joined in the gesture of consoling all living beings.[142]

---

137. Granoff 1968–1969: 81–95.

138. For an early listing, see *Foshuo ba jixiang shenzhou jing* 佛說八吉祥神咒經, attributed to Zhi Qian 支謙 (fl. 222–253), T427:14.72b–73a. For a more common listing of the eight bodhisattvas, see *Foshuo ba da pusa jing* 佛說八大菩薩經, T490:14.751b–752a.

139. For example, *Ba da pusa mantuluo jing* 八大菩薩曼荼羅經, translated by Amoghavajra, T1167:20.675a–676a; *Foshuo dasheng ba da mannaluo jing* 佛說大乘八大曼拏羅經, translated by Faxian 法賢 (ca. 1000), T1168A:20.676a–c.

140. For a reproduction of the painting, see Whitfield 1982–1985: vol. 1, pl. 17; Kawahara 1974: 108. For a detailed description, see Waley 1931: 83–84.

141. *Ba da pusa mantuluo jing*, T490:14.751b–c; cf. *Foshuo dasheng ba da mannaluo jing*, T1168A:20.676b.

142. *Ba da pusa mantuluo jing*, T1167:20.675c. The gesture described is the *anwei yin* 安慰印; see Saunders 1960: 66–69. Descriptions of the eight bodhisattvas' hand gestures are not given in the *Foshuo dasheng ba da mannaluo jing*, T1168A.

Apparently there existed more than one iconographical tradition for representing Dizang as a member of the eight bodhisattvas. Based on the Tibetan characters, the nature of the pigments used, and other details, scholars are inclined to date the Stein painting to the Tibetan occupation of Dunhuang, which occurred sometime around the ninth century.[143]

Another representation of the cult of eight great bodhisattvas, believed to have been executed in the eighth century, is a partially damaged wall mural on the east side of cave 25 in the Yulin ku.[144] Only four bodhisattvas and a central deity, Vairocana, remain of the original painting. Identified in a cartouche, Dizang is dressed in princely garb, his hair pulled back in a coiffure. His left hand forms the gesture of meditation *(dhyānamudrā)*, while his right, grasping a jewel, is raised to his chest. The three other bodhisattvas are Ākāśagarbha, Mañjuśrī, and Maitreya (see Figure 31.)

In addition to paintings, stone carvings of the eight great bodhisattvas have also been found in China. At the Slope of the Reclining Stūpa (Daota po 倒塔坡) in Dazu stands an octagonal pagoda built in the Song period. On the first level are chiseled eight niches, each enshrining a bodhisattva. Chinese art historians have identified these images as the eight great bodhisattvas.[145] Dizang, outfitted in an ornate headpiece and flowing garments, holds a staff and a jewel (now eroded), from which radiates two beams of light to the exterior of the niche.[146]

Together with artistic representations of the eight bodhisattvas, there exists an important piece of material evidence that places Dizang worship in the everyday practice of esoteric ritual: Pelliot 4514.5, a woodblock print consisting of an image of Dizang and liturgical text. The print is mounted on a scroll, which was evidently used for ritual veneration and belongs to a set of similar xylographs recovered from Dunhuang, all containing an image of a particular deity matched with a mantra and dedication verse.[147] Although largely undated, these prints probably appeared no earlier than the Song, when woodblock printing became integral to daily culture and life in China.

In P 4514.5 Dizang is identified in a cartouche as "The Great Saint Dizang Bodhisattva" (*dasheng dizang pusa* 大聖地藏菩薩). He is dressed in royal robes and heavily decorated with jewelry; his long hair cascades down to his shoulders from beneath an ornamented headpiece. Sitting on a lotus with both legs crossed, his right hand forms the gesture of fearlessness and his left holds an alms bowl. The following liturgy appears in the lower portion of the print:

143. Waley 1931: 84.

144. For the dating, see Dunhuang yanjiuyuan 1996: 213; and pl. 37. For more detailed reproductions of the painting, see Duan 1993: 26–27.

145. Liu, Hu, and Li 1985: 505–506.

146. Guo 1999b: 132, pl. 140.

147. For a survey of Dunhuang woodcut prints preserved in the British Museum and the Bibliothèque Nationale de Paris, see Kikutake 1975: 3–35.

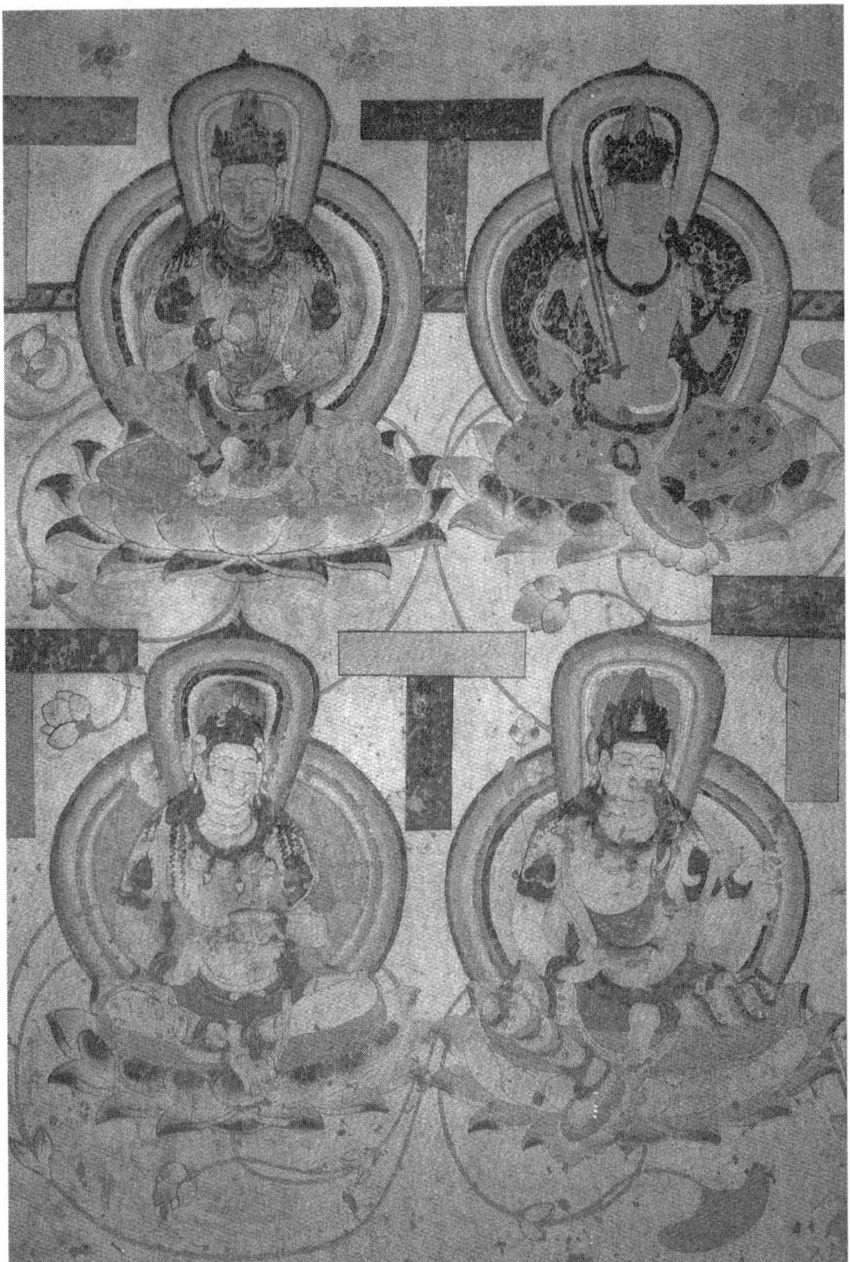

FIGURE 31. Remains of the Maṇḍala of Eight Great Bodhisattvas. Yulin cave 25, Anxi, Gansu. Photograph courtesy of Dunhuang Research Academy.

> *An Abbreviated Version of the Dizang Ritual* (*Dizang lueyi* 地藏略儀)
> Single-heartedly I take refuge with my life and prostrate to all the Tathāgatas, who are of equal nature and of the same body.
> Great compassionate saint, the Bodhisattva Mahāsattva Dizang,
> I, together with living beings—may we all take refuge with our lives, and by the transference of merits may [all] be reborn in the Land of Peaceful Joy (*anle guo* 安樂國). (prostrate ten times)
> Next, my mind totally resolute and singularly fixed on the deity, I recite
> The Mantra of Dizang Bodhisattva's Dharmakāya for
> Extinguishing and Determining Karmic Obstacles:
> *An boluomotani suofuhe* 唵 鉢囉沫他鶇 娑縛賀.
>
> This *mantra* clearly possesses great austere power to extinguish and determine grave sins and karmic obstacles; it is able to eliminate disaster and epidemics, extend the life span, and protect the body. The fourfold congregation [monks, nuns, laymen, and laywomen] are universally encouraged to recite and observe [this *mantra*] with a resolute mind and to transfer merits [so that all] may together be reborn in the Land of Immeasurable Life Span (*wuliangshou guo* 無量壽國).

P 4514.5 obviously does not promulgate the kind of systematized esoteric practices associated with Amoghavajra and other Tang esoteric teachers. In the broader religious setting, the esoteric practices were absorbed by and merged with the exoteric—as in the ritual text above, which incorporates Pure Land imagery. Originating in Mahāyāna scriptures, *mantra* and *dhāraṇī* recitation is claimed by esoteric Buddhism as one of its core practices. Precisely because of its more diffused origins, *mantra* recitation swiftly became a vehicle for spreading esoteric teachings and practices and an indispensable part of daily religious praxis for monastic and lay practitioners alike.[148] Woodblock printing facilitated the mass production of images and *mantras* for daily worship. P 4514.5 is an example of this kind of production featur-

148. *Mantra* recitation was so widely circulated in the medieval milieu that it was incorporated into the daily routine of Chinese Buddhist monasteries of the period. The Chinese translation of the *Susiddhikara* (*Suxidijieluo jing* 蘇悉地羯囉經), an esoteric text, contains a chapter titled "Chapter on Observing Precepts" (Chijie pin 持戒品), which outlines the use of *mantra* recitation in everyday monastic life. See T893:18.606a–608a. The text prescribes *mantras* for a repertory of daily activities, including morning ablutions, eating, and so forth, as it aims to ritualize and sanctify the mundane by transforming the secular into the sacred. This kind of alternative practice for Chinese monastics is not unusual, and modern scholarship has produced several studies on the Chan disciplinary code (e.g., Foulk, 1995, 454–472). The esoteric contribution to modern Chinese monastic codes is significant and needs to be more fully explored. It would be interesting to examine to what extent the chapter on precepts from the *Susiddhikara* was actualized in the medieval Chinese context. Monastic use of *mantra* recitation in daily activities is an important antecedent for similar practices found in a later genre of Chinese disciplinary literature called *pini riyong* 毘尼日用, or "*vinaya* for daily functions," which emerged during the Ming.

ing, in this case, the Bodhisattva Dizang as the patron saint for daily worship, combined in an ad hoc fashion with esoteric and Pure Land elements.

Forgotten Images in Religious Artifacts

Visual and epigraphic evidence shows that Dizang worship rapidly expanded across north central China to the western borders of Gansu and Sichuan. In Longmen sculpture, Dizang was first represented in the princely householder's guise typical of bodhisattvas before a special iconography was introduced. The *Scripture on the Ten Wheels* provides the *śramaṇa* iconography, as well as the imagery of the six paths of rebirth and the wish-granting jewel. Moreover, Longmen art and epigraphy tie Dizang to other cults, especially Guanyin and the Amitābha triad.

From the eighth century on, the western regions of Sichuan and Dunhuang became the centers of Dizang art. Substantial increases in the size and number of niches and sculptures reflect the growth of Dizang cults in the area. Sichuan and Dunhuang art also captured critical moments in Dizang's history. In Dunhuang the veneration of Dizang as Lord of the Underworld came into its own, drawing on medieval afterlife concepts such as the Ten Kings and the Bodhisattva Yinlu. Parallel developments occurred in Sichuan: In Anyue province, Dizang and the Ten Kings iconographies borrowed elements from Mulian mythology, an important source for Tang imaginings of the afterlife. To what extent these religious currents, particularly as they relate to the underworld, were molded by Central Asian cultures requires further research. Undoubtably, the staff and hood of the itinerant monk braving the sandy deserts of Central Asia were adopted by Chinese Buddhists in their visualizing of the Bodhisattva Dizang, the afterlife savior who guides travelers through the six paths of rebirth, promising mercy to the deceased as they stumble through the dark realm of the Ten Kings. The coming together of Dizang worship and the Ten Kings, while not clearly articulated in textual sources, is attested to in visual materials. In Dizang art from Dunhuang and Sichuan, hell imagery became the focus of depictions of the six paths of rebirth, culminating in Baoding shan cave 20's panoramic display of hell tortures from the Southern Song (1127–1279). Also on the western borders the combination of the jewel and staff remained constant in Dizang's iconography.

Vestiges of a possible link between Dizang and Bhaiṣajyaguru are discernible in Sichuan and Dunhuang art, especially in a pair of tableaux inspired by the *Scripture on the Healing Buddha* at Beishan Fowan. Although Bhaiṣajyaguru never gained the same level of prominence as Amitābha, he appears consistently in East Asian Buddhist art. As the buddha of healing and prolonging life, he appealed to medieval Chinese, with their penchant for the mantic arts and magico-religious techniques for healing and exorcism such as those detailed in the indigenous scripture *The Exorcism Method*. Given their iconographic similarities, it is not surprising that Sichuan devotees of Bhaiṣajyaguru and Dizang addressed their prayers for assistance in combating the evils of this world, procuring benefits for family members, and bringing about a good rebirth for the dead to both deities. No textual evidence exists, however, of a connection between these two cults. This "lost" relationship may have been the inspiration behind the birth of Enmei Jizō (Life-Prolonging Jizō) in Japanese Buddhism in the twelfth century. In medieval China, there temporarily flourished a life-prolonging bodhisattva called Yanming pusa 延命菩薩 who evolved, like the Bodhisattva Yinlu, from the personification of an attribute from the array of generic functions shared by all bodhisattvas. These "generic" bodhisattvas were eventually absorbed by the cults of more prominent Buddhist deities.

Finally, among artistic and epigraphical materials we find an "esoteric" Dizang as a member of the eight bodhisattvas, forming a *maṇḍala* with a buddha or receiving veneration as the presiding deity in esoteric rites. Although my survey is hardly exhaustive, it does indicate that such esoteric expressions are relatively few in number when compared to other iconographies, notably the underworld Dizang. As one of the eight bodhisattvas, Dizang usually appears as a householder bodhisattva who more or less resembles the other members of the entourage. His iconography is hardly uniform: His hand gestures and accessories are varied and rarely coincide with textual renditions. An intriguing iconography is the octagonal pagoda at the Daota po in Dazu Baoding shan, which bears little resemblance to *maṇḍala* designs seen in Japanese Shingon Buddhism. Here Dizang carries the staff and jewel, which are more commonly associated with his underworld aspect than his membership in the cult of the eight bodhisattvas. Other evidence of Dizang as the patron deity of esoteric rites can be found in Dunhuang woodblock print P 4514.5. This print verifies that the so-called esoteric rites enumerated in *A Ritual Manual*, especially in the abbreviated version of P 4514.5, were practiced in an everyday context and the text was frequently printed in large quantities. In the abbreviated version, Dizang was venerated using a ritual formula that draws on image contemplation, *mantra* recitation, and the goal of rebirth in the Pure Land, all of which are broadly disseminated religious elements that cannot be relegated to a single tradition.

CHAPTER 5
Narrative Literature

THE NEED TO MOVE beyond an exclusive focus on the written word in the study of medieval religion and culture has been voiced repeatedly in modern scholarship. But the study of the oral aspect of medieval culture poses its own methodological problems. Aaron Gurevich, an expert in the field of western medieval popular culture, frames the problem as follows:

> The oral tradition of the distant past could not be directly recorded, and everything we learn of it in the sources, the texts of the literary tradition, is only an indirect reflection. What is more, this reflection of the oral through the written, which is always and inevitably transformed and distorted, has been filtered through ecclesiastical ideology.
>
> Given that this is the case, is it then possible to "dig down" to the level of popular culture?[1]

In response, Gurevich proposes that scholars "take account of such works as the lives of saints, *exempla*, descriptions of the wanderings of souls through the other world, sermons, texts of vulgar theology, 'confession books'—handbooks for confessors—that is, the genres of middle Latin literature intended for the broad mass of the population."[2] He further argues that it is precisely through "a symbiosis with the scholarly tradition" that popular culture could exist in the medieval period.[3]

Gurevich's observations may be applied also to medieval China: One can approximate some kind of anthropological reconstruction of daily attitudes and practices by investigating its popular literary genres. To understand the Dizang cult as it functioned in the daily life of medieval society, this chapter studies the genre of Chinese narratives broadly referred to as "miracle tales." Buddhist miracle tales usually fall into three categories: accounts of divine intervention in times of need, usually initiated by appeals to a deity; illustrations of the efficacy of Buddhist piety, often through descriptions of the inexorable workings of the law of karmic retribution; and miracle prodigies, often famous monastics or laypeople who have demonstrated advanced spiritual attainments.[4] Broadly speaking, the term "miracle" in

1. Gurevich 1992: 50.
2. Ibid.: 51.
3. Ibid.: 64.
4. Cf. Gjertson 1981: 296.

western religious history refers to the suspension of the laws of nature or some form of divine intervention in the workings of the cosmos ultimately attributed to the power or grace of the cosmic creator.[5] Buddhist cosmology stipulates a universe revolving around the paths of rebirth dictated by the rational workings of *karma,* a principle of moral causation.[6] Against this cosmological background, a so-called "miraculous experience" is in some sense always bound to the principle of moral causation insofar as the spiritual efficacy or "numinous verification" (*lingyan* 靈驗)—however strange or inexplicable at first glance—is always *caused,* so to speak, by the worship of a deity or scripture or through the observance of some form of religious practice. Precisely because of this "hidden" pattern of causation, the common Chinese term used for collections of miracle tales is a pair of Chinese causal concepts that can be literally translated as "stimulus and response" *(ganying).*[7] But insofar as the experiences recounted are viewed as extraordinary in the sense of extending beyond daily functions and normal patterns of rationality, it is appropriate to call them "miracle tales." This usage is especially apt for narratives relating uncommon experiences attributed to divine intervention, which results from sincere veneration of a deity.

Miracle stories as they have been transmitted to us have undergone considerable editing or collation. They usually originated as oral narratives and were disseminated locally. Only after a deity or religious practice had gained considerable sway among believers were the stories edited, compiled, and canonized by the tradition. After compilation, miracle tales continued to be transmitted orally until the cult disappeared from the religious scene. They thus serve as fairly reliable mirrors of religious attitudes and practices observed by the larger population across the diverse social strata of medieval Chinese society. Hence, Chinese Buddhist miracle tales offer a de facto vehicle for accessing otherwise elusive dimensions of daily medieval life.

Chinese Buddhist miracle tales can often be traced to translations, beginning as early as the third century, of Buddhist narratives known as *avadāna.*[8] Shortly afterward, indigenous collections and writings were composed; by the Tang period a substantial corpus of Buddhist miracle tales ex-

---

5. Note that even in the context of the history of western religion, this broad definition of "miracle" does not allow for subtle refinements or explications. For the nuances underlying the theory of miracles in medieval western religion, see Ward 1982: 3–19.

6. For the problems in using "miracle" to translate the Japanese concept *ryōi,* see LaFleur 1983: 33–34.

7. Several scholars have discussed the problem of translating *ganying* and similar usages as "miracle"; see, for instance, Birnbaum 1986: 137; Kieschnick 1997: 97–101.

8. Gjertson 1989: 8–9. The oldest surviving Chinese translations of Indian Buddhist tales actually date from the late second century, but these translations are mostly interspersed in doctrinal materials. It is not until the mid-third century that the Chinese translation of Indian Buddhist tales begins with a translation of the *Avadānaśataka, Zhuanji baiyuan jing* 撰集百緣經 (T200:4.203a–257a), by the third-century Indo-Scythian layman Zhi Qian 支謙. Also see Campany 1991.

isted.[9] Their rise was probably in part spurred by a growing interest in another genre called "strange writing" or "anomaly accounts" (*zhiguai* 志怪).[10] Introduced between the fourth and the fifth centuries, these writings narrate human encounters with irrational and supramundane forces. Another catalyst was undoubtedly the transmission of Mahāyāna Buddhism with its pantheon of celestial bodhisattvas presented as omnipotent saviors. As early as the fourth century, miracle tales recording the numinous efficacies of the Bodhisattva Guanyin were circulating in China.[11] Components of cultic worship, such as making and venerating images, copying and reciting scriptures, and incanting the deity's name, became key motifs in miracle stories.

The earliest compilation of Dizang miracles, the *Dizang pusa xiang lingyan ji* (A Record of Numinous Verifications of Images of Dizang Bodhisattva), was completed in 989. Prior to it, miracle tales featuring Dizang already existed, scattered and preserved in Buddhist and non-Buddhist records. Those included in non-Buddhist compilations are especially valuable because they must have been sufficiently widespread to warrant the attention of elite Chinese authors, who might or might not have been Buddhists.

The Earliest Dizang Miracle Tale

Previously I noted Dizang worship and the efficacies of Dizang images in seventh-century Buddhist texts such as *The Pearl Forest of the Dharma Grove* and the *Continued Biographies of Eminent Monks.* However, the earliest miracle tale referring to Dizang occurs in the early eighth century in the *Huayan jing zhuanji* 華嚴經傳記 (Chronicles of the Flower Adornment Scripture), by the famous Huayan patriarch Fazang 法藏 (643–712).[12]

This Huayan compendium of miraculous stories includes a short narrative concerning a Mr. Wang's encounter with Dizang Bodhisattva in hell. It is the earliest documentation of Dizang's role in the netherworld, and it recurs in subsequent collections of miracle tales. Fazang records the story as follows:

> In the first year of *wenming* 文明 [684], a metropolitan person, one Mr. Wang, whose first name is today not known, did not cultivate good acts and moreover was lacking in moral conduct. When he died of illness, two persons came to lead him to the entrance of hell, where they encountered a monk who said, "I

9. Gjertson 1981: 287.

10. For a study of this literary genre, see Campany 1996b.

11. Several titles in Gjertson's survey of early Chinese collections of Buddhist miracle tales celebrate the miraculous potency of Guanyin Bodhisattva; see Gjertson 1981: 292–296; Makita 1970: 13–108.

12. *Huayan jing zhuanji*, T2073:51.153a–173a. The *Tang da Jianfu si guzhu fanjing dade fazang heshang zhuan* 唐大薦福寺故主翻經大德法藏和尚傳 states that Fazang died before completing the *Huayan jing zhuanji*. Evidently, his disciples completed the work and added their own commentaries and eulogies (T2054:50.283a). Scholars agree that the *Huayan jing zhuanji* was mostly authored by Fazang and that the "accretionary layers" added by his disciples contributed very few changes to Fazang's work; see Takamine 1963: 213.

> am the Bodhisattva Dizang." [The bodhisattva] then taught Mr. Wang to recite a line of verse, which states: "If a person seeks to apprehend all the buddhas of the three realms, he or she should contemplate thus: It is the mind that creates all *tathāgatas*." After delivering the scriptural line, the bodhisattva addressed him, saying, "Recitation of this *gāthā* can dissipate [the fate of] hell." Mr. Wang recited most earnestly, and then he was brought to meet King Yama. The king asked, "What merits does this person possess?" Wang replied, "Only the observance of the above *gāthā* of four phrases." The king subsequently released and pardoned him. At the time when this *gāthā* was recited, in the places where the recitation could penetrate, all those suffering obtained liberation. After three days, Mr. Wang revived. Recalling his observance of this *gāthā*, he spoke of it to all the monks. Searching for the text of the *gāthā*, they then realized that it occurred in the "Chapter on the Preaching of Teachings at the Cloud Assembly of All the Countless Bodhisattvas in the Suyama Celestial Palace" (*Yemo tiangong wuliang zhu pusa yunji shuofa pin* 夜摩天宮無量諸菩薩雲集說法品) from the twelfth fascicle of the *Avataṃsaka-sūtra* (*Huayan jing* 華嚴經, Flower Adornment Scripture). Mr. Wang himself told it all to the monk Dingfa 定法 from the Monastery of Contemplating Emptiness (Kongguan si 空觀寺).[13]

This story is later cited almost verbatim in a commentary on the *Huayan jing* composed by the Huayan patriarch Chengguan 澄觀 (738–839).[14] In Chengguan's treatment, the story is said to have come from the *Zuanling ji* 纂靈記 (Compendium of Numinous Records), evidently a variant name for the *Chronicles of the Flower Adornment Scripture.*[15] The story appears again in a tenth-century collection of Dizang miracle tales, *A Record of Numinous Verifications.*[16] As recorded in Huayan writings, the role of Dizang is minimal: He appears as one who teaches the mind-only doctrine of Huayan to those reborn in hell.

Mention of Dizang in Huayan writings poses several questions. Françoise Wang-Toutain explains that Huayan had a close relationship with Sanjie jiao and thus might have been molded by Sanjie jiao's penchant for Dizang worship.[17] But the perplexing fact is that Fazang's writing constitutes the earliest extant record of Dizang's underworld function—before it became an explicit theme in art, inscription, or other nonsectarian Buddhist collections of miracle tales. No evidence suggests that Sanjie jiao might have already promoted Dizang's underworld character. More likely, Fazang extrapolated the basic narrative of the underworld sojourn from contemporary sources before recasting it as propaganda for Huayan teachings. Narratives recounting un-

13. *Huayan jing zhuanji*, T2073:51.167a.

14. *Da fangguang fo huayan jing suishu yanyi chao* 大方廣佛華嚴經隨疏演義鈔, T1736:36.1a–701a. The story occurs twice in this commentary: T1736:36.116b–c, 324b.

15. For an occurrence of this variant title of the *Huayan jing zhuanji*, see *Tang da Jianfu si guzhu fanjing dade fazang heshang zhuan*, T2054:50.283a.

16. See record 5, *Lingyan ji*, 356a–b.

17. Wang-Toutain 1998: 144.

derworld journeys were common in medieval China and constituted a genre that modern scholarship refers to as "return-from-death narratives."[18] The motif of returning from death can be traced to the third century BCE in China.[19] By the seventh century, the Buddhist monk who performs a panoply of ritual functions, including funerary rites, is a familiar figure. The association of the Buddhist monk with death, particularly the belief that the monk's merits could bring salvation to the deceased, was already integral to Tang religion. A well-known example is the Mulian story, discussed previously, which furnishes the mythology for the Ghost Festival, a ritual for making offerings to the *saṅgha* to accrue merit for deceased ancestors and particularly to liberate the suffering of those reborn as hungry ghosts. The association of the monastic establishment with the afterlife is further reflected in popular stories. For example, in a return-from-death narrative collected in the late fifth-century text the *Mingxiang ji* 冥祥記 (Auspicious Records in the Dark Terrain), monks operate as important agents in the proper running of a highly bureaucratic administration that dispensed karmic retribution in the subterranean lands.[20] In particular, the monk Sengda 僧達 decides to prolong the protagonist's life and permits his return to the living world.[21] Numerous examples, too many to recount here, are recorded in various collections of Chinese narratives.

Another example from Huayan literature is the *Da fangguang fo huayan jing ganying zhuan* 大方廣佛華嚴經感應傳 (Biographies of the Responses Stimulated by the Great Extended Buddha Flower Adornment Scripture), composed by Fazang's disciple, the eighth-century monk Huiying 惠英 (d.u.). This narrative relates the return-from-death experience of a donor named Guo Shenliang 郭神亮, who lived in the Quarter of Benevolent Peace (Xian'an fang 賢安坊) in Chang'an.[22] Guo describes his own death experience: Upon his death in 687, he was led by three messengers to the abode of the Impartial King (Pingdeng wang 平等王), who determined that he be sent to hell for his wrongdoings.[23] At the entrance to hell, Guo encounters a miracle:

18. For example, Campany 1990.

19. Among the excavated finds from the Fangmatan tombs, dated to the fourth century BCE, is a petition directed to underworld authorities urging the resurrection of a dead man. For a discussion of this document, see Harper 1994: 13–28. For return-from-death narratives in medieval China, see Campany 1990, 1995.

20. The *Mingxiang ji* is said to have been compiled by Wang Yan 王琰 (fl. 424–479). Precisely when it was written is unclear, but the extant work refers to a date as late as 485, and it was known to have been in circulation by 501. See Campany 1996a: 82–83.

21. Recorded in the *Mingxiang ji*, this story is cited in two anthologies: *Fayuan zhulin*, T2122:53.988c–989a, and *Taiping guangji*, 379: 3014. Minor discrepancies in wording exist among these versions, but the story's content is basically the same. For a translation of the entire story, see Campany 1995: 351–353.

22. For the complete narrative, see *Da fangguang fo huayan jing ganying zhuan*, T2074: 51.175b–c.

23. The Impartial King is usually listed as the eighth of the Ten Kings. His origins are unclear, but an Impartial King also exists in Manichaean cosmology; see *Bosijiao can jing* 波斯教

> He suddenly saw a monk, who said, "Because I wish to save you from the suffering of hell, I shall teach you to recite a line." Astonished, Shenliang asked the monk to save and protect him and to bestow the *gāthā*. Reciting the *gāthā*, the monk stated, "If someone desires to apprehend all the buddhas of the three realms, one should thus contemplate that the mind creates all *tathāgatha*s." Shenliang then resolutely recited this *gāthā* numerous times. Consequently, Shenliang obtained liberation, together with numerous thousands of billions of people who were all undergoing suffering, and he did not [have to] enter hell.[24]

This story is strongly reminiscent of Mr. Wang's return-from-death experience, except for the identity of the monk: The monk Mr. Wang encountered is recognized as the Bodhisattva Dizang, whereas Guo met an ordinary, nameless cleric who held the key to the salvation of denizens in the underworld.

A parallel between these two return-from-death stories recorded in separate Huayan works suggests how Dizang's connection with the underworld may have evolved in medieval China. In Fazang's version of Mr. Wang's story, Dizang appears as a monk at the entrance to hell: There is no indication that he necessarily resides or presides there. Dizang's appearance seems no different from that of any other bodhisattva assisting living beings in dire need. The sectarian import of the story is obvious: Dizang is represented as the agent who delivers the teaching of mind-only, which enables living beings to elude the horrible destiny of rebirth in hell. In Guo's story, a nameless monk assumes this role. By replacing a generic monk with Dizang, a bodhisattva monk, the story of Mr. Wang may have captured a historic moment in Chinese underworld development—that is, between the late seventh and eighth centuries, the subtle shift in narrative accounts that resulted in Dizang assuming a role formerly ascribed to an average Buddhist monk, namely, the task of assisting those reborn into the underworld.

Non-Buddhist Records

From the eighth-century *Chronicles of the Flower Adornment Scripture* to the tenth-century compilation *A Record of Numinous Verifications*, other miracle tales mention Dizang, but these were recorded outside the Chinese Buddhist canon. The inclusion of such stories in any non-Buddhist compilation confirms that they were sufficiently disseminated in the larger milieu and that a non-Buddhist author would be familiar with them. A set of narratives from a tenth-century compilation, the *Taiping guangji* 太平廣記 (Extensive Records

---

殘經, T2141B:54.1282c. On the relations between Manichaeism and Buddhism, see Bryder 1985: 102–103.

24. *Da fangguang fo huayan jing ganying zhuan*, T2074:51.175c.

from the Taiping Era), and a return-from-death narrative retrieved from Dunhuang relate stories in which Dizang plays a central role.

Compiled by Li Fang 李昉 (925–996) from 977 to 978, the *Extensive Records from the Taiping Era* is an extensive collection of anecdotes and stories.[25] In one story dating to 746 and derived from the *Jiwen* 紀聞 (Records of Hearsay), a monk named Qizhi 齊之 enjoyed socializing with the upper classes and neglected monastic discipline. He was summoned to the underworld when a recently deceased maidservant from his monastery mistakenly accused him of causing her death. After the case was resolved and Qizhi was about to return to the world of the living, he met Dizang, in the guise of a monk, who explained that Qizhi had died on account of his lack of merit. Dizang exhorted Qizhi to correct his bad habits and live a secluded life.[26] Here Dizang is not cast as Lord of the Underworld; instead, he appears as a moral agent delivering injunctions to perform good deeds and observe monastic values. This treatment portrays the underworld bureaucracy as no different from the human institutions of law and order, which were prone to error. Except for Dizang's intervention, the otherworldly bureaucrats would have allowed the course of *karma* to play itself out.

The next story is about an official, Li Siyuan 李思元, who reportedly died and was later revived in 746. The narrative describes Siyuan's encounter with underworld bureaucrats, ranging from official underlings, who solicited bribes, to the underworld king, who allowed Siyuan to return to the realm of the living. On his way home, Siyuan passed through the gates of hell, where he encountered the Bodhisattva Dizang:

> At the west wall of the gate a door stood facing east. Outside the door were several hundreds of multitudes of monks holding banners and flowers to welcome Siyuan. They said, "The bodhisattva wishes to see you." Siyuan entered the cloister. Lucid ponds covered the entire grounds. The hall and balcony were all made of seven precious substances.[27] In the hall was a monk wearing a robe with golden designs and sitting on a bejeweled couch. Siyuan paid respect to him. [The monks] on both sides said, "This is the Bodhisattva Dizang." Siyuan then knelt down. The monks all composed eulogies, and on hearing them Siyuan shed tears. The bodhisattva told the congregation, "Do you see this person shedding tears? This person will depart in a short while. It is because he hears the singing of praises to the Buddha that he is crying."

25. Li Fang headed the editorial committee compiling and editing the *Taiping guangji*. The task was decreed under imperial auspices in 977 and completed the following year. This encyclopedic work amounts to a repertory of extracts from strange tales and stories of the supernatural, constituting a great source of material on the social history of medieval China. About one third of its entries are said to be from the Tang; most belong to the Han and the Six Dynasties, and a handful are from the tenth century. See Teng and Biggerstaff 1971: 125; Hervouet 1978: 341.

26. *Taiping guangji*, 100: 672.

27. *Qibao* 七寶 (*saptaratna*) in Buddhist texts usually refers to gold, silver, lapis lazuli, crystal, red pearl, agate, and mother-of-pearl.

> He told [Siyuan], "You have seen the affairs of this realm. When you return to the human world, you should accordingly speak about it and let people of the [living] world hear about it [that they might] correct their conduct and cultivate good deeds. If in this life you do not have disorderly conduct and always maintain correct thoughts, you can come here again." He then commanded all the monks to escort [Siyuan on his] return. When Siyuan woke up, he [had his family] prepare a meal for thirty people as well as separately prepare meat and wine for two persons. As a result, they all received gifts and benefits.
>
> Siyuan lived for seven days. After hosting a great vegetarian feast, Siyuan died again. But reviving at daybreak, he said that he had been summoned to Dizang's place, where [Dizang] reprimanded Siyuan, saying, "I commanded you to report the affairs of retribution in hell; why did you not talk about it?" [Dizang] was about to have him whipped, [but] Siyuan pleaded for forgiveness and was released. Because Siyuan usually did not consume wine and meat, he was again revived. He finally purified himself and became a vegetarian, and his family refrained from eating past noon. Also every time Siyuan was at a place where a crowd gathered, he would definitely report the netherworld incident. The people were all converted by it.[28]

In this story, Dizang's abode is located on the fringes of the underworld, where afterlife decisions and grisly penal tortures take place. The description of his lodgings, with their ponds and buildings made of precious substances, is reminiscent of the stock descriptions of paradise in Buddhist cosmology, although neither the term "paradise" nor "Pure Land" actually occurs here. Because most texts locate Dizang either in the land of Kharādīya in the south or in the western Land of Bliss, the association with the east is puzzling.[29] Moreover, Dizang seems to have under his command a throng of monks who live with him in his paradisal residence. Garbed in ornate robes, Dizang is thus presented as *the* monk of monks: The bodhisattva-monk is the monk par excellence.[30] This image of Dizang presiding over a host of monks on the fringes of the underworld is most likely an extension of the tendency to connect monks with the salvation of the dead. Compared to other accounts, Siyuan's story assigns a larger role to Dizang and further introduces echoes of Pure Land. Dizang's abode seems to be located immediately outside the underworld, between King Yama's court and the realm of the living. As I will show later, the *A Record of Numinous Verifications* contains a narrative

28. *Taiping guangji*, 100: 670–671.

29. The use of the eastern direction might well come from indigenous Chinese cosmography. The seat of otherworldly administration in early China, Mount Tai, is located in the east. In pre-Buddhist China, mortuary rites invoked a series of paradises, among them the Palace of the Eastern King presided over by the King Father of the East.

30. We are reminded here of the honors, especially the special monastic robe of royal purple, that the imperial Chinese court sometimes bestowed on a famous monk to signal courtly approbation and recognition of his accomplishments.

that presents lesser-known destinations of rebirth in Dizang worship; these are cast as semiheavenly abodes located in the subterranean geography on the return route from hell to the living realm.[31]

The third narrative from the *Extensive Records from the Taiping Era* was originally recorded in the ninth-century collection the *Youyang zazu* 酉陽雜俎 (A Miscellany on the Setting Sun).[32] It relates the otherworldly sojourn of Sun Xian 孫咸, a low-ranking general who, sometime between the late ninth and the beginning of the tenth century, reportedly died and was subsequently revived. The event is said to have occurred at Chongyi 崇義 in Xiang prefecture. In the story, Sun Xian is summoned to hell to verify the claim of a corrupt monk who falsely maintains that while alive he urged Sun Xian to copy the *Lotus Scripture.* Sun Xian's prolonged confrontation with the monk concludes only with the intervention of a monk who turns out to be Dizang. After the court hearing, Dizang leads Sun Xian on a guided tour of hell:

> Upon arriving at the gate, smoke and flames were blazing brightly, making a noise that sounded like wind and thunder. [Sun Xian] was apprehensive and dared not look. Just before him he saw a cauldron of boiling soup. The foam bubbled up and dripped onto his left thigh. The pain seared his heart and [pierced his] marrow. Dizang instructed a messenger to send [Sun Xian] back and forbade [Sun Xian] to divulge any underworld affairs. [Sun Xian] revived as if from a dream. . . . The spot where the drop had fallen in the dream formed a scar that remained throughout his entire life.[33]

Another story of Dizang in the underworld is a return-from-death narrative, the *Huanhun ji* (Record of a Returned Soul, S 3092), from Dunhuang.[34] Here the protagonist is Daoming, a monk from the Monastery of Kaiyuan Era (Kaiyuan si 開元寺) in Xiang prefecture.[35] The underworld sojourn reportedly occurred in 778:

31. See *Lingyan ji*, 362a–363a.

32. The *Youyang zazu* was a collection of anecdotes and stories composed by Duan Chengshi 段成式 (d. 863).

33. *Taiping guangji*, 106: 717.

34. For an unannotated transcription of the *Huanhun ji*, see Wang 1982: 173. However, Wang's transcription omits lines from the original texts. Stephen Teiser has edited and translated a portion of the narrative according to the manuscript copy S 3092; see Teiser 1988a: 448–449, 464.

35. The name "Daoming" was fairly common and surviving sources contain biographies of over a dozen Buddhist monks with this name. The recurrence of the name among Buddhist monks was acknowledged in the *Record of a Returned Soul* that relates how the netherworld authorities mistook Daoming of Kaishan si for Daoming of Longxing si 龍興寺; for a discussion of the various Daomings related to death and afterlife, see Teiser 1994: 66–69. In subsequent extensions of Dizang mythology in conjunction with the cult of Mount Jiuhua, Daoming was the name of a character in the Golden Dizang legend. He was the son of a local village elder, a patron of Kim Chijang, who subsequently received ordination from Kim.

Having been granted a clean slate, Daoming was overcome with emotion {as he left the king} to return to the human world. Lifting his head and turning to the west, he saw a meditation monk with eyes like blue lotus and a face like the full moon. Replete with jewels and lotuses, majestically adorned with fringe, by shaking the metal rings of his staff he could gather and disperse clouds and water. The bodhisattva asked Daoming, "Do you recognize me?" Daoming replied, "My eyes and ears are common and low. I do not recognize your venerable countenance."

[The monk said], "Take a good look, I am Dizang."

[Daoming said], "The way you look in the other world is different from this."

[The bodhisattva said], "How do I look on Jambudvīpa?"

[Daoming said], "Your body {is concealed under a big} gown, you hold rare jewels in your hands, and your head is exposed, not covered with hanging pearls and flower tassels."

[The bodhisattva said], "Those who hand down this tradition are in error! [Images of me] in the chambers and halls of {temples} must be odd in the same way. Most of the sentient beings of Jambudvīpa would not recognize me! You must observe closely the appearance {of my demeanor and comportment}, noting clearly my proportions one by one, so that you can transmit them to the world. Admonish all sentient beings to chant my true words [mantra]—at the {top of their voices}! The sins of those who hear my name shall be wiped away, blessings shall accrue to those who see my appearance; and I vow that I shall without fail bring salvation to those who {meet me in} this hall."

Having received these enticing instructions, Daoming was happy to put into practice what is hard {to practice. With devotion and} sincerity he accepted the bodhisattva's grace.

As he was about to take his leave Daoming went again to study the bodhisattva's venerable countenance, and only then did he see that there was a lion {at his side}. Daoming asked the bodhisattva, "What animal is this that dares to approach the Worthy Sage? When it comes time for me to transmit and copy [your likeness], I must know where [this animal] comes from."

"I suppose you do not recognize him," [replied the bodhisattva]. "This is the transformation body in the present of the Great Sage, Mañjuśrī Bodhisattva. He and I together in the dim dark world bring salvation to all in distress."

Daoming left, and within an instant he was back in the temple of his old home, breathing once again. There he set to work mixing his paints, passing down to the world the portraits he had copied of [Dizang's] true countenance.[36]

The date of this text is uncertain, but it was probably copied in the ninth century.[37] The narrative not only points to Dizang's role in the underworld but

36. Translated in Teiser 1988a: 448–449.
37. Ibid.: 447.

also sheds further light on the evolution of the underworld Dizang's iconography. The return-from-death narratives all portray Dizang as a *śramaṇa* in the netherworld. The image of Dizang as a monk must have been a critical factor in the articulation of his underworld function. However, the *Record of a Returned Soul* seems to indicate that at some point after his underworld role was established, there was a concerted effort to reinforce the bodhisattva aspect of Dizang's personality by reinstating the jewels and ornamented headdress typical of a bodhisattva. A similar iconography of the monk Dizang wearing a celestial coiffure is prescribed in *A Ritual Manual*. The *Record of a Returned Soul* was probably written no earlier than the end of the eighth century, after Dizang had already gained a firm foothold in the larger religious milieu. In other words, both the ritual and narrative date roughly to the same period, but because we do not have firm dating for either, it is hard to say how exactly one was influenced by the other. The narrative insists on the priority of Dizang by making another great bodhisattva, Mañjuśrī, his attendant animal. The lion-dog "vehicle" occurs only in late medieval iconography of Dizang in association with his underworld function. Dunhuang and Sichuan art certainly furnishes examples of the monk Dizang adorned with jewels and attended by an animal. Whether or not these motifs emerged first in art or narrative, it is impossible to ascertain.

These stories recorded outside the Chinese Buddhist canon are return-from-death narratives that focus on the underworld. Except for the last story, all are from the *Extensive Records from the Taiping Era*, which in turn extrapolated the stories from other non-Buddhist collections. The non-Buddhist origins of the sources suggest that Dizang's underworld aspect belonged not only to the Buddhist population in medieval society, but also to a wider audience.

A Buddhist Compilation of Dizang Miracle Tales

Compiled by the monk Changjin 常謹 (d.u.), the earliest extant collection of Dizang miracle tales, *A Record of Numinous Verifications*, was completed in 989.[38] Changjin explains in his preface that he was summoned by the court to compile the text. The preface does not explain the rationale for the project, but one may assume that Dizang worship was sufficiently widespread in the tenth century to merit compiling miraculous accounts of his images. Changjin observes that there exists an overwhelming number of incidents attesting to Dizang's numinous efficacy transmitted orally or through written records, of which he has only compiled thirty-two. Little is known about Changjin. Except for *A Record of Numinous Verifications*, no other work is attributed to him, although a brief mention in one source tells us that in 982, he was attached to an imperially sanctioned translation

38. At the close of the preface, the compiler notes that his task was completed in the second year of *duangong* 端拱; see *Lingyan ji*, 354a.

bureau in Kaifeng 開封 (in modern-day Henan).[39] He refers to himself as "a *śramaṇa* who transmits the teachings" (*chuanjiao shamen* 傳教沙門).[40] Changjin probably belonged to the elite class of literate monks, which included copyists and translators engaged in the transmission and propagation of Buddhism in China.

As previously mentioned, the *Scripture on the Ten Wheels* frequently served as the scriptural core for the early development of Dizang Bodhisattva. But in a shift that probably took place in late medieval China, the *Scripture on the Past Vows* increasingly emerged as the new scriptural source for Dizang imagery. Changjin indicates early in his preface that the *Scripture on the Past Vows* was a salient influence on his compilation of Dizang miracle tales. He recalls events from the scripture, especially the scene of its preaching in Trāyastriṃśa heaven.[41] His recounting of this scene quotes almost verbatim lines from the *Scripture on the Past Vows*, establishing a connection with the scripture that canonized Dizang's role as savior of the living beings of the Sahā world during the interval between Śākyamuni and Maitreya. After invoking the myth of Dizang's origin, Changjin then explains Dizang's special affinity with this world and its inhabitants and that there are countless believers who have received miraculous assistance from him. Changjin's compilation of Dizang miracle tales is then presented as a record of some of these incidents.[42]

The narratives reflect a wide range of themes that locate Dizang in more various religious developments than those found in miracle tales from non-Buddhist sources. To facilitate my discussion, I have organized Changjin's work around four sets of recurring themes.

Rebirth in the Pure Land and Heavenly Abodes

Three narratives (records 9, 11, and 26) in *A Record of Numinous Verifications* confirm Dizang's connection with Pure Land, which, as we have seen, is apparent in art, epigraphy, and other texts. Record 26 is especially important for its Pure Land echoes. The protagonist in this story is an exemplary Buddhist nun, Zhizang 智藏, who lived in the chaotic times surrounding the year 980. As part of her aspiration to be reborn in the Pure Land, Zhizang commissions and worships a painting portraying the Buddha Amitābha flanked by Dizang and Guanyin. Her deathbed scene is described as follows:

> On the twenty-third day of the second month in the seventh year, she informed her friends that "It has been decided that I will die the next day, and the Bodhisattva Dizang shall lead me to the Pure Land." She burnt

39. *Fozu tongji*, T2035:49.398a.

40. *Lingyan ji*, 354a.

41. Changjin especially invokes the events of Chapter 2, "The Assembly of the Emanation Bodies" (*Fenshen jihui pin er* 分身集會品二), in the *Benyuan jing*, T412:13.779a–c. Literally, "Trāyastriṃśa deva" refers to the thirty-three gods in Vedic lore. In Buddhist cosmology, it is the second of six heavens in the realm of desire (*yujie* 欲界; Skt. *kāma-dhātu*).

42. *Lingyan ji*, 354a.

> incense, scattered flowers, intoned the names of the holy triad 108 times each. Then she sat upright, palms joined, faced west, and passed away.[43]

Granted that this description has undergone editing to better reflect the normative views of the elite Chinese Buddhist community, it is nonetheless one vignette, albeit idealized, of Buddhist death rites practiced in late medieval times. Here the paradigm invoked is the death rites and deathbed testimonials from the Amitābha Pure Land tradition flourishing in medieval China.[44] Dizang appears as a psycho pomp leading the dying devotee to the Pure Land as in the *Scripture on the Bodhisattva Dizang*. This miracle tale shows a medieval Chinese nun venerating Dizang as one of the Pure Land triad: In her conception of the afterlife and her preparatory rite for rebirth, Dizang is an integral element of her Pure Land devotion. As a miracle tale, this story very likely reflects the afterlife beliefs and practices observed by Buddhists in late medieval China.

Another example is record 24, which describes cultic life in the city of Liao 遼 also around 980.[45] The religious practices in that city are described thus:

> In a village in Liao, more than one thousand families of the past [and up to] about two thousand families of the present generation had always served the Great Dharma. Also they always had faith in Guanyin and Dizang. They took refuge under the monks and nuns and were strongly predisposed to the *Guanyin Scripture* and the *Scripture on the Ten Wheels*. There was an ancient *saṅghārāma* with three bays and four sides. In the renovated green-tiled hall, two statues of Guanyin and Dizang, their bodies seven feet five inches high, were placed on the left and right, and an image of Amitābha stood in the middle, one *zhang* and six feet tall. All [three] were divinely auspicious images, sculpted in the past by Liu Dengdu 留鄧度.[46]

The passage records the shrine arrangement in what was probably the main hall of a rural monastery in tenth-century China. Whether or not the monastery in question actually existed, the description certainly mirrors to a greater or lesser degree the socio-cultural and religious realities of late medieval China. My previous discussion of cave temple art already uncovered several instances of this triad, although examples from cave temple art cannot conclusively establish whether the triad was actually used for daily worship. Both narratives concerning the nun Zhizang and Liao city indicate

43. Ibid., 367a.

44. On Pure Land death rites and deathbed testimonials in medieval China, see Stevenson 1995a, 1995b; Huang 1998. On this genre of writings, see Lai 1996.

45. The chaotic times mentioned in the story of the nun Zhizang also appear in record 24: "During the reign of Taizong 太宗 in the period of *taiping xingguo* 太平興國 (976–984), an epidemic raged" (*Lingyan ji*, 366b).

46. *Lingyan ji*, 366a–b

that the triad was employed for personal and communal ritual in the tenth-century. In other words, Dizang's connection with Amitābha's Pure Land was not an abstract theoretical formulation but rather existed as part of daily religious practice in medieval society.

In *A Record of Numinous Verifications*, those who worship Dizang may also be reborn in Maitreya's abode, Tuṣita heaven. For example, in record 13, a filial daughter, Miss Zhang 張, makes a Dizang image on behalf of her mother, who has been reborn as a hungry ghost:

> After that, in her dream, [Miss Zhang] saw her mother, her body emitting radiance and dwelling in space. [Her mother] said, "[Because of] the power of the good merits you cultivated [on my behalf], I was swiftly reborn into heaven. If you prostrate and pay homage to this image with a reverent heart, we will together dwell in the abode of Maitreya Bodhisattva and will listen together to the teachings."[47]

In another record, a regional inspector named Zu 祖 makes an image of Dizang for his parents and succeeds in converting them to Dizang worship before his father passes away. In a dream, his deceased father appears before Zu, saying:

> "I was reborn in the Fourth Heaven. The Bodhisattva Dizang led and guided [me] to serve [the future buddha Maitreya], who has only one more rebirth (Ch. *buchu* 補處; Skt. *ekajātipratibaddha*). People reborn in that heaven are mostly led and guided by this Great Being. He who has only one more rebirth applauds, saying, 'The Great Being can never neglect the injunction of all the buddhas!'"[48]

In record 6 the monk Dingfa 定法, who worships Dizang, dreams of a prophetic voice that declares:

> "[Because] you have traced and copied my form numerous times, you will never fall into the three evil paths [of rebirth]. When you die, you shall be born in Tuṣita heaven. On the day the Compassionate One [Maitreya] descends, you shall receive a prediction obtained from the Buddha."[49]

In record 11 the protagonist has a miraculous encounter with Dizang, following which he becomes a monk named Fashang 法尚, who builds the Monastery of the Wisdom Sun (Huiri si 慧日寺). At seventy-eight, he reports to the other monks of his monastery a vision in which Dizang predicts that he will attain awakening at one of the preaching assemblies Maitreya holds on

47. Ibid., 360b. Although the name of Maitreya's abode is not specified, we can assume that the passage refers to Tuṣita heaven, the dwelling of the future buddha.

48. Ibid., 355b.

49. Ibid., 356b.

earth; in the meantime, however, he will be reborn into the pleasures of Trāyastriṃśa heaven.[50]

In addition to Tuṣita, Trāyastriṃśa is another heavenly realm held out as a place of rebirth for devotees of Dizang Bodhisattva. The emphasis on rebirth in Trāyastriṃśa heaven, as previously mentioned, can be ascribed to the influence of the *Scripture on the Past Vows.* For instance, in record 12 a filial daughter named Miss Chen 陳 makes an image on behalf of her deceased mother. She later dreams that a *śramaṇa* tells her he has braved the flames of the Scorching and Burning hell (*jiaore diyu* 焦熱地獄) to preach to her mother, who is consequently reborn into the Trāyastriṃśa heaven.[51] In record 18 a husband commissions an image of Dizang for his deceased wife; as a result, she is reborn into Trāyastriṃśa heaven, where, on the twenty-fourth day of each month, boundless transformation bodies of Dizang appear to preach at the Hall of Excellent Dharma (Shanfa tang 善法堂).[52]

At least two narratives (records 9 and 11) suggest some kind of rivalry between the cults of Amitābha and Maitreya in the medieval period. Record 9 relates how a poor widow is miraculously impregnated after dreaming that a monk opened her mouth with a staff to place a precious gem in it. She subsequently gives birth to two children, a boy named Dizang (Earth Treasury) and a girl named Ruyi 如意 (Wish-Granting). The girl's name deliberately invokes the jewel frequently associated with Dizang Bodhisattva. The children disappear and on their return:

> The mother queried the cause [of their disappearance]. The boy said, "I went to the Pure Land of Peace and Joy in the west, where I presented myself to the congregation of bodhisattvas and saints. Mother should aspire to be reborn in that land," and so forth. The girl said, "I went to Tuṣita heaven and presented myself to Maitreya. The place was filled with men and women. Will mother aspire to be reborn there?" The mother said, "I loathe the female body, so I do not delight in the enjoyments of heaven. Should I be reborn in heaven, I fear I may receive the female form [again]. I should [therefore] aspire to be reborn in the western Pure Land.[53]

The underlying polemical intent is quite evident: Rebirth in the western Pure Land implicitly guarantees release from the female body, an advantage over Tuṣita, which belongs to the heavenly sphere of enjoyments where gender differentiation still exists. In record 11, Fashang asks to be reborn in the western Pure Land, thereby rejecting the prospect of rebirth in Trāyastriṃśa for fear of being distracted from the path. Fashang further explains: "Moreover, the time [of the coming] of the future buddha is still

50. Ibid., 360a.
51. Ibid., 360a–b.
52. Ibid., 364a–b.
53. Ibid., 358b.

distant, so I aspire only to be reborn in the Western Land of Bliss."[54] Present again is the criticism of rebirth in the heavenly realms, this time directed at Trāyastriṃśa rather than Tuṣita. Such rebirth is associated with the mythology of Maitreya's descent. The final verdict in these stories emphasizes the advantages of being reborn in the Pure Land. Even the promise of achieving awakening in the future cannot enhance the goal of heavenly rebirth. Rebirth in the Pure Land is not, however, always pitted against rebirth in Maitreya's realm. In record 16 the two are held out as complementary soteriological destinations and devoted patrons of Dizang images may be reborn in either of them:

> Among the donor-disciples of Dizang Bodhisattva who make offerings, those who had emphasized [the commission of] paintings and images are mostly reborn in the Pure Land or Tuṣita heaven.[55]

Finally, record 16 introduces new afterlife destinations as part of the otherworldly geography traversed by the protagonist, Cui Lixi 崔李係, referred to as Xi. Having witnessed a variety of tormenting hells, Xi, accompanied by escorts, heads back to the world of the living. En route he encounters two places that sharply contrast with the terrifying scenes of hell he had witnessed earlier:

> I saw green-tiled houses of sand, elegantly piled up with seven- or eight-inch thick beams of precious substances. On the left and right of the side paths were jeweled trees interspersed with a variety of fruits. Therefore, I immediately questioned the two historiographers, who answered, "Those disciples of Dizang who, among acts of service and donation, in particular emphasize [commission] paintings and images will mostly be reborn in the Pure Land or Tuṣita heaven in accordance with their aspiration. But the majority of those who do not believe in images but serve [Dizang] will dwell in this abode."
>
> We proceeded further and saw a precious hall in the middle of a great city. Hundreds and thousands of millions of men and women were frolicking [in the hall]. I also saw my parents, brothers, relatives, and so forth, who, in delight, paid respects [to me]. All the men and women said, "We were previously in hell. Because your lordship taught us to chant [the name of] Dizang Bodhisattva, we were relieved from afflictions and reborn in this huge hall." Parents, brothers, and relatives joyously said to me, "Your lordship's kindness has brought about Dizang Bodhisattva's transformation, so we were able to escape from [hell] sufferings and be reborn in here."
>
> Again I asked, "Where is this place?" They answered, "It is called Merit Lodge (*fushe* 福舍), and those who live here experience longevity and are removed from all sufferings. Although we are reborn in this place, we will

54. Ibid., 360a.
55. Ibid., 364a.

> definitely meet Maitreya in the three assemblies and exhaust the time of suffering." I asked, "Who established this land?" They answered, "In the past, when Dizang Bodhisattva was in the world, he received an injunction from the Buddha. [Dizang] told the Buddha, "The four groups of disciples should not fall into the evil paths [of rebirth]. In the period of fifty-six hundred and seven millions of years, from the time of the Buddha to Maitreya's birth [into this world], those with scarce merits who desire to be reborn in the Pure Land and the fourth heaven will all reside in this Merit Lodge and will not return to the evil paths [of rebirth]. They will be made to wait only for the future buddha." We returned to the commanding governor, who dispatched the two previous [officials] to escort me back.[56]

Although the descriptions echo those of paradise, the two new afterlife destinations are evidently "low" in the ranks of Buddhist heavenly realms; they are not on par with Tuṣita or Amitābha's Pure Land.

A brief look at similar concepts in the tradition of Amitābha's Pure Land may shed light on the quasiheavenly realms encountered in Xi's story. The Chinese translation of the *Larger Sukhāvatīvyūha-sūtra,* attributed to Saṅghavarman, speaks of the Palace of Seven Jewels (*qibao gongdian* 七寶宮殿) as the place "where persons of faltering faith are reborn in the Land of Bliss."[57]

> These living beings will be reborn in one of these palaces, and will spend in it five hundred years of their life span without seeing the Buddha, without hearing the teaching of the scriptures, without seeing the holy assemblies of bodhisattvas and disciples. This is why we speak about rebirth in a womb in that country. . . .
>
> Those who are reborn in a womb inhabit flying palaces of a hundred leagues or five hundred leagues; and in those palaces each and every one experiences all manner of delightful pleasures; and, again, all of these they experience spontaneously, exactly as in the Heaven of the Thirty-Three Gods.[58]

The Palace of Seven Jewels performs the same function in the Pure Land as borderlands (Ch. *piandi* 遍地; Skt. *pratyantajanapada*) in the cosmography of our Sahā world. Borderlands such as the higher heavens and the northern continent of Uttarakuru are conceived as paradisal lands in this world system, where one does not encounter Buddhist teachings.[59] There are parallels between the concepts of borderlands and the Palace of Seven Jewels on the one hand, and the two quasiheavenly realms Xi encounters on the other. Adherents lacking faith in the efficacy of Dizang icons or adequate merits will be reborn in the garden of green-tiled sand houses or in

56. Ibid., 363a.

57. Gómez 1996: 314.

58. Translated in ibid.: 217.

59. On the concept of borderlands, see ibid.: 286.

the city of Merit Lodge. In either situation, their flaws are such that they cannot be reborn in Amitābha's Pure Land or Maitreya's Tuṣita heaven. In other words, because of their weaknesses these devotees cannot encounter the buddha—be it the Buddha Amitābha or the future Buddha, Maitreya. These believers can, however, receive the assurance that they will meet Maitreya when he attains buddhahood in Jambudvīpa, which is similar to the promise given to those reborn in the Palace of Seven Jewels—that they will eventually meet the Buddha Amitābha and his saintly congregation after five hundred years.

The geography of these two alternate destinations of rebirth for Dizang devotees is somewhat perplexing. The narrative does not indicate that Xi exited the subterranean territory where the infernal regions are situated, and the new places of rebirth are presented as if they were spatially continuous with the terrifying hells Xi just visited. Perhaps one can assume that these two anomalous afterlife destinations are located in the subterranean realm. Although the exact location of the hells is not specified in Chinese Buddhism, they are supposedly located under the earth. In classic Indian Buddhist cosmology, the hells of this world system (*sahāloka*) are located beneath Jambudvīpa; in early China, several terms are coined for "underworld," all of which invoke the earth as a referential location: for example, the earliest usage of "below the earth" (*dixia* 地下); or "earth prefecture" (*tufu* 土府) like in the *Scripture of Great Peace* (*Taiping jing* 太平經); or "prison in the earth" (*diyu* 地獄), which occurs frequently as the translation for Buddhist hells.[60] One can therefore presume that the hells Xi visits, as well as the new afterlife destinations that are depicted as spatially continuous with the hells, are all situated in a subterranean region. In other words, the garden of green-tiled houses and Merit Lodge are underground paradises that rank lower than the Buddhist heavens. They are somewhat akin to the underground grotto paradises imagined by Chinese thinkers. For example, as early as the late third and early fourth centuries, Tao Yuanming 陶淵明 (365–427) envisioned a grotto paradise called the Peach Flower Font (Taohua yuan 桃花源).[61] Southern developments of Daoism created an entire mythology of underground grotto paradises located in the mountains and connected to one another by passageways.[62] In medieval Chinese mythology, "the city" subsequently displaced earlier pastoral imagery as the principal metaphor for paradise.

The garden of green-tiled houses and Merit Lodge probably resulted from a synthetic combination of Buddhist paradises like the borderlands or the Palace of Seven Jewels with underground heavenly grottoes. It is especially appropriate that Dizang should be the deity associated with these two idyllic subterranean realms; his name literally means "storehouse of the earth." As alternative destinations for devotees of Dizang, they are not men-

60. See Seidel 1987a: 187. In ancient western cosmologies, the Greek Pluto and the old Norse Hel are located underground.

61. On Tao Yuanming and the Peach Flower Font, see Bokenkamp 1986.

62. Ter Haar 1998: 91–95.

tioned in other literature. Given the paucity of sources, it would seem that these elaborations of otherworldly geography never took root in China. Hence the Dizang narratives offer a glimpse into neglected features of medieval imaginings of the afterlife.

The Underworld Connection

In *A Record of Numinous Verifications*, a number of stories (records 3, 5, 8, 10, 14, 16, 17, 21, 24, and 32) are presented as return-from-death narratives. With few exceptions, the portrayal of the underworld in these tales is fairly standardized. The infernal bureaucracy is present at the beginning of the underworld voyage in the form of messenger officials, sometimes on horseback, pursuing and bringing victims to court. At times other court attendants such as scribes and officials who keep records of allotted life spans may also appear. Record 16 depicts an expanded administration, including court historians and local magistrates, which mirrors the Chinese imperial bureaucracy. Ever present is the underworld sovereign, referred to simply as "the king" or at times more specifically as "King Yama." The authority of the king varies but misjudgment and error on his part as well as the various court members is common. Dizang's role is seldom amplified: His presence is frequently an intrusion into the routine functioning of the infernal judiciary, although he is often represented as a fixed element in the subterranean framework. For instance, in record 8, during his underworld journey, Deng Zong 鄧宗 encounters a monk who identifies himself as Dizang:

> "I am the Bodhisattva Dizang of the Monastery of Founding a Mountain (Kaishan si 開山寺). To rescue living beings in the three realms of suffering, Zhiman 智滿, a disciple of the monk Zhizang 智藏, has sculpted my image in the past, and I heard his prayers. At an appointed hour each day, I enter the eighteen hells and the numerous smaller hells to teach and guide [living beings]."[63]

In record 13 a daughter learns of Dizang's role in the subterranean realm from her mother, who has been reborn as a hungry ghost:

> The daughter saw her mother, who appeared before her as a great malevolent spirit. [The mother continued,] "Except for a day every month in the human world, I cannot eat at all. I am referring to the morning of the twenty-fourth day of [each] month. A monk enters the city [of hell] and bestows food [on hungry ghosts], causing them to be satiated. Other than this day, I cannot be exempted from this [kind of] suffering. At that time, the monk recites these words, 'I am the Bodhisattva Dizang, and I am now entering the Hell of Hungry Ghosts. I can bestow great peace and joy. All of you should arouse the mind of awakening.'"[64]

63. *Lingyan ji*, 357b.
64. Ibid., 360b–361a

In both these versions, Dizang is integrated into the routine structure of the underworld, manifesting as a savior at a specific hour or day to bring relief to those undergoing torments in hell.

A Record of Numinous Verifications does not allude to the Ten Kings of purgatory except for one prominent mention in record 29. The narrative offers an origin myth for the iconic representation of the Bodhisattva Dizang together with the Ten Kings. A *śramaṇa* from the western region named Zhiyou 智祐 supposedly came to China and lived in the Monastery of the Qingtai Era (Qingtai si 清泰寺) in the middle of the *tianfu* 天福 reign era (936–944):

> Among the images and scriptures [Zhiyou] brought with him were a transforming image of Dizang Bodhisattva and a *Scripture on the Merit of [Dizang's] Past Vows* bound in Brāhma-style boards. The special marks of the image were that in the central circle the Image of the Bodhisattva was drawn wearing a cap and carrying a jewel and metal staff. To the sides were images of the Ten Kings, five on each side . . . and each accompanied by the Officer of Life Span and the Officer of Emoluments, magistrates, and various administrators.
>
> Zhiyou explained their origins. He said, "Formerly in western India there lived a Bodhisattva who was compassionate and brought salvation to the world. He took a great vow to paint an Image of Dizang in order to bring salvation to living beings suffering in the three paths. He went to the city of the Ten Kings and declared, 'I have aspired to bring salvation to the suffering of the three paths. I seek your help in bringing benefit to those who suffer.' The Ten Kings assented respectfully by bringing their palms together. They lined up in order to the left and the right and told the Image [of Dizang]. 'All living beings belong to the Great Sage. If you should wish to transform them, we will serve as companions to help in the process of sagely transformation.' At that time the Image gave a subtle smile [and said], 'Excellent! The sinful acts of living beings will soon be lessened.' Then it emitted a beam of light that illuminated the suffering vessels in the three paths. All of the sufferings of the living beings who received illumination were relieved."
>
> [Zhiyou continued,] "Such is the great profit that was bestowed when the Indian Bodhisattva entered the *samādhi* of bringing benefit to living beings and prayed to the Ten Kings. That Bodhisattva himself made into a picture the forms that he had seen and added the Ten Kings and the others to the original Image. This [painting that I have brought from the West] is the numinous image."[65]

Indian origins are assigned to both the scripture and the icon. In light of the urgent need to establish an authoritative source for the icon and scripture and the text's sophisticated literary style, this genesis legend was undoubt-

65. Ibid., 367b–368a; adapted from the translation by Teiser (1994: 44–45).

edly the work of literate clergy attempting to explain and incorporate popular beliefs—in this case the cult of the Ten Kings. By the tenth century, iconic paintings of Dizang together with the Ten Kings were circulating in China; they were a common motif in Dunhuang scroll paintings and ceiling paintings over grotto passageways.[66] The popularity of these depictions may have warranted attention from the clerical establishment, who sought to "authenticate" the practice as part of its transmitted heritage.

Another aspect of Dizang's underworld function is introduced in record 17, which presents King Yama as a manifestation of Dizang. This text narrates the experience of Guo Xu'an 郭徐安, a regional inspector in Yi prefecture (modern-day Chengdu), who fell very ill and died in 950. He is subsequently resurrected and records King Yama as saying: "I am the true body of the abode of King [Dizang] who, in order to make living beings experience the penalties of their actions, had manifested as King Yama. In reality I am the Dharma King."[67] The merging of King Yama and Dizang, originally two separate Buddhist personages, might have contributed to the development of the image of Dizang as a sovereign. This fusion of identities offers a possible Chinese antecedent for the subsequent Japanese doctrine of *honji suijaku* 本地垂迹, which correlates indigenous deities with Buddhist deities to form pairs of emanations and essence bodies.[68]

Demonology and Extending the Life Span

I have already highlighted the themes of warding off illness, averting death, and prolonging the life span in connection with Dizang Bodhisattva. Two narratives (records 22 and 32) in Changjin's collection confirm that venerating Dizang brought about the goal of prolonging life. In record 22 an acolyte averts death and has his life span lengthened after he practices drawing Dizang's image with his fingernail:

> In the great Song, Shi Huiwen 釋惠溫 was a monk of the Monastery of Kaibao Era (Kaibao si 開寶寺). There was an acolyte there whose name was unknown. When the acolyte was fourteen years old, he met Jian Zhen 健真, a fortuneteller, who [forewarned], "This child's life span is exceedingly short, and he has only one month of life remaining." Hearing Jian Zhen's words, the teacher let the acolyte return to his immediate family. On the way, it rained heavily and there was no through road leading to his home or [to the monastery]. [Hence] the acolyte lodged at an artist's house for the night. [The acolyte] saw a drawing of an image of Dizang Bodhisattva and used his fingernail to copy the image on the wall. The weather cleared, the rain ceased, and he returned home. After more than a month, he returned to Kaibao si. Rejoicing, Huiwen said, "What Jian Zhen said was false." He immediately summoned Zhen to let

66. See Chapter 4 for a discussion on the iconography of Dizang and Ten Kings.
67. *Lingyan ji*, 363b.
68. For a study of *honji suijaku*, see Matsunaga 1969.

> him see the child. [Zhen] said, "This child's life has been extended and he will [live to be] fifty years old. I do not really know the reason." The acolyte himself said, "That very night after I used my fingernail to draw Dizang's image, the monk sleeping by my side spoke to me, saying, 'You will [live to be] fifty, fifty [years old].' Thus he spoke thrice. Except for this, I have practiced no other good deed." The teacher and fortune-teller exclaimed, "The saint's power is inconceivable!" Subsequently, the acolyte was ordained, received full precepts, and became the Reverend Huizang 惠藏.[69]

In record 32 a filial son, Chen Jian 陳健, sets up a shrine room for his parents with the images of Dizang and Guanyin. In the fourth year of *qiande* 乾德 (966), he dies and subsequently revives to relate how he was brought to the netherworld for questioning by King Yama.[70] The two images he commissioned for his parents appear and protest that he will not be released back to the living world because he has yet to complete his filial practice and that he has accrued significant merits from image-making. Consequently, King Yama bestows another forty years of life on Chen so that he may fulfill his practice of filial piety; he further spares Chen's son from an early death so that Chen may enjoy his due of filial piety from his son. Of course, prolonging the life span is a generalized religious function attributed to both Buddhist and non-Buddhist deities and thus should not be regarded as the special domain of the Bodhisattva Dizang.

A few stories in *A Record of Numinous Verifications* are preoccupied with a set of thematic concerns that could be broadly classified under "demonology." One aspect of Dizang's personality, set forth in the *Scripture on the Ten Wheels*, emphasizes his mastery of *dhāraṇī*, which enables him to dispel all natural and supernatural harm and to bring about various benefits for living beings. In the *Section on the Sumeru Treasury*, Dizang is the subduer of calamities, especially those unleashed by fiendish demons and spirits. One may recall that in the same vein, *The Exorcism Method* explains how Dizang trained, in a past life, under a skilled saint to master an array of magico-religious techniques to help those persecuted by demons, ghosts, and other harmful spirits. During the time of the Buddha, he uses his skill to liberate a family from fiendish spirits. Record 7 in *A Record of Numinous Verifications* refers to an anecdote from the indigenous scripture *The Exorcism Method*:

> A Tang layman, Li Xinsi 李信思, was from Lushui 瀘水. The men and women in his family were vexed by fiendish ghosts. More than thirty people, without cause, were in pain or vomited blood, and the majority were suffocated to death. At that time, Xinsi was perturbed and questioned a monk, "Do you have methods and ways to save them?" The monk thought for a very long while and told him, "In the past, when the Tathāgata was in the world, in the

69. *Lingyan ji*, 365b–366a.
70. Ibid., 368b–369a.

> country of Magadha at the foot of Mount Vipula, a malevolent ghost that was vexing the family of Elder Qiaoti 橋提 exhaled its last vital vapor.[71] For ten days, five hundred members of his family were all strangled to death without cause. At that time, the Bodhisattva Dizang was roaming and performing supernormal feats in all the lands. Arriving at the elder's house, he aroused the mind of great compassion and recited incantations to save them. Instantly, all [ailments] were eradicated and they recovered. Relying on that teaching, you should take refuge in the venerated Dizang." [Li], in a blink of an eye, thought and rejoiced. He delighted in selecting beautiful [images] and used his wealth to make [copies].[72] For fifty years after that, the Lushui district was immune from the terrors of epidemics. All that remains is the efficacious image, which still exists.[73]

The experience of Li Xinsi is deliberately presented as continuous with the events related in *The Exorcism Method.* It cannot be ascertained whether the compiler deliberately incorporated the anecdote from *The Exorcism Method,* but we do know that in medieval China, among the techniques used to vanquish demons and ghosts, was an expanding set of devices associated with Dizang: intoning his *dhāraṇī,* reciting his name, making images of him. Two stories in *A Record of Numinous Verifications* state that venerating Dizang may avert calamities wrought by malevolent spirits. In the tale of Kang Jutong 康居通 (record 14), a regional inspector in Lu 路 prefecture, the following anecdote is included:

> In the first year of *guangming* 廣明 (880), during the reign of Emperor Xizong 僖宗 (r. 873–888), great turmoil was caused by malevolent spirits. In the country, there was an epidemic that caused the numbers of dead to rise as high as a mountain peak. Tong dreamt that hundreds of thousands of blue-colored spirits, who happened to pass by his gate, said, "This household is the chamber of Dizang Bodhisattva. We and our subordinates should not enter this gate." [Tong] awoke and greatly rejoiced. He and his family members were [thus] able to remain free of demonic calamities.[74]

Record 24 also mentions the return-from-death experience of a heretical shamaness who died from the plague. She explains that while a fiendish spirit was strangling her, a *śramaṇa* appeared. On seeing the *śramaṇa,* the spirit fled in fear, and the *śramaṇa* then disclosed that he was Dizang Bodhisattva.[75]

---

71. Mount Vipula is in the city of Rajagṛha (Wangshe cheng 王舍城), located in present Bihar (eastern India).

72. An editorial annotation states that the phrase *quanshi* 泉失 is ambiguous. I have translated it as "used his wealth."

73. *Lingyan ji,* 356b–357a.

74. Ibid., 361a–b.

75. Ibid., 366b.

Image-Making and Icon Worship

The title of *A Record of Numinous Verifications* signals its preoccupation with recording and exalting the miraculous power of Dizang images. The potency of icon worship has always been a salient factor in cult formation. To the believer, the icon is more than a mere replica of the deity; through the icon, the deity is transformed into a living presence amidst daily life. Not surprisingly, image-making, in the form of sculpting statues or drawing pictures, is a central theme underscoring all the stories collected in *A Record of Numinous Verifications.*

Making and venerating images of Dizang is also emphasized in the *Scripture on the Past Vows.* According to this text, in certain past lives, the Bodhisattva Dizang appeared as the filial Brāhman daughter Luminous Eyes, who renounced all her wealth to sculpt an image of the past Buddha and dedicated herself completely to pious contemplation of the image to rescue her deceased mother from the sufferings of hell.[76] Such accounts connect the practice of Buddhist filial piety and the making and worship of Dizang images attested to in records 4, 9, 12, 13, 20, and 32 of *A Record of Numinous Verifications.* Records 12, 13, and 20 in particular relate how filial daughters made and venerated images of Dizang to liberate their deceased mothers from the evil paths of rebirth. Both in its narrative structure and contents, record 12 closely parallels the story of the Brāhman woman as told in the *Scripture on the Past Vows*:

> It was said that a commander-in-chief in Chen 陳 city had a young daughter whose last name was Chen. (Her first name is not known.) As her mother had died when she was very young, the daughter fretted day and night that she had never known [her mother]. The commander-in-chief advised her, "If you yearn for your deceased mother, you should forge [an image of] the Bodhisattva Dizang to venerate and aspire to relieve [your mother] from suffering." She immediately donated five hundred in cash to employ an artisan to sculpt a three-foot image. . . . The daughter venerated [the image] and made offerings day and night. She prayed and vowed to save her mother from suffering. She dreamt that she saw a *śramaṇa*, who told her, "Your mother was [reborn] in the Scorching and Burning hell." [The daughter replied], "I am a woman. My father's name is Śilasudarśana [Shiluoshanxian 尸羅善現] and my mother is called Yuedili 悅帝利." The *śramaṇa* said, "I sought the place of your mother's rebirth and saw her suffering. [Because] I have vowed to arouse the mind of awakening to help living beings and have been moved by your filial heart, I myself entered hell to emit light and preach the Dharma. Your mother has been released from sufferings and has been reborn in Trāyastriṃśa." Seeing that the *śramaṇa*'s clothes were burnt and damaged, the daughter Chen immediately enquired the reason. The *śramaṇa* said, "When I entered hell, there were only raging flames." When the daughter

76. *Benyuan jing*, T412:13.778b–779a, 780c–781b.

> awoke, she was both sad and happy. A crowd gathered and saw that the image's robes appeared to have been scorched. Family members said it was an extraordinary event. On hearing [what had happened], many duplicated the image hoping to save their parents from suffering.[77]

Here we have a reenactment of Dizang's descent into hell during his previous life as the filial Brāhman daughter. The names of Chen's parents are the same as those of the Brāhman's parents. In all likelihood, the story of Daughter Chen was a colloquial retelling of the Dizang *avadāna* in the *Scripture on the Past Vows.* Nonetheless, it is important to note deviations that the miracle tale introduces. In the miracle tale, for example, Dizang appears not as the filial daughter but as the patron deity who manifests himself as a *śramaṇa* to enter hell in response to a filial daughter's prayers.

Here, too, one encounters the theme of the icon springing to life: Religious devotion and filial piety transmute the image so that the material object becomes the embodied flesh of the deity who performs the supernormal act of braving the raging flames of hell. The image verifies the miracle by its scorched robes—a visual confirmation of its own efficacy that in turn attracts adherents to venerate the image. The particular image through which the deity is venerated in daily religious practice often becomes the form through which the deity manifests itself to the worshiper, thereby driving home the point that the icon has indeed come alive. For example, in record 32 a filial son, Chen, forged twin images of Dizang and Guanyin for his parents before dying in 966. He revived two hours later and reported that when he was brought to the underworld court, the exact two images he had commissioned arrived to intervene on his behalf and secured his release back to the realm of the living.[78]

In *A Record of Numinous Verifications,* potency is not restricted to formal objects of worship. In fact, Dizang icons sketched at leisure are equally efficacious and bring about numinous experiences. In the previous story of the young acolyte, he is not only spared, but has his life extended after he casually traces an image of Dizang with his fingernail.[79] In another narrative, a sudden thunderstorm breaks out while some youths play at tracing a Dizang icon in the sand; as the terrified youths flee in different directions, Dizang simultaneously manifests himself to each one and guides them to safety.[80] The import of these stories is evident: Images of Dizang are so powerful that even idly drawing his form brings religious protection and otherworldly assistance.

Seeing a deity in the flesh is a highly coveted experience interpreted as a verification of one's spiritual state. One example from *A Record of Numinous*

---

77. *Lingyan ji,* 360a.
78. Ibid., 368b-369a.
79. Ibid., 365b-366a.
80. Ibid., 367a-b.

Verifications is the story of the monk Dingfa 定法, who earnestly prayed for a chance to witness a manifestation of the Bodhisattva Dizang:

> After a full three years, during which nothing happened, a novice monk came asking for lodging at the monastery. Overhearing this conversation in the corridor, Dingfa politely came out to make inquiries. Before speaking more than a few words, [the monk] abruptly vanished. People were baffled by this and questioned Dingfa: "Who was that *śramaṇa* guest?" [Dingfa] replied, "The *śramaṇa* spoke [to me] thus: '[Your] wondrous vow has already been fulfilled. Why is your resolve so deficient?' and so forth." All those who heard this said, "You were anxious to see Dizang, but you did not attend to the essential matter of transcendence. Hence, the bodhisattva manifested his body and questioned your lack of resolve." Ding[fa] cried out, "A miracle!" [Dingfa] aroused the aspiration for awakening and earnestly pursued the Unsurpassed Awakening. Consequently, he stimulated a response [in the form of] a dream [in which a voice] said: "The previous *śramaṇa* was I, Dizang Bodhisattva. You sought to see my bodily manifestation, [but] you did not engender the mind of awakening. For this reason, I [appeared as a monk to] awaken you. [Because] you have traced and copied my form numerous [times], you will never fall into the three evil paths [of rebirth]. When you die, you will be born in Tuṣita heaven. On the day the Compassionate One descends, you should receive a prediction from the Buddha. I will follow you as shadow follows form and as water takes [the shape of its] vessel."[81]

Here the patron deity, Dizang, manifests himself in everyday life and instructs Dingfa to discriminate the true essence from the material form of the sacred. The story draws on controversial points regarding image worship, probably reflecting larger debates in the Buddhist intellectual milieu. Venerating images implies an attachment to material form as well as the anticipated merits and efficacies. In the narrative, Dingfa is criticized for being overly attached to "seeing" the deity's form and neglecting the path to awakening. Ultimately, the story affirms the practice of venerating images because Dingfa is compensated in the afterlife for piously copying images of Dizang.

At times, a particularly efficacious image of a deity verifies its potency through visible signals. For example, records 1, 2, 3, 6, 15, 26, 28, and 29 all speak of Dizang images that miraculously emanate lights and are particularly efficacious in assisting or granting the prayers of devotees. The notion of icons emitting light was a familiar one in medieval China, and both Dizang and Guanyin were known to do so.[82] As illustrated in records 1, 2, 28, and 29, the practice of tracing and duplicating images was especially associated with Dizang icons that emitted light. In records 1 and 2, wall paintings

81. Ibid., 356b.

82. A famous example is the Dunhuang scroll painting titled "Painting of Bodhisattvas Radiating Light" (*Fangguang pusa tu* 放光菩薩圖), now preserved in Japan.

in certain monasteries known to emanate light prompted widespread copying. Even venerating replicas caused them to emanate light and stimulate numinous efficacies.

Another widespread practice associated with image worship is the invocation of the deity's name. In the retelling of Cui Lixi's 崔李係 otherworldly journey (record 16), as Cui visits each of the hells he exhorts those suffering to invoke the name of Dizang in their appeals for relief. In a story (record 20) that invokes Dizang's past life as the filial daughter Luminous Eyes in the *Scripture on the Past Vows*, an orphaned girl seeks out a *śramaṇa*, who teaches her to recite the name of Dizang. After doing so, the girl is able to ascend to heaven and meet her mother. In record 26 the nun Zhizang recites the name of Dizang and, as a result, she miraculously recovers a drawing of the Pure Land triad that she had lost.

Finally, *A Record of Numinous Verifications* indicates the growing practice of consecrating specific days of the month to the worship of Dizang. Venerating particular deities on assigned days was a prevalent practice in late medieval China; this can be seen in the widespread observance of the Ten Feast Days. Depending on the version of the text used, the twenty-fourth or the twenty-third day of the month was usually consecrated to the worship of the Bodhisattva Dizang.[83] Two narratives in *A Record of Numinous Verifications* signal the growing association of Dizang worship with the twenty-fourth day of the month. In record 18 a deceased wife is liberated from hell and reborn in the heavenly realm after her husband worships Dizang on her behalf. She describes how the emanation bodies of Dizang appear in heaven on the twenty-fourth day of each month:

> Now that you, my husband, have constructed the holy image on my behalf, as a result of this good deed, my [bad] *karma* is eliminated and I have been reborn into Trāyastriṃśa heaven. . . . On the twenty-fourth day of each month, a trichiliocosm of numerous and limitless transformation bodies of Dizang, measureless and boundless, assemble inside the Hall of Good Deeds (Shanye tang 善業堂) of that heaven. They completely spread out under the Tree of No Worries to preach teachings for the benefit of living beings. [The emanations] are all gold and in the form of a monk. Once when they preached the teachings to me, they informed me, "You, [both] husband and wife, have made [the Dizang statue], and on account of [this] practice of the teaching, you were freed from the realm of suffering and reborn in heaven.[84]

Also in record 13 a filial daughter dreams of her deceased mother, reborn as a hungry ghost, who says that on the twenty-fourth day of each month,

83. For example, see the Dunhuang manuscript *Dizang pusa shizhai ri* (S 2568), transcribed in T2850:85.1300a–b. In this version, the twenty-fourth day of the month is consecrated to Dizang veneration; incanting Dizang's name will prevent one from falling into the Hell of Being Chopped in Two and will efface a thousand aeons of wrongdoings.

84. *Lingyan ji*, 364a–b.

Dizang himself enters the Hell of Hungry Ghosts to bring temporary respite and satiate the acute hunger of the beings there.[85]

In summary, *A Record of Numinous Verifications* suggests that by the tenth century a full-fledged Dizang cult was in existence. Making Dizang icons, copying images, contemplating his image, incanting his name, reciting scriptures, abstaining from meat on a specific day of the month—these were all practices that flourished in late medieval China. The diverse social backgrounds of the devotees indicates the dissemination of Dizang worship across varied sectors of Chinese society. Female devotees include a maidservant, a poor widow, a Buddhist nun, the daughter and mother of a government official, even Empress Wu herself. Most male worshipers—who frequently appear as husbands, fathers, or sons—possess official titles or are members of the Buddhist clergy; a goose hunter and a fisherman, however, are also found among them.

The Canonization of a Buddhist Cult

Miracle tales are important sources for studying the underworld Dizang cult and its function in medieval society. The earliest story, of Mr. Wang's voyage, may denote a historic moment in the medieval Chinese conception of the afterlife, signaling a shift from the generic Buddhist monk to the Bodhisattva Dizang the monk-bodhisattva responsible for the salvation of the dead, especially those reborn in the subterranean realm. At first glance, it may seem that the shift hardly constitutes a major transition and only supplies a name and personality for the generic monk responsible for the salvation of those reborn as ghosts or in hell. On reflection, however, introducing Dizang in place of a generic monk does bring about a paradigmatic shift—a move from the monastic establishment to the savior bodhisattva cult as the site of Buddhist afterlife practice. The result is a new Chinese afterlife cult centered on a set of fairly generic Buddhist practices, such as image-making and veneration, recollecting the deity's name, scripture recitation, ritual confession, and the observance of vegetarianism. These practices are Mahāyāna insofar as they were subsumed under the savior bodhisattva Dizang.

As stated previously, medieval Chinese, inspired by new Buddhist concepts, fashioned visions of death and the afterlife that brought together threads from various religious sources. In keeping with Indian practices of making and transferring merits, Chinese Buddhists regarded the monk as a specialist in the affairs of death and the afterlife. The Ghost Festival reflects the successful integration of the Buddhist *saṅgha* into medieval Chinese economic and institutional structures centered on the enterprise of caring for the dead. In the late seventh and early eighth centuries, with the growing importance of Buddhist savior cults, it was critical that Buddhist piety root itself

85. Ibid., 360b–361a.

in the sphere of death and afterlife practices, which were so germane to everyday religion in medieval China. Because Buddhist monks had by then established a reputation for delivering the deceased from undesirable realms of rebirth, the *śramaṇa* iconography of the Bodhisattva Dizang made him the logical candidate for an afterlife bodhisattva cult and eased the transition from the monastic to the bodhisattva paradigm. Discernible in the *Scripture on the Ten Wheels,* Dizang's *śramaṇa* iconography emerged in Chinese Buddhist art in the seventh century—the same period as Fazang's record of Mr. Wang's underworld voyage. The image of Dizang the *śramaṇa* had a lasting impact on Chinese Buddhists and drove home his dual role as both bodhisattva and monk.

The tale of Mr. Wang's journey heralds the beginning of what would be a lasting connection between Dizang and Chinese imaginings of the underworld. Derived from earlier collections, miracle tales in the tenth-century *Extensive Records from the Taiping Era* indicate that this association was continuously enlarged upon so that by the time the *Extensive Records from the Taiping Era* and *A Record of Numinous Verifications* made their appearance in the second half of the tenth century, Dizang was already recognized across sectors of Chinese society as an integral part of the underworld. The stories preserved in non-Buddhist collections are usually styled as accounts of return-from-death experiences. Thus Dizang's underworld character was most likely first elaborated in a diffused religious setting where miracle tales spring up and are transmitted. Return-from-death narratives were a literary genre in early medieval China, and Buddhist return-from-death narratives soon appeared as a subgenre operating as a forum for negotiating the imaginings of the afterlife, especially the underworld. From the eighth century on, this subgenre served as the stage for scripting Dizang's underworld character. In return-from-death accounts collected in the *Extensive Records from the Taiping Era,* Dizang possesses considerable status in the underworld; he resides in a palatial residence located immediately outside or in the precincts of the subterranean realm.

The third body of evidence discussed in this chapter is *A Record of Numinous Verifications,* a tenth-century Buddhist compilation of Dizang miracle tales. Orally transmitted from disparate geographical regions, the stories can hardly be expected to be consistent or compatible with one another. Yet the collection exhibits a remarkable degree of thematic consistency, suggesting that the compiler, a member of the elite literate clergy, had a hand in reshaping the narration. The overall picture of the Dizang cult in the narratives, especially its afterlife aspects, is relatively systematized and coherent. Moreover, the stories frequently invoke themes consistent with scriptural lore and imagery, especially the *Scripture on the Past Vows.* In fact, *A Record of Numinous Verifications* evinces a decided preference for the *Scripture on the Past Vows* as the scriptural core for the Dizang cult. This canonical compilation of Dizang miracles, unlike non-Buddhist anthologies, includes several themes in addition to underworld concerns.

The rich diversity of the Dizang cult is still evident in the collection despite editorial efforts to maintain thematic unity. Several themes have been reiterated, some obviously continuous with motifs from Dizang Bodhisattva scriptures, art, and epigraphy. The Pure Land connection, for instance, surfaces in several stories and is considerably expanded so that one catches glimpses of Dizang's relationship with both Maitreya and Amitābha. *A Record of Numinous Verifications* states that Dizang devotees attain rebirth either in Amitābha's Pure Land or Maitreya's Tuṣita. Trāyastriṃśa heaven is introduced as another rebirth destination for Dizang devotees; this addition can probably be traced to the *Scripture on the Past Vows.*[86] Other lesser-known afterlife destinations are invoked. The differentiated goals of rebirth held out to adherents of Dizang worship suggest the existence in medieval times of a rich afterlife geography, which for the most part remains obscure to us.

86. In the *Scripture on the Past Vows,* the Buddha visits Trāyastriṃśa heaven, where he preaches to his deceased mother, the Lady Māyā; see *Benyuan jing,* T412:13.779c–780b.

CONCLUSION
Reassessing Dizang, Lord of the Underworld

IN THE MODERN encounter described in the Introduction, Dizang Bodhisattva presides over a set of afterlife rites, all of which were introduced by Tang Buddhism. On the thirtieth day of the seventh lunar month, Dizang's birthday, local temple celebrations seamlessly synchronize a medley of rites for feeding deceased ancestors reborn as hungry ghosts and hell dwellers.[1] The observances of the Ghost Festival, the Buddho-Daoist purgatorial rites of Universal Salvation, the esoteric rite of liberating flaming mouths, and the *Scripture on the Past Vows*—all converge into a single vision of afterlife redemption, at the crucible of which stands Dizang, Lord of the Underworld. Dizang reigns over this synthetic reconfiguration of afterlife rites as the patron deity. Avalambana and its more widespread manifestations (the Middle Primordial and Universal Salvation rites) traditionally take place on the fifteenth day of the seventh lunar month. In local temples, however, these rites are subsumed beneath the ceremonies honoring Dizang's birthday—a testament to Dizang's centrality in death and afterlife practices in Chinese religion today. Dizang's sovereignty over the underworld is so much an accepted fact that ritual actors and audience alike presume that it is Dizang who is opening and closing the gates of hell during the ritual.

Casting Dizang as *the* savior of the damned in all situations has also pervaded modern scholarship, and scholars are predisposed to reconstruct Dizang's early history largely from the perspective of his role as Lord of the Underworld. Analyzing Dizang Bodhisattva through this lens, however, superimposes over the evidence a preconceived trajectory that culminates in Dizang's crowning as an underworld sovereign. Such a perspective necessarily predetermines the selection, reading, and analysis of source materials. This study has so far avoided viewing Dizang's early history as an evolution of his underworld character and has instead let the evidence speak for itself and shape the discourse. Medieval sources all suggest variegated historical situations and make apparent how inadequate the paradigm of the Lord of the Underworld is for describing the formative historical relationships that Dizang worship forged with other religious components in medieval China. From the sixth to the tenth century, Dizang was an important image, facili-

1. For a listing of birthdays of prominent buddhas and bodhisattvas, see Zhong 2000: 186.

tating and embodying a dynamic interplay of relationships among religious forms often thought of as autonomous and separate from one another. In this environment, Dizang developed a series of complicated associations with Sanjie jiao, Pure Land, esoteric Buddhism, the cults of Bhaiṣajyaguru, Guanyin, Maitreya, the Ten Kings, and Mulian mythology, as well as commonplace practices such as ancestral worship, filial piety, demonology, use of the mantic arts, and abstaining from eating meat.

Medieval sources, nonetheless, indicate that by the end of the eighth century, Dizang worship melded with other death and afterlife cults, especially in Dunhuang and Sichuan, where the bodhisattva shows up frequently in portrayals of afterlife judgment. This concluding chapter will piece together the relevant evidence to map out Dizang's trajectory as Lord of the Underworld and then reevaluate the extent to which this role describes the medieval Dizang cult. What is it about Dizang that captured the attention of medieval Chinese, who reconfigured this bodhisattva to play a part in the afterlife? To what extent was he internalized to form the array of concepts and practices conjured up to confront the anxieties of dying and secure salvation for the dead? Approaching the study of Dizang Bodhisattva from the material evidence before scrutinizing his emergence as the Lord of the Underworld ultimately lays out the larger significance of studying the medieval Dizang cult.

Afterlife Practices in China

Afterlife beliefs and practices in early China can be classified as public or private. In the public sector were the cults of ancestral worship and popular sacrifices. Rites of feeding and propitiating ancestral spirits were held in the precincts of ancestral temples and were accessible only to the aristocracy. The larger population fed and appeased the restless spirits of the dead by conducting sacrifices of meat and wine presided over by village shamans. Afterlife practices from their inception were intertwined with those of filial piety and the family, which forms the institutional core of Chinese society. Tomb excavations in the twentieth century reveal that the interval between the Warring States and the Han saw a rise in the performance of funerary rites spurred on by a new spiritual concern with the fate of the individual after death. This growing consciousness of individuality led to an investigation of the composition of the self, which came to be equated with the ethereal (*hun* 魂) and earthly (*po* 魄) spirits. Funerary and mortuary practices often reflect the desire for an idyllic existence beyond death and the urgent need not only to pacify the dead (conceived of as disembodied spirits), but also to separate them from the living. Imaginings of life beyond the grave were linked to quests for immortality and otherworldly paradises, as well as the burying of material provisions for the use of the dead in the afterlife.[2] Appeasing the restless dead and separating them from the living are themes

2. For early pre-Buddhist Chinese attitudes toward death and the afterlife, see Poo 1998.

that resonate in many traditional societies.[3] Early Chinese conceptions of the underworld were prompted by a need to seal off the dead in a remote place, away from the world of the living.[4] Mirroring the political reality of Chinese society, an underworld bureaucratic administration surfaced early on, undoubtably created to bring a sense of order to the unpredictability of death and the potential havoc it can unleash.

The transmission of Buddhism to China at the beginning of the common era introduced the principles of *karma* and rebirth, the heart of the Buddhist afterlife. Although the six paths of rebirth was a new concept to the Chinese, the realm of hungry ghosts immediately struck a resonating chord because of its similarities to traditional ideas of the dead as wandering, disembodied spirits; similarly the bureaucratic metaphor was transposed onto Buddhist retributive hells.[5] The Ghost Festival constitutes one medieval Chinese Buddhist reimagination of the familiar theme of feeding ancestral spirits in association with making offerings to the *saṅgha* and transferring merits. The Ten Kings function as another formula that creatively envisions the passage from death to rebirth; it furnishes a ritual solution offering salvation to the deceased through liturgical penances on their behalf. The Dizang cult represents another strand of afterlife imaginings in this malleable environment, where variant permutations of death and life beyond the grave were played out.[6]

Dizang's afterlife connection is present in his early image as the savior of the six paths of rebirth from the *Scripture on the Ten Wheels*. This role situates him at the heart of the Indian Buddhist view of the afterlife, founded on the principle of *karma* and rebirth. In the sixth century, Dizang as overseer of the six paths of rebirth was germane to his function as the savior of this Sahā world in the age of the five turbulences, a role especially conducive to the religious and intellectual ethos in fifth- and sixth-century China. Exacerbated by the Northern Zhou persecution of Buddhism and the widespread sociopolitical chaos on the eve of the Sui unification of China, sixth-century Chinese Buddhists were convinced that the decline of Buddhism prophesied in the scriptures had arrived. In this volatile atmosphere, Dizang was the savior who possessed the key to salvation, a function that forged ties between Dizang worship and Sanjie jiao. However, during the period of political stability and prosperity following the unification of China between the seventh and the eighth centuries, in his capacity as the savior of the six paths of rebirth, Dizang interacted with prevalent afterlife expressions to produce both a desire for an afterlife in paradisal abodes and a deep-seated phobia of rebirth in hell.

3. For the ancient Greek concept of neutral death, see Bernstein 1993: 21–49; for the restless dead in ancient Greek religion, see Johnston 1999.

4. For a study of Chinese conceptions of the underworld before Buddhism, see Harper 1994; Seidel 1982, 1987a; Thompson 1989.

5. Teiser 1994: 171–195.

6. For another example, see Wu (1996), who discusses what he calls "secularized or vulgarized Buddhism" (*shishu fojiao* 世俗佛教) through a study of Tang tomb documents.

The pursuit of an idyllic afterlife is expressed fairly early in Dizang worship. Inscriptions indicate that from its inception, Dizang images were commissioned in the hope that the deceased or sponsor might be reborn in the Pure Land. Moreover, Buddhist art and epigraphy reveal that the earliest phase of Dizang art at Longmen, dating to the seventh and eighth centuries, evinced a Pure Land connection, beginning with the appearance of Dizang in Amitābha triads. Such Pure Land iconography also occurs in the miracle tales collected in the tenth-century *A Record of Numinous Verifications.* Dizang figures as an addition to the Amitābha Pure Land triad as well. This quartet is invoked, for instance, in the writing of the eighth-century Pure Land thinker Fazhao. His *Jingtu wuhui nianfo lue fashiyi zan* 淨土五會念佛略法事儀讚 (Hymns from the *Abridged Procedure for the Five-Cadence Buddha Incantation of the Pure Land*) calls on followers to "recite [the names of] the Buddha Amitābha and the bodhisattvas Guanyin, Mahāsthāmaprāpta, and Dizang, each hundred and fifty times."[7] A similar quartet of Pure Land deities occurs in Dunhuang liturgical writings, namely the *Tankuang wen* 嘆壙文 (A Tomb Eulogy, S 4474).[8]

Dizang was further connected to other forms of Pure Land, notably the cults of Maitreya and Bhaiṣajyaguru.[9] *A Record of Numinous Verifications* sug-

---

7. *Jingtu wuhui nianfo lue fashiyi zan,* T1983:47.475a. In the preface to this text, Fazhao explains that the ritual assembly of the five-cadence Buddha incantation is found in an original three-fascicle text titled *Wuhui fashiyi* 五會法事儀. The five cadences here refer to five basic melodic rhythms for reciting the Buddha's name, which Fazhao himself is alleged to have personally heard from Amitābha during a visionary journey to Sukhāvatī.

8. The *Tankuang wen* states:

> Homage to the Great Compassionate Buddha Amitābha in the Western Land of Bliss (repeat 3 times);
> Homage to the Great Compassionate Bodhisattva Guanyin in the Western Land of Bliss (repeat 3 times);
> Homage to the Great Compassionate Bodhisattva Mahāsthāmaprāpta in the Western Land of Bliss (repeat 3 times);
> Homage to the Great Compassionate Bodhisattva Dizang (repeat 1 time). (Wang 1995: 7)

As a eulogy, the *Tankuang wen* brings together several cultic strands. In the above verses, Dizang is appended to the triad of the Western Land of Bliss, although his position as an "interloper" in this tradition is perhaps indicated by the fact that his name is incanted only once. The eulogy concludes with a description of Guanyin and Mahāsthāmaprāpta coming to lead the way to the Western Land of Bliss, where one will meet the future Buddha Maitreya and listen to his teachings.

9. Narratives in *A Record on Numinous Verifications* hold out rebirth in Maitreya's land, Tuṣita, as a reward for venerating Dizang; see *Lingyan ji,* records 9, 11, 14, 16, and 26. This connection follows logically from Dizang's role as the savior of this Sahā world in the period before Maitreya's advent, a function canonized in the *Scripture on the Past Vows.* The scripture states:

> You should recollect my painstaking injunction at the Palace of Trāyastriṃśa and cause all living beings in the Sahā world, *until the appearance of Maitreya in this world,* to attain liberation, to leave suffering eternally, to encounter the buddhas, and to receive prophecies [of their buddhahood]. (*Benyuan jing,* T412:13.779b–c; my italics)

gests that Dizang worship was, moreover, associated with rarely documented anomalous afterlife destinations.[10] Constructed as heavenly subterranean realms (the Buddhist counterparts to Daoist paradisal grottoes), these abodes are presented as temporary residences for those adherents of the Dizang cult who possessed scarce merit or lacked faith in the efficacy of Dizang images. They apparently did not take root in the Buddhist context, and their presence in medieval Dizang literature serves as a portal to lesser-known aspects of the medieval afterlife geography.

The underworld Dizang becomes increasingly discernible from the late eighth century. Except for an early allusion in *The Exorcism Method*, the first phase of Dizang's underworld theme is largely elaborated in the return-from-death narratives, which tell of encounters with Dizang during journeys to the subterranean realm. Dizang normally appears in hell as an intercessor, a ray of mercy and redemption in the afterlife judiciary process over which King Yama or the Ten Kings presided. Because these return-from-death narratives are preserved in non-Buddhist and Buddhist anthologies, they affirm that Dizang worship was observed across the boundaries of organized religions; this may also explain how Dizang's underworld character was disseminated in medieval society. The *Record of a Returned Soul* in particular belongs to a genre of tales and ballads recovered from Dunhuang manuscripts that were frequently used in storytelling.[11] In short, the underworld Dizang was defined and disseminated in a malleable religious landscape that absorbed and intermingled doctrines and practices extracted from a wealth of diverse sources.

After his introduction, the underworld Dizang generated new motifs and interacted with other underworld cults. Iconography captures themes not often acknowledged in writing, such as the amalgamation of the Ten Kings with Dizang Bodhisattva in Dunhuang and Sichuan. In *A Record of Numinous Verifications*, one story associates an icon of the Ten Kings with an Indian copy of the *Scripture on the Past Vows*.[12] Dunhuang art also introduces Dizang's entourage, which includes the acolytes who record good and bad deeds, the monk Daoming, the lion-dog, and the Ten Kings and their court attendants.[13] These characters became permanent fixtures in Chinese underworld mythology. Sculpture from the Yuanjue dong at Anyue documents an encounter with another afterlife cult, the Ghost Festival, and its foundational myth, Mulian's descent to hell. The ambiguous identity of the main figure (is it Mulian or Dizang?) in the sculpture suggests that the two underworld cults may have overlapped in late medieval China. Precisely because Mulian and Dizang are both frequently illustrated as monks bear-

10. See *Lingyan ji*, record 16, 362a–363a.

11. On Dunhuang transformation texts, see Mair 1983, 1989; for the pan-Asian origins of Chinese storytelling and performance, see Mair 1988.

12. Record 29, *Lingyan ji*, 367b–368b.

13. For the iconography of Dizang's acolytes, see Soymié 1996, 1967.

ing staffs, it is often difficult to distinguish one from the other without a corroborating inscription.[14] In the fifteenth century, the *Sanjiao yuanliu soushen daquan* 三教源流搜神大全 (The Complete Collection of the Investigation of Spirits Originating in the Three Teachings) matter-of-factly names Mulian as one of Dizang's past lives.[15]

The growing status of Dizang's underworld image probably prompted the monastic establishment to produce scriptural legitimization and canonize this aspect of his cult. The *Scripture on the Bodhisattva Dizang* and, quite likely, the *Scripture on the Past Vows* represent efforts to rearticulate and normalize novel expressions, to make them conform to accepted discourse, interpretations, and practices.[16] King Yama's role as head of the underworld bureaucracy and the existence of administrative errors in the afterlife judiciary process were "canonized" in this fashion. Juxtaposition of beatific visions of Pure Land against the ghastly terrors of hell may signal differentiated aspects of complex medieval Chinese attitudes toward death and the afterlife: Did Dizang devotion become a conduit for dealing with the residual guilt and anxiety that even a strong faith in Amitābha could not entirely erase? Whatever the catalysts, Tang Buddhists added Dizang to the pantheon of deities invoked to bring about rebirth in the Pure Land, thereby continuing trends in Indian Pure Land.

In Tang afterlife practices, filial piety and the salvation of deceased kin were channels through which Buddhism permeated the family, the institution at the heart of Chinese society. In this context, Dizang was one of several key symbols in Chinese reimaginings of Mahāyāna Buddhism, especially the bodhisattva doctrine. The question must then be raised: Why Dizang—and not other bodhisattvas like Mañjuśrī, who also attracted widespread devotion during the Tang period?[17] Dizang's cultic status in Tang society certainly catalyzed his steady assimilation into afterlife practices. He already possessed a natural affinity with the afterlife as the savior of the six paths of rebirth in the *Scripture on the Ten Wheels*. But the critical factor was no doubt Dizang's physical appearance as a monk bodhisattva, introduced early on in the *Scripture on the Ten Wheels*. In medieval Chinese society, Buddhist monks quickly established themselves as ritual specialists in the cult of the dead;

14. For a discussion of this sculpture, see Howard 2001: 157–159.

15. *Sanjiao yuanliu soushen daquan* is an encyclopedia of 181 deities found in the Three Teachings *(sanjiao)*: Buddhism, Confucianism, and Daoism. It was composed in the late Ming, probably after the *yongle* 永樂 era (1402–1424), and is based on an earlier work, the *Soushen guangji* 搜神廣記, dating to the Yuan (1280–1368). *Sanjiao yuanliu soushen daquan* is especially useful because it includes a set of woodblock illustrations of the deities. The text hails Dizang as the Bodhisattva King Dizang (Dizang wang pusa 地藏王菩薩); besides naming Mulian as one of Dizang's past lives, the record briefly narrates the legend behind the establishment of his cult on Mount Jiuhua; see the *Sanjiao yuanliu* in Wang and Li 1989: vol 3, 304.

16. One cannot conclusively make this claim for the *Scripture on the Past Vows* given the ambiguities surrounding its composition.

17. On the flourishing of Mañjuśrī worship in medieval China, see Birnbaum 1983; Gimello 1992, 1994, 1997; Gu n.d.

they were in competition with indigenous Chinese experts like village shamans and Daoist priests. The myth of Mulian and the Ghost Festival exemplify the Buddhist monastic establishment's successful intrusion into Chinese family religion centered on procuring purgatorial cleansing and afterlife salvation for dead ancestors. For a savior bodhisattva to secure a similar foothold in medieval Chinese religion, it was imperative that he should also be inextricably tied to the range of concerns about death and the salvation of deceased family members. Although several bodhisattva cults, notably Guanyin, did form relationships with the cult of the dead, the monk bodhisattva Dizang furnished the most effective imagery in this cultic contest between holy monk and savior bodhisattva. Dizang's iconography as a monk eases the paradigmatic shift from the holy monk to the savior bodhisattva, implanting Mahāyāna cultic practices permanently in the landscape of Chinese afterlife religion. If Dizang's identity as a monk helped connect him with the cult of the dead, then it was his status as a bodhisattva that allowed him to execute the marriage of indigenous death and afterlife concepts to those practices rudimentary to a savior cult like copying and reciting scripture, making and venerating images, and incanting *dhāraṇī* or the deity's name.

Female Practice of Filial Piety

The marriage of afterlife practice and the cult of filial piety has always been a salient characteristic of Chinese religion. Although filial piety was known in India, Chinese Buddhists emphatically stressed providing for the welfare of ancestors and relatives in the afterlife to accommodate indigenous practices. Afterlife rites advocating Dizang worship as a form of filial behavior are documented in non-Buddhist historical records, especially memorials composed for the eminent or virtuous. The practice of embroidering Dizang images on behalf of the deceased is recorded in three memorial eulogies collected in the *Wenyuan yinghua* 文苑英華 (A Literary Grove of Elegant Flowers) and the *Sikong Biaosheng wenji* 司空表聖文集 (A Collection of Essays by Sikong Biaosheng).[18]

One of the two records from *A Literary Grove* is titled *Xiu Dizang pusa zan* 繡地藏菩薩讚 (Hymn to the Embroidery of Dizang Bodhisattva), attributed to the Tang scholar Mu Yuan 穆員 (ca. 790), who belonged to a family of civil officials living in the era of *zhenyuan* 貞元 (785–805).[19] The hymn memorializes the sewing of Dizang images on behalf of the deceased. Sometime around 790, Mu Yuan's family suffered a series of deaths. His mother first embroidered a Dizang image on behalf of his dying younger sister, a nun liv-

18. Sikong is the author's last name or family name; Tu 圖 is his given name, and Biaosheng is his courtesy name (*zi* 字), usually coined at the age of twenty.

19. *Wenyuan yinghua*, fasc. 782, collected in *Wenyuange siku quanshu, yingyin* (影印)文淵閣四庫全書, 1340: 607. I have translated *zan* here as "hymn" because the piece is styled as a prayer to the deity Dizang for assistance in the afterlife. For biographical details on Mu Yuan, see *Xin Tang shu*, 16: 5015–5016; *Jiu Tang shu*, 13: 4114–4117.

ing at the Monastery of Pacifying the Nation (Anguo si 安國寺). Later his youngest sister dreamt of their elder sister reporting that this image of Dizang kept watch over her. The youngest sister then embroidered another image and the older sister subsequently died. Mu Yuan eulogizes Dizang as the bodhisattva unsurpassed in relieving the three unfortunate paths of rebirth (hell, ghost, and animal realms) and dispelling the grief of those mourning the loss of loved ones. He beseeches the deity to cause the desolate dark realms to quake (*shengling cui zhen you* 聖靈萃振幽).

Another record, the *Dizang pusa zan* 地藏菩薩讚 (Eulogy to the Bodhisattva Dizang), composed by Liang Su 梁肅 (753–793), praises a daughter for embroidering an image of Dizang on behalf of her deceased mother in addition to observing Confucian rites of mourning.[20] A distant relative of the family, who happened to be vice director of the palace library, reported her actions to the imperial court. Consequently, the filial daughter was officially lauded and memorialized in Liang Su's verse. Born in Anding 安定 (modern-day Jinchuan 涇川 in Gansu), Liang Su became a lay disciple of the Tiantai 天台 monk Zhanran 湛然 (711–782), composed several Tiantai works, and wrote a stele inscription to honor his religious teacher. His numerous ties to the literati and the court must have facilitated the Tang revival of Tiantai associated with Zhanran.[21] It is no coincidence that Liang Su was a prominent member of literati circles, particularly a group that harmonized Confucian and Buddhist concepts to reiterate the position that "patriotism and filial piety are innate to the nature of mind" (*xinxing ben ju zhong xiao* 心性本具忠孝).[22] In the late eighth and ninth centuries, the largely male court literati envisioned living out an integration of Confucian, Daoist, and Buddhist teachings and saw literati education as beginning with Confucian, then Daoist, and finally Buddhist learning.[23] Arising from these broader intellectual trends, Liang Su's *Eulogy to the Bodhisattva Dizang* furnishes a rare glimpse of the male literati spelling out ways for elite court women to embrace a combination of Buddhist piety and Confucian social norms in keeping with the intellectual changes in late Tang society.

---

20. *Wenyuan yinghua*, fasc. 781, *Wenyuange siku quanshu, yingyin*, 1340: 602. I have translated *zan* here (and also in the title of the next piece by Sikong) as "eulogy" because this text formally praises the virtues of the woman who embroidered the image and is not a prayer to the deity. It is unclear whether it was ever read in a ritual context.

21. Liang Su held several posts in the central government: Palace Library Secretariat, Investigation Censor, Rectifier of Omissions of the Right, the Prince's Reader-in-Waiting, and Scholar of the Hanlin Academy. Tiantai Buddhism enjoyed the patronage of the Sui court. In their ascent to power, Tang rulers were at first reluctant to promote this form of Buddhism because of its association with the former dynasty. Consequently, Tiantai Buddhism suffered a short decline only to be revitalized in the late eighth century with the rise of Zhanran and his supporters. For Liang Su and Tiantai thought, see Pan and Wu 2001: 326–336.

22. The literati thinkers frequently associated with Liang Su include Li Ao 李翱 (774–836) and Liu Zongyuan 柳宗元 (773–819), both of whom were also drawn to Buddhist teachings on the nature of the mind. See Pan and Wu 2001: 336–349.

23. On Tang literati and Buddhism, see Guo Shaolin 1993; Zhang Gong 2003.

The third piece, the *Jin xiangguo Dizang zan* 今相國地藏贊 (Eulogy to the Dizang [Image Made for] a Tang Statesman), was composed by Sikong Tu 司空圖 (837–908), a late Tang poet and statesman.[24] Although Sikong's essays and poems mostly treat secular topics, a few of his essays do reflect his interest in Buddhism and his participation in religious rituals.[25] In his preface to the eulogy, Sikong explains that he was invited (*deqing* 得請) to compose the piece in praise of his younger sister-in-law's embroidery of a Dizang image for his dead father-in-law, a duke in the Ministry of Personnel.[26]

The triple worlds [operate on] the same principle.[27]
The six directions are without bounds.[28]
For sages there is the cause for buddhahood
The culmination of which cannot be obstructed.
The forms are imperceptible.
The principle is inexhaustible.
For humans there is sincere reverence.
Arousing [this emotion] can access [the supernormal].
Filial piety is truly the teacher of women.
The merit can only be a female virtue.
Its accomplishment is most admirable
[One should] go to all lengths to respectfully report it.[29]

Like Liang Su, Sikong Tu seems less concerned with venerating Dizang than lauding and promoting the embroidering of Buddhist images as a filial behavior appropriate for women.

These three compositions suggest that Dizang worship was recognized

24. *Sikong Biaosheng wenji*, fasc. 9, *Wenyuange siku quanshu, yingyin*, 1083: 538. For a modern annotated edition, see Zu and Tao 2002: 304–305. The exact reference of the phrase *Jin xiangguo* is unclear; I have translated it as "a Tang statesman" to refer to the deceased man, Sikong's father-in-law. The *Xin Tang shu* states that Sikong was born in present-day Shanxi but the *Jiu Tang shu* speaks of him as coming from Linhuai 臨淮 (present-day Jiangsu). Modern scholars believe that Linhuai was in fact his ancestral home and the poet associated himself with the place as a form of respect for his ancestors. See Zu and Tao 2002: 5–6.

25. For instance, Sikong wrote the *Guanyin chanwen* 觀音懺文, the *Yingxiu shihui zhai* 迎修十會齋, the *Shihui zhaiwen* 十會齋文, and the *Yuntai sanguan tang* 雲臺三官堂. For a modern annotated edition of these essays, see Zu and Tao 2002: 314–318.

26. Neither the preface nor the verse tells us who invited Sikong to compose the eulogy. Given his in-laws' affiliations with the court, he was most probably addressing an elite audience that included court officers and aristocrats.

27. The "triple worlds" (Ch. *san jie* 三界; Skt. *tri-dhātu*) is a Buddhist usage referring to the realm of desire (Ch. *yu jie* 欲界; Skt. *kāma-dhātu*), the realm of form (Ch. *se jie* 色界; Skt. *rūpa-dhātu*), and the realm of formlessness (Ch. *wuse jie* 無色界; Skt. *ārūpya-dhātu*).

28. In indigenous Chinese thought *liuyou* 六幽 is a cosmological term referring to the six directions: zenith, nadir, north, south, east, and west.

29. The text reads *shenbao* 申報, a reverential way of saying "to report to superiors." Given that he refers to his in-laws by their official titles, Sikong could be reporting his sister-in-law's filial practice to the court.

as a component of death and afterlife rituals in late eighth- to ninth-century China. All three records focus on the families of officials. Evidently, sewing Dizang images, as an act of transferring merit to a dying or deceased relative, was a practice prescribed to and adopted by women of elite families in the eighth and ninth centuries. Although the eulogies are addressed to Dizang Bodhisattva, they frequently exalt female filial piety in afterlife practices. In the example recorded in Liang Su's eulogy, court recognition of an elite woman's practice of filial piety points to official sanction of the amalgamation of Buddhist and Confucian afterlife observances involving filial behavior. Ornate embroidery of Buddhist images was already practiced in pre-Tang times and was in vogue especially in the Tang court; sewing images of Dizang on behalf of the dead probably began only in the Tang, which witnessed the ascendancy of Dizang worship in connection with afterlife practices. Other Buddhist deities, notably Amitābha, Bhaiṣajyaguru, Guanyin, and Vairocana, also appeared as subjects of needlework undertaken for the spiritual welfare of deceased family members or relatives.[30] Using needlework to convey Buddhist piety may have flourished as a way for women to participate in a religious environment that encouraged variegated combinations of afterlife and filial practices.

Given this background, it is necessary to address the gender implications in the rise of Dizang worship in Tang society. In Japan, Dizang (known as Jizō) is famous for his role in female religiosity in the late Heian and Kamakura periods.[31] Female expressions of the Dizang cult are naturally traced to the *Scripture on the Past Vows*' portrayal of Dizang as a filial daughter who braves the fiery descent into hell to rescue her deceased mother. *A Record of Numinous Verifications* includes colloquial versions of this prototypical practice of Buddhist filial piety, where the female protagonist commissions and venerates an image of Dizang, thereby successfully liberating her deceased mother from hell.[32] In view of the eulogies and narratives, it is tempting to regard the flourishing of female veneration of Dizang as anticipating later Japanese trends. But prudence must prohibit one from reading too much into the relationship between the cult of Dizang and women in medieval China. After all, embroidering Buddhist images was a common practice among women of elite families, and the image chosen was not always Dizang Bodhisattva. The historical situation is really more nuanced, and the afterlife of Dizang furnishes a paradigm that particularly but not exclusively accentuates female filial behavior.

Investigating a set of indigenous Chinese Buddhist texts like the Mu-

30. For a listing of embroidered images of Amitābha, Bhaiṣajyaguru, and Guanyin, see *Wenyuan yinghua*, fasc. 782, *Wenyuange siku quanshu, yingyin*, 1340: 602.

31. Glassman (2002) has investigated the nude Jizō in Denkōji, proposing a connection between Jizō worship and women in Kamakura Buddhism. It is also in Japan that we see an array of Jizōs dealing with pregnancy, childbirth, and abortion during the late Heian period. For a popular account of the feminine aspects of Jizō, see Bays 2002: 81–93.

32. *Lingyan ji*, records 12, 13, and 20.

lian myth, all of which speak to the mother-son relationship in afterlife soteriology, Alan Cole has argued that medieval Chinese fabricated a Buddhist model of filial piety centered on mothers and sons. For Cole, this Buddhist emphasis on a mother-son paradigm intentionally contrasted and competed with the father-son relationship in normative Confucian models.[33] Similarly, the *Scripture on the Past Vows* can be regarded as a means to combine an alternative filial behavior with Buddhist afterlife observances, one that emphasizes the mother-daughter relationship. But it should be cautioned that these alternate forms of filial piety accentuating the mother-son or mother-daughter relationship are not uniquely Buddhist; they rearticulate the plural paradigms of filial behavior circulating in Chinese society. From the perspective of gender, the *Scripture on the Past Vows* deliberately pits the filial daughter bodhisattva at the crux of the afterlife Dizang cult against the filial son monk of the Ghost Festival, thus introducing the female savior, who is at once a filial daughter and a virtuous saint, in contrast to the wretched mother engulfed in the retributive afflictions of hell. Sophia Lai notes that the mother-son paradigm in the story of Mulian still subscribes to a fundamentally patriarchal structure that lodges "Father in Heaven, Mother in Hell."[34] In these versions, the sinful mother has to depend on male offspring for her spiritual salvation, thus reinforcing the Confucian social hierarchy that always subordinates a woman to the men in her life.[35] The *Scripture on the Past Vows* deliberately shifts the responsibility of the mother's salvation from the son to the daughter. However, it is crucial to realize that the text ultimately conforms to and deliberately invokes norms of womanhood associated with Confucian orthodoxy. The filial daughter belongs to a category of exemplary women exalted in texts known as *Lienü zhuan*, which first appear at the beginning of the common era and were eventually integrated into standard dynastic histories.[36] The contrast between the saintly daughter and the fallen mother thus explicitly draws on themes familiar to a Chinese audience schooled

---

33. Cole 1998: 3.

34. Lai 1999: 187–213. Lai uses the phrase in the title of her article.

35. In keeping with the Confucian "three obediences," a woman lives under perpetual male protection and authority, defined according to three stages of her life, furnished first by her father, then her husband, and finally her son.

36. In the *Lienü zhuan*, Liu Xiang 劉向 (77–76 BCE), a Confucian historian, compiled 104 tales of virtuous women from antiquity up to his time. The work includes only a few exemplary daughters who saved their fathers from some peril or other. For a study of the filial daughter in medieval China, especially the period 200–600, see Knapp 2005: 164–186. Knapp concludes that in early medieval China, the examples of female filial piety were significantly fewer than those of filial sons; they mostly centered on the daughters-in-law rather than daughters. It may be useful to further explore how Buddhist narratives and practices might have addressed this lack in medieval China. As a preliminary note, it is important that the theme of female filial piety was expressed in the Dizang cult only in late medieval China, just before or about the same time when another Buddhist model of female filial piety was introduced: the Miaoshan story of the Guanyin cult that highlights the father-daughter relationship. Were Buddhists intentionally responding to the needs of women in medieval China?

for centuries in normative portrayals of female virtuosity. Precisely because of its compatibility with the prescribed norms of female behavior in Tang society, embroidering Dizang for a dead parent met with approbation by the court and the largely male elite literati (*wenren* 文人), for whom this practice was mostly meaningful as yet another conduit for disseminating and perpetuating a praiseworthy female virtue.

The *Scripture on the Past Vows* and the miracle tales all reiterate the mother-daughter relationship, whereas the eulogies collected in non-Buddhist historical records contain both mother-daughter and father-daughter relationships. The link between Dizang and the mother-daughter model of filial piety was never intended as absolute; it is better understood as a normative paradigm scripted into the *Scripture on the Past Vows*. The gender shift from the filial son to daughter did not necessarily correspond to actual practice. Historical records indicate that men and women in different kinship settings venerated Dizang. In the records by Sikong Tu and Liang Su a daughter sewed an image of Dizang for her dead father, while in Mu Yuan's eulogy, the images are embroidered by a mother for her deceased daughter and by one sister for another. Finally, in Liang Su's account, the Buddhist combination of filial piety and afterlife observance apparently received court approbation and was practiced alongside Confucian mourning rites. Hence one must conclude that the rivalry between Confucian and Buddhist articulations, which Alan Cole presumed, cannot completely render the complicated array of historical and social relationships that interconnected divergent forms of religion in Tang society. The hymn and eulogies feature poets, scholars, and officials from the Tang court; they make sense of the afterlife Dizang cult and recast the practices for a broader (and not necessarily Buddhist) audience. Applying the lens of filial behavior in a sense rationalizes and elevates the "cultic" and "vulgarized" connotations of the afterlife Dizang, reorienting the worship to a moral discourse and agenda on cultivating filial piety.[37] In this regard the literati Liang Su exemplifies how a lay Buddhist thinker was involved in reimagining Dizang through the broader intellectual trends in the late Tang court. Similarly, Buddhist clerics probably felt encumbered to reimagine parts of Dizang mythology and practices that would illuminate affinities between Dizang worship and observances of filial piety. Examples are Changjin's compilation *A Record of Numinous Verifications* and his preface,

37. After its initial incorporation into Tang religion, filial piety remained a salient dimension of the Dizang cult, often highlighted by Buddhist exegetes anxious to elevate and reinstate the relevance of Dizang Bodhisattva in the societies of their time. There exist several Qing commentaries on the *Scripture on the Past Vows* like the *Dizang benyuan jing ke* 地藏本願經科 (*XZ* 35: 393–408), *Dizang benyuan jing ke zhu* 地藏本願經科註 (*XZ* 35: 409–438), and *Dizang benyuan jing lunguan* 地藏本願經綸貫 (*XZ* 35: 439–671). Similarly contemporary Chinese Buddhist teachers, propagating a form of Buddhist humanism (*renjian fojiao*), speak of Dizang Bodhisattva as the Buddhist paragon of filial piety; examples include Yinshun 1989 and Zhengyan 2003.

which frames Dizang miracles against the preaching of the *Scripture on the Past Vows*. The *Scripture on the Past Vows* (or portions of it) may have been rewritten to bolster and disseminate the revisioning of the afterlife Dizang via the lens of filial behavior. It is therefore impossible to map religious change on a linear trajectory of influences. Instead, as the cult to Dizang eloquently shows, religion is perpetually remaking itself, innovatively drawing from and profoundly embedded in a rich pluralism of genres and traditions.

Ritual Divination, Exorcism, and Healing

Even if one were to recast Dizang, Lord of the Underworld, more broadly as a Buddhist afterlife deity, the title still cannot do justice to the many diverse functions this bodhisattva assumed in medieval religion. An important dimension not entirely explicable or subsumable under the rubric of "afterlife religion" is Dizang's association with a body of ritual techniques for combating malicious forces, healing disease, prognosticating the past and the future, and prolonging the life span, some of which in modern times have been designated as (for example, in the Taishō canon) "esoteric teachings" (Ch. *mijiao* 密教; J. *mikkyō*). In other words, Dizang is integrally linked to a cluster of religious concerns and thaumaturgic techniques that adhered themselves to and grew up around *dhāraṇī* teachings.

Dizang's association with *dhāraṇī* was established in China in the earliest scriptural accounts of this bodhisattva (no later than the sixth century): the *Scripture on the Ten Wheels* and the *Section on the Sumeru Treasury*. Both texts associate Dizang with *dhāraṇī* teachings that can effect miraculous healing, spiritual protection, fulfillment of desires, and even removal of mental afflictions. In the *Section on the Sumeru Treasury*, Dizang subjugates malevolent dragons in a spirit world where dark forces wreak havoc. Originating in early Indian Mahāyāna, *dhāraṇī* recitation was conceived as a "quick fix" technique for the inevitable ills of earthly existence; it coexisted with the practice of "medicine" in a broad religious milieu to counteract fears of death, catastrophe, ailments, poverty, and malicious spirits.[38] After its introduction to China, *dhāraṇī* incantation melded with indigenous methods for healing and expelling ghosts, which included the use of potent utterances and other forms of breath magic.

The centrality of *dhāraṇī* to the Dizang cult is most apparent in the existence of a small corpus of Dizang *dhāraṇī* texts, mostly recovered from Dunhuang manuscripts or Japanese archival collections. Varying in length, these *dhāraṇī*s are frequently associated with the *Scripture on the Ten Wheels*. The shorter texts are meaningless phonetic characters strung together, supposedly utterances by Dizang; the longest comprises the prefatory chapter on Dizang from the *Scripture on the Ten Wheels* with some additions. Clearly, the

38. Schopen 1978: 271–275.

dhāraṇī originally attributed to Dizang in the *Scripture on the Ten Wheels* had come alive in medieval cultic life. From the Tang period on, incantations from the scripture were extrapolated for independent circulation, sometimes with substantial changes most likely for usage in rituals, thus engendering a subset of Dizang *dhāraṇī* texts. The *dhāraṇī* appears to function as a statement of the quintessence of a scripture or a series of scriptures, much like the collection of *Prajñāpāramitā* literature was reduced to the *Heart Scripture*, which in turn was further narrowed down to an efficacious *mantra*. Ritual efficacy was probably an important catalyst in the production of *dhāraṇī* texts. In Tang society, the written *dhāraṇī* was most likely looked upon as a material token of numinous protection—a counterpart to the talisman—and deployed as a charm or amulet.

Related to *dhāraṇī* literature are scriptures and ritual texts composed on Chinese soil, which mobilize indigenous resources to reimagine Dizang as the bringer of otherworldly assistance in a world of uncertainties populated by destructive spirits. An early Tang composition, *The Exorcism Method*, expanded the *dhāraṇī* teaching to encompass a repertoire of rituals (hand gestures, spitting, clapping teeth, composing talismans), all of which Dizang, envisioned as a Buddho-Daoist exorcist expert, deployed to battle demonic forces and reestablish health, longevity, peace, and prosperity in this world. The *Scripture on Divination*, composed in the late sixth century, also endeavored to broaden the scope of techniques associated with Dizang Bodhisattva, integrating repentance rites and the mantic arts. Although this scripture technically does not belong to the class of *dhāraṇī* literature, it is similar to *The Exorcism Method* insofar as they both illustrate the medieval Chinese use of indigenous formulae to connect Dizang Bodhisattva to the task of minimizing uncertainties and misfortunes and maximizing worldly enjoyment.

Along the same vein, *A Ritual Manual* provides guidelines for performing rites to Dizang Bodhisattva as a patron deity. The term *yigui* 儀軌, or *sādhana*, in its title places the text in the subgenre of ritual manuals on venerating and visualizing deities in esoteric rites. *A Ritual Manual* invokes the ritual structures and terminology typically associated with the esoteric cosmology of salvation articulated by the Indian esoteric masters of the Tang court: visualizing the deity, making the deity's *mudrā*s, incanting the deity's *mantra*s, and performing *homa* rites to the deity. Despite this "esoteric" overlaying, the text really evinces marked similarities with the kind of religion we have mapped out thus far, manifesting the same propensity for formulaic ritual solutions to remedy ills and reap boons in daily life. For instance, *homa* offerings, which entail the use of medicinal herbs and plants, resemble prescriptions for curative and demonofugic purposes rooted in early Chinese medical practices and employed in medieval Daoist rituals.

But it is also equally important to note that in the so-called "esoteric soteriology," the pursuit of secular gain is formalized as a legitimate religious goal known as *laukika siddhi*, or "worldly accomplishment." The religion of practical benefits and its paraphernalia of magical properties were thus grafted onto systematized visions of Buddhist soteriology, which are hailed today as esoteric teachings. This acknowledgment of the validity of the worldly or conventional existing alongside the transcendental or the absolute is hardly novel; it was spelled out previously in Indian Mahāyāna as the teaching of two truths (*er di* 二諦). What is perhaps unique to the esoteric formula of the twofold *siddhi* is its translation of the two truths to soteriological, or more specifically ritual, terms.[39] The ritual emphasis would have been particularly attractive to indigenous religions like Heavenly Master Daoism which emphasize ritual performance. Except for being framed within explicitly esoteric terminology and liturgical structures, most of the religious components in *A Ritual Manual* like hand gestures, magical incantations, and deity visualization were fairly ubiquitous practices in the larger cultic milieu and not confined to any single religious tradition.[40] Our sources really do not yield treatments of Dizang in relation to the two *maṇḍala*s at the heart of Japanese Buddhist esoterism.[41] Iconographic and epigraphic materials point to Dizang's presence in the Maṇḍala of the Eight Bodhisattvas, but examples are relatively few and are mostly concentrated (during the ninth and tenth centuries) in Dunhuang and less frequently in Sichuan. Moreover, this *maṇḍala* has its origins in the Mahāyāna concept of the eight bodhisattvas, conceived as a group of protective spirits to whom prayers for blessing and protection are addressed. More comprehensive investigation must be conducted before establishing conclusions on the medieval esoteric Dizang cult. For now, the medieval sources seem to suggest that venerating

39. Charles Orzech (1989) has highlighted the fallacies of viewing the achievement of secular benefits and the attainment of liberation as two mutually exclusive goals in esoteric practice. According to him, this erroneous conception springs from employing taxonomies polarizing "pure" against "miscellaneous," "the elite" against "the popular," distinctions that obscure the nature of Chinese Vajrayāna. Orzech argues that Vajrayāna instead exists in China primarily in a series of esoteric yet popular rituals in which enlightenment is identified with "mundane" pursuits such as the healing of diseases and the expulsion of enemy armies or epidemics.

40. Recent studies have disputed the "existence" of esoteric teaching (also known as Tantra and Vajrayāna) as an independent, distinctive movement with a clearly defined institution and audience; see Sharf 2002a: 263–278; McBride 2004.

41. The *maṇḍala*s of the Diamond Realm (Ch. Jinggang jie 金剛界; J. Kongōkai; Skt. Vajradhātu) and the Matrix Realm (Ch. Taizang jie 胎藏界; J. Taizōkai; Skt. Garbhadhātu) constitute the core interpretative lens in Japanese esoteric Buddhism. Modern scholarship often uncritically accepts the Japanese Shingon's biased account of the history of these two *maṇḍala*s, which posits their origins in the heyday of Chinese esoteric Buddhism and attributes them to the great Indian esoteric teachers of the Tang court. Based on this perspective, older Japanese scholarship understands the esoteric Dizang in Tang Buddhism via Jizō in one or both of the *maṇḍala*s; see Hatta 1968. Modern studies still tend to include the texts for the *maṇḍala*s in their overview of the esoteric Dizang; see Zhuang 1999: 162–167. Dizang does appear in the esoteric scripture on which the Matrix Realm Maṇḍala is based, the *Mahāvairocana-abhisaṃbodhi-vikurvita-adhiṣṭāna-sūtra* (*Da Piluzhena chengfo shenbian jiachi jing* 大毘盧遮那成佛神變加持經, T848:18.1a–55a), attributed to Śubhakara. In addition to the uncertainty of dates and composition, Dizang art and epigraphy contain little if any record of practice in relation to this text.

Dizang in the esoteric context, whether as the deity of a self-contained cult (*bie zun* 別尊) or as a member of the eight bodhisattvas, really derived from the broader cultic milieux and was perpetuated in those settings.

In this regard, woodblock print P 4514.5 from Dunhuang further affirms the diffused nature of esoteric rites in late medieval China. The print describes a common rite (one in a series devoted to several different deities) that involves contemplating the deity through *mantra* recitation to eliminate sins, karmic obstacles, disasters, and epidemics; to extend the life span; and even to achieve rebirth in the Western Paradise. It is within this broader cultic context—where the mantic arts, medicine, ritual magic, and the quest for immortality interact with one another—that the Sichuan visual imaginations of Bhaiṣajyaguru, Dizang, and the *Buddhoṣṇīṣa Dhāraṇī* as seen in Beishan Fowan niches 279 and 281 are best understood. Demonology and healing also figure in *A Record of Numinous Verifications*, dated to the tenth century; several stories relate how Dizang worship enables adherents and their families to escape epidemics and demonic assaults or have their life spans extended.

Dizang's early representation as the savior of this world in an age without the Buddha left a profound imprint on the Chinese religious imagination; it repeatedly surfaces in the history of this bodhisattva even after his cult took on strong afterlife colorings in the eighth century. The historical sources reveal the fluid imagination of medieval Buddhists, who drew on a rich variety of resources to conjure multiple personalities and roles for Dizang Bodhisattva, which are linked to a greater or lesser extent to his early scriptural associations with a wish-granting and antidotal *dhāraṇī*. A cluster of practices—ritual healing, exorcism, divination, longevity techniques—surfacing in variant permutations with impressive consistency across different genres of evidence shows how profoundly embedded Dizang was in the broader cultic milieu of the Tang. The image of the afterlife bodhisattva, therefore, cannot map Dizang's trajectories as the patron saint of Buddhist divination and repentance or as a Buddho-Daoist priest who employs spells and talismans to subjugate demons and recruit their services to assist and benefit living beings. These dimensions of the Dizang cult continued to exist long after the dominion of Dizang's afterlife function and remain discernible in East Asian religion today.[42]

The Daoist Savior of Hells

A short digression at this point to discuss the emergence of a Daoist savior of hells may be in order as Daoist parallels may further elucidate Dizang's history as Lord of the Underworld. In Chinese religion today, the Great Unity Heavenly Worthy Who Relieves Suffering (Taiyi Jiuku tianzun 太一救苦天尊)

42. See the Introduction for examples of modern occurrences of these lesser-known aspects of Dizang Bodhisattva.

is the Daoist savior of hells.[43] Although the epithet "Taiyi jiuku tianzun" occurs only in the Song period, the deity Heavenly Worthy Who Relieves Suffering (Jiuku tianzun) appears as early as the sixth century. In a mid-sixth-century text titled *Taishang dongxuan Lingbao yebao yinyuan jing* 太上洞玄靈寶業報因緣經 (Scripture of the Most High from the Dongxuan Lingbao Canon Regarding Retribution and Karmic Causes), it is stated that when one approaches death, one should first forge an image of the Heavenly Worthy Who Relieves Suffering, copy the scripture, and engage in recitation all day long.[44] Medieval Chinese heeded the instruction to commission images of the Heavenly Worthy on behalf of the deceased; this is apparent from an early inscriptional reference to this deity in Anyue, which attributes the engraving of the image in 748 to a certain Wang family.[45] Fascicle 6 of the scripture states:

> Single-mindedly prostrate before the Heavenly Worthy in the east who compassionately relieves suffering;
> Single-mindedly prostrate before the Heavenly Worthy in the south who relieves suffering out of his fondness for living beings;
> Single-mindedly prostrate before the Heavenly Worthy in the west who impartially relieves suffering;
> Single-mindedly prostrate before the Heavenly Worthy in the north who relieves suffering with great love;
> Single-mindedly prostrate before the Heavenly Worthy in the northeast who universally relieves suffering;
> Single-mindedly prostrate before the Heavenly Worthy in the southeast who immeasurably relieves suffering;
> Single-mindedly prostrate before the Heavenly Worthy in the southwest who relieves suffering contemplating the equality [of all beings];
> Single-mindedly prostrate before the Heavenly Worthy in the northwest who relieves suffering through the transformation of grace;
> Single-mindedly prostrate before the Heavenly Worthy at the zenith who relieves suffering with pervasive love;
> Single-mindedly prostrate before the Heavenly Worthy at the nadir who relieves suffering through boundless assistance.
> After completing the prostrations respectfully, each should then bow with head to the ground and for a long time kneel, reciting thrice: The Great Supreme Worthy Who Relieves Suffering in the Ten Directions.[46]

43. Sometimes written as 太乙救苦天尊.

44. *Taishang dongxuan Lingbao yebao yinyuan jing*, HY30900, 6: 7a–b. Note that all my translations of titles of Daoist texts follow or modify those used in Schipper and Verellen 2005.

45. According to the inscription, the image shows the Heavenly Worthy Who Relieves Suffering riding on a nine-headed dragon in one of the grottoes engraved by members of the Wang family, evidently on the behalf of their mother. The Wangs carved several niches to memorialize their deceased mother, including the niche with the image of the Heavenly Worthy; see Yusa 1989: 25.

46. *Taishang dongxuan Lingbao yebao yinyuan jing*, HY 30900, 6: 4a–b.

If one were to substitute the Heavenly Worthy with one of the Buddhist deities, the above liturgical sequence could have been excerpted from a Buddhist confession rite. This liturgical formula is also reminiscent of Sichuan's visual representations of Dizang and Guanyin with the cult of multiple buddhas, including the buddhas of the ten directions. Like Dizang and Guanyin, the Heavenly Worthy is the divine intercessor mediating relations between this world and all otherworldly realms, this life and the afterlife. Like the two bodhisattvas, this Daoist deity ultimately holds out the promise of a good conclusion to this life—that is, passage to one of the paradisal lands.

In the above liturgical invocation, the Heavenly Worthy comes across as a generic savior. In his early phase, he resembled the Buddhist deity Guanshiyin, Perceiver of the Cries of the World, apparent from the appellation Heavenly Worthy Who Relieves Suffering through Locating the Cries for Help (Xunsheng Jiuku tianzun 尋聲救苦天尊). But over time, the Heavenly Worthy's functions expanded and he was increasingly defined as the Daoist savior of hells. In this vein, the *Daojiao lingyan ji* 道教靈驗記 (Record of Numinous Verifications in Daoism), a collection of miracle tales compiled after 905 by Du Guangting 杜光庭 (850–933), includes four stories on the Heavenly Worthy Who Relieves Suffering under the category "numinous verifications of the worthies' images" (*zun xiang lingyan* 尊像靈驗).[47] One story, the return-from-death experience of a Daoist priest, Zhang Renbiao 張仁表, obviously resonates with the *Record of a Returned Soul,* which relates the monk Daoming's meeting with Dizang Bodhisattva.[48] Zhang falls ill and the Director of Destiny (*siming* 司命) guides him to the underworld, where Zhang is surprised to come upon a palatial complex. Upon learning that it is the residence of the Great Unity Heavenly Worthy, he intones the deity's name and the deity manifests itself in a halo of light attended by a retinue of more than a thousand followers. The Great Unity Heavenly Worthy extends Zhang's life span by seven years and instructs him to return to the living to correct and propagate the deity's iconography. Awakening in this world, Zhang exhausts his wealth by commissioning statues and paintings of Great Unity Heavenly Worthy and devotes himself to copying scriptures. He dies seven years later.

Other stories in *A Record of Numinous Verifications in Daoism* share conspic-

47. Born in the region of Chuzhou 處州 in Zhejiang, Du Guangting was raised in the Confucian classics. After failing the *mingjing* 明經 examinations, he went to Mount Tiantai to receive Daoist training and ordination. Hearing of his abilities, Emperor Xizhong 僖宗 (r. 873–888) summoned Du to the imperial court, where he served as court priest. In 881, he fled with the court in exile to Sichuan during the Huangchao 黃巢 rebellion (874–884). When the civil war ended, Du stayed on in Sichuan and became the spiritual leader of the Shu 蜀 kingdom. He helped restore Daoist collections destroyed during the political chaos and was the first to have the works he edited printed for wider dissemination. In terms of his work, he was an expert in Lingbao liturgy and was also reputed for his versatile synthesis of Confucian and Daoist thought. See Schipper and Verellen 2005: 1259–1260.

48. *Daojiao lingyan ji*, HY9983, 5: 1a–3a. For parallels between the Buddhist and Daoist stories, see Yusa 1989: 27.

uous parallels with those collected in *A Record of Numinous Verifications.* In *A Record of Numinous Verifications in Daoism* Yuan Feng 袁逢 encounters a tidal wave while sailing one day.[49] In the face of disaster Yuan incants the Great Unity Heavenly Worthy's name a hundred times. The deity reveals himself in a stream of light and averts the danger. This story corresponds to record 1 of *A Record of Numinous Verifications,* which narrates how Wang Ji 王記, who regularly copies and venerates Dizang images, is miraculously saved when he encounters danger at sea.[50] Another story in *A Record of Numinous Verifications in Daoism* tells of a dead wife suffering punishment in hell at the hands of an ox-headed warden. She obtains respite after her husband forges and venerates an image of Great Unity Heavenly Worthy.[51] In *A Record of Numinous Verifications* a deceased wife suffering in hell instantly ascends to Trāyastriṃśa heaven after her husband commissions an image of Dizang on her behalf.[52] Finally, in *A Record of Numinous Verifications in Daoism,* a large family escapes from harm during an epidemic simply because its head, Sun Jingzhen 孫靜真, is reputed for his reverence to Heavenly Worthy.[53] Similarly, in *A Record of Numinous Verifications,* the family of Kang Jutong was also spared during an epidemic because the demons recognized him as a pious devotee of Dizang Bodhisattva.[54] In all of these miracle tales, the Heavenly Worthy Who Relieves Suffering gradually becomes a Daoist savior of the underworld not unlike Dizang Bodhisattva. Because Du compiled his work sometime in 905–933, while Changjin completed his work in 989, one may be tempted to conclude that the miracle tales on Dizang Bodhisattva were latter derivations based on the Daoist collection. But one must bear in mind that return-from-death narratives about an underworld Dizang were already circulating prior to the tenth century. Hence, given the frequent oral sources of narrative literature, it is more prudent to resist making general assumptions about the direction of influence and recognize that the overlap in these two sets of Buddhist and Daoist miracle tales places their origins in a broader cultic setting in which the boundaries of organized religions blur and lose their sharp distinctions.

The Heavenly Worthy, the savior of hells, is sometimes juxtaposed with the Ten Kings, as in the *Taishang Jiuku tianzun shuo xiaoqian miezui jing* 太上救苦天尊說消愆滅罪經 (Scripture on the Great Supreme Heavenly Worthy Who Relieves Suffering Explaining How to Extirpate Guilt).[55] Another example connecting the Heavenly Worthies of the Ten Directions to purga-

49. *Daojiao lingyan ji,* HY 9983, 5: 3a–b.

50. *Lingyan ji,* 354a–b.

51. *Daojiao lingyan ji,* HY 9983, 5: 3b–5a.

52. *Lingyan ji,* 364a–b.

53. *Daojiao lingyan ji,* HY 9983, 5: 5a–6b. In the story of Sun, the deity is known as the Heavenly Worthy Who Relieves Suffering; the other three stories refer to the deity as the Great Unity Heavenly Worthy.

54. *Lingyan ji,* 361a–b.

55. *Taishang Jiuku tianzun shuo xiaoqian miezui jing,* HY 30900, 1a–3b. In this text, the Heavenly Worthy delivers as sermon to an audience of celestial dragons, the Ten Kings, and

torial visions and afterlife salvation is a twelfth-century work titled *Yuanshi Lingbao ziran jiutian shenghua chaodu yinlian mijue* 元始靈寶自然九天生化超度陰煉秘訣 (Private Tutor of the Nine Spontaneously Generating Lingbao Heavens of Primordial Commencement: On Latent Refinement for Transcendent Salvation and Vitalizing Transformation).[56] This text describes a liturgical visualization where the Daoist master imagines the cosmos within his own body and, through this rite, visualizes the path of salvation for souls lost in the depths of purgatory. For the lay sponsors of the ritual, the rite becomes a staged public enactment of one's ancestral spirits advancing to paradise. The Heavenly Worthy, who started his career as a generic savior, gradually developed associations with the underworld and emerged after the tenth century as *the* Daoist deity of the underworld—a transformation comparable to Dizang in the Buddhist pantheon. Given the dates, the Heavenly Worthy's transfiguration probably occurred on the heels of Dizang's success as Lord of the Underworld. Once the underworld Heavenly Worthy was introduced, these two saviors of hells evolved in close association with each other in late medieval China.

The Cult of Mount Jiuhua

A final discrepancy between the modern and the medieval Dizang cult needs to be addressed: namely, the emergence of Mount Jiuhua as a pilgrimage center of Dizang worship. As mentioned earlier, Mount Jiuhua, located in southern Anhui (eastern China), is one of the four famous Buddhist mountains and is specifically consecrated to Dizang Bodhisattva. The *cultus locus* for this site is an eighth-century Korean monk named Kim Chijang, who was said to be Dizang's earthly incarnation. Early biographical records situate Kim at Mount Jiuhua, but they contain no explicit allusion to Dizang Bodhisattva. The earliest of these records is an essay relating the coming of Kim to Mount Jiuhua. It is titled *Jiuhua shan Huacheng si ji* 九華山化城寺記 (Record of the Monastery of the Manifested City at Mount Jiuhua) and was authored in 813 by Fei Guanqing 費冠卿 (fl. 807–822), a member of the literati from Qingyang 青陽 in Chizhou 池州, Anhui.[57] Born a prince in the Silla court, Kim became a monk and moved to China, where he settled at Mount Jiuhua. He supposedly possessed unusual bone structure, measured seven feet tall, and was known for his incredible strength. The text describes Kim's encounter with a lovely mountain goddess who recognized the monk, made offer-

---

Directors of Destiny, in which he explains the performance of penance rituals for liberating all "solitary souls" (*gu hun* 孤魂) from hells.

56. *Yuanshi Lingbao ziran jiutian shenghua chaodu yinlian mijue*, collected in *Lingbao wuliang duren shangjing dafa* 靈寶無量度人上經大法, HY 219, 57: 2b–5b. See Boltz 1983 for a study and translation of this text. I use her translation of the title (1983: 496).

57. Fei's essay is collected in the *Qinding quan Tang wen* 欽定全唐文, 694: 10–12. Grieving over his mother's death, Fei retreated to Mount Jiuhua, where he evidently lived in seclusion and even rejected a summons in the year 823 to assume a court appointment.

ings, and manifested a gushing spring for his nourishment.[58] Kim retreated to a grotto, where he practiced meditation and observed a rigorous ascetic regimen, cooking meager meals of millet mixed with white clay in a cracked pot. Attracted to his religious aura, villagers built a temple for him, and, as Kim's reputation grew, it was expanded in 780 and named Huacheng si by imperial decree.[59] The charismatic monk attracted hundreds of followers, who flocked to the mountain. Kim died at the age of ninety-nine, an event marked by omens including a sudden earthquake that caused the temple bell to fall without a sound.[60] His corpse, sitting in meditation with legs crossed, was interred in a cave. When the cave was reopened three years later, Kim's body had self-mummified and "the bones rattled like golden chains."[61] His body is now interred in a pagoda on the hills overlooking the basin of the Monastery of the Manifested City. Similarly, shorter accounts of Kim's life are preserved in the *Song gaoseng zhuan* 宋高僧傳 (Biographies of Eminent Monks of the Song Dynasty), a work completed in 988 by Zanning 贊寧 (919–1001), and the *Shenseng zhuan* 神僧傳 (Biographies of Holy Monks), composed in the fourteenth century.[62]

However, in all of these records, Kim really does not have any intrinsic relationship with Dizang Bodhisattva except for a shared name. Biographical records do refer to monks whose religious names are Guanyin or Puxian, and it is clear that Chijang was Kim's religious name because Fei refers to him as such (*seng* Dizang 僧地藏).[63] Similarly, in his record, Zanning refers to Kim as "Shi Dizang" 釋地藏.[64] Moreover, in the *Shenseng zhuan*, the entry simply titled "Dizang" identifies the monk as coming from the royal clan of the Kim (Jin) in Silla. Observing an ascetic life on the mountain, he came to be known in the south as "the solitary withered one" (*ku gao* 枯槁) who was venerated by all.[65] No mention is made of him as Dizang Bodhisattva's incarnation, and in the rest of the text he is simply referred to as "Zang." Very likely the character "Di" was omitted because it was common to all the ordination names in the tonsure lineage to which Kim belonged. Finally a Ming visitor by the name Liu Cheng 劉城 recorded that previously in the Song people

58. The goddess is Jiuzi shen 九子神, or the Spirit of the Mountain of Nine Sons. The ancient name of Mount Jiuhua is Mountain of Nine Sons (Jiuzi shan 九子山).

59. The monastery's name, Huacheng (Manifested City), is borrowed from the parable of the phantom city in the *Lotus Scripture*. At Mount Jiuhua today, a monastery with this name still exists, although the original buildings have been rebuilt and expanded.

60. According to Fei's dating, Kim passed away in 794 (*Qingding quan Tang wen*, 694: 10–12). Zanning, in the *Song gaoseng zhuan* (T2061:50.839a), dates Kim's death to 803.

61. In Chinese Buddhist mythology, a person whose skeleton is interlocked like a golden chain is understood to have achieved a high level of spiritual attainment. For instance, the *Song gaoseng zhuan* states that ten-stage bodhisattvas leave behind a "linked skeleton" (十地菩薩骨節解盤龍相結), while a buddha's entire body is a *śarīra* (*sheli* 舍利). See T2061:50.830a.

62. *Song gaoseng zhuan*, T2061:50.838c-839a; *Shenseng zhuan*, T2064:50.1000b.

63. For a reference to the meditation monk (*chan seng* 禪僧) Guanyin, see *Song gaoseng zhuan*, T2061:50.896a; for the occurrence of "Puxian" in a list of monks, see T2061:50.875b.

64. *Song gaoseng zhuan*, T2061:50.709b.

65. *Shenseng zhuan*, T2064:50.1000b.

noted the confusion of names that led to the Silla prince Kim Chijang being equated with the Bodhisattva King Dizang when they were really two separate personalities. This was verified by an in situ stele inscription on Mount Jiuhua, which addressed Kim as "the meditation monk Dizang" (*chan seng* Dizang 禪僧地藏).[66] The hagiographies cast Kim Chijang in the guise of a holy monk (*shenseng* 神僧), one of the charismatic wonder-workers who attract large followings across social strata. They often enjoyed imperial patronage and on their death left behind "flesh bodies" (*roushen* 肉身) as tokens of their superior spiritual achievement.[67] Over time, a number of these eccentric monks were canonized as living incarnations of Buddhist saints.[68] Pilgrimage practice thus started at Mount Jiuhua in connection with venerating charismatic monks and their flesh bodies. However, over time, Kim Chijang was recognized as a living incarnation of Dizang Bodhisattva, and his story conveniently localizes and sacralizes Mount Jiuhua as the pilgrimage site for the Dizang cult.

But this transfiguration of Mount Jiuhua most likely did not take place until the Ming period. It was during the time of the Ming emperor Shenzong 神宗 (1572–1619) that Mount Jiuhua gained national prestige as a pilgrimage site and was added to the list of famous Buddhist mountains (Mount Emei, Mount Putuo, and Mount Wutai). In 1599 Shenzong presented the Buddhist canon as offerings to shrines on the four mountains in token of his public patronage of Buddhism.[69] The reimagining of Mount Jiuhua as a pilgrimage site for Dizang worship was no doubt connected with Ming Buddhist revivals. A key Buddhist reformer of the period, Zhixu, who promoted the *Scripture on Divination*, stayed on Mount Jiuhua on several occasions and composed commentaries on Dizang scriptures.[70] Another factor was the

---

66. In the *You jiuhua ji*, Liu Cheng comments: 宋人有言，新羅王子金地藏，非佛國地藏王也，按之九華碑版亦然. See *Jiuhua shan zhi* 九華山志, fasc. 7, collected in *Si da mingshan zhi* 四大名山志, 1: 300.

67. Veneration of the bodies of great teachers particularly flourished in Chan Buddhism in connection with the contestation and legitimation of religious powers. The installation of "flesh bodies" also became a means of sacralizing a religious site and therefore generating economic revenue from the pilgrimage circuit; see Faure 1992: 167–180. Also see Ritzinger and Bingenheimer 2006. For a study of mummy worship in contemporary Taiwan, see Gildow 2005.

68. For example, after their deaths, the two monks Baozhi 寶誌 (425–514) and Sengqie 僧伽 (617–710) were deified and believed to be manifestations of Guanyin. An early biography of Baozhi is collected in the *Gaoseng zhuan* (T2059:50.394a–395a), which contains no mention of Guanyin. It is only in the Tang period that the story of Baozhi tearing off his own face to reveal the form of a multiheaded Guanyin was recorded. Early records of Sengqie speak of him as the eccentric thaumaturge who founded the Monastery of the King of Universal Light (Puguangwang si 普光王寺) in Sizhou 泗州 (modern-day Jiangsu). The first mention of him as a manifestation of Guanyin occurs in the *Taiping guangji*, compiled in the tenth century; see *Taiping guangji*, 2: 638–639. Zanning also refers to Sengqie as the emanation of the eleven-headed Guanyin, an association that would become definitive of Sengqie; see *Song gaoseng zhuan*, T2061:50.822a–823a.

69. See *Jiuhua shan zhi*, fasc. 5, in *Si da mingshan zhi* 四大名山志, 1: 213–214.

70. The role of Zhixu is evident in subsequent Chinese Buddhist history. For example, the talented artist-turned-monk Hongyi 弘一 (1880–1942), who lived during the Qing

mummification of the Buddhist monk Wuxia 無瑕 (1513–1623). Arriving at the mountain during the *wanli* era (1573–1620), Wuxia built a hermitage, practiced asceticism, ate only berries and fruits, and copied scriptures with a mixture of his own blood and golden powder. Three years after his death at the age of 110, his body was discovered intact; it was subsequently gilded and installed in the Palace of a Hundred Years (Baisui gong 百歲宮).[71] An imperial decree issued in 1630 by Emperor Yizong 毅宗 (r. 1628–1644) announced that Wuxia was "an emanation body of a bodhisattva" (*yingshen pusa* 應身菩薩).[72] Although the cult of Wuxia does not directly pertain to Dizang worship, Wuxia clearly followed in Kim's footsteps, and his rise to cultic status no doubt contributed to Mount Jiuhua's fame as a Buddhist pilgrimage site.

Judging from the evidence, one must be careful not to make too much of the medieval connection between the Mount Jiuhua cult and Dizang worship despite the fact that Kim lived during the eighth century. Mount Jiuhua's transition from the site of a local cult to a place of national pilgrimage, the locus of Dizang worship, unfolded only in the Ming period, which explains why medieval sources on Dizang Bodhisattva contain no allusion to Mount Jiuhua.

Rethinking Tang Buddhism

After traversing the polychromatic landscape of the Dizang cult in medieval China, what can one conclude about the history of Chinese Buddhism in general? Ultimately, Dizang's history corroborates the conclusions that western scholars have recently brought to the fore: namely, that much of Chinese Buddhist history, as transmitted by the tradition today, is "constructed" only after the tenth century. In the last fifteen years, a steady stream of western revisionist studies on Song Buddhism has dismantled the old picture of Chinese Buddhist history, which crowns Tang Buddhism as the epitome, giving rise to "uniquely Chinese" forms of Buddhism configured as different lineages (*zong* 宗).[73] The growing corpus of excellent studies on Song Buddhism

(1644–1912), attributed his veneration of Dizang to Zhixu's influence. Hongyi wrote two essays exalting Dizang Bodhisattva: *Dizang pusa shengde daguan* 地藏菩薩聖德大觀, and *Hongyi dashi puquan jingzong daolu jian chisong Dizang jing* 弘一大師普勸淨宗道侶兼持誦地藏經 (collected in Huimen 1989: 109–180). In addition he composed the *Dizang pusa Jiuhua chuiji tuzan* 地藏菩薩九華垂跡圖讚, a set of ten verses to accompany the illustrations of Kim's biography drawn by one of his contemporaries, the layman Lu Shihou 盧世侯 (d.u.). Hongyi's verses are also reprinted in Luo Weiguo 1998: 158–163.

71. On the legend of Wuxia, see *Jiuhua shan zhi*, fasc. 2, 3, 4, in *Si da mingshan zhi*, 1: 130, 141, 178. Also see Bao and Hu 1996: 164–166.

72. *Jiuhua shan zhi*, fasc. 4, in *Si da mingshan zhi*, 1: 178, 205.

73. Older scholarship viewed Chinese Buddhist history through the lens of traditional Chinese historiography, which espouses a model of dynastic cycle from prosperity to decadence. A classic example is Kenneth Ch'en's work *Buddhism in China: A Historical Survey*, which basically outlines Chinese Buddhist history through phases of growth and domestication, maturity and acceptance, and finally, decline. Ch'en calls the Tang dynasty the "apogee" of Buddhist history in China, the flowering of the "authentic" Chinese Buddhist schools

has cast doubt on the existence of Buddhist "schools" in the Tang period and has shown lineages and patriarchates to be largely retroactive fabrications instituted in the Song to solidify the lineage's identity and thereby legitimize claims to orthodoxy and state patronage.[74] Scholars now recognize that much of Chinese Buddhism as it exists today was in fact largely created during the Song period, and our knowledge of its history up to the tenth century has been substantially mediated by Song reconstructions of the past.

The same can be said for the medieval Dizang cult, although we are dealing with rearticulations that date also to the Ming, which witnessed a renewed vigor in the cult. I deliberately began this study with Dizang as he is now known in Chinese religion so as to underline how these impressions have so pervasively colored modern approaches to the study of this bodhisattva. The two prevalent images of Dizang in Chinese religion today are no doubt his functions as the Buddhist sovereign of the underworld and the patron saint of the Mount Jiuhua pilgrimage. I have already indicated that the ties between Dizang worship and Mount Jiuhua were largely created in the Ming period. Further research must be undertaken to ascertain the extent to which Kim Chijang's hagiography was enlarged to accommodate his transfiguration into the Bodhisattva Dizang's earthly incarnation and to redefine Mount Jiuhua as a pilgrimage site for Dizang worship.[75] One example is the designation of the thirtieth day of the seventh month as the day when Kim Chijang achieved awakening. As we have seen in the seven-month temple rituals described in the Introduction, this day is consecrated as Dizang's

like Huayan, Chan, Pure Land, and Tiantai. In this framework, the Song period introduced a path of steady retrogression that led to "recession and decline" in the Ming and Qing dynasties, which necessitated the Buddhist reforms and changes of the modern period. Arthur Wright's *Buddhism in Chinese History* also classifies the history of Chinese Buddhism into periods of preparation, domestication, independent growth, and appropriation. Daisaku Ikeda's *The Flower of Chinese Buddhism* basically adopts the same classification of Chinese Buddhist history and assumes that the Tang period is the "flower" of Chinese Buddhism. Early scholars mistakenly translated *zong* as "sect," but as used in Chinese Buddhism, the term rarely implies institutional affiliations pertaining to a sect and more accurately denotes "clan" or "lineage"; see Weinstein 1987: 482.

74. Scholars like Daniel Getz, Griffith Foulk, Huang Chi-chiang, Morton Schlütter, and Brook Ziporyn have critically reexamined Song Buddhism and their findings have conclusively revised the perspective of Chinese Buddhist history. See their important contributions collected in Gregory and Getz 1999. Ironically, the rhetoric of lamentation over "the lost golden era" discerned in Song Buddhist writings instigated an outburst of Buddhist activities during that period. If any era deserves to be called "the golden age" of Chinese Buddhist history, it would have to be the Song because it is only then that the so-called "schools" of Buddhism came into their own as full-fledged, distinguishable movements.

75. Initial research, for example, indicates that Kim might have been given the name Qiaojue 喬覺 later in history as it surfaces no earlier than the Ming. Zang Weixi points out that in the Qing and Republican editions of the *Jiuhua shan zhi,* the name is used inconsistently as his dharma name or secular name in different contexts. It is especially telling that even in the Qing compilations of the *Jiuhua shan zhi,* there is still confusion as to how this name fit into Kim Chijang's legend, which may mean that his hagiography was still undergoing reconstruction and expansion. See Zang 1993: 45.

birthday. But there is really no medieval precursor for choosing the thirtieth day of the seventh month as Dizang's birthday.[76] If in the medieval sources there is a day in the calendar associated with Dizang worship, it has to be the twenty-fourth day of each month. A story collected in *A Record of Numinous Verifications* asserts that on the twenty-fourth day of each month, Dizang's numerous emanations, appearing as golden monks, assemble to preach in the Hall of Excellent Dharma in the Trāyastriṃśa heaven.[77] Another narrative in the same collection declares that on the twenty-fourth day of each month, Dizang himself goes to the Hell of Hungry Ghosts to relieve the suffering and satisfy the hunger of those reborn in this hell.[78] The source for the twenty-fourth day is the medieval observance of the Ten Feast Days, which stipulates days of the month for observing vegetarianism, a cleansing of one's moral conduct in preparation for celestial inspection. In certain renditions of the Ten Feast Days, the practitioner is also urged to recite a different Buddhist deity's name on each of these days, and Dizang Bodhisattva is assigned the twenty-fourth day.[79]

The other dominant aspect of the Dizang cult today—his manifestation as Lord of the Underworld—did take shape in the medieval period, but in the eighth century and as one of several dimensions of his cult. By the late Tang, several aspects of the underworld Dizang cult such as associations with the Ghost Festival and the Ten Kings, ancestral worship, filial piety, and abstaining from eating meat were present, but they were rarely consistently or systematically packaged to produce the standardized and cohesively woven pictures of afterlife prevalent in Chinese religion today. It is also only in the tenth century (for instance, in Dunhuang art) that a relatively consistent representation of Dizang's relationship with the Ten Kings is established. Full-fledged, cohesive statements such as the monumental sculpting of grotto 20 at the Mount Summit of Treasures in Sichuan—where hell punishments, the Ten Kings, Dizang Bodhisattva, and the Ten Buddhas were reconfigured into a single vision of the passage from death to rebirth—occur after the tenth century. This should not be surprising because modern Chinese imaginings of the paths to rebirth are mostly traced to the Song period, when the spread of printing furnished the essential medium for the large-scale production and standardization of ideas, images, and texts.[80] Especially in the realm of everyday religion, where afterlife practices normally flourish, the

76. In the late Ming compilation *Sanjiao yuanliu soushen daquan*, Jin Dizang of Mount Jiuhua appears as an incarnation of the bodhisattva, was born on the thirtieth day of the seven lunar month; see the *Sanjiao yuanliu* in Wang and Li 1989: vol 3, 304.

77. *Lingyan ji*, 364a–b.

78. Ibid., 360b–361a.

79. For example, *Dizang pusa shizhai ri*, Dunhuang S 2568, transcribed in T2850: 85.1300a–b.

80. See Teiser 1993: 115. For example, a key source for modern Chinese imaginings of the passage of death is the *Yu li* 玉曆 (Jade Emperor's Calendar), a series of Buddho-Daoist works belonging to a noncanonical literary genre called "morality books" (*shan shu* 善書). The *Jade Emperor's Calendar* consists of illustrations and text and is comparable to "hellfire and damna-

invention of mass printing was a decisive tool for standardizing common expressions.

Furthermore, the sovereign imagery commonly associated with the iconography of Dizang was probably introduced during the tenth century. Today the underworld Dizang is unmistakenly regarded as a sovereign, hailed in modern Buddhist liturgies as the Bodhisattva King Dizang. For Chinese today, the image of a monk wearing fine robes and a five-buddha golden crown is automatically associated with Dizang as Lord of the Underworld. Thus, for example, in the esoteric rite of feeding hungry ghosts at the local temple, the ritualist's wardrobe should cue his audience that he is enacting the part of Dizang closing the gates of hell. However, in medieval art, whenever Dizang is depicted wearing a headpiece, it is usually a cloth mantle wrapped around his head or a celestial coiffure (*tianguan*) of the type that princely bodhisattvas normally wear and rarely a five-buddha crown, a sign of kingship. The creation of the five-buddha crown and its symbolism requires further research, but this iconography seems to have surfaced later in Dizang's history, after his underworld aspect had gained prominence. Use of regal imagery in literary records of Dizang occurred at the close of the tenth century; even when the appellation "king" was employed either in an epigraphical or narrative context, the bodhisattva was not necessarily shown as a sovereign wearing the five-buddha crown. The inscribed texts at Sichuan Beishan Guanyin po niche 1 label images as "The Bodhisattva King Dizang" and "The Bodhisattva King Yinlu," but the sculpture is unfortunately too badly damaged to discern Dizang's iconography.

Studies of Song Buddhism have shown that the Tang Buddhist landscape was not organized into schools and lineages in the manner that retroactive Song reimaginings would have us believe. Given this revelation, how then should we reexamine Tang Buddhism to highlight its fluidity and complexity, both of which elude the categories typically used to analyze religious history? Revised studies were initiated by Robert Gimello and Peter Gregory, who, respectively, studied the practical and social dimensions of Huayan Buddhism during the Tang.[81] Recent scholarship has fruitfully probed cultic perspectives as windows to complex and dynamic religious realities. Examples are Bernard Faure's investigation of cultic aspects of Chan; Raoul Birnbaum's writing on deity cults, sacred mountains, and vision quests; and Stephen Teiser's work on afterlife practices. [82] One should also add to this list Koichi Shinohara's studies of the visionary and thaumaturgic strains in the writings of Daoxuan, who is celebrated chiefly as the founder of the Southern Mountain Vinaya (Nanshan lü 南山律).[83]

tion" tracts in the west. Not incidentally, *the Jade Emperor's Calendar* was first composed in the Song and widely distributed by the Ming. On this text and related literature, see Pas 1989.

81. See Gimello 1983; Gregory 1983.

82. Faure 1991, 1992; Birnbaum 1979, 1983, 1984, 1986; Teiser 1988b, 1994.

83. Shinohara 1988, 1990, 1991. Following Shinohara's lead, scholars have continued to plumb the depths of Daoxuan's work to reveal the encompassing nature of this great medi-

Following in the same trajectory, my study shows the medieval Dizang cult to be one of several lenses that reveal the kaleidoscopic interplay of variegated religious elements and practices that underpin reimaginings of the savior bodhisattva in medieval China. Dizang Bodhisattva, as a focus of piety, was hardly a marginalized phenomenon on the peripheries of more "formative" or "substantive" Buddhist developments. The Dizang cult really cannot be explained by the usual typologies used to classify Chinese Buddhist history. Instead, Dizang operated as a key symbol in medieval religion, a multivalent image embodying the fertile cross-interactions of religious and cultural components like ancestral worship, filial piety, demonology, the mantic arts, and underworld concepts and Buddhist movements like Sanjie jiao, Pure Land, esoteric Buddhism, and the cults of Bhaiṣajyaguru, Guanyin, and Maitreya. Some aspects of Dizang are not mentioned in the transmitted archives of the Buddhist canon, notably the relationship with Amitābha and Maitreya worship.[84] Although attenuated with the passing of time so that few traces now exist in the preserved canon of Pure Land writings, the medieval link between Dizang and forms of Pure Land worship did survive in Japan and Korea.[85] If not for the noncanonical literature and art-historical sources, these missing pieces in medieval Chinese Pure Land would have been completely overlooked, and we would have presumed that Dizang's connection with Pure Land had evolved outside China. The study of Dizang thus functions as a corrective lens that illuminates the complicated historical realities and dynamics of medieval Chinese religion as well as continuities across Buddhist cultures.

A major challenge in modern scholarship is to find a method that transcends the disciplinary constraints imposed by the choice of the subject for investigation and is able to elucidate the sophisticated manner in which religious imagery functions in different spheres. Surveying the field of Chinese Buddhism, John McRae points out the need to coin methods of studying religion that "take into account the dynamic relationships that occur between the so-called doctrinal, practical, and popular realms, which of course were never as isolated from each other as they sometimes appear in modern scholarship."[86] This is especially true for the Tang period prior to Song formulations of separate lineages and schools. A Buddhist cult like that of Dizang Bodhisattva substantiates the ways in which "the so-called doctrinal, practical, and popular realms" are inseparably interwoven to shape a religious

eval Buddhist thinker. For example, see Eric Reinders's (1997) discussion on Daoxuan's understanding of ritual space and Zhihui's (2002) dissertation on Daoxuan's vision of Jetavana as an ideal Buddhist monastery.

84. Zhiru 2001–2002, 2005.

85. In modern Chinese Buddhism, an occasional glimpse of Dizang's Pure Land association surfaces. For instance, a modern compilation of Dizang miracle tales includes a story relating how the bodhisattva Dizang led a woman to rebirth in the Western Pure Land; see Xinran 1995: 94–95. However, overall, this link has been largely forgotten in the modern period.

86. McRae 1995: 362.

phenomenon. Dizang Bodhisattva imagery manifests across various spheres (art, doctrine, mythology, ritual, soteriology), thereby allowing the mapping of the encompassing nature of religion as it is being made.

Consider, for instance, the religio-cultural amalgamation that created the image of Dizang, Lord of the Underworld. An early, brief allusion to Dizang in the underworld occurs in the indigenous scripture *The Exorcism Method*, which speaks of the temporary transfiguration of hells when the bodhisattva recites his *mantra.* Dizang's underworld character is elaborated in popular narratives, particularly in the subgenre of return-from-death tales. Within this narrative context, Dizang Bodhisattva is considerably reimagined in the underworld mythology circulating in medieval Chinese society, and he is scripted into lasting relationships with a host of afterlife dignitaries. From the perspective of ritual, Dizang worship was steadily interfused with afterlife cults like the Ghost Festival, the observance of the Ten Feasts, and the Ten Kings of purgatory, all of which accentuate practices of filial piety and merit-making for one's deceased family and ancestors. In the sphere of art and iconography, the underworld Dizang was combined with visualizations of hells and paradises, Mulian's descent to hell, and the dark courts of the Ten Kings. Finally, in the realm of texts, one witnesses efforts by the Buddhist establishment to canonize Dizang's underworld connection as illustrated by the *Scripture on the Past Vows* and the *Scripture on the Bodhisattva Dizang* as well as Changjin's tenth-century compilation of Dizang miracle tales. In short, the image of Dizang, Lord of the Underworld, encompasses a broad range of dynamic interactions among differentiated afterlife concepts and practices, complementing or competing with one another, in the Tang milieu.

This study of the medieval incarnation of Dizang Bodhisattva reinforces conclusions about Tang Buddhism that western scholars have come to anticipate—namely, that the Tang Buddhist landscape was not divided into clearly demarcated lineages but possessed a fluidity that lent itself to negotiation, experimentation, and changes across disparate religious forms. In this malleable religious environment, not only do Buddhist doctrines defy rigid classification, but Buddhist cultic behavior, as the Dizang cult shows, is also intrinsically embedded in a web of differentiated religious expressions, undermining the polarity of the categories used for the study of religion such as elite versus folk, doctrine versus practice, canonical versus noncanonical, textual versus visual. The success of Dizang as a Chinese reimagining of the savior bodhisattva lies precisely in his ability to encompass these complex interrelationships in Tang China.

APPENDIX 1

The Scripture on the Ten Wheels

Reevaluating the Traditional Dating

TRADITIONAL BUDDHIST scholarship regards the *Scripture on the Ten Wheels* as an Indian composition first translated into Chinese under the title *Da fangguang shilun jing* during the Northern Liang. However, in light of the ambiguities surrounding the text's origin raised in the Introduction, it is imperative to reevaluate this conventional dating of the scripture's first appearance in China.

Among the catalogs, the *Lidai sanbao ji* (Chronological Record of the Three Jewels), compiled in 597 by Fei Changfang, first introduced a seven-scroll *Da fangguang shilun jing* under the category "anonymous translations" (*shiyi* 失譯) of Mahāyāna scriptures.[1] Earlier catalogs such as the *Chu sanzang jiji* 出三藏記集 (A Compilation of Notices on the Translation of the Tripiṭaka, ca. 515), compiled by Sengyou, and the *Zhongjing mulu* (Catalog of Scriptures) compiled in 594 by Fajing and others, do not list the *Da fangguang shilun jing*. Because Fajing's *Catalog of Scriptures* was compiled just three years prior to Fei's work, it seems suspicious that Fajing would neglect to acknowledge the existence of the *Da fangguang shilun jing* if the text was really an established translation of an Indian original in the sixth century. Fajing's omission is baffling especially in light of the fact that by all accounts, Sanjie jiao's founder, Xinxing, supposedly relied on the *Da fangguang shilun jing* in his writings and was known to have composed two commentaries to the scripture.[2] In other words, the scripture was circulating in the second half of the sixth century. Fajing's silence on the *Da fangguang shilun jing* thus remains an enigma and certainly calls into question traditional claims made on its origin and date.

Moreover, the *Chronological Record of the Three Jewels* frequently deploys sources that were either unspecified or lost, and Fei's ascriptions were already debated during the Tang period.[3] He was evidently prone to "correct" previous designations of scriptures as suspect and preferred to argue for their authenticity, enumerating only three titles as forgeries. Kyoko Tokuno proposes that Fei's liberal attitude toward canonizing scriptures may have sprung from a polemical intent to expand the Buddhist canon to counteract the massive production of Daoist scriptures during his

---

1. *Lidai sanbao ji*, T2034:49.112b.

2. Xinxing extensively cited the *Da fangguang shilun jing* in his early work the *Sanjie fofa* (Three Levels of Buddhist Teachings). Moreover, the *Record of the Kaiyuan Era* credits Xinxing with the composition of two commentaries on this scripture: the *Shilun yi yi li ming* and the *Shilun luechao*. See *Kaiyuan shijiao lu*, T2154:55.678c.

3. Tokuno 1990: 44.

time.[4] She also notes that because Fei had suffered under the Northern Zhou persecution of Buddhism, during which he was forced to return to lay life, he was especially anxious to enhance the credibility of the Buddhist textual transmission by minimizing dubious or spurious scriptures. In light of these circumstances, it is only natural that Fei would have included in his catalog texts like the *Scripture on the Ten Wheels* and the *Section on the Sumeru Treasury*, both of which strongly endorse the supremacy of the monastic vocation and insist on state protection of the monastic community. However, it should also be reiterated that the *Scripture on Divination (Zhancha jing)*, which promoted Dizang worship in connection with the mantic arts and ritual confession, was mentioned also for the first time in Fei's catalog.[5] The text appears as one of three works that Fei dismissed as forgeries.[6] Thus one can conclude that Dizang Bodhisattva was present in a number of ways in the late sixth-century milieu. These elaborations of Dizang Bodhisattva may well have been fairly new because the statuses of the scriptures in which this bodhisattva appeared seem controversial. The next Sui catalog, the *Zhongjing mulu* 衆經目錄 (Catalog of Scriptures), compiled in 602 by Yancong 彥琮 (557–610), includes a ten-scroll *Da fangguang shilun jing* under the category "Mahāyāna scriptures available in single editions" (*Dasheng jing dan ben* 大乘經單本).[7]

The Tang catalogs further introduce another "translation" of the *Scripture on the Ten Wheels* titled *Dasheng daji shilun jing*, attributed to the great pilgrim monk Xuanzang. The *Gujin yijing tuji* 古今譯經圖紀 (A Record of Past and Present Translated Scriptures), compiled by Jingmai 靖邁 (fl. 627–649), lists one *Dasheng daji dizang shilun jing* without referencing the earlier *Da fangguang shilun jing* version.[8] Compiled in 663 by Jingtai 靜泰 (d.u.), the *Zhongjing mulu* 衆經目錄 (Catalog of Scriptures) lists both titles under "Revised translations of Mahāyāna scriptures" (*Dasheng jing chongfan* 大乘經重翻) and explains their relationship as follows:

> *Da fangguang shilun jing* in eight scrolls; the *Dasheng daji dizang shilun jing* in ten scrolls, translated by Xuanzang during the *yonghui* 永徽 reign (650–655) of the Tang period; these two titles are variant translations of the same text.[9]

All subsequent catalogs are fairly consistent in giving the number of scrolls of the earlier anonymous edition as eight and the Tang edition as ten and accepted the pronouncement that the two titles were "variant translations of the same text."

Compiled by Daoxuan in 664, the *Datang neidian lu* 大唐內典錄 (The Great Tang Record of Buddhist Scriptures) repeatedly cites both versions of the *Scripture on the*

---

4. Ibid.: 46–47.

5. For the *Scripture on Divination*, see the previous discussion in Chapter 3.

6. The other two texts are *Tiwei Boli jing* 提謂波利經 and *Saporuotuo juanshu zhuangyan jing* 薩婆若陀眷屬莊嚴經; see *Lidai sanbao ji*, T2034:49.85b, 97b.

7. *Zhongjing mulu*, T2147:55.152c. No other information was gleaned about this scripture. Recounting Yancong's life, the *Xu gaoseng zhuan* says: 仁壽二年下敕更令撰衆經目錄 乃分為五例 (T2060:50.437b–c).

8. *Gujin yinjing tuji*, T2151:55.367b.

9. *Zhongjing mulu*, T2148:55.189b.

Ten Wheels under different scriptural categories.[10] For Daoxuan, the eight-scroll *Da fangguang shilun jing* was the first translation for which the date and translator were unknown; the *Dasheng daji Dizang shilun jing* was a revised translation undertaken by Xuanzang during 650–655 at the Monastery of Great Compassionate Kindness (Da ci'en si 大慈恩寺) in the Tang capital, Chang'an.[11] Daoxuan also pronounced "the two scriptures" to be "variant translations of the same edition."[12]

Another interesting entry is collected in the *Dazhou kanding zhongjing mulu* 大周刊定眾經目錄 (A Catalog of Scriptures Authorized by the Great Zhou), compiled in 695 by Mingquan 明佺 (d.u.) and others, which records both editions of the *Scripture on the Ten Wheels* and provides more information concerning the eight-scroll *Da fangguang shilun jing*.[13] Curiously, the catalog ascribes the *Da fangguang shilun jing* to the Northern Liang monk Dharmakṣema and named the place of translation as Guzang 姑臧 (modern Wuwei 武威 in Gansu), which was the capital of the Later Liang Dynasty (386–403)—a piece of information the catalogers claimed to have "extracted from [Fei] Changfang's catalog."[14] This claim is inaccurate because Fei's record (at least as it is extant today) only characterizes the *Da fangguang shilun jing* as a seven-scroll anonymous translation. Subsequent compilers seem to have doubted Mingquan's ascription of authorship to Dharmakṣema, and the catalogs after the *Catalog of Great Zhou* do not name the translator.

The *Kaiyuan shijiao lu* 開元釋教錄 (The Kaiyuan Record of Śākyamuni's Teachings), completed in 730 by Zhishen 智昇 (fl. 669–740), registered an eight-scroll *Da fangguang shilun jing* (translator unknown) and a ten-scroll *Dasheng daji Dizang shilun jing* by Xuanzang. Zhishen noted that the anonymous edition was, in his day, traced to the Northern Liang.[15] A similar entry appeared in the *Zhenyuan xinding shijiao mulu* 貞元新定釋教目錄 (A Newly Revised Catalog of Śākyamuni's Teachings from the Zhenyuan Era), completed in 799 by Yuanzhao 圓照 (fl. 778), a monk from the Monastery of Western Luminosity (Ximing si 西明寺).[16]

In summary, the catalog literature indicates that the traditional dating of the *Da fangguang shilun jing* to the Northern Liang period was a retroactive addition by Tang catalogers, probably after the mid-seventh century. Earlier Sui catalogs provide no dating and the number of scrolls varies. In fact, the scripture was listed regularly in catalogs only from 597, beginning with Fei's *Chronological Record of the Three Jewels*. Not incidentally, Fei's catalog is known for conferring canonicity to an extensive number of controversial titles, thereby multiplying the number of works included in the corpus of Buddhist literature. That the *Scripture on the Ten Wheels* and the *Sec-*

10. The date of the compilation is announced in the preface; see *Datang neidian lu*, T2149:55.219a; for its listing of the two versions of the *Scripture on the Ten Wheels*, see 286c, 303a, 305b, 314a.

11. Ibid.:55.314a.

12. Ibid.:55.286c: 二經同本異譯.

13. *Dazhou kanding zhongjing mulu*, T2153:55.384a, 384c, 461a, 461b.

14. Ibid., T2153:55.384a: 大方廣十輪經一部八卷 北涼沙門曇無讖於姑臧譯 出長房錄.

15. *Kaiyuan shijiao lu*, T2154:55.702b: 大乘大集地藏十輪經十卷 唐三藏玄奘譯 大方廣十輪經八卷 失譯今附北涼錄; cf. 523a, 555c, 588c, 681b.

16. *Zhenyuan xinding shijiao mulu*, T2157:55.917b; cf. 1024c. The introduction to the catalog gives the date of the compilation (771c–772a).

tion on the Sumeru Treasury were "canonized" only in Fei's catalog may therefore reflect the ambiguities surrounding their claims to be Chinese translations of Indian texts. The inconsistencies in Sui catalog descriptions of the *Da fangguang shilun jing* further problematize its claim as a translated work.

Based on the catalog entries, one can only confirm that the *Da fangguang shilun jing* was present in Chinese Buddhist circles during the late sixth century and not necessarily the fifth century as traditional dating would have it. Although the dating to the Northern Liang period is obviously problematic, the contents of the *Scripture on the Ten Wheels* do align it with the works of Indian and Central Asian translators in the northwestern region of China during the fifth and sixth centuries. One such work is the *Section on the Sumeru Treasury*, the other early scriptural source for Dizang, attributed to Narendrayaśas. Moreover, the evidence does not allow us to conclude authoritatively that the *Da fangguang shilun jing* was a translation of an Indian or Central Asian composition.

APPENDIX 2

Antecedents of Dizang?

Kṣitigarbha in India and Central Asia

As MENTIONED in the Introduction, Dizang Bodhisattva is generally assumed to have started out as Kṣitigarbha, a minor bodhisattva appearing sporadically in Indian literature, before emerging as a major deity in China in the seventh century.[1] Buddhism was transmitted from its homeland in India to China by way of Central Asia and the oasis towns along the Silk Road. A number of factors operated in the transmission process so that the Buddhism that finally made its way into Chinese society was not purely Indian, but also included accretions of Central Asian elements. Logically speaking, if Kṣitigarbha is part of the Buddhist heritage transmitted from India to China, vestiges of this bodhisattva should be present along the route of transmission and even on the Indian subcontinent. But as indicated below, evidence of Kṣitigarbha in India or Central Asia is fraught with too many historical problems to verify conclusively the existence of Kṣitigarbha prior to Dizang's appearance in China.

India

The earliest mention of Kṣitigarbha in Sanskrit writings occurs in the works of the eighth-century Indian author Śāntideva, who invokes Ākāśagarbha and Kṣitigarbha, together with Samantabhadra, Mañjughoṣa, and Avalokita, in his *Bodhicaryāvatāra*.[2] Another of his works, the *Śikṣāsamuccaya*, quotes passages from the *Āryakṣitigarbha-sūtra*, which is actually a version of the *Scripture on the Ten Wheels*.[3] Citation of the *Scripture on the Ten Wheels* in an Indian work may seem, at first glance, to confirm its pre-Chinese origin, but it should be cautioned that Śāntideva's works are almost two centuries later than the oldest extant Chinese *Scripture on the Ten Wheels*, and so they cannot verify that this scripture was composed in India. Śāntideva's mention of Kṣitigarbha can only confirm that by the eighth century the elite monastic community at Nalanda knew of this bodhisattva.

Lacking Indian literary evidence, scholars turn to iconography and point to the presence of Kṣitigarbha in the nine-square *maṇḍala* at Ellora cave 12 (ca. 730), a re-

1. See, for instance, the entry on Dizang in Levering 1987: 392. Also see De Visser 1914: 20.

2. *Bodhicaryāvatāra* 3.52 in Crosby and Skilton 1996: 18.

3. See the translation by Bendall and Rouse 1922: 14, 72 (passages on sin and penance); 90, 102, 171 (passages on abstaining from killing and theft). The similarities are evident when we compare the relevant passages in the Chinese translation of the *Śikṣāsamuccaya* with extant Chinese translations of the *Daśacakrakṣitigarbha-sūtra*. At one point, the Chinese translation of *Śikṣāsamuccaya* actually cites the *Dizang shilun jing* in place of the *Kṣitigarbha-sūtra (Dizang jing)* in the Sanskrit version; see *Dasheng ji pusa xue lun* 大乘集菩薩學論, T1636:32.78b.

lief engraving of the Maṇḍala of the Eight Great Bodhisattvas (*aṣṭamahābodhisattva maṇḍala*).[4] The art historian Geri Malandra, moreover, identifies the shrines of Ellora cave 12, which contain groups of eight large bodhisattvas flanking a central buddha image, as early sculptural representations of the Maṇḍala of the Eight Great Bodhisattvas.[5] This identification is based on a set of esoteric textual descriptions of the Maṇḍala of the Eight Great Bodhisattvas, the earliest of which are Chinese works dating to the eighth century, although later Sanskrit sources do exist.[6] Within these variant textual renditions, roughly the same eight bodhisattvas appear, though disparities in the order of enumeration, as well as in their names and attributes, may exist.[7] One common listing, from the *Ba da pusa mantuluo jing* (Scripture on the Maṇḍala of the Eight Great Bodhisattvas) attributed to Amoghavajra, lists the bodhisattvas as Avalokiteśvara (Guanzizai), Maitreya (Cishi), Ākāśagarbha (Xukongzang), Samantabhadra (Puxian), Vajrapāṇi (Jinggangshou), Mañjuśrī (Manshushili), Sarvanivaraṇaviṣkambhin (Chugaizhang), and Kṣitigarbha (Dizang).[8]

The Ellora examples again date no earlier than the seventh or eighth century—that is, at least a century or two after the *Scripture on the Ten Wheels* makes its appearance in the Chinese Buddhist milieu. Moreover, when one traces the Maṇḍala of the Eight Bodhisattvas to the cult of the eight bodhisattvas in early Mahāyāna, Kṣitigarbha does not appear in the listings.[9] For example, the *Foshuo ba jixiang shenzhou jing* 佛說八吉祥神咒經 (Scripture on the Buddha Preaching the Numinous Mantra of the Eight Auspices), first translated into Chinese in the third century by the Scythian translator Zhi Qian 支謙 (fl. 222–253), speaks of eight bodhisattvas as protective dei-

4. Wang-Toutain 1998: 263; De Visser 1914: 17–18.

5. For a study of the sculptures of the *aṣṭamahābodhisattva maṇḍala* in the Ellora Caves, see Malandra 1993. An earlier study of the *aṣṭamahābodhisattva maṇḍala* pointed to this possibility; see Granoff 1968–1969: 94. Other iconographical representations of the *aṣṭamahābodhisattva maṇḍala*, dating from the eighth to the ninth century, have been discovered outside of Ellora in the eastern Orissan sites of Ratnagiri, Lalitagiri, and Udayagiri. For a brief overview, see Malandra 1993: 114–116. The Lalitagiri site has preserved three sets of the *aṣṭabodhisattva* group, dating from the eighth and ninth centuries, which may contain three carvings of Kṣitigarbha; see Malandra 1993: 115.

6. Examples of the Chinese works are the *Ba da pusa mantuluo jing (Aṣṭamahābodhisattva-maṇḍala-sūtra)*, said to have been translated by Amoghavajra in 746–771; and the *Da Piluzhena chengfo shenbian jiachi jing* 大毘盧遮那成佛神變加持經 (*Mahāvairocanābhisambodhi-sūtra*), ascribed to Śubhakara. Examples of Sanskrit texts include the *Niṣpannayogāvalī*, the *Piṇḍikrama Sādhana*, and the *Sādhanamālā*.

7. The identity and gesture of the central buddha figure, however, varies from text to text. Variation in the central buddha's identity was common throughout the development of the *aṣṭamahābodhisattva maṇḍala*; see Granoff 1968–1969: 92–93

8. *Ba da pusa mantuluo jing*, T1167:20.675b–c; cf. *Foshuo ba da mannaluo jing*, T1168A:20.676a–c. There also exists a *sidhaṃ* version titled *Ba mantuluo jing* 八曼荼羅經, T1168B:20.676c–677b.

9. For a study that traces the origin of the *aṣṭamahābodhisattva-maṇḍala* to the cult of the eight bodhisattvas, see Granoff 1968–1969: 81–95. Mention of the eight bodhisattvas occurs, for instance, in the *Bhaiṣajyaguru-sūtra*, although the names are rarely listed. In its early manifestations, the eight bodhisattvas seem to appear as protective spirits who ward off illness and misfortune. In the earlier Mahāyāna version, the identity of the eight bodhisattvas is not rigidly fixed, whereas the latter *aṣṭamahābodhisattva maṇḍala* exhibited a considerable degree of systematization. For a short follow-up to Granoff's study, see Pal 1972–1973: 71–73.

ties of eight buddha-lands who can secure mundane benefits for their devotees and will descend to guide them upon death. The eight bodhisattvas are relatively unknown and differ from those usually named in the Maṇḍala of the Eight Great Bodhisattvas.[10] The cult of the eight bodhisattvas, Phyllis Granoff argues, began more as a general belief of the efficacy of a group of four or eight beings as protectors, connected with the directional or astronomical symbolism of quadruples—hence the relative anonymity of the bodhisattvas in early listings.[11] This concept of the eight bodhisattvas in early Mahāyāna was adopted in esoteric Buddhist development, and the bodhisattvas appeared as the entourage flanking the central buddha in the Maṇḍala of the Eight Great Bodhisattvas. Their identities might have been standardized only after they had been established in the *maṇḍala*. Inclusion of Kṣitigarbha in the *maṇḍala* most likely took place in Indian esoteric development—that is, later than Dizang's appearance in China in the sixth century.[12]

The Indian subcontinent, therefore, yields little evidence of Kṣitigarbha. Both literary and visual sources date no earlier than the late seventh century or early eighth century. Moreover, travelogues of famous pilgrims to India, like the *Datang xiyu ji* 大唐西域記 (The Great Tang Dynasty Record of the Western Regions), composed in 646 by Xuanzang, and the *Nanhai jigui neifa zhuan* 南海寄歸內法傳 (A Record of Travels to the Southern Seas in Search of Buddhist Teachings), authored by another renowned pilgrim Yijing 義淨 (634-713), make no mention of Kṣitigarbha worship in India.[13] It is thus plausible that in seventh-century India, this bodhisattva still had not attracted widespread devotion. If he was venerated at all, it was largely as a member of the cult of the Maṇḍala of the Eight Great Bodhisattvas.

Central Asia

One encounters few records when searching for Kṣitigarbha among Central Asian Buddhist writings. He occurs briefly in the so-called *Book of Zambasta*, a Khotanese work probably dating to the beginning of the eighth century, as well as in Üighur texts accompanying illustrations of the Ten Kings of purgatory, which are late

10. *Foshuo ba jixiang shenzhou jing*, T427:14.73a. The bodhisattvas are Batuohe pusa 颰陀和菩薩, Luoliannajie pusa 羅憐那竭菩薩, Qiaoridou pusa 橋日兜菩薩, Naluoda pusa 那羅達菩薩, Xushenmi pusa 須深彌菩薩, Mohe xuhesahe pusa 摩訶須和薩和菩薩, Yinqida pusa 因祇達菩薩, and Heluntiao pusa 和輪調菩薩.

11. Granoff 1968–1969: 92–93.

12. Another problem of note: The task of identifying Kṣitigarbha among the eight bodhisattvas in any portrayal of the *maṇḍala* is arbitrated by the textual description invoked for the purpose of identification. Because the texts themselves are no earlier than—and are, in fact, frequently later than—the Indian iconographical depictions, this method of dating the iconography is hardly satisfactory and cannot be conclusive. For instance, identification of Kṣitigarbha at Orissa is based on a relatively late Sanskrit text, the *Niṣpannayogāvalī*; see Malandra 1993: 115. The iconographies of the bodhisattva images frequently do not correlate exactly with any one textual rendition, so more than one text must be used for identification purposes. Not surprisingly, art historians seldom agree on the individual identities of the sculptural figures in the Maṇḍala of the Eight Great Bodhisattvas.

13. This point, reiterated in previous scholarship on the subject, was first mentioned by De Visser 1914: 19–20.

sources, dating after the tenth century.[14] Moreover, Françoise Wang-Toutain calls attention to the Tibetan annals of Li-yul, which were likely first composed in Khotan in the eighth century.[15] In the annals, the eight bodhisattvas, whose names are not given, are entrusted with the task of protecting Khotan, but some pages later Kṣitigarbha Bodhisattva appears independently as the protector of certain sites.[16] Based on this evidence, Wang-Toutain argues that although Kṣitigarbha originally existed in India as a member of the eight great bodhisattvas, he did not as yet possess a distinctive character and only acquired one in Central Asia, specifically in Khotan. She believes that the Goddess Pṛthivī, an Indian earth spirit, as well as astrological connections in the cult of the eight bodhisattvas, contributed to the elaboration of Kṣitigarbha's character in Central Asia.[17]

Wang-Toutain's use of Khotanese evidence is, however, problematic for two reasons. First, the Khotanese works were written no earlier than the first half of the eighth century, so we are again dealing with compositions that obviously postdate early Chinese materials on Dizang.[18] Second, by the time Kṣitigarbha appeared in the Maṇḍala of the Eight Great Bodhisattvas in the seventh and eighth centuries,

14. The text itself did not bear any title. Sir H. W. Bailey named it after the official who commissioned the text, a certain *Ysaṃbasta*; see Emmerick 1968: vii. The dating follows R. E. Emmerick, who believed that the language and orthography of the *Book of Zambasta* signaled its belonging to the oldest layer of Khotanese literature. Kṣitigarbha Bodhisattva appears twice in Chapter 2 of the *Book of Zambasta*, which contains the tale of Bhadra: first, as a member of a bodhisattva entourage comprising Mañjuśrī, Samantabhadra, and Maitreya (Emmerick, 37); and, second, in the formal role of a questioner (Emmerick, 172). For Üighur sources, see Gabian 1973, 1977.

15. That is, the *Li-yul lung-bstan-pa* (Prophecy of Khotan) and the *Li-yul chos-kyi lo-rgyus* (The Religious Annals of Khotan); see Emmerick 1967. Emmerick also provides an English translation of the first text with an accompanying glossary. For translations of both texts, see Thomas 1935–1963: 89–136, 303–323.

16. Thomas 1935–1963: 96–97; Emmerick 1967: 13, 35, 55, 82.

17. Wang-Toutain 1998: 87–88. It is often thought that in the first phase of defining Dizang's personality, some form of earth deity (such as the Indian earth goddess Pṛthivī) was used as a prototype. On the rise of Pṛthivī, see Pintchman 1994. However, Dizang is significant because he represents the transformation of the deity into the classic Mahāyāna paradigm of the bodhisattva ideal. This perhaps accounts for the fact that the earth deity did not entirely vanish after Dizang appeared on the Chinese Buddhist scene; it was perpetuated independently under various appellations such as Chidi pusa 持地菩薩 (Bodhisattva Who Supports the Earth), Ditian 地天 (Earth Deity), or simply Dishen 地神 (Earth Spirit). Wakamori (1984) first proposed a Brahmanical astrological connection. The standard Indian elaboration enumerates nine planetary deities: Sūrya (the Sun); Candra (the Moon); Maṅgala (Mars); Budha (Mercury); Brhaspati (Jupiter); Śukha (Venus); Śaṇi (Saturn); Rāhu (The Demon of Eclipses); and Ketu (The Personification of Comets). On the Indian planetary deities, see Markel 1995. Although the solar and lunar deities form obvious corollaries with two of the bodhisattvas, Sūryagarbha and Candragarbha, the names of the other planetary deities offer no immediate or obvious counterparts for Kṣitigarbha and Ākāśagarbha.

18. Nattier 1991: 188–189, 199–200. The *Li-yul chos-kyi lo-rgyus* is not included in the Tibetan canon but was recovered from the Dunhuang manuscript P 960. An attached colophon announces it to be "a mere epitome, newly translated by the preceptor Mo-rgu-bde-shil, from the texts of the Dharma-sūtras *Sūryagarbha*, *Candragarbha*, and *Vimala[prabhā-pari]pṛcchā*." According to Jan Nattier, although the manuscript gives no indication of the date of its composition or translation, it can be assumed that the original was composed no

Dizang worship was well established in north central China. Visual evidence shows that the cult to the eight bodhisattvas, in the more or less standardized form that includes Dizang, was acknowledged first in Dunhuang between the eighth and ninth centuries, shortly after or coinciding with the appearance of the *Scripture on the Maṇḍala of the Eight Great Bodhisattvas*. But because Longmen and north central Buddhist sites contain a sizeable collection of Dizang art dating to the second half of the seventh century and early eighth century, Dizang Bodhisattva must have already been thriving as a relatively independent cult in central China prior to the burgeoning of the eight bodhisattvas in the *maṇḍala* version, be they of Indian or Chinese origin. Iconography further supports this conclusion: Images of Dizang in north central China reflect the existence of an iconographical tradition flourishing fairly independently of the grouping of the eight bodhisattvas, which resulted in the novel representation of Dizang, Lord of the Six Paths, which in turn gave way to Dizang, Lord of the Underworld. These separately evolving iconographies of Dizang do meet and meld on the western borders of Dunhuang and Sichuan. The number of occurrences, in both artistic and textual representations, of Dizang as a member of the eight bodhisattvas, is relatively few compared to other iconographies of Dizang. Hence, Wang-Toutain's explanation fails to address the anomaly of early Chinese sources predating non-Chinese evidence.

In contrast to the paucity of texts, a sizeable collection of visual materials exists in the case of Central Asia. For instance, representations of Kṣitigarbha as a monk have been recovered in Toyuk, Bäzäklik, and Chotstco.[19] Paintings of this bodhisattva wrapped in a head mantle, the so-called "hooded" Kṣitigarbha, have been found in Turfan, Khaladik, and Khotan.[20] Turfan too has produced books illustrating Kṣitigarbha in the company of the Ten Kings of purgatory.[21] Although the presence of regional elements should be acknowledged, Central Asian iconography of Kṣitigarbha on the whole resembles Chinese portrayals of Dizang.[22] The bulk of visual materials from Central Asia cannot be conclusively dated, and the earliest pieces

---

earlier than the second half of the eighth century because the text deals with events known to have taken place during the reign of Mes-'ag tshoms.

19. In a painting uncovered in Toyuk, despite numerous mutilations, it is possible to distinguish a figure resembling Dizang. The lower portion of the attached cartouche reads *zang pusa*; see Wang-Toutain 1998: 269, n. 1015. For Kṣitigarbha in Bäzäklik art, see Gaulier, Jera-Bezard, and Maillard 1976: fig. 69. A beautiful piece was found in Chotstcho by Le Coq during his expedition to Gaochang 高昌; it must have been the right side of a wooden triptych that formed part of a small portable altar. In it is Kṣitigarbha with his head shaven, seated with one leg pendant and holding a *cintāmaṇi*; see Le Coq 1913: pl. 57c; reproduced in Granoff 1968–1969: 84, fig. 6. Granoff points out that the greatest number of portable shrines have been found in Central Asia, where they may have originated.

20. For the use of this phrase, see Matsumoto 1937. For the bodhisattva in Khaladik, see Gaulier, Jera-Bezard, and Maillard 1976: fig. 68. For Kṣitigarbha in Khotan, see Williams 1973: 131–132, and fig. 35.

21. See Gabian 1973: 47–71.

22. For instance, see ibid.: 50; 1977: 27. I thank Sabine Wilms for her help in reading Gabian's German article. In Gabian's studies of the Üighur illustrations of Buddhist purgatory, he was able to identify the presence of local elements by comparing them to similar Chinese representations in Dunhuang; see Gabian 1973: 70; 1977: 33.

date no earlier than the eighth century—that is, after Chinese elements had crept into Central Asian Buddhist culture.[23] Central Asian art, therefore, does not allow us to extract information about, let alone to reconstruct, pre-Chinese manifestations of this bodhisattva. The only conclusion one can deduce from the state of the evidence is this: By the eighth century in Central Asia, Kṣitigarbha had emerged as an autonomous object of worship.

Finally, Central Asia has also yielded non-Buddhist references to this bodhisattva, a testament to his sway over that region. His name is used, along with Buddhist terminology, to translate Manichaean concepts. Manichaeism flourished in parts of Central Asia and emerged as the state religion of the Üighur empire between the eighth and ninth centuries and was also introduced to China.[24] Two Chinese Manichaean texts, salvaged from manuscripts recovered at Dunhuang in the twentieth century, mention an Envoy of Light Dizang (Mingshi Dizang 明使地藏) in connection with the Manichaean notion of the Five Sons of the Living Spirit—or, in Chinese, of the Pure Wind.[25] The Five Sons figure in Manichaean cosmology, each playing a role to ensure the order of the universe.[26] Again, these Manichaean usages throw no light on Central Asian developments (if any) before the eighth century.

Like the Indian sources, Central Asian materials on Kṣitigarbha are equally beset with historical problems, among which are the fragmented nature of the

23. According to Gabian 1977: 25, the Üighur illustrations of Buddhist purgatory date approximately from the eleventh to the thirteenth centuries.

24. For a brief history of the transmission, see Lieu 1979: 1–18. On Manichaeism in Central Asia and China, see Lieu 1998.

25. They are the *Bosijiao can jing* 波斯教殘經 (edited in T2141B:54.1281a–1286a) and the *Monijiao xiabu zan* 摩尼教下部讚 (edited in T2140:54.1270b–1279c). A passage from the *Bosijiao can jing* states:

> The New Man, defending against enemies and hatred, relies on the five kinds of strength as if they were the symbols of the Holy Ones of the macrocosm. Pity symbolizes the Envoy of Light Who Upholds the World. Good faith symbolizes the Great King of the Ten Heavens. Contentment symbolizes the Vanquishing Envoy Who Subdues the Demons. Patience symbolizes the Envoy of Light Who Is the Receptacle of the Earth [Dizang]. Wisdom symbolizes the Envoy Who Accelerates Brightness. (T2141B:54.1282c; English translation adapted from Liu 1976: 50)

A similar occurrence is found in the *Monijiao xiabu zan*, T2140:54.1273b; see Tsui 1943–1946: 174–219.

26. See Lin 1987: 16–17. Following Latin sources, Lin lists the Five Sons of the Pure Wind and their various macrocosmic functions as follows: Splenditens, in charge of upholding the world like a lamp suspended in his hand; Rex Honoris, responsible for utilizing his radiance to absorb fragmented light particles; Adam, armed with spear and shield, drives away the demonic army of Darkness; Glorius Rex, in charge of making the heavenly bodies revolve; and lastly, Atlas, responsible for carrying the entire world on his shoulders. There is some controversy as to exactly which of the five sons Dizang represents: For Chavannes and Pelliot, Dizang represents Atlas (Mānbēd), who carries on his shoulders the eight worlds; for Waldschmidt and Lentz, Dizang represents Gloriosus Rex, or King of Glory (Zanbēd), who is responsible for the movements of the heavens. More recently, Bryder, in his study of Chinese Manichaean terminology, proposes that Envoy of Light Dizang is the Sogdian name for the King of Glory, the Earth Spendārmad (Bryder 1985: 102–103).

sources and lack of accurate chronology. Furthermore, as Jan Nattier cautions, China was never "merely the recipient of Buddhist traditions from the Western Regions," but also became, as early as the sixth century, "the source of certain elements in the later history of Central Asian Buddhism."[27] In other words, Central Asian evidence of Kṣitigarbha, dating no earlier than the eighth century, mirrors a state of Buddhism that implicated a conglomeration of Indian, Chinese, and Central Asian cultures. Hence, the dating and nature of Central Asian sources naturally disqualify them as evidence of the pre-Chinese origin of Dizang as Kṣitigarbha.

Pre-Chinese Scriptural Representations?

From this survey, one must conclude that the Chinese canon contains the earliest evidence on Dizang, dating to no later than the sixth century. Previous scholarship on Dizang Bodhisattva acknowledges this fact but regards the early Chinese materials as translations of Indian originals—that is, as evidence of Kṣitigarbha in India. However, it is necessary to reevaluate whether this claim of pre-Chinese origin is justified for the texts in question. For example, frequently cited as early evidence of Dizang in China, the *Jingang sanmei jing* (Scripture on the Adamantine Concentration), a text allegedly translated in the Northern Liang, has been established as a later Korean composition more accurately dating to about 685.[28]

Two other Chinese scriptural treatments of Dizang profess to be translations of pre-Chinese works: the *Scripture on the Ten Wheels* and the *Section on the Sumeru Treasury*. The textual history of the *Scripture on the Ten Wheels* is fraught with questions; the geography and date of composition are controversial. A survey of catalogs shows that the traditional dating of the translation to the Northern Liang is problematic; the text really can be dated with certainty only to the second half of the sixth century (see Appendix 1). In other words, one cannot affirm or deny this scripture's claim to be translated from an Indian original.

The *Section on the Sumeru Treasury* belongs to a small cluster of scriptures attributed to the Central Asian monk Narendrayaśas, which are collected in a larger work, the *Da fangdeng daji jing (Mahāvaipulya-mahāsaṃnipāta-sūtra)*, a compendium of Mahāyāna texts compiled in China.[29] Said to be translated in 559, the *Section on the*

27. Nattier 1990: 211–212. Through studying the issue of language in Central Asian Buddhism, Nattier demonstrates that China began asserting its influence on parts of Central Asian Buddhist culture sometime after the beginning of the sixth century.

28. Buswell 1989: 3–73. Dizang figures briefly in this text as an interlocutor; see *Jingang sanmei jing*, T273:9.372c–374b. Some scholars regard this scripture as early evidence of Dizang Bodhisattva; see Gaulier, Jera-Bezard, and Maillard 1976: 14; Wang-Toutain 1998: 82–84.

29. The compilation of the *Da fangdeng daji jing* took place in China over a considerable period of time. The extant version, consisting of seventeen scriptures in sixty scrolls and dated 594, is traditionally attributed to Sengjiu 僧就 (fl. 586–594). However, the *Chu sanzang jiji* 出三藏記集, written by Sengyou 僧祐 in 514, mentions the *Da fangdeng daji jing*, which consists of twelve works translated by Dharmakṣema, the Central Asian translator from Kashmir. Sengjiu's later compilation probably added texts translated by others to the original corpus by Dharmakṣema. However, this process may have taken place over time and probably not in a rigorous manner because the varying lists of texts given in catalogues seems to suggest a lack

Sumeru Treasury is listed for the first time in the *Chronology of the Three Jewels*, a catalog composed in 597.[30]

Because the *Mahāsaṃnipāta* is a compendium of scriptures including several of Central Asian origin, some scholars believe that the *Scripture on the Ten Wheels* and the *Section on the Sumeru Treasury* should be traced to Central Asia. Françoise Wang-Toutain, for instance, argues for their Central Asian origins on the grounds of thematic parallels with two other scriptures attributed to Narendrayaśas, the *Rizang fen (Sūryagarbha-sūtra)* and the *Yuezang fen (Candragarbha-sūtra)*, both of which were composed in Central Asia.[31] However, the complexity and ambiguity of *Mahāsaṃnipāta*'s textual history renders this argument problematic. Because the *Mahāsaṃnipāta* itself was compiled and enlarged in sixth-century China, parallels in thematic concerns across the various scriptures do not necessarily reflect a common origin but may actually reflect the tendency of Chinese compilers to put together a set of scriptures ascribed to various authors.

Moreover, although there is no dearth of Central Asian geographical or linguistic markers in the *Sūryagarbha-sūtra* and the *Candragarbha-sūtra*, the *Scripture on the Ten Wheels* and the *Section on the Sumeru Treasury* do not contain explicit regional markers. In fact, the origin of the *Scripture on the Ten Wheels* remains controversial, and the possibility that it may have been composed at least in part in China cannot be ruled out. Alexander Soper, for instance, observes that Dizang seems to have "no necessary connection with the subject matter" of the *Scripture on the Ten Wheels* in general. He questions whether this bodhisattva's presence "is not the result of a relatively late addition, made in the hope of launching a new cult."[32] Furthermore, the Tibetan version of the *Scripture on the Ten Wheels* has an attached colophon noting its translation from a Chinese text.[33] Rather than assume that the *Section on the*

---

of standardized citation. For a short history on the compilation of the *Da fangdeng daji jing*, see Mochizuki 1958–1963: 3422c–3423b; Wang-Toutain 1998: 16–22. There exists a fairly late Tibetan translation cited in the Otani catalogue as *'Dus-pachen-po then-pa chen-po'i mdo-sde-las De-bzhin-gshegs-pa'i dpa-gyi dam-tshig ces-bya-ba theg-pa chen-po'i mdo* (Skt. *Mahāsaṃnipātān mahāyāna-sūtrāt tathāgata-śrī-samaya-nāma-sūtra*). However, given the later date of the text, the Tibetan version has no bearing on our discussion.

30. *Lidai sanbao ji*, T2034:49.87b.

31. For the presence in both texts of linguistic and geographical data reflecting Central Asian associations, see Lévi 1904, 1905; cf. Wang-Toutain 1998: 67–71. Central Asian manuscripts of both scriptures have been found, thus reinforcing the Central Asian links. Khotanese versions of both scriptures exist; see Wang-Toutain 1998: 46. A small fragment of a Sanskrit manuscript of the *Candragarbha-sūtra*, discovered in Chinese Turkestan, corresponds to a section of the Chinese *Yuezang fen*, thus demonstrating that at least part of the Chinese text once existed in Sanskrit. For a transcription and translation of this fragment, see Hoernle 1916: 103–108. The relevant Chinese passage was located by Judith Boltz, who found that Hoernle's Sanskrit fragment corresponds to T13.306a–c; see Nattier, 1991: 174, n. 70.

32. Soper 1959: 210.

33. Please see previous discussion of the Tibetan version of this scripture and its colophon in the Introduction, p. 8, n. 20. As previously mentioned, a few passages from an *Āryakṣitigarbha-sūtra* that seem to be some version of the *Scripture on the Ten Wheels* are cited in Śāntideva's *Śikṣāsamuccaya*, but this Indian work clearly postdates the Northern Liang Chinese translation by a few centuries and cannot qualify as verification of the text's pre-Chinese origin. Hadani Ryōtai has indicated the possible existence of an Iranian version of the

Sumeru Treasury must be of Central Asian origin—like the *Sūryagarbha-sūtra* and the *Candragarbha-sūtra* simply because they were all authored by Narendrayaśas—one should stress that a translation often involves accretionary layers in response to changes in religious and cultural settings. Nattier has shown, comparing variant versions of the *Candragarbha-sūtra*, that Narendrayaśas incorporated new themes into his Chinese translation of this scripture. Because Dizang appears in the *Section on the Sumeru Treasury* as a subsidiary figure, and sometimes only in passing, one must entertain the possibility that Narendrayaśas may have added the treatment of Dizang in his translation of the *Section on the Sumeru Treasury*. As it is difficult to distinguish the original substratum from accretionary layers in a text, one cannot ascertain the existence of pre-Chinese versions of Dizang using only Chinese works.

An Audience Bodhisattva

Finally, several Chinese translations of early Mahāyāna texts mention Dizang when listing members of the bodhisattva entourage who graced the *dharma* assemblies where the Buddha delivered his teachings.[34] Lewis Lancaster calls this category of largely neglected bodhisattvas "audience bodhisattvas." They often have only nominal existences and are perpetuated through the directories preserved in Mahāyāna scriptures.[35] Most of the names of audience bodhisattvas were based on the prose metrics, rhythm, and style of the text in question. Early occurrences of Dizang as an audience bodhisattva occur in Chinese translations of the *Gaṇḍavyūha-sūtra*, an early Indian work dating to no later than the second century. Four Chinese translations of this text exist today (translation dates are given in parentheses): The oldest is by Shengjian 聖堅 (385–388), and the remaining three are by Buddhabhadra 佛陀跋陀羅 (418–420), Śikṣānanda 實叉難陀 (695–699), and Prajñā 般若 (796–798). All four begin by listing the audience bodhisattvas present at the preaching assembly. First, bodhisattvas whose names end with *chuang* 幢 *(dhvaja)* appear, then those whose names end with *zang* 藏 *(garbha)*, and so forth.[36] In P. L. Vaidya's edition of the Sanskrit manuscript, Dizang's counterpart is not Kṣitigarbha but Dhāraṇīgarbha.[37] Because there is no extant Sanskrit manuscript of the *Gaṇḍavyūha-sūtra* earlier than the

Scripture on the Ten Wheels, but we know almost nothing about this source; see Hadani 1937: 38.

34. These occurrences have led some scholars to conclude that Kṣitigarbha first appeared as a minor figure in the early bodhisattva pantheon in India; see Levering 1987: 392.

35. Lancaster 1981: 155.

36. *Da fangguang fo huayan jing* 大方廣佛華嚴經, T278:9.676a–b. Some of these "*dhvaja* bodhisattvas" have names like Bodhisattva Banner of Night Light (Yeguangchuang pusa 夜光幢菩薩) and Bodhisattva Banner of Mount Sumeru (Xumichuang pusa 須彌幢菩薩). Similar listings, with some variants, are found in other Chinese translations of a chapter from the *Ru fajie pin (Gaṇḍavyūha-sūtra)*: T279:10.319a–b (translated by Śikṣānanda); T293:10.661a–c (translated by Prajñā). Another listing of bodhisattva names that includes Dizang is found in the Chinese translation of a chapter from the *Da boaji jing* 大寶積經 *(Mahāratnakuṭa-sūtra)*; see T310:11.3a–c; cf. *Da fangguang sanjie jing* 大方廣三戒經, T311:11.687c.

37. *Gaṇḍavyūha-sūtra*, Vaidya 1960: 2.

eleventh century, this seemingly anomalous usage may be explained as a later interpolation—except that Shengjian's fourth-century translation, the *Foshuo luomoqie jing* 佛說羅摩伽經 (Scripture on the Buddha's Preaching on Luomoqie), uses "Chidizang" (Dhāraṇīgarbha), not "Dizang" (Kṣitigarbha).[38] The word *chi* 持 ("to hold," "to maintain," or "to support") is frequently used to translate word forms derived from the root verb *dhṛ*, "to support." One of the several meanings of the noun *dhāraṇī* is "earth."[39] Could Shengjian have deliberately used *chidi* as a binome to capture both the verbal and noun usages of *dhāraṇī?*

Shortly thereafter, Buddhabhadra's fifth-century translation of the *Gaṇḍavyūha-sūtra* uses "Dizang" rather than "Chidizang."[40] It is unclear whether this use of "Dizang" reflects an actual change in the Indian usage (from "Dhāraṇīgarbha" to "Kṣitigarbha") or is merely the translator's abbreviation for "Chidizang" as a translation of "Dhāraṇīgarbha." After its adoption, "Dizang" occurs frequently, not only in all subsequent translations of the *Gaṇḍavyūha-sūtra,* but also in other Mahāyāna scriptures. The introduction of *Scripture on the Ten Wheels* in China prior to the sixth century then represents a transformation of Dizang Bodhisattva; no longer merely a name in bodhisattva directories, he is evolving a history and an identity. At the same time, in the Indian context, "Kṣitigarbha" was coined, probably in connection with the cult of the Eight Great Bodhisattvas. However, because Indian and Central Asian evidence postdates the Chinese version of the *Scripture on the Ten Wheels,* it is difficult to ascertain to what extent Dizang's personality had been fleshed out before his appearance in China.

Does Kṣitigarbha Antedate Dizang?

Given the present state of evidence, we obviously face an anomaly in which Chinese evidence of Dizang Bodhisattva predates the datable sources from India and Central Asia. Dizang's geographical origins remain unclear; if he has antecedents known as Kṣitigarbha in Indian or Central Asian Buddhism, they are not recoverable from the evidence. In the Indian context, all that we know for certain is that Kṣitigarbha was known by the eighth century in particular circles of Indian Buddhists like the Nalanda community and that he received veneration as a member of the cult of the eight bodhisattvas, especially in the esoteric form of the Maṇḍala of the Eight Great Bodhisattvas. In the case of Central Asia, again by the eighth century, he was venerated not only through the cult of the eight bodhisattvas, but also as an independent focus of Buddhist piety. On the other hand, it is clear that by the

38. *Foshuo Luomoqie jing* 佛說羅摩伽經, T294:10.851c.

39. *Dhāraṇī,* in its nominal sense of "that which supports," is used to refer to the earth because it supports all life.

40. In Buddhabhadra's version, the list of *garbha* bodhisattvas is enumerated as follows: Great Dizang Bodhisattva, Xukongzang Bodhisattva, Lianhuazang Bodhisattva, Baozang Bodhisattva, Rizang Bodhisattva, Jingdezang Bodhisattva, Fayinzang Bodhisattva, Mingjingzang Bodhisattva, Qizang Bodhisattva, Lianhuazang Bodhisattva 大地藏菩薩 虛空藏菩薩 蓮華藏菩薩 寶藏菩薩 日藏菩薩 淨德藏菩薩 法印藏菩薩 明淨藏菩薩 臍藏菩薩 蓮華藏菩薩 (T278:9.676a).

eighth century in China, Dizang worship had established itself as a major Buddhist cult in its own right, replete with iconography, mythology, rituals, and texts. Dizang Bodhisattva has certainly undergone significant changes since his first appearance in China between the end of the fourth century and the beginning of the fifth, and his emergence as a cultic object is significantly defined by Chinese culture, religion, and society. Hence, if he has Indian or Central Asian antecedents as Kṣitigarbha, he also has his own history in China, where he evolved fairly independently of Kṣitigarbha's trajectory in India and Central Asia. Sometime in the eighth century, Indian and Central Asian developments, especially those of esoteric Buddhism, would make their way into Chinese society, where they creatively melded with existing forms of Dizang worship.

Beginning our investigation with the question of whether antecedents to Dizang exist in India or Central Asia, we discover that the evidence really does not provide a conclusive answer. The making of a religious phenomenon is a truly complicated process; in endeavoring to reconstruct religious history, we often can only catch partial glimpses of the complicated history depending on the sources that survived. As pointed out in the Introduction, the search for Indian origins in the study of Chinese Buddhism inaccurately prioritizes Indian Buddhism as the source by which the "authenticity" of Chinese Buddhist expressions is measured. In fact, Chinese Buddhist history—as we have seen in our investigation of Dizang Bodhisattva—unfolds in multiple directions. It does not progress in a strictly linear fashion from India to Central Asia to China, but includes retroactive and simultaneous developments across Buddhist cultures.

APPENDIX 3
Translations of Scriptures

Dizang dadao xin quce fa 地藏大道心驅策法 (The Exorcism Method of Dizang's Aspiration Toward Great Awakening), T1159A:20.652c–5a.

ONCE, WHEN THE Tathāgata was residing at Mount Vulture Peak (Gṛdhrakūṭa), he sat on a lion throne under the Bhagavan tree.[1] At the assembly were hundreds of ten million of a hundred million *nayuta* of congregations from other [lands], all of whom received consecration in the [final] stage of never-receding [in the bodhisattva's career].[2] Their reputations greatly surpassed Mount Sumeru. They circumambulated hundreds of thousands of times along the four directions of the Buddha and then sat down silently. At that time, the bodhisattva [Dizang] was roaming the countries, teaching and transforming living beings, when he arrived at the foot of Mount Vipula and came upon Elder Gaoti's household. At the elder's house, numerous malevolent ghosts had snatched the vital vapor of five hundred family members, all of whom were suffocated without knowing it. Ten days passed before the Bodhisattva Dizang learned of this matter, and he instantly contemplated, "It is indeed sorrowful and excruciating that there should exist in this world unspeakable acts like this! I commiserate with these living beings and would like to relieve their suffering." Saying this, he arose and proceeded to Mount Vulture Peak. Arriving at the Tathāgata's resi-

My translation of the *Dizang dadao xin quce fa* is based on the Taishō edition of the text, which in turn is based on the copy printed in the *Dainihon zokuzōkyō* (henceforth, *ZZ*). This edition has a colophon that records 1087 as the year when it was copied at the Śūraṅgama Cloister (Shuryōgon-in). The framing narrative at the beginning of the text is recorded as story 35 titled *Dizang pusa ju qiaoti zhangzhe jia e'gui nan ganying* in the *Sanbao ganying yaolue lu* (T2084:51.855a–b), compiled by Feizhuo. See previous discussion of *The Exorcism Method* in Chapter 3.

1. Mount Vulture Peak is located northeast of the city of Rājagṛha, the capital of Magadha (roughly corresponding to the modern Patna and Gaya districts of Bihar), in northeastern India. It is frequently mentioned in Buddhist scriptures as one of the sites where the Buddha Śākyamuni delivered his teachings.

2. The Taishō edition corrects *shu* 輸 *(ZZ)* to *zhuan* 轉, the reading used here. The text thus reads: 皆是灌頂轉不退轉. The *Mahāvastu* (1: 46) speaks of four stages in the bodhisattva's career: *prakṛiti-caryā*, or the "natural career;" *praṇidhāna-caryā*, or the stage of making resolution; *anuloma-caryā*, or the conforming stage; and *anivartana-caryā*, or the non-receding stage). In the first three stages, the bodhisattva perfects the ten *pāramitā*s, advancing through the grounds of attainment, or *bhūmi*s. On completion, he attains the stage of non-receding (*butuizhuan* 不退轉), at which point it is impossible for the bodhisattva to abandon the path. The bodhisattva is anointed (*abhiṣeka*; *guanding* 灌頂) by a buddha as his immediate successor and will be reborn in Tuṣita to await the descent to achieve buddhahood in the world. For a discussion of these four stages in Maitreya's bodhisattva career, see Padmanabh 1988: 55–56.

dence, he prostrated his head at the feet of the Buddha and then circumambulated a hundred thousand times,[3] before standing to one side and addressing the Buddha:

"World-Honored One, I was traveling from country to country, teaching and transforming living beings, when I arrived at the foot of Mount Vipula. There I came upon the Elder Gaoti's household, where more than five hundred people had their vital vapor snatched away by malevolent ghosts. Suffocated, they swooned to the ground and laid there. After several days had passed, I saw what had happened; this gave rise to commiseration, love, and the intent to offer protection. May the World-Honored One only permit me to deliver a salvation technique that will expel all the malevolent ghosts from the people in whom they have concealed themselves. [The method] will enable practitioners to exorcise [the ghosts], and allow the elder to return to life as usual."

At that time, the World-Honored One emanated rays of light from his head extending to eighty thousand feet and illuminating the Bodhisattva Dizang's body.[4] The bodhisattva then understood that the Tathāgata's has permitted [him] to preach.[5] At that moment, the multitude gathered in the great assembly said to one another, "Now that the Tathāgata has emitted rays of light illuminating the bodhisattva's body, this bodhisattva should accomplish the great *dharma* of teaching and transforming living beings." The Bodhisattva Dizang then arose from his seat, went before the Buddha, and addressed him:

"World-Honored One, ages ago I received teachings from the Buddha. Once again before the Buddha today I will espouse some teachings to enable all living beings to abandon the bondage of the five hindrances (*wu gai* 五蓋) and establish peace and stability again in this world so that it will be free from corruption and disaster.[6]

"World-Honored One, now I possess a numinous spell that can ward off malicious intentions and can further ward off malevolent ghosts and so forth, enabling living beings to be free from all obstructions. If a practitioner is troubled by various demons, he should perform this method of mine without breach. If one wishes to ward off and dispatch all ghosts and spirits, in accordance to one's wish and need they must each be identified. If one incants this spell and this rite, one will attain accomplishments in three days and nights. World-Honored One, if one wishes to avert and eliminate catastrophes, or if one desires to know the future or penetrate the knowledge of the mortal conditions of the self and others in previous lives (*tong suming zhi* 通宿命智), or have spontaneous knowledge (*ziran zhi* 自然智), one will possess these three [abilities].[7] Moreover, [this teaching] will enable those who

3. Here I adopt the alternative reading first proposed in the *ZZ* annotation, which substitutes *da* 達 for *rao* 遶.

4. The text says "ten thousand *xun* 尋"; one *xun* is equivalent to eight feet.

5. Here I adopt the reading in the *ZZ* annotation, which substitutes *shuo* 說 for the lacuna.

6. The five hindrances are desire, anger, drowsiness, excitability, and doubt.

7. The Sanskrit is usually cited as *pūrva-nivāsānusmṛti-jñāna-sakṣāt-kriya-vidyā*; the full translation into Chinese should be *suzhu suinian zhi zhengming* 宿住隨念智證明. But the shortened phrase *suming zhi* or *tong suming zhi* is more commonly deployed, as in this text. It refers to the knowledge of one's or others' past lives, up to ten thousand million lives ago. In the Chinese canon, there exists a very short text titled *Suming zhi tuoluoni jing* 宿命智陀羅尼經 (T1382:21.904a), attributed to the Song monk Faxian 法賢 (d. 1001). In this scripture, the

have not met to come together and appease those who have not been pacified. World-Honored One, this teaching can endow one with boundless knowledge and limitless abilities. If a lay or monastic practitioner were to practice this method at a person's residence, that person will definitely achieve the goal.

"World-Honored One, a measureless and boundless time ago, there was a buddha named King Radiance of the Sun (*ridengguang wang* 日燈光王). This buddha was endowed with the ten epithets and he employed the teachings of the Three Vehicles to convert living beings. After this buddha entered *nirvāṇa*, I dwelled at the stage of the worldly beings in the period of the Semblance Dharma.[8] There was a saint (*xian* 仙) at Mount Kuṭṭāra (Juteluo 俱特羅) who was skilled in the art of magic.[9] I encountered living beings who were afflicted by malevolent ghosts just like those in the Elder's household. At that time I made the following aspiration, 'May I meet the learned one who should be able to teach the method for subjugating [ghosts].' Having said this, I immediately headed for Mount Kuṭṭāra[10] to visit the sage. Seeing him, my heart rejoiced and I immediately inquired about the method. At that time the sage taught me [the method] so I was able to apprehend it within three days. I had to know all the good and bad news within the circumference of ten thousand miles. Moreover, all malevolent ghosts congregated at my abode and, relying on my teacher's method, I tamed their hearts and enabled them to aspire to the path of awakening. Again I incanted this spell, and in a split second the living beings undergoing tortures in all the hells obtained relief from various sufferings, and each of them appeared seated[11] on a lotus.

"When he saw I had attained these supernatural abilities, the sage bestowed

---

Buddha teaches Ānanda to observe a *dhāraṇī* that not only can dispel one's heavy transgressions, but also enable one to know events in numerous past lives.

Svayambhū-jñāna, or *ziran zhi* 自然智, refers to the wisdom that spontaneously arises when one attains buddhahood. According to the seventh-century monk Kuiji, when the Buddha achieves awakening, he naturally possesses wisdom that arises from contemplations of the emptiness and existence of all phenomena in this world, referred to as the Buddha's *ziran zhi*. See *Miaofa lianhua jing xuanzan* 妙法蓮華經玄贊, T1723:35.755b.

8. *Xiangfa* 像法 is the second of three periods in the Chinese Buddhist history of its religion. The first is the Correct Dharma (*zhengfa* 正法), the period when the Buddha is alive, the Buddhist teachings flourish, and the Buddha's disciples are capable of achieving awakening. The second is the Semblance Dharma (*xiangfa*), when the outward appearances of the religion (scriptures, texts, the monastic community) are present, but the religion has embarked on a path of spiritual degeneration, monastics are vulnerable to corrupting forces, and the goal of awakening appears unattainable. The last period is the Final Dharma, a degenerate time when the demise of the Buddhist religion has truly begun.

9. As I pointed out earlier, *xian* 仙 is used frequently to translate *ṛṣi*, the wise seer in Indian religions. In the indigenous Chinese religions, *xian* is used to refer to an immortal who has transcended death and lives forever. In religious Daoism, the search for immortality is part of its vision of salvation, and Daoist sainthood is often conceived of as a hierarchy of rankings of *xian*, or immortals. As deployed in this text, *xian* effectively juxtaposes the Indian and Chinese usages of the word to create a hybrid Chinese Buddhist saint who is at once the ascetic seer of the Indian religions and a Daoist immortal living as a recluse in the mountains.

10. I follow the *ZZ* reading, which substitutes *shan* 山 for *suo* 所.

11. Here I adopt the alternative reading in the *ZZ* annotation and substitute *cheng* 乘 for *cheng* 承.

on me a prophecy proclaiming, 'Immeasurable, limitless ages ago the Buddha had already bestowed a prophecy to you. You were then named Dizang. Among the humans and gods in the chaotic era of the five turbulences, Dizang frequently transforms his body to liberate and free living beings from calamities.'[12] The sage [thus] delivered the prophecy to me, and I have since striven even harder to practice this method. What I saw today at the elder's [residence] is the same as in the past. If a practitioner requests and receives [the teaching], I will arrive at his or her dwelling and assemble and register [the ghosts] for him or her. All the ghosts will simultaneously appear to be dispatched as desired, and it shall be exactly the same as if I were performing the method."

At that time, after speaking those words, Dizang Bodhisattva pronounced this spell in the presence of the Buddha: "*Nanmo naluo sanpotuoye juliu pomo canduman* (3 times) *suopohe* (4 times)."[13] After reciting it, [Dizang] said to the Buddha:

"World-Honored One, where one desires to perform the method, one should first prepare five types of wondrous incense: first, white sandalwood (one ounce); second, resinous [sandalwood] (one ounce); third, cloves (one ounce); fourth, green wood (one ounce); and, fifth, lily (one ounce). After obtaining these five types of wondrous incense, pulverize and blend them with white honey. Place each form of incense on a white cloth[14] without raising it to the nose and refrain from smelling. Remove all dirt to ensure it is fragrant. Recollect my name until the blending is complete. Then go to one's own room, or a bright spot of wilderness, or some high plateau: It should be a place of the practitioner's choosing. To perform the rite do the following: Take a clean cloth seven feet long and seven shallow cups of milky porridge. Perform [the rite] atop an immaculate cloth on which is placed an incense burner made of white porcelain. This incense will summon various ghosts when you recite the name "*Naluosu naluosu*."[15] Repeat these words. After three summons, incant the spell three hundred times. Before performing the rite, one should not incant the spell, [not even] once. After the three summons and the three hundred recitations, again incant the spell two hundred times. Then perform again the previous three summons, followed by a hundred recitations of the spell, and then perform again the three summons. You should do it thrice in three days, the same day and night. During the rest of the day or night, recite Dizang's name.

"World-Honored One, the ritualist [will experience] an omen each day: On the first day, clouds of wondrous hues shall rise from a peak and there will be an extraordinary fragrance; on the second day, a hundred bejeweled lotuses will appear in space as well as a wish-granting jewel; on the third day, the ringing of bells will sound in the skies accompanied by rain showers[16] and strong breezes. If the practitioner perceives these signs, he or she will be assured of various kinds of

12. I follow the suggestion in the annotation that *jiao* 交 should perhaps read *zai* 災 to make better sense with the next character, *nan* 難.

13. 南謨那羅三婆陀耶俱留婆摩糝都滿 三 娑婆訶四.

14. I adopt the alternate reading of *bu* 布 instead of *shi* 市. This is clearly an error; a few lines later, the text refers to "the unstained cloth" (*jing bu* 淨布).

15. 那邏速 那邏速.

16. As the *ZZ* annotation suggests, *liang* 兩 should be read as *yu* 雨.

heavenly assistance. Accordingly, at this time the ghosts and spirits of this world will all assemble like a gathering of clouds and pervade the space. The practitioner perceives that the ghosts and spirits have arrived but cannot really see them distinctly. Should one wish to see them, one should incant the spell one or two hundred times in the previous manner of the three summons. Then the forms of the ghosts will become slightly evident but still not clearly manifested.

"At this point, the bodhisattva then performs the rite that enables one to be fearless while encountering ghosts (*jian gui wuwei fa* 見鬼無畏法). World-Honored One, the practitioner of this method has assembled the ghosts, and in an effort to make the ghosts manifest themselves he or she should procure clear water and spit at the ghosts. Then one should make the all-embracing gesture (*doushe yin* 都攝印): first, slightly raise the left foot and stand upright, resting on the right foot; then bend the left hand with the thumb grasping the forefinger (*touzhi* 頭指), which is pressed against the lower joint (of the finger); then clutch the right fist and suspend it. Now invoke the previous name three times.[17] The ghosts will manifest themselves and may strike terror. Then one should immediately incant the previously stated spell while [the ghosts] are manifesting themselves. After a round of incantation,[18] point to the ghosts and sit silently without uttering a single word.

"When the ghosts and spirits manifest their forms, one who has no fear should then make the gesture for liberating and encompassing [living beings] as one wishes (*suixin jiushe yin* 隨心救攝印): Directly in front, slightly bend the left foot and place together the left and right palms; one will no longer be afraid. The method of the rite is as follows: If one wishes to converse with the ghosts, perform fifteen times the rite of 'clapping the teeth' (*kouchi* 叩齒).[19] Open the mouth and pronounce loudly in the following manner: '*Du* 咄! *Du*! Who is it that has arrived? I have a numinous spell that can eliminate malevolent ghosts. If you are not eradicated and subjugated, then you will instantly die! *Du! Du!*' On uttering these words, the ghosts will bump [their faces on the ground] in fear. [The practitioner] recites single-mindedly and all the ghosts abandon their malicious intentions. When you have incanted these words thrice, the ghosts will declare that they possess deadly transgressions

"World-Honored One, those ghosts and spirits experience fear. Having subjugated them, [the practitioner] should then cause them to rejoice by forging the gesture of [bestowing] fearlessness (*wuwei yin* 無畏印): namely, stand with the two feet close together, the right hand pendant at the side, while the left hand is raised upward to the heart; then bend the last finger and fourth finger toward the middle of

17. The text says to invoke the previous name (*ming* 名), which probably means the previous spell: 那邏速 那邏速.

18. As suggested in the *ZZ* annotation, I substitute *zhou* 咒 for the lacuna.

19. The rite of clapping the teeth occurs frequently in Daoist liturgies. An early mention is found in the *Baopuzi neipian*, an early Daoist text attributed to Ge Hong 葛洪 (283–343). It instructs the ritualist to hit the upper and lower rows of teeth against each other to produce a clattering sound; see *Baopuzi neipian*, HY50211, 15: 12a. The *Zhengao*, a compilation completed in 490 by Tao Hongjin 陶弘景 (456–536), explains that the sounds of clapping teeth and magical utterances strike fear in malignant ghosts and spirits; see *Zhengao*, HY71294, 15: 10a–b.

the palm, with the thumb pressing the joints.[20] Summon the name three times as before.

"The ghost will then approach the practitioner and say: 'Great Being! Possessing the form of a ghost, I undergo immensely heavy retribution and am constantly afflicting and troubling living beings. I yearn for humans to have shortened life spans, and I perpetually feed on the blood of living beings from their vital points without even temporary respite. [Today][21] on account of the Great Being, his power has penetrated me and enabled me to come here and aspire to the path of awakening. Even if I were to smash this body into minute dust motes, it would be difficult to repay[22] completely my gratitude to the Great Being. May the Great Being preach to me a teaching that will exonerate my wrongdoings so that I may be released from this vile body.' As requested, the practitioner delivers the Buddhist teachings that enable [the ghosts] to attain awakening, and hearing the teachings the ghosts rejoice. They speak to the practitioner on worldly matters concerning the teaching and transforming of living beings so as to satisfy accordingly the desires [of living beings].

"In a split second, the practitioner says,[23] 'You and all the ghosts should not fear.[24] Forever, each of you[25] will be my spiritual friend and we together will liberate living beings. In accord with the wishes of all living beings, we will together bestow benefits to them.' Further [the practitioner] says, 'If there are living beings seeking various knowledge and the arts of magic, we will together go to teach them and satisfy their desires and requests according to their wishes. If there are living beings suffering various bodily afflictions, or living beings undergoing capital punishment by kings and officials, or living beings plagued by flood or fire; or if there are nasty beasts, venomous dragons, resentful robbers, and stealthy bandits; or if there are similar situations, we should together go to assist and provide relief. If there are things that living beings wish for, we will rejoice in bestowing them and establish peace and joy.

"World-Honored One, if the practitioner wishes to dispatch ghosts, he or she must employ vermilion sand to write out a talisman, then stamp it with a seal three times. One should swallow nine slips [of the talisman] and thus carry them [in one's body].[26] Subsequently, perform the rite that causes the ghosts to bustle around everywhere, dispatching services. Everything will be successful.[27] World-Honored One, if you want to employ the ghost to divine future affairs—for example, to determine on which day and month and where the Tathāgata will enter *nirvāṇa* after his appearance in the world—then one should summon the ghosts to make inquiries and within seconds [the ghosts] will report and all will be revealed.[28]

---

20. The gesture of fearlessness is known in Sanskrit as *abhayamudrā*. It is most commonly made with the right hand raised, palm outward, fingers stretched and joined. However, the description in the text differs markedly.

21. As the *ZZ* annotation suggests, *ling* 令 should be *jin* 今.

22. As the *ZZ* annotation suggests, *zhi* 執 should be *bao* 報.

23. As the *ZZ* annotation suggests, *qu* 去 should be *yun* 云.

24. As the *ZZ* annotation suggests, the lacuna should be substituted with *bu* 怖.

25. As the *ZZ* annotation suggests, *ru yi* 汝一 should be *yi ru* 一汝.

26. As the *ZZ* annotation suggests, *shi jiu mei* 世九枚 should be read as *dai jiu mei* 帶九枚.

27. As the *ZZ* annotation suggests, the lacunae should be replaced with 百事無失.

28. As the *ZZ* annotation suggests, the lacunae should be replaced with 如來出世後.

"World-Honored One, if the practitioner [wishes to] dispatch a ghost to obtain knowledge about past, present, and future events, he or she should summon the ghost, pose the query, and within seconds [the ghost] will report the good and the bad. World-Honored One, if the practitioner is attacked and ruined by ill-intentioned people, summon and speak to the ghost, then all the officials and those who have banded together to harm him or her will be afflicted with nonhuman diseases.[29] World-Honored One, if birds and beasts encircle a practitioner of this teaching and desire to harm him or her, summon and speak to the ghost. The heads of the malicious beasts and others will split into seven parts.

"World-Honored One, when the practitioner goes to the great ocean to collect treasures, and if various vile venomous dragons, malicious beasts, sea turtles, water reptiles, and so forth should desire to harm him or her, summon and speak to the ghost. All the malicious beasts and so forth will all sink into the mud and never surface again. World-Honored One, if[30] there is a practitioner who received curses and oppression at the hands of others, if he or she were to recite my name[31] in the five paths of rebirth and call on heaven and earth to make a declaration, within seconds of summoning and speaking to the ghost,[32] the malicious people and others will be bound up and prohibited from talking. Their eyes will bleed and a giant serpent will crawl out of the ears; their limbs will become fastened by a serpent that coils itself around them. There will be sufferings like these! World-Honored One, if one wishes to be freed, summon and address the ghost and to obtain release, one says, '*Su* [ ] *luli* 速□嚕利.' On uttering this, one should be released[33] immediately. World-Honored One, if one who observes this teaching encounters resentful robbers and seeks escape, one should summon and address the ghost. Within that day, [the robbers] will be tied up and brought to the practitioner's residence. Should one wish to release [the robbers], one [only needs] to summon and speak [to the ghost].

"World-Honored One, if the practitioner lives in an age of famine, summon and address the ghost. The ghost can procure delicacies[34] from worlds in the other directions[35] and present them to the practitioner to enjoy. World-Honored One, if a practitioner lives in a time of epidemics, he or she should summon[36] and address[37] the ghost, then everyone will have nothing amiss and it will be the same as before the disease; there will not be even the slightest damage.[38] World-Honored One, if the practitioner lives in a world in which the body is burning in flames for

29. The *ZZ* annotation suggests reading *cha* 差 for *zhuo* 著.

30. The *ZZ* annotation suggests reading *ruo* 若 for the lacuna.

31. The *ZZ* annotation suggests reading the lacunae as *nian wo ming* 念我名.

32. Pointing to heaven and calling on earth as a witness is part of the ritual of making a vow. When the Buddha was born, he is said to have walked seven steps, pointed with one hand up at heaven and the other down at the earth, and delivered the pronouncement that he was the lord of humans and gods.

33. The *ZZ* annotation suggests reading the lacuna as *tuo* 脫.

34. As the *ZZ* annotation suggests, *cheng* 承 should be read as *mei* 美.

35. As the *ZZ* annotation suggests, *wu* 五 should be read as *ta* 他.

36. The *ZZ* annotation suggests substituting *zhao* 召 for the lacuna.

37. I follow the *ZZ* reading, which adds *yu* 語 after *yu* 與.

38. I follow the suggestion in the *ZZ* annotation to read the lacunae as 無病不損.

a *kalpa,* he or she should summon and address the ghost. One will obtain cooling respite and the fire will do no damage. World-Honored One, if the practitioner is adrift in waters, he or she should summon and address the ghost. A hundred jeweled lotuses will spring forth from the ground. The practitioner and living beings in the worlds of other directions will avoid water catastrophes.

"World-Honored One,[39] if a person has troubles with ghosts, the reciter of the spell[40] should summon and address the ghost. If it is not effective, the ritualist together with the ghost[41] should visit the dwelling of the afflicted person, incant the previously mentioned spell seven times, and an improvement in the condition will occur immediately. World-Honored One, if the practitioner [wishes to] heal those who are constantly sick, summon the ghost and question it. For those who can be cured, take a bunch of yew branches[42] and boil it. Take a handful and administer it [to the sick] while incanting the spell seven times. Some change in the condition will occur immediately. World-Honored One, if the practitioner [wishes to] cure various kinds of maladies associated with the wind, he or she should summon the ghost and question it. Administer water to [the sick] over which the spell was incanted and some change in the condition will take place immediately.[43] World-Honored One, if the practitioner wishes to heal various kinds of head sicknesses,[44] he or she should summon and question the ghost. Incant [the spell over some boiled] rhubarb[45] and administer it [to the sick], and instantly there will be some change in the condition. World-Honored One, if the practitioner [wishes to] heal eye diseases and various kinds of blindness, those with eyes and those without, one should summon and question the ghost. Identifying the curable, one should obtain a young *harītakī,*[46] crush it for its milky sap, then mix the sap and apply it to the eye. Then one should incant the spell fourteen times, and one should perceive some difference within three days. World-Honored One, if a practitioner [wishes to] heal those possessed by ghosts, he or she should summon the ghost and question it. Incant [the spell] seven times[47] and some change will immediately occur.

"World-Honored One, if one were to describe the causes of all the illnesses,[48] it would be difficult to exhaust their number even in a limitless aeon. But if the practitioner wishes to cure [a malady], he or she should first summon and question[49] the

---

39. I follow the suggestion in the *ZZ* annotation that there should be no lacunae here.

40. I follow the suggestion in the *ZZ* annotation to read the lacunae as *zhe songzhou* 者誦咒.

41. I follow the suggestion in the *ZZ* annotation to read the lacunae as 若無效者咒人共.

42. *Pai* 棑, more commonly written as *fei* 榧, is a yew tree with the scientific name *Torreya nucifera*. It is sometimes called *yeshan* 野杉, or "wild *Cunninghamia*." Its nuts are collected and eaten by the Chinese, and they are valued as an anthelmintic. See Stuart 1928: 439–440. I have therefore translated *pai zhi* 棑枝 as "yew branches."

43. In the *ZZ* edition the lacuna is read as *ji cha* 即差; my translation follows this reading.

44. In the *ZZ* edition the lacuna is read as *toubing* 頭病; my translation follows this reading.

45. In the *ZZ* edition the lacuna is read as *dahuang* 大黃; my translation follows this reading.

46. *Harītakī* (*helile* 訶梨勒) is the Sanskrit name for the yellow myrobalan tree *(Terminalia chebula),* whose fruit is frequently used as a dye and a laxative.

47. The *ZZ* annotation suggests substituting *qi* 七 for the lacuna.

48. In the *ZZ* edition the lacuna is read as *duo zhu bing* 多諸病; my translation follows this reading.

49. The *ZZ* annotation suggests substituting *wen* 問 for the lacuna.

ghost and then proceed to heal the illness. [This method] is unfailingly effective in all situations. Again, if a practitioner, in accordance with the ailments of all living beings, repeatedly weighs their seriousness[50] and subjects them to clinical observation and questioning, this method [ensures] all will not die. World-Honored One, [ ] today I am only inquiring for the practice, the observance of which will immediately[51] yield results. World-Honored One, one who wishes to observe the teaching without any contamination should first incant the spell, then write out the talisman,[52] and then carry the talisman everywhere to perform the practice. It is efficacious in all situations.[53]

"World-Honored One, when performing the rite, according to convenience one should practice it free from notions of purity and impurity. Whether it is in the main living or sleeping chamber, a separate chamber, a buddha pagoda, the wilderness, or on a sanctified mountain—at all these various sites one should accordingly perform the rite as is convenient, discriminating according to the exigency of the situation. The performance of this rite[54] accomplishes instant results. Whether it is in a crowded or secluded place, whether one is single or has a spouse and children, all these various factors really do not matter. But when mental urgency is present and without straining the physical limits, one will accomplish [the goals] in three days and nights. Then one should recite the name of the Bodhisattva Dizang. World-Honored One, when the practitioner is engaged in this rite, I will always be with this person. The path that I have pointed out is a byway that should not be disclosed. Furthermore, the practitioner of this method[55] employs the ghosts and spirits as servants and thereby secures rapid prowess. [The practitioner] makes [the ghost] report every single affair[56] that occurs in the dark realm and thus gains knowledge about the realm of the dead while [still] living.[57] Performing this teaching [for a dying person] will hasten his or her departure from this world.

"World-Honored One, whoever wishes to incant the spell and practice the various rites should selectively incant the spell and call the ghost. The practitioner should carry this out in secrecy, without making any noise. When he or she calls for and dispatches [the ghost], it should be conducted according to one's spontaneous intention, without hesitation. If attachment arises, one should perform purification for an extended period. If one is still not purified,[58] then one should continue to perform [the penance] carefully. Should attachment to the wondrous fragrance arise, greed, hatred, and ignorance will manifest.[59] Do not allow a practitioner with these

50. The *ZZ* annotation suggests substituting *qing* 輕 for *jing* 經.

51. The *ZZ* annotation suggests substituting *zhi* 直 for the lacuna.

52. I follow the suggestion in the *ZZ* annotation to read the lacunae as 誦咒後書.

53. I follow the suggestion in the ZZ annotation to read the lacunae as 皆悉有驗.

54. In the *ZZ* edition the lacuna is read as *suozuo* 所作; my translation follows this reading.

55. In the *ZZ* edition the lacuna is read as *xiufa ren* 修法人; my translation follows this reading.

56. In the *ZZ* edition the lacuna is read as 一一報示; my translation follows this reading.

57. The *ZZ* annotation suggests placing *zhi* 知 before *sheng* 生.

58. In the *ZZ* edition the lacuna is read as *ruo buran* 若不然; my translation follows this reading.

59. In the *ZZ* edition the lacuna is read as 滑或著妙香生欲. I follow the reading of the original edition.

obstructions on the path to practice [the rite]. World-Honored One, this teaching can be practiced and accomplished by inhabitants of the defiled lands (*huiguo* 穢國), but should the living beings in pure lands (*qingjingguo* 清淨國) practice it, they would be tainted by defilements and fall into the three evil paths of rebirth. World-Honored One, they do not deviate from the four phrases.[60] As long as one deeply engages in the practice all the goals can be accomplished.

"World-Honored One, again one[61] reciting the spell should not wear miscellaneous clothing. If one does not have adequate money to obtain new clothing,[62] the garments that one is wearing should be acceptable as long as they are not [made of] leather, fur, felt, and so forth. It is fine to wear these kinds of clothing when one is not engaged in the art of magic. World-Honored One, again, concerning the practice of the teaching—whether there are many or few ritualists, whether the rite is performed in a public or private site—it is all for the practitioner performing the rite to decide. So long as the ghost manifests and converses with the practitioner, he or she can be assured of success. Consequently practitioners come from distant places to inquire about the method of knowing the various[63] events and *karma* in past and present lives, all of which are generally predisposed toward the human realm. [ ] the name, the dispatcher very quickly explains to the practitioner.

"World-Honored One, when a practitioner who possesses knowledge of the future up to ten thousand years sees those who are undergoing pain, sicknesses, or disasters, he or she should write a talisman and dispatch it so that it will fly a thousand miles and be recompensed. When the talisman lands in the hearts of those who have died for a day, they will be resurrected. During the practice of this method, if the talisman is written on the first day of the year, all goals will be accomplished. On this day one should write out a thousand slips [ ] [ ] of talisman that will be sufficient for a year's use. Using the talisman from the first day of the year to this date[64] [in the next year], one will experience great efficacy from its use. The first day of the year varies: In India, the beginning of the year is the first day of the third month, whereas to the east in China, the beginning of the year is [the first day of] the first month. All should perform according to the custom of their country. After this date the talismans will lose their functionality.

"World-Honored One, for the above, there are forty types of talisman. The first twenty numinous talismans can ward off all calamities. If[65] the practitioner is treating the illnesses of living beings, he or she should write a thousand slips of talisman. After they are written, they should be swallowed and thus carried [within one's

60. It is unclear what the text really means here. "Four phrases" (*siju* 四句) is usually understood as an abbreviation of *siju fa* 四句法, or *siju fenbie* 四句分別, which refers to the four modes of existence: existence (*you* 有); non-existence (*wu* 無); existence and non-existence (*yi you yi wu* 亦有亦無); neither existence nor non-existence (*fei you fei wu* 非有非無).

61. The *ZZ* annotation suggests substituting *zhe* 者 for the lacuna.

62. In the *ZZ* edition the lacunae is read as 資若不足調新衣.

63. The Taishō edition contains a lacuna, but I am reading this according to the *ZZ* annotation, which states that there should be no missing characters.

64. The *ZZ* annotation suggests reading the lacunae as *yong chu nian* 用初年.

65. I follow the suggestion in the *ZZ* annotation to read the lacuna as *ruo* 若.

body].[66] For all those who have morbid illnesses and malignant tumors, write talismans with vermilion sand and [place them] facing the sick; there will be a difference immediately. World-Honored One, for all illnesses of living beings, regardless of what it is or how severe it is, immediate effect will be experienced upon the writing of the talismans. Should it not be efficacious, I [Dizang] shall abandon my bodhisattva's form before the Tathāgata and will undertake the suffering on behalf of that living being. On account of their observance of this method, the practitioners will not be assaulted by [demons].[67]

"World-Honored One, the remaining twenty talismans can eliminate degeneration and calamity within ten days.[68] If the practitioner wrote them in vermilion [sand] and carried them for forty-one days,[69] he or she would possess supernormal powers. One would attain the four knowledges of non-obstruction (*si wu'ai zhi* 四無礙智)[70] and would transcend life and death, emerging from the mire [of cyclic existence]. All the buddhas will praise and the bodhisattvas will keep vigil over [those who observe this method]. For a hundred days his distant relatives and close kin of the five clans will also realize the intuitive tolerance of the birthlessness of all phenomena (*anutpattika-dharma-kṣānti*; *wusheng fa ren* 無生法忍).[71] Every one of them will spread out their body and fly away. Again if the practitioner carries [the talisman] for up to fifty days,[72] his or her body (even the small finger) will then emit light and it will naturally become lucid and transparent like pure glass. All the kings, princes, officials, and citizens of the country where the practitioner lives will venerate and submit to him or her; insects, beasts, birds, the four-legged that dwell on the ground, all will bring incense and flowers to make offerings. All the heavens will scatter flowers and make the music of the great teachings so that the sound reaches the worlds of the ten directions. All those hearing [the sounds][73] will receive offerings of excellent delicacies and beverages."

After these words were spoken,[74] [the elder] then prepared various kinds of delicacies and beverages and proceeded to Mount Vulture Peak. He then prostrated and circumambulated a hundred thousand times before sitting down to one side and ad-

66. I follow the suggestion in the *ZZ* annotation to read the lacunae as 千枚符書之.

67. I follow the suggestion in the *ZZ* annotation to read the lacunae as *qinrao* 侵擾.

68. I follow the Taishō editors' suggestion that there might be the phrase *ruoganshu* 若干數 (that is, "a number of") before *chuxun* 除旬.

69. The *ZZ* annotation suggests substituting *fu* 符 for *cun* 村.

70. The *Abhidharmakośa* defines the four wisdoms of non-obstruction as (1) *dharma-pratisaṃvid* (*fa wu'ai* 法無礙), or ability to deploy language in a skillful manner to enable living beings to attain awakening; (2) *artha-pratisaṃvid* (*yi wu'ai zhi* 義無礙智), or command of all the intrinsic meanings of all the teachings without any uncertainty; (3) *nirukti-pratisaṃvid* (*ci wu'ai zhi* 詞無礙智), or versatility in different geographical dialects and the use of languages with any obstacles; (4) *pratibhāna-pratisaṃvid* (*bian wu'ai zhi* 辯無礙智), or eloquence that delights in preaching the Buddhist truths with great skill and effect.

71. A Buddhist technical term for the tolerance or patience *(kṣānti)* that enables one to remain in a state of equanimity after one apprehends that all phenomena in this world ultimately are not produced or annihilated (*bu sheng bu mie* 不生不滅).

72. I follow the suggestion in the *ZZ* annotation to read the lacunae as *shi ri qi* 十日其.

73. I follow the suggestion in the *ZZ* annotation to read the lacunae as *wen zhe xi* 聞者悉.

74. I follow the suggestion in the *ZZ* annotation that there should be no lacuna.

dressing the Buddha: "World-Honored One, from a long time ago, I and others have been telling all our households always to cultivate the ten good actions.[75] Today why did we die, resurrect,[76] and again see the Tathāgata? May you please resolve my doubts." At this time, the Tathāgata spoke these causes and conditions so as to remove my doubts.[77] The elder and so forth listened to the teachings and rejoiced. Finally, they attained arhatship, whereupon they spread out their bodies and flew away. At this time, the bodies of the four congregations rose into the void and in the air they prostrated at the feet of the Buddha.[78] All rejoiced and accepted the teaching.

The Exorcism Method of [Dizang's Aspiration Toward] Great Awakening. The dharma-transmitter Ācarya Keiyū 慶有 wrote out [this copy] at Śūraṅgama Cloister.[79] It was completed on the twenty-fifth day of the seventh month in the first year of the *kanji* 寛治 era [1087]. In the autumn of the third year of the *kyōhō* 亨保 era [1718] Bushin 武親 was decreed to copy the text based on the copy in the Mount Togao 栂尾 collection.[80] However, this copy was damaged by grub worms and was very difficult to read, so he obtained a good copy for revising.

75. *Daśakuśala-karmāni*, or *shi shan ye* 十善業, translated as "the ten good actions," is a set of physical, verbal, and mental actions concieved to contrast the ten negative actions (*Daśākuśala-karmāni*, or *shi e ye* 十惡業). The ten good actions are not to kill, not to steal, not to commit adultery, not to lie, not to slander, not to criticize others, not to mock others, not to manifest greed and desire, not to give way to resentment, and not to engage in heterodox views. The ten good actions are discussed in detail in a work attributed to Śikṣānanda, the *Shi shan yedao jing* 十善業道經, T600:15.157c–9b.

76. Here I adopt the alternative reading first proposed in the *ZZ* annotation, which substitutes *sheng* 生 for *zhu* 主.

77. According to the annotation, the original edition suggests that instead of the lacuna there are characters: *po yihuo shuo* 破疑惑說. I follow the reading of the original edition.

78. *Si zhong* 四衆, or the fourfold congregation of monks, nuns, laymen, and laywomen.

79. Śūraṅgama Cloister, also known as Yokowa 横川 Hall, is part of the temple complex of Enryaki-ji 延暦寺 on Mount Hiei, the headquarters of Japanese Tendai 天台, located in Kyoto. The cloister is one of three main pagoda buildings and was established by the monk Ennin 圓仁 (793–864). It houses an extensive collection of Buddhist writings.

80. Located in Kyoto, Mount Togao, also known as Kōzan-ji 高山寺, is a center that bridges Shingon 真言 and Kegon 華厳 Buddhism. The temple was founded by the famous Kegon monk Myōe (1173–1232), who served as its abbot for the latter half of his life. It houses archival collections that include Song Buddhist paintings and texts.

Dizang pusa yigui 地藏菩薩儀軌 (A Ritual Manual on the Bodhisattva Dizang), T1158:20.652a–c. Translated by Śubhakara from Central India

At that time Śākyamuni was preaching the Dharma on Mount Kharādīya surrounded by numberless bodhisattvas, ten *koṭī*s of *bhikṣu*s and *bhikṣuṇī*s, *deva*s, *nāga*s, and others of the eight classes of living beings, various demons and spirits, all together with countless hundreds of thousands in the great congregation.[81]

At that time a Great Being named Dizang bared his right shoulder and knelt with his right knee on the ground amidst the multitude. He placed his palms together and reverently requested of the Buddha: "I wish to preach numinous *mantra*s for the benefit of all beings. I only wish the World-Honored One would kindly listen and accede to my desire to preach the numinous *mantra*s." The Buddha told Dizang Bodhisattva, "You all should hasten to preach [the *mantra*s] so as to benefit all living beings." At that time, Dizang Bodhisattva ascended into the air, gave praise to and took refuge in the World-Honored One, exhibited countless supernormal powers in the air, and uttered a *mantra* through his divine mouth: *An yanmota anmoer jubi jubi sanmanduo suopohe.*[82] Then he uttered the middle-length *mantra*: *An yanmantazhe suopohe.*[83] Then he uttered[84] twice the shortest *mantra*: *An shisi.*[85] Upon his recitation of these *mantra*s, the great bodhisattvas of the tenth stage and so forth lost their original aspiration to awakening and became confused. The *deva*s, *nāga*s, and others of the eight classes, *yakṣa*s, demons, and spirits, fled in great apprehension and collapsed to the ground. The sun, moon, and stars lost their luminosity and darkness pervaded the sky. Showers of precious flowers rained down. Even if one were to discourse on the power of the *mantra*s for an entire aeon, one cannot exhaust [this subject].

[Dizang Bodhisattva] then explained the method of painting the image [of Dizang]. Forge an image of a *śrāvaka* wearing a *kāṣāya* robe, the end of which covers his left shoulder. He should be seated on a lotus flower, his left hand holding a flower in full bloom and his right hand in the gesture of bestowing fearlessness (*shi wuwei yin* 施無畏印; *abhayaṃdadamudrā*). Next, a second description: Forge[86] a seated image of the Great Being wearing a celestial coiffure and a *kaṣaya* robe; he should hold in his

The Taishō editors based their edition on the manuscript copy kept in the library of Hōzan University, dated to the Kyōho period (1716–1736). The editors also cross-referenced their work with a collated text copied in the fifth year of the Eikyū 永久 period (1113–1118) and now in the Dōzan sanmitzu 東山三密. I should thank Professor Chen Ming, a specialist in Indian and Chinese Buddhist medicine, for extensive help in translating the plants and herbs listed in the *homa*.

81. I follow the reading in the Hōzan edition, which does not have the name Dizang 地藏 in this line.

82. 唵 閻摩他嚩摩爾 俱苾 俱苾 三曼多 娑婆賀.

83. 唵 炎曼他啫 娑婆賀.

84. I follow the Dōzan edition's suggestion to read *shuo* 說 after *ci* 次.

85. 唵 [illegible]呬 二合. The text describes this *mantra* as *xin zhong xin zhou* 心中心咒, literally "the heart of heart *mantras*." Each deity has *mantra*s of varying lengths often characterized as long, middle, and short.

86. I follow the Dōzan edition's suggestion to read *zuo* 作 before *ju* 居.

left hand a lotus flower with leaf and stalk,[87] while his right hand makes the previous [gesture of fearlessness]. He should be seated on a lotus platform of nine grades. Nine grades is said to be nine layers or a middle platform with eight leaves.

Then [Dizang] explained the *mudrā* and *mantra:* The two hands[88] [are brought together to make a hollow between the palms] in the *saṁpuṭāñjaliḥ mudrā;*[89] motion the ring fingers (the right signifies precepts and the left expedient means) downward to the inside of the palms; incant this *mantra*: *An yanmozhili suopohe.*[90] Next he explained the *mudrā* of universal offering: The two hands are in *saṁpuṭāñjaliḥ;* motion to-and-fro with the thumbs (the right signifies meditation and the left wisdom);[91] [incant this *mantra*]: *An nanremoni suofuhe.*[92] He then summarized the general *mudrā:* The hands are in *saṁpuṭāñjaliḥ;* motion to-and-fro with the index fingers (the right signifies diligence and the left strength); twice [incant] this *mantra*: *An jiezhiniye suofuhe.*[93] Then [he explained] the *mudrā* for inviting and praising [the deity]: The hands are in *saṁpuṭāñjaliḥ mudrā;* motion to-and-fro with the index fingers, gesturing repeatedly. By using the visualization of hand [gestures] one advances into [states of] concentration.[94]

Again [Dizang] explained the *siddhi* methods. If one thinks of procuring great blessing and virtue, one must perform the offering (*homa*) of *aka* wood seventy thousand times. If one thinks of obtaining the harvest of the five grains, one

---

87. I follow the Hōzan edition's suggestion to read *yejing* 葉莖 for *cha* 茶. The Dōzan edition reads *zuo* 作 for *cha* 茶.

88. In ritual language *eryu* 二羽 is a technical term for the two hands as well as the ten *pāramitā*s. In esoteric ritual the ten fingers signify the ten *pāramitā*s (giving, precepts, patience, effort, meditation, wisdom, expedient means, aspiration, knowledge). The right hand represents merit (*fu* 福) and the left wisdom (*zhi* 智). The mapping of the ten *pāramitā*s is discerned in esoteric ritual texts like the *Niansong jiehufa putong zhubu* 念誦結護法普通諸部, attributed to Vajrabodhi (Jingangzhi 金剛智, 671?–741), and the *Jingangding jing duoluo pusa niansongfa* 金剛頂經多羅菩薩念誦法, attributed to Amoghavajra. Hand symbolism was subsequently integrated into the *fang yankou* ceremony. Diagrams of hand symbolism and *mudrā*s are included in a modern reprint of a Qing text titled *Yuqie yankou shisi yaoji* 瑜伽焰口施食要集, produced by and used at Baohua si 寶華寺. This text, also nicknamed the *Huashan yankou* 華山焰口, is a revised edition completed in 1693 by Deji Ding'an 德基定庵 (1634–1700), who was ordained from an early age at Baohua si. Contemporary performances of the *fang yankou* are usually based on this Qing text. See *Yuqie yankou shisi yaoji,* 10.

89. *Sanbuzha* 三補吒, the transliteration for *saṁpuṭāñjaliḥ,* is one of the twelve gestures of placing the palms together (*añjaliḥ*). Its Chinese name is *xuxin hezhang* 虛心合掌.

90. 唵 炎摩智利 娑婆賀.

91. The *mudrā* of the universal offering, or *pu gongyang yin* 普供養印, is forged while making offerings to the deities. This hand gesture varies from rite to rite. For a description of the hand gesture in the Garbhadhātu rites, see Devi 1999: 47–48; for the Vajradhātu rites, see ibid.: 80, 85.

92. 唵 喃惹摩尼 娑嚩賀.

93. 唵 嘱只禰耶 娑嚩二合賀.

94. In Chinese it is the *qingzan yin* 請讚印. "Invitation and praise" refers to *gāthā*s extolling the merits of the deity and inviting the deity to descend to the ritual sanctuary. For descriptions of hand gestures of invitation in the *homa* rite to Agni, the astral deities, and others, see Devi 1999: 92–94. For the Garbhadhātu, see ibid.: 48–49; for the rite of Vajradhātu, see ibid.: 81.

must perform the rice spike (*daoshi hua* 稻實華) *homa*.[95] If one thinks of [bestowing] merits and virtue on another, one must perform a *homa* with ashes from the stove of that person's house. If one thinks of obtaining eminent status and virtue,[96] one must perform a *homa* with *bili* 比哩 flowers.[97] If one thinks of subduing enemies in all of one's births, one must rigorously practice wood *homa*. If one thinks of conquering malicious spirits and inauspicious vapor,[98] one must perform a *homa* with poisonous odors. If one thinks of curing insanity, fits,[99] and [other] illnesses, one must perform a *homa* with lotus, fruits, and herbs thirty thousand times. If one thinks of extinguishing evil, producing good, and [attaining] rebirth in paradise after death,[100] one must perform a *homa* with herbs thirty thousand times. If one thinks of reversing a curse on the wicked person who spells the curse, one must perform a *homa* by throwing tape grass (*ku cao* 苦草) into the fire thirty thousand times.[101] If one thinks of procuring immeasurable glorious achievements and an official salary, one must perform a *homa* with white flowers and bird grass (*bai hua niao cao* 白華鳥草) thirty thousand times.[102] If one thinks of becoming a virtuous person who has the ability of *samaya* debate (*sanmei biancai* 三昧辨才),[103] one must per-

95. The *daoshi hua* does not appear in glossaries of Chinese medicine and plants. Chen Ming calls attention to two close correlates, *daogu hua* 稻穀華 and *dao hua* 稻華 in esoteric Buddhist texts. The *Jianlao ditian yigui* 堅牢地天儀軌, a text attributed to Śubhakara, speaks of the *daogu hua* and explains the method of accomplishing the *homa* as follows: "Through performing the *homa* of the rice spike *(daogu hua)* one attains the *siddha* of harvesting the five grains" (T1286:21.355a). There are two occurrences of *dao hua* in Buddhist texts. The first is in the *Shisong lü* 十誦律: "At that time when the Buddha was in the land of Somāpatra, the elder *bhikkhu* Aniruddha became ill, and after consuming some medication, his heart was stifled. The Buddha said, 'Give him the decocted rice spike *(dao hua)* juice.'" (T1435:23.462a). The second example of *dao hua* is found in the *Foshuo dalun jingang zongchi tuoluoni jing* 佛說大輪金剛總持陀羅尼經, which prescribes a method to rid oneself of prolonged illness caused by spirits and the use of witchcraft: "Then, in front of the buddha image, one should prepare beforehand burnt incense. Blend it together with butter, honey, curd, rice spike grains, and sesame. Burn [the mixture] in the fire and recite the *mantra* for seven days and seven nights. Prepare in advance offerings and then swallow the fragrant pill with water drawn from the well. One will instantly eliminate any irregular condition" (T1230:21.165c).

96. I follow the Dōzan edition's suggestion to read *er* 二 as *gao* 高.

97. Another unknown plant. Chen Ming speculates that *bili hua* may be an abbreviation for one of two Indian plants: *bi[kouli]jia* 畢[口栗]迦, or *spçkkā*; and *biliyunyu* 畢哩孕愚, or *priyaṛgu*. *Biliyunyu* occurs in the *Shiyimian Guanzizai pusa xin miyan niansong yigui jing* 十一面觀自在菩薩心密言念誦儀軌經, attributed to Amoghavajra: "Using two ounces of green wood incense, etc., four ounces of *priyaṛgu*, and eight ounces of *turuṣka*, pound and sieve thoroughly, and grind again with water" (T1069:20.145b).

98. I follow the Dōzan edition's suggestion to read *jia* 家 as *qi* 氣.

99. I follow the Dōzan edition's suggestion to read *e* 痾 as *xian* 癇.

100. I follow the Hōzan edition's suggestion to read *sheng* 生 as *she* 捨.

101. The medicinal term for *ku cao* is *Valliseneria spiralis*, a tape grass (also known as eel grass) that grows to the length of two or three feet in ponds and marshes. It is prescribed, together with sesamum, for leucorrhoea. Made into a tea or masticated together, the two are used to increase the appetite; see Stuart 1928: 452.

102. Chen Ming proposes that *bai hua niao cao* should perhaps be separated into *bai hua* and *niao cao*.

103. The Hōzan edition has *cai* 財, which the Dōzan edition correctly reads as *cai* 才.

form a *homa* with skeletal grass (*gulou cao* 骨婁草) thirty thousand times.[104] If one thinks of transforming and converting all beings, removing them from suffering and attaining happiness, one must perform a *homa* with white mustard seeds thirty thousand times. If one thinks of transforming and converting the beings in the buddhaless world, one must perform a *homa* with *shijia* grass (*shijia cao* 尸迦草)[105] thirty thousand times.[106] If one thinks of producing the five grains from an infertile field, one must consecrate an old rape turnip (*manqing* 蔓青);[107] where it is scattered, those sites will be consecrated.[108] If one worries about the ten thousand kinds of diseases, one must perform a *homa* with hyssop (*niuxi cao* 牛膝草) thirty thousand times.[109] If one worries about the assorted diseases caused by the three colds (*san yin* 三陰) and the four heats (*si re* 四熱), one must perform a *homa* with a variety of herbs yielding dryness.[110] If a husband and wife are at odds with each other, one must perform a *homa* with *bizui* 比罪 grass thirty thousand times; then they will be in harmony.[111] If one's wicked and good friends are caught in conflict, one must perform a *homa* with

104. Chen Ming speculates that *gulou cao* 骨婁草 may be *jinglou cao* 兢婁草, but he cautions that further investigation should be undertaken to see if the phonetics supports this. In the *Jianlao ditian yigui*, the *jinglou cao* is prescribed for a *homa*: "Again, through the method of offering *jinglou* grass, one procures boundless wealth in the form of the six domestic animals" (T1286:21.355a).

105. Chen Ming speculates two possibilities: On the one hand, *shijia cao* 尸迦草 may be an incorrect inversion of *jiashi cao* 迦尸草, identified as *Saccharum spontaneum*, a plant that appears frequently in Buddhist texts. On the other hand, *shijia cao* may also be an abbreviation of *yishijia cao* 伊師迦草, a plant mentioned in the *Mahāparinirvāṇa-sūtra* (*Da boniepan jing* 大般涅槃經; see T375:12.717c). Commentaries provide glosses of this plant. For example, in the *Da boniepan jing jijie* 大般涅槃經集解, it is said that *yishijia* grass has a firm, solid internal skin and a soft, crispy external one; see T1763:37.510c. A glossary on phonetical usages in Buddhist texts, the *Yiqie jing yinyi* 一切經音義, states that *yishijia grass* is a foreign medicinal plant, which Hexi monks say possesses a firm exterior and soft interior; T2128:54.475a. This grass also appears in the *Fan fanyu* 翻梵語; see T2130:54.1049a.

106. I follow the Hōzan edition's suggestion and omit *qi* 七 as it is not in the text.

107. This plant, also written as *manjing* 蔓荊, is the *Vitex trifolia* or *Vitex incisa*. It grows in abundance in north China and produces bland, odorless berries that are supposed to have curative abilities, particularly for headache, catarrh, and watery eyes. In folk medicine *manqing* is also believed to catalyze the growth of male facial hair; see Stuart 1928: 457.

108. I follow the Hōzan edition's suggestion to add *qisuo* 其所 after *san* 散. *Jiachi* 加持 or *adhiṣṭhana*, translated here as "consecrate," is a ritual term used in esoteric texts in connection with purification and empowerment rites. To perform consecration, the ritualist sanctifies the chosen object through mental visualization, often accompanied by *mantra* recitation.

109. This plant is *Achyranthes bidentata Bl.* It is an amarantaceous plant possessing greenish-purple stems. Its Chinese name, which literally means "ox knee," comes from its large joints, which resemble the knee of an ox. The plant is reputed to have antirheumatic and anodyne properties and is prescribed for ague, fever, urinary problems, and puerpal and cutaneous diseases; see Stuart 1928: 6–7.

110. *San yin* refers to the three kinds of ailments caused by an excess of cold phlegm in the body. The four heats are brought on by a bodily imbalance due to excessive heat. The *āyurveda* literature usually speaks of eight heat ailments. But this text refers to only four, which Chen Ming identifies as those caused by the three types of bodily fluid plus the ailment arising from heat catalyzed by a combination of fluids.

111. *Bizui cao* is not cited in the literature on Chinese medicine and herbs.

rattan leaves (*tengye cao* 藤葉草) thirty thousand times.[112] If one cultivates according to the above methods on the eighth, fourteenth, and fifteenth days of the first half of the month, one is sure to attain accomplishment.

A Ritual Manual on the Bodhisattva Dizang[113]

112. This plant is not listed in dictionaries on Chinese medicine and herbs. The word *tengye* occurs in a Buddhist text attributed to Yijing, the *Genben shuoyiqieyou bu baiyi jiemo* 根本說一切有部百一羯磨: "Moreover, at several holy sites, aristocrats and lowly people at that time all chewed a concoction of betel nuts and rattan leaves, mixed with white ashes and fragrances, which they regarded as a delicacy. If a *bhikṣu*, wishing to eliminate mouth odors caused by illness, is advised by a physician to ingest this [concoction], this does not constitute a transgression [of the *vinaya*]" (T1453:24.498c).

113. The Taishō editors note that the Dōzan edition had a colophon stating the text was copied and proofread on the twenty-third day of the seventh month during the fifth year of Eikyū 永久 (1113–1118).

Dizang pusa jing 地藏菩薩經 (Scripture on the Bodhisattva Dizang), Dunhuang manuscript S 6257, transcribed in T2909:85.1455b–c.

At that time, Dizang Bodhisattva was residing in the Lapis Lazuli Realm in the south, and he deployed his pure celestial eye to contemplate living beings undergoing tortures in hell: Iron mortars were pounding; trip-hammer pestles were grinding; iron plowshares were furrowing while iron saws were sawing away; the broth in the cauldrons was simmering and gushing over while a raging fire rose into the sky.[114] When hungry, [the beings] swallowed scathing iron pellets; when thirsty, they drank molten bronze. They underwent afflictions without respite.

Unable to endure these sights, Dizang Bodhisattva came from the south and arrived in hell. He assumed a separate seat in the same place as King Yama. [He came] for four reasons: First, he feared that King Yama's judgment of crimes would be unreliable; second, he feared that the written documents could have been confused; third, he was concerned for those who died in an untimely fashion; and fourth, he [desired that] those who had received their punishments would be able to leave the riverbanks of hell.

If there is a good man or woman who has carved images of the Bodhisattva Dizang, copied the *Scripture on the Bodhisattva Dizang*, and recited the Bodhisattva Dizang's name, he or she will surely attain rebirth in the Land of Supreme Bliss in the west. [He or she will travel] from one buddha-land to another buddha-land, from one heaven to another heaven. If there is a person who has carved images of the Bodhisattva Dizang, copied the *Scripture on the Bodhisattva Dizang*, and recited the Bodhisattva Dizang's name, this person will surely attain rebirth in the Land of Supreme Bliss in the west. On the day when this person dies, the Bodhisattva Dizang himself will come to welcome him or her, and he or she will always be in the same place as the Bodhisattva Dizang.

After hearing the Buddha's preaching, all rejoice immensely, accept [the teaching] with faith, and reverently uphold it.

According to a Taishō annotation, the original version is manuscript S 197 from the Dunhuang collection kept in British Museum. But Wang-Toutain has established this to be the wrong manuscript; the one actually used was S 6257 (1998: 146, n. 581).

114. The southern direction is consistent with the opening scene in the *Scripture on the Ten Wheels*, which describes Dizang Bodhisattva and his retinue arriving from the south to attend the Buddha's assembly; see *Da fangguang shilun jing*, T410:13.681a–b; *Dasheng daji Dizang shilun jing*, T411:13.723b.

Works Cited

Primary Texts

Anle ji 安樂集. Daochuo 道綽 (562–645). T1958:47.4a–22a.

Ba da pusa mantuluo jing 八大菩薩曼荼羅經. Attributed to Amoghavajra (Bukong jingang 不空金剛, 705–774). T1167:20.675a–676a.

Ba mantuluo jing 八曼荼羅經. T1168B:20.676c–677b.

Baiqian song daji jing Dizang pusa qingwen fashen zan 百千頌大集經地藏菩薩請問法身讚. Attributed to Amoghavajra (Bukong jingang 不空金剛, 705–774). T413: 13.790a–792c.

Baopuzi neipian 抱朴子內篇. HY 50211.

Beihua jing 悲華經. Dharmakṣema (Tanwuchen 曇無讖, 385–433). T157:3.167a–233c.

Bodhicaryāvatāra of Śāntideva with the Commentary Pañjikā of Prajñākaramati. P. L. Vaidya, ed. Buddhist Sanskrit Texts, no. 12. Darbhanga, Bihar: The Mithila Institute, 1988.

Bosijiao can jing 波斯教殘經. T2141B:54.1281a–1286a.

Brahmājāla-sūtra. See Davids, T. W. Rhys.

Chang ahan jing 長阿含經. Buddhayaśas (Fotuoyeshe 佛陀耶舍, fl. 408–412), Zhu Fonian 竺佛念 (fl. 365–384) et al., trans. T1:1.1a–149c.

Chu sanzang jiji 出三藏記集. Sengyou 僧祐 (445–518), comp. T2145:55.1a–114a.

Chūshin hossō shū shōsho 注進法相宗章疏. Zōshun 藏俊 (1104–1180). T2181: 55.1141b–1144c.

Da baoji jing 大寶積經. Attributed to Bodhiruci (Putiliuzhi 菩提流志, fl. 693–727) et al. T310:11.1a–685a.

Da boniepan jing 大般涅槃經. Huiyan 慧嚴 (363–443) et al. T375:12.605a–852b.

Da boniepan jing jijie 大般涅槃經集解. Baoliang 寶亮 (444–509). T1763:37.377a–611a.

Da fangdeng daji jing 大方等大集經. Attributed to Dharmakṣema (Tanwuchen 曇無讖, 385–433) et al. T397:13.1a–407a.

Da fangguang fo huayan jing 大方廣佛華嚴經. Buddhabhadra (Fotuobatuoluo 佛陀跋陀羅, 359–429). T278:9.395a–788b.

Da fangguang fo huayan jing 大方廣佛華嚴經. Prajñā (Bore 般若, b. 734). T293: 10.661a–851c.

Da fangguang fo huayan jing 大方廣佛華嚴經. Śikṣānanda (Shicha'nantuo 實叉難陀, 652–710). T279:10.1b–444c.

Da fangguang fo huayan jing ganying zhuan 大方廣佛華嚴經感應傳. Huiying 惠英 (fl. 687). T2074:51.173b–178b.

Da fangguang fo huayan jing suishu yanyi chao 大方廣佛華嚴經隨疏演義鈔. Chengguan 澄觀 (738–839). T1736:36.1a–701a.

Da fangguang sanjie jing 大方廣三戒經. Dharmakṣema (Tanwuchen 曇無讖, 385–433). T311:11.687a–704b.

Da fangguang shilun jing 大方廣十輪經. T410:13.681a–720a.

Da Piluzhena chengfo shenbian jiachi jing 大毘盧遮那成佛神變加持經. Attributed to Śubhakara (Shupojialuo 輸婆迦羅, 637–735). T848:18.1a–55a.

Dabei jing 大悲經. Narendrayaśas (Naliantiyeshe 那連提耶舍, 517–589). T380:12.945b–973a.

Daojiao lingyan ji 道教靈驗記. Du Guangting 杜光庭 (850–933), comp. HY 9983.

Daozang zimu yinde 道藏子目引得. Weng Dujian 翁獨健, ed. Harvard-Yenching Institute Sinological Index Series, no. 25. Beijing: Yanjing University, 1925. Reprint, Taipei: Xinwenfeng chuban gongsi, 1988.

Dasheng daji Dizang shilun jing 大乘大集地藏十輪經. Xuanzang 玄奘 (602–664), trans. T411:13.721a–777c.

Dasheng fajie wujinzang fa shi 大乘法界無盡藏法釋. S 721, Giles 5563. In *Sangaikyō no kenkyū* 三階教の研究, edited by Yabuki Keiki 矢吹慶輝, Appendix, 161–176. Tokyo: Iwanami Shoten, 1927.

Dasheng ji pusa xue lun 大乘集菩薩學論. Dharmarakṣa (Damoluocha 達磨羅刹, a.k.a. Zhu Fahu 竺法護, fl. 265–313). T1636:32.75b–145a.

Datang neidian lu 大唐內典錄. Daoxuan 道宣 (596–667), comp. T2149:55.219a–342a.

Datang xiyu ji 大唐西域記. Xuanzang 玄奘 (602–664). T2087:51.867b–947c.

Dazhou kanding zhongjing mulu 大周刊定衆經目錄. Mingquan 明佺 (Tang) et al., comps. T2153:55.372c–476a.

Dizang dadao xin quce fa 坔䧈大道心驅策法. T1159A:20.652c–655a.

Dizang lueyi 地藏略儀. P 4514.5. *DHBZ* 133: 283.

Dizang pusa benyuan jing 地藏菩薩本願經. Attributed to Śikṣānanda (Shicha'nantuo 實叉難陀, 652–710). T412:13.777c–790a.

Dizang pusa hushen tuoluoni 地藏菩薩護身陀羅尼. S 431. *DHBZ* 3: 484.

Dizang pusa shizhai ri 地藏菩薩十齋日. S 2568. Transcribed in T2850:85.1300a–b.

Dizang pusa tuoluoni 地藏菩薩陀羅尼. S 4543. *DHBZ* 36: 517.

Dizang pusa xiang lingyan ji 地藏菩薩像靈驗記. Changjin 常謹 (Song), comp. *XZ* 149: 352a–369b.

Dizang pusa yigui 地藏菩薩儀軌. Attributed to Śubhakara (Shupojialuo 輸婆迦羅, 637–735). T1158:20.652a–c.

Dizang pusa zan 地藏菩薩讃. Li Bai 李白 (699–762). *Wenyuange siku quanshu, yingyin* (影印)文淵閣四庫全書, 1066: 415. Taipei: Taiwan shangwu yinshuguan, 1986.

Dizang pusa zan 地藏菩薩讃. Liang Su 梁肅 (753–793). *Wenyuange siku quanshu, yingyin* (影印)文淵閣四庫全書, 1340: 602. Taipei: Taiwan shangwu yinshuguan, 1986.

Dongxuan lingbao ziran jiutian shengshen zhang jing 洞玄靈寶自然九天生神章經. HY 1821.

Dunhuang baozang 敦煌寶藏. Huang Yongwu 黃永武, ed. 140 vols. Taipei: Xinwenfeng chuban gongsi, 1981–1986.

Fan fanyu 翻梵語. T2130:54.981a–1054c.

Fanwang jing 梵網經. Kumārajīva (Jiumoluoshi 鳩摩羅什, 343–413). T1484:24.997a–1010a.

Fayuan zhulin 法苑珠林. Daoshi 道世 (d. 683), comp. T2122:53.269a–1030a.

Foshuo ba jixiang shenzhou jing 佛說八吉祥神咒經. Zhi Qian 支謙 (fl. 222–253). T427: 14.72b–73a.

Foshuo dalun jingang zongchi tuoluoni jing 佛說大輪金剛總持陀羅尼經. T1230:21.161b–166b.

Foshuo dasheng ba da mannaluo jing 佛說大乘八大曼拏羅經. Faxian 法賢 (d. 1001). T1168A:20.676a–c.

Foshuo Dizang pusa jing 佛說地藏菩薩經. S 431. *DHBZ* 3: 484.

Foshuo Dizang pusa jing 佛說地藏菩薩經. S 6257. *DHBZ* 45: 176–177. Transcribed in T2909:85.1455b–c.

Foshuo Dizang pusa tuoluoni jing 佛說地藏菩薩陀羅尼經. T1159B:20.655b–660a.

Foshuo guan wuliangshou fo jing 佛說觀無量壽佛經. T365:12.340b–346b.

Foshuo Luomoqie jing 佛說羅摩伽經. Shengjian 聖堅 (Eastern Jin). T294:10.851c–876a.

Fozu tongji 佛祖統紀. Zhipan 志磐 (fl. 1258–1269). T2035:49.129a–475c.

Gaṇḍavyūha-sūtra. P. L. Vaidya, ed. Buddhist Sanskrit Texts, no. 5. Darbhanga, Bihar: The Mithila Institute, 1960.

Gantong lu 感通錄. Daoxuan 道宣 (596–667). T2106:52.404a–435a.

Gaoseng zhuan 高僧傳. Huijiao 慧皎 (497–554). T2059:50.322c–423a.

Genben shuoyiiqeyou bu baiyi jiemo 根本說一切有部百一羯磨. Yijing 義淨 (635–713). T1453:24.455c–500b.

Guan Xukongzang pusa jing 觀虛空藏菩薩經. Dharmamitra (Tanmomiduo 曇摩蜜多, 356–442). T409:13.677b–680c.

Guang hongming ji 廣弘明集. Daoxuan 道宣 (596–667). T2103:52.97a–361a.

Gujin yijing tuji 古今譯經圖紀. Jingmai 靖邁 (fl. 627–649), comp. T2151:55.348a–367c.

Hongming ji 弘明集. Sengyou 僧祐 (445–518). T2102:52.1a–95b.

Hossō shū shōsho 法相宗章疏. Recorded by Byōso 平祚. T2180:55.1138b–1140b.

Huanhun ji 還魂記. S 3092. *DHBZ* 25: 667–668.

Huayan jing zhuanji 華嚴經傳記. Fazang 法藏 (643–712), comp. T2073:51.153a–173a.

Jianlao ditian yigui 堅牢地天儀軌. Attributed to Śubhakara (Shupojialuo 輸婆迦羅, 637–735). T1286:21.354b–355b.

Jin guangming jing 金光明經. Dharmakṣema (Tanwuchen 曇無讖, 385–433). T663: 16.335a–359b.

Jin xiangguo Dizang zan 今相國地藏贊. Sikong Tu 司空圖 (837–908). *Wenyuange siku quanshu, yingyin* (影印)文淵閣四庫全書, 1083: 538. Taipei: Taiwan shangwu yinshuguan, 1983.

Jingang sanmei jing 金剛三昧經. T273:9.365c–374b.

Jingangding jing duoluo pusa niansongfa 金剛頂經多羅菩薩念誦法. Attributed to Amoghavajra (Bukong jingang 不空金剛, 705–774). T1102:20.454a–457b.

Jingtu wuhui nianfo lue fashiyi zan 淨土五會念佛略法事儀讚. Fazhao 法照 (fl. 766–804). T1983:47.474b–490c.

Jiu Tang shu 舊唐書. Liu Xu 劉昫 (887–946). 200 vols. Beijing: Zhonghua shuju, 1975.

Jiuhua shan zhi 九華山志. 1938 edition. Revised by Yinguang 印光 (1861–1940). In Vol. 1, *Si da mingshan zhi* 四大名山志. 4 vols. Taipei: Fojiao chubanshe, 1978.

Kaiyuan shijiao lu 開元釋教錄. Zhishen 智昇 (fl. 669–740), comp. T2154: 55.477a–723a.

Lidai sanbao ji 歷代三寶紀. Fei Changfang 費長房 (ca. 597), comp. T2034:49.22c–127c.

Lingbao wuliang duren shangjing dafa 靈寶無量度人上經大法. HY 219.

Miaofa lianhua jing 妙法蓮華經. Kumārajīva (Jiumoluoshi 鳩摩羅什, 343–413). T262: 9.1a–62c.

Miaofa lianhua jing xuanzan 妙法蓮華經玄贊. Kuiji 窺基 (632–682). T1723:34.651a–854b.

Monijiao xiabu zan 摩尼教下部讚. T2140:54.1270b–1279c.

Nanhai jigui neifa zhuan 南海寄歸內法傳. Yijing 義淨 (634–713). T2125:54.204c–234a.

Nianfo jing 念佛鏡. Daojing 道鏡 (Tang). T1966:47.120a–133c.

Niansong jiehufa putong zhubu 念誦結護法普通諸部. Vajrabodhi (Jingangzhi 金剛智, 671?–741). T904:18.900a–909b.

Qianshou qianyan Guanshiyin pusa zhibing heyao jing 千手千眼觀世音菩薩治病合藥經. Bhagavat-dharma (Qiefandamo 伽梵達摩, Tang). T1059:20.103c–105c.

Qinding quan Tang wen 欽定全唐文. Dong Gao 董誥 (1740–1818), comp. 200 vols. Guangdong: Guangya shuju, 1901.

Qishu jiyuan tu 祇樹給園圖. Daoxuan 道宣 (596–667). T1899:45.882c–895c.

Renji lu yi zhu dasheng jing zhong lue fayuan fa 人集錄依諸大乘經中略發願法. Dunhuang manuscript *bei* 北 8422. *DHBZ* 110: 272–277.

Renwang borepoluomi jing 仁王般若波羅蜜經. Attributed to Kumārajīva (Jiumoluoshi 鳩摩羅什, 343–413). T245:8.825a–834a.

Ruhe xiuchi Dizang jing 如何修持地藏經. Hong Yuanyin 洪緣音. Fojing xiuchi fa, no. 12. Taipei: Quanfo wenhua chubanshe, 1995.

Sanbao ganying yaolue lu 三寶感應要略錄. Feizhuo 非濁 (d. 1063), comp. T2084: 51.826a–856c.

Sanjie fofa 三階佛法. S 2084. In *Sangaikyō no kenkyū* 三階教の研究, edited by Yabuki Keiki 矢吹慶輝, Appendices, 9–47. Tokyo: Iwanami Shoten, 1927.

*Sanjie jiao can juan*三階教殘卷. In *Sangaikyō no kenkyū* 三階教の研究, edited by Yabuki Keiki 矢吹慶輝, Appendices. Tokyo: Iwanami Shoten, 1927.

Sanjiao yuanliu shengdi fozu soushen daquan 三教源流聖帝佛祖搜神大全. In Vol. 3, *Zhongguo minjian xinyang ziliao huibian* 中國民間信仰資料彙編, edited by Wang Qiugui 王秋桂 and Li Fengmao 李豐楙. Taipei: Taiwan xuesheng shuju, 1989.

Shami shijie bing weiyi 沙彌十戒并威儀. T1471:24.926a–932b.

Shenseng zhuan 神僧傳. T2064:50.948b–1015a.

Shi jingtu qunyi lun 釋淨土群疑論. Huaigan 懷感 (Tang). T1960:47.30c–76c.

Shi shan yedao jing 十善業道經. Śikṣānanda (Shicha'nantuo 實叉難陀, 652–710), trans. T600:15.157c–159b.

Shijia fangzhi 釋迦方志. Daoxuan 道宣 (596–667). T2088:51.948a–975a.

Shike shiliao xinbian 石刻史料新編. Series 2. Taipei: Xinwenfeng chuban gongsi, 1979.

Shimen zijing lu 釋門自鏡錄. Huaixin 懷信 (fl. 843). T2083:51.802a–826a.

Shisong lü 十誦律. Puṇyatara (Foruoduoluo 弗若多羅, fl. 399–415), Dharmaruci (Tanmoliuzhi 曇摩流支, fl. 405–?), Vimalākṣa (Beimoluocha 卑摩羅叉, fl. 406–413), and Kumārajīva (Jiumoluoshi 鳩摩羅什, 343–413). T1435:23.1a–470b.

Shiyimian Guanzizai pusa xin miyan niansong yigui jing 十一面觀自在菩薩心密言念誦

儀軌經. Attributed to Amoghavajra (Bukong jingang 不空金剛, 705–774). T1069:20:139c–149a.

Sifen lü 四分律. Buddhayaśas (Fotuoyeshe 佛陀耶舍, fl. 408–412) et al., trans. T1428: 22.567a–1014b.

Sifen lü shanfan buque xingshi chao 四分律刪繁補闕行事鈔. Daoxuan 道宣 (596–667). T1804:40.1a–156c.

Song gaoseng zhuan 宋高僧傳. Zanning 贊寧 (919–1001), comp. T2061:50.709b–900a.

Suming zhi tuoluoni jing 宿命智陀羅尼經. Faxian 法賢 (d. 1001). T1382:21.904a.

Suxidijieluo jing 蘇悉地羯囉經. Śubhakara (Shupojialuo 輸婆迦羅, 637–735). T893: 18.603a–633c.

Taiping guangji 太平廣記. Li Fang 李昉 (925–996), comp. 5 vols. Reprint, Beijing: Renmin wenxue, 1959.

Taishang dongxuan Lingbao yebao yinyuan jing 太上洞玄靈寶業報因緣經. HY 30900.

Taishang Jiuku tianzun shuo xiaoqian miezui jing 太上救苦天尊說消愆滅罪經. HY 30900.

Taishō shinshū daizōkyō 大正新修大蔵経. Takakusu Junjirō 高楠順次郎 and Watanabe Kaigyoku 渡邊海旭, eds. 100 vols. Reprint, Taipei: Xinwenfeng chuban gongsi, 1983.

Tang da Jianfu si guzhu fanjing dade Fazang heshang zhuan 唐大薦福寺故主翻經大德法藏和尚傳. Ch'oe Ch'i-won 崔致遠 (857–904?). T2054:50.280a–289c.

Tōiki dentō mokuroku 東域伝燈目録. Eichō 永超 (b. 1014). T2183:55.1145c–1165b.

Xianyu jing 賢愚經. Huijue 慧覺 (fl. 445) et al., trans. T202:4.349a–445a.

Xifang yaojue shiyi tonggui 西方要決釋疑通規. Kuiji 窺基 (632–682). T1964: 47.104a–110b.

Xifang zanwen, Shinian wen 西方讚文、十念文. S 4474. *DHBZ* 36: 276–277.

Xin Tang shu 新唐書. Ouyang Xiu 歐陽修 (1007–1072), comp. Beijing: Zhonghua shudian, 1975.

Xinbian wanzi xuzang jing 新編卍字續藏經. Reprint of *Dainihon zokuzōkyō* 大日本続藏経. 151 vols. Taipei: Xinwenfeng chuban gongsi, 1993.

Xinxing kouji zhenrushi guan qi xu 信行口集真如實觀起序. In *Sangaikyō no kenkyū* 三階教の研究, edited by Yabuki Keiki 矢吹慶輝, Appendix, 189–199. Tokyo: Iwanami Shoten, 1927 .

Xiu Dizang pusa zan 繡地藏菩薩讚. Mu Yuan 穆員 (ca. 790). *Wenyuange siku quanshu, yingyin* (影印)文淵閣四庫全書, 1340: 607. Taipei: Taiwan shangwu yinshuguan, 1983.

Xu gaoseng zhuan 續高僧傳. Daoxuan 道宣 (596–667), comp. T2060:50.425a–707a.

Xukongyun pusa jing 虛空孕菩薩經. Jñānagupta (She'najueduo 闍那崛多, 523–600). T408:13.667c–677a.

Xuming jing 續命經. T2889:85.1405a.

Xumizang fen 須彌藏分. See *Da fangdeng daji jing* 大方等大集經.

Yaoshi liuliguang rulai benyuan gongde jing 藥師琉璃光如來本願功德經. Xuanzang 玄奘 (602–664). T450:14.404c–8b.

Yiqiejing yinyi 一切經音義. Huiling 慧琳 (737–820). T2128:54.311a–933b.

Yuanshi Lingbao ziran jiutian shenghua chaodu yinlian mijue 元始靈寶自然九天生化超度陰煉秘訣. HY 219.

Yuezang fen 月藏分. See *Da fangdeng daji jing* 大方等大集經.

Yuqie jiyao jiu Anan tuoluoni yankou guiyi jing 瑜伽集要救阿難陀羅尼焰口軌儀經. Attributed to Amoghavajra (Bukong jingang 不空金剛, 705–774). T1318:21.468c–472b.

Yuqie jiyao yankou shishi yi 瑜伽集要焰口施食儀. T1320:21.473c–84a.

Yuqie yankou shisi yaoji 瑜伽焰口施食要集. Deji 德基 (1634–1700). Reprint, Singapore: Guoying.

Yuqie lunji 瑜伽論記. Dun Lun 遁倫 (Tang), comp. T1828:42.311a–868b.

Za ahan jing 雜阿含經. Guṇabhadra (Qiunabatuoluo 求那跋陀羅, 394–468), trans. T99:2.1a–373b.

Zanli Dizang pusa chanhui fayuan fa 讚禮地藏菩薩懺悔發願法. Dunhuang manuscript *zhong* 重 22 or *bei* 北 8422. *DHBZ* 110: 277–279. In *Dunhuang foxue—foshi pian* 敦煌佛學. 佛事篇, edited by Wang Shuqing 王書慶, 118–119. Gansu: Gansu minzu chubanshe, 1995.

Zengyi ahan jing 增一阿含經. Gautama Saṃghadeva (Jutan sengqietipo 瞿曇僧伽提婆, fl. 383–397), trans. T125:2.549a–830b.

Zhancha shan'e yebao jing 占察善惡業報經. Attributed to Bodhidīpa(?) (Putideng 菩提燈, Sui). T839:17.901c–910c.

Zhengao 真誥. HY 71294.

Zhenyuan xinding shijiao mulu 貞元新定釋教目錄. Yuanzhao 圓照 (fl. 778). T2157: 55.771a–1048a.

Zhong ahan jing 中阿含經. Gautama Saṃghadeva (Jutan sengqietipo 瞿曇僧伽提婆, fl. 383–397), trans. T26:1.421a–809c.

Zhongjing mulu 眾經目錄. Fajing 法經 (fl. 594) et al., comps. T2146:55.115a–218a.

Zhongjing mulu 眾經目錄. Jingtai 靜泰 (Tang), comp. T2148:55.189a–218a.

Zhongjing mulu 眾經目錄. Yancong 彥琮 (557–610), comp. T2147:55.150a–180b.

Zhouye liushi fayuan fa 晝夜六時發願法. Dunhuang Manuscript *bei* 北 8422. *DHBZ* 110: 272. Taipei: Xinwenfeng chuban gongsi, 1984. Also in *Dunhuang foxue—foshi pian* 敦煌佛學. 佛事篇, edited by Wang Shuqing 王書慶, 94–95. Gansu: Gansu minzu chubanshe, 1995.

Zhuanji baiyuan jing 撰集百緣經. Zhi Qian 支謙 (fl. 222–252). T200:4.203a–257a.

Secondary Sources

Acker, William R. B. 1954. *Some T'ang and Pre-T'ang Texts on Chinese Painting*. Leiden: E. J. Brill.

Ahn, Hwi-joon. 1986. "Painting." In *Korean Art Treasures*, edited by Roderick Whitfield and Pak Young-Sook, 31–90. Seoul: Yekyong Publications.

Almond, Philip C. 1988. *The British Discovery of Buddhism*. Cambridge: Cambridge University Press.

Alphen, Jan van, ed. 2001. *The Buddha in the Dragon Gate: Buddhist Sculpture of the 5th–9th Centuries from Longmen, China*. Antwerp: Ethnografisch Museum.

Amanō Denchū 天納伝中. 1988. "Shakujō no ichi kōsatsu 錫杖の一考察." *Indogaku bukkyōgaku kenkyū* 印度学仏教学研究 37.1: 285–291.

———. 1989. "Shakujō to kinjō no kankei ni tsuite no ichi kōsatsu 錫杖と金杖の関係についての一考察." *Eizan gakuin kenkyū kiyō* 叡山学院研究紀要 20: 69–78.

Andrews, Allan A. 1993. "Lay and Monastic Forms of Pure Land Devotionalism." *Numen* 40: 16–37.

Bai Ziran. 1985. *Les Sculptures Millénaires de Dazu.* Beijing: Editions en Langues Étrangères.

Balazs, Etinne. 1964. *Chinese Civilization and Bureaucracy.* New Haven and London: Yale University Press.

Bao Lixin 鮑立新 and Hu Jun 胡峻, eds. 1996. *Jiuhua shan de chuanshuo* 九華山的傳說. Hefei: Huangshan shushe.

Bays, Jan Chozen. 2002. *Jizo Bodhisattva: Modern Healing and Traditional Buddhist Practice.* Boston: Tuttle Publishing.

Bell, Catherine. 1989. "Religion and Chinese Culture: Toward an Assessment of 'Popular Religion.'" *History of Religions* 29.1: 35–57.

Bendall, Cecil, and W. H. D. Rouse, trans. 1922. *Śikṣā Samuccaya: A Compendium of Buddhist Doctrine.* Reprint, Delhi: Motilal Banarsidass, 1981.

Bernstein, Alan E. 1993. *The Formation of Hell: Death and Retribution in the Ancient and Early Christian Worlds.* Ithaca: Cornell Universiy Press.

Bielefeldt, Carl. 2005. "Practice." In *Critical Terms for the Study of Buddhism*, edited by Donald S. Lopez, 229–244. Chicago: University of Chicago Press.

Birnbaum, Raoul. 1979. *The Healing Buddha.* Boulder: Shambala.

———. 1983. *Studies on the Mysteries of Mañjuśrī: A Group of East Asian Maṇḍalas and Their Traditional Symbolism.* Society for the Study of Chinese Religions Monographs, no. 2. Boulder: Society for the Study of Chinese Religions.

———. 1984. "Thoughts on T'ang Buddhist Mountain Traditions and Their Context." *Tang Studies* 4: 5–23.

———. 1986. "The Manifestation of a Monastery: Shen-ying's Experience on Mount Wu-T'ai in Tang Context." *Journal of the American Oriental Society* 106.1: 119–137.

Bokenkamp, Stephen R. 1983. "Sources of the Ling-pao Scriptures." In *Tantric and Taoist Studies in Honor of R. A. Stein*, edited by Michel Strickmann, 2: 434–486. Mélanges chinois et bouddhiques, no. 21. Brussels: Institut Belge des Hautes Études Chinoises.

———. 1986. "The Peach Flower Font and the Grotto Passage." *Journal of the American Oriental Society* 106.1: 65–77.

———. 1989. "Death and Ascent in Ling-Pao Taoism." *Taoist Resources* 1.2: 1–20.

———. 1990. "Stages of Transcendence: The *Bhūmi* Concept in Taoist Scripture." In *Chinese Buddhist Apocrypha*, edited by Robert E. Buswell, 119–148. Honolulu: University of Hawai'i Press.

———. 1997. *Early Daoist Scriptures.* Berkeley: University of California Press.

Boltz, Judith M. 1983. "Opening the Gates of Purgatory: A Twelfth-Century Taoist Meditation Technique for the Salvation of Lost Souls." In *Tantric and Taoist Studies in Honor of R. A. Stein*, edited by Michel Strickmann, 2: 488–510. Mélanges chinois et bouddhiques, no. 21. Brussels: Institut Belge des Hautes Études Chinoises.

Boucher, Daniel J. 1996. "Buddhist Translation Procedures in Third-Century China: A Study of Dharmarakṣa and His Translation Idiom." Ph.D. diss., University of Pennsylvania.

———. 1998. "Gāndhārī and the Early Chinese Buddhist Translations Reconsidered: The Case of the *Saddharmapuṇḍarīkasūtra*." *Journal of the American Oriental Society* 118.4: 471–506.

Bryder, Peter. 1985. *The Chinese Transformation of Manichaeism: A Study of Chinese Manichaean Terminology*. Loberod: Bokförlaget Plus Ultra.

Buswell, Robert E. 1989. *The Formation of Ch'an Ideology in China and Korea: The Vajrasamādhi-Sūtra, a Buddhist Apocryphon*. Princeton: Princeton University Press.

———. 1990. "Introduction: Prolegomenon to the Study of Buddhist Apocryphal Scriptures." In *Chinese Buddhist Apocrypha*, edited by Robert Buswell, 1–30. Honolulu: University of Hawai'i Press.

Campany, Robert Ford. 1990. "Return-from-Death Narratives in Early Medieval China." *Journal of Chinese Religions* 18: 91–125.

———. 1991. "Notes on the Devotional Uses and Symbolic Functions of Sutra Texts as Depicted in Early Chinese Buddhist Miracle Tales." *Journal of the International Association of Buddhist Studies* 14.1: 28–72.

———. 1993a. "Buddhist Revelations and Taoist Translation in Early Medieval China." *Taoist Resources* 4.1: 1–29.

———. 1993b. "The Real Presence." *History of Religions* 32: 233–272.

———. 1995. "To Hell and Back: Death, Near-Death and Other Worldly Journeys in Early Medieval China." In *Death, Ecstasy, and Other Worldly Journeys*, edited by John J. Collins and Michael Fishbane, 339–360. Albany: State University of New York Press.

———. 1996a. *Strange Writing: Anomaly Accounts in Early Medieval China*. Albany: State University of New York Press.

———. 1996b. "The Earliest Tales on Bodhisattva Guanshiyin." In *Religions of China in Practice*, edited by Donald S. Lopez, Jr., 82–96. Princeton: Princeton University Press.

———. 2002. *To Live as Long as Heaven and Earth: A Translation of Ge Hong's Traditions of Divine Transcendents*. Berkeley and Los Angeles: University of California Press.

Cao Shibang 曹仕邦. See Tzo Sze-bong.

Cedzich, Ursula-Angelika. 1993. "Ghosts and Demons, Law and Order: Grave Quelling Texts and Early Taoist Liturgy." *Taoist Resources* 4.2: 23–35.

———. 2001. "Corpse Deliverance, Substitute Bodhies, Name Change, and Feigned Death: Aspects of Metamorphosis and Immortaility in Early Medieval China." *Journal of Chinese Religions* 29: 1–68.

Chan, Alan K. L., and Tan Sor-hoon, eds. 2004. *Filial Piety in Chinese Thought and History*. New York: Routledge Curzon.

Chan, Beverly. 1996. "Shuiyue Guanyin in China: The Way of Compassion." Ph.D. diss., California Institute of Integral Studies.

Chandra, Lokesh. 1988. *The Thousand-Armed Avalokiteśvara*. New Delhi: Abhinav Publications.

Chang, K. C. 1983. *Art, Myth, and Ritual: The Path to Political Authority in Ancient China*. Cambridge, MA: Harvard University Press.

Chang Qing 常青. 1993. "Longmen shiku Dizang pusa ji qi youguan wenti 龍門石窟地藏菩薩及其有關問題." *Zhongyuan wenwu* 中原文物 4: 27–34.

———. 1995. "Hangzhou Ciyun ling Zixian si moya kanxiang 杭州慈雲嶺資賢寺摩崖龕像." *Wenwu* 文物 10: 70–79.

———. 1998. *Binxian Dafo si zaoxiang yishu* 彬縣大佛寺造像藝術. Beijing: Xiandai chubanshe.

Chanrui 禪叡, ed. 1996. *Dunhuang baozang yishu suoyin*《敦煌寶藏》遺書索引. Taipei: Fagu wenhua.

Chappell, David W. 1980. "Early Forebodings of the Death of Buddhism." *Numen* 27: 122–153.

Chavannes, Édouard. 1910. *Le T'ai chan: Essai de monographie d'un culte chinois*. Annales du Musée Guimet, no. 21. Paris: Ernest Leroux.

———. 1914. *Six monuments de la sculptures chinoise*. Brussels and Paris: G. van Oest and Cie.

Chen, Jinhua. 2002. "*Pusaseng* 菩薩僧: A Peculiar Monastic Institution at the Turn of the Northern Zhou (557–581) and Sui (581–618) Dynasties." *Journal of Chinese Religions* 30: 1–22.

Ch'en, Kenneth. 1964. *Buddhism in China: A Historical Survey*. Princeton: Princeton University Press.

———. 1968. "Filial Piety in Chinese Buddhism." *Harvard Journal of Asiatic Studies* 28: 81–97.

———. 1973. *The Chinese Transformation of Buddhism*. Princeton: Princeton University Press.

Chen Mingguang 陳明光. 2002. "Chongqing Dazu Baoding shan Dafo wan di 20 hao kan yicun jingbian zaoxiang de diaocha yu yanjiu—jian tan 'shiwang jing bian' yu 'diyu bian' de yitong 重慶大足寶頂山大佛灣第20號龕遺存經變造像的調查與研究—兼探<十王經變>與<地獄變>的異同." *Yishu shi yanjiu* 藝術史研究 4: 325–363.

Chen Zuolong 陳祚龍. 1979. "Shi Feizhuo xinzhuan 釋非濁新傳." In *Zhonghua fojiao wenhua shi sance* 中華佛教文化史散策, 2: 123–124. Taipei: Xinwenfeng chuban gongsi.

Ching, Julia, and R. W. L. Guisso, eds. 1991. *Sages and Filial Sons: Mythology and Archaeology in Ancient China*. Hong Kong: Chinese University Press.

Chou, Yi-liang. 1945. "Tantrism in China." *Harvard Journal of Asiatic Studies* 8.3 and 8.4: 241–333. In Chinese: *Tangdai mizong* 唐代密宗, translated by Qian Wenzhong 錢文忠. Shanghai: Yuandong chubanshe, 1996.

Cohen, Alvin P., trans. 1982. *Tales of Vengeful Souls: A Sixth Century Collection of Chinese Avenging Ghosts Stories*. Taipei: Ricci Institute.

Cohen, Richard S. 1995. "Discontented Categories: Hīnayāna and Mahāyāna in Indian Buddhist History." *Journal of the American Academy of Religion* 63.1: 1–25.

Cole, Alan. 1996. "Upside Down/Right Side Up: A Revisionist History of Buddhist Funerals in China." *History of Religions* 35.4: 307–338.

———. 1998. *Mothers and Sons in Chinese Buddhism*. Stanford: Stanford University Press.

Crosby, Kate, and Andrew Skilton, trans. 1996. *The Bodhicaryāvātara*. Oxford: Oxford University Press.

Davids, T. W. Rhys. 1899. *Dialogues of the Buddha: Translated from the Pali of the Dīrgha Nikāya*. London: Pali Text Society.

Dayal, Har. 1932. *The Bodhisattva Doctrine in Buddhist Sanskrit Literature*. London: Routledge and Kegan Paul. Reprint, Delhi: Motilal Banarsidass, 1970.

De Groot, J. J. M. 1892–1910. *The Religious System of China*. 6 vols. Leiden: E. J. Brill.

De Mallman, Marie Thérèse. 1948. *Introduction à l'étude d'Avalokiteçvara*. Paris: Civilisations du Sud.

———. 1964. *Étude iconographique sur Mañjuśrī*. Paris: École française d'Extrême-Orient.

Devi, Gauri. 1999. *Estoric Mudrās of Japan: Mudrās of the Garbhadhātu and Vajradhātu maṇḍalas, of Homa and Eighteen-step Rites, and of Main Buddhas and Bodhisattvas, Gods and Goddesses of Various Sūtras and Tantras*. New Delhi: International Academy of Indian Culture and Aditya Prakashan.

Dewoskin, Kenneth, and J. I. Crump, Jr., trans. 1996. *In Search of the Supernatural: The Written Record*. Stanford: Stanford University Press.

Dien, Albert E. 2002. "Turfan Funeral Documents." *Journal of Chinese Religions* 30: 23–48.

Ding Mingyi 丁明夷. 1988. "Sichuan shiku zashi 四川石窟雜識." *Wenwu* 文物 8: 46–58.

———. 1990. "Chuanbei shiku zhaji: Cong Guangyuan dao Bazhong 川北石窟札記: 從廣元到巴中." *Wenwu* 文物 6: 41–53.

Donner, Neal, and Daniel B. Stevenson. 1993. *The Great Calming and Contemplation: A Study and Annotated Translation of the First Chapter of Chih-i's Mo-ho chih-kuan*. Honolulu: University of Hawai'i Press.

Du Doucheng 杜斗城. 1989. *Dunhuang ben foshuo shiwang jing jiaolu yanjiu* 敦煌本佛說十王經校錄研究. Lanzhou: Gansu jiaoyu chubanshe.

———. 1995. *Beiliang yijing lun* 北涼譯經論. Lanzhou: Gansu wenhua chubanshe.

———. 1998. *Beiliang fojiao yanjiu* 北涼佛教研究. Taipei: Xinwenfeng chuban gongsi.

Duan Wenjie 段文傑, ed. 1990a. *The Appreciation of Dunhuang Art* (Vol. 3, Book 7, Cave 384) 敦煌石窟鑒賞叢書第三輯第七分冊第384窟. Lanzhou: Gansu renmin meishu chubanshe.

———. 1990b. *Zhongguo bihua quanji 9: Dunhung Wudai, Song* 中國壁畫全集 9: 敦煌五代. 宋. Shenyang: Liaoning meishu chubanshe.

———. 1993. *Dunhuang shiku yishu: Yulin ku di ershiwu ku* 敦煌石窟藝術: 榆林窟第二十五窟. Nanjing: Jiangsu meishu chubanshe.

Dudbridge, Glen. 1978. *The Legend of Miao-shan*. London: Ithaca Press.

———. 1995. *Religious Experience and Lay Society in T'ang China: A Reading of Tai Fu's Kuang-i chi*. Cambridge: Cambridge University Press.

———. 1996–1997. "The General of the Five Paths in Tang and Pre-Tang China." *Cahiers d'Extrême-Asie* 9: 85–98.

Dunhuang yanjiuyuan 敦煌研究院, ed. 1996. *Dunhuang shiku neirong zonglu* 敦煌石窟內容總錄. Beijing: Wenwu chubanshe.

———. 1997. *Zhongguo shiku: Anxi Yulin ku* 中國石窟: 安西榆林窟. Beijing: Wenwu chubanshe.

Dunnell, Ruth W. 1996. *The Great Stage of White and High: Buddhism and State Formation in Eleventh-Century Xia*. Honolulu: University of Hawai'i Press.

Dutt, Nalinaksha. 1930. *Aspects of Mahāyāna Buddhism and Its Relation to Hīnayāna*. Calcutta Oriental Series, no. 23. London: Luzac.

Dykstra, Yoshiko Kurata. 1978. "Jizō, the Most Merciful: Tales from *Jizō Bosatsu Reigenki*." *Monumenta Nipponica* 33.2: 179–200.

Ebrey, Patricia B., and Peter N. Gregory, eds. 1993. *Religion and Society in T'ang and Sung China*. Honolulu: University of Hawai'i Press.

Elverskog, Johan. 1997. *Uygur Buddhist Literature*. Silk Road Studies, no. 1. Turnhout: Brepols.

Emmerick, R. E., ed. and trans. 1967. *Tibetan Texts concerning Khotan*. London: Oxford University Press.

———. 1968. *The Book of Zambasta: A Khotanese Poem on Buddhism*. London: Oxford University Press.

———, trans. 1970. *The Sūtra of Golden Light: Being a Translation of the Suvarṇabhāsottamasūtra*. London: Luzac.

Fan Wenlan 范文瀾. 1979. *Tangdai fojiao [fu: Sui Tang Wudai fojiao dashi nianbiao]* 唐代佛教 [附：隋唐五代佛教大事年表]. Beijing: Renmin chubanshe.

Faure, Bernard. 1991. *The Rhetoric of Immediacy: A Cultural Critique of Ch'an/Zen Buddhism*. Princeton: Princeton University Press.

———. 1992. "Relics and Flesh Bodies: The Creation of Ch'an Pilgrimage Sites." In *Pilgrims and Sacred Sites in China*, edited by Susan Naquin and Yü Chün-fang, 150–189. Berkeley: University of California Press.

Feuchtwang, Stephan. 2001. *Popular Religion in China: The Imperial Metaphor*. Richmond: Curzon Press.

———. 2003. "The Avenging Ghost: Paradigm of a Shameful Past." In *Belief, Ritual and Society: Papers from the Third International Conference on Sinology, Anthropology Section*, edited by Mei-rong Lin, 7–36. Taipei: Academia Sinica.

Finney, Paul Corby, ed. 1999. *Seeing Beyond the Word: Visual Arts and the Calvinist Tradition*. Grand Rapids, MI: Eerdmans Publishing.

Forte, Antonino. 1988. *Mingtang and Buddhist Utopias in the History of the Astronomical Clock: The Tower, Statue and Armillary Sphere Constructed by Empress Wu*. Paris: École française d'Extrême-Orient.

Foulk, Theodore Griffith. 1987. "The 'Ch'an School' and Its Place in the Buddhist Monastic Tradition." Ph.D. diss., University of Michigan.

———. 1993. "Myth, Ritual, and Monastic Practice in Sung Ch'an Buddhism." In *Religion and Society in T'ang and Sung China*, edited by Patricia Buckley Ebrey and Peter N. Gregory, 147-208. Honolulu: University of Hawai'i Press.

———. 1995. "Daily Life in the Assembly." In *Buddhism in Practice*, edited by Donald S. Lopez, 454–472. Princeton: Princeton University Press.

———. 1999. "Sung Controversies concerning the 'Separate Transmission' of Ch'an." In *Buddhism in the Sung*, edited by Peter N. Gregory and Daniel A.

Getz, Jr. Kuroda Institute Studies in East Asian Buddhism, no. 13, 220–294. Honolulu: University of Hawai'i Press.

Foulk, Theodore Griffith, and Robert H. Sharf. 1993–1994. "The Meanings and Functions of Ch'an Portriature in Medieval China." *Cahiers d'Extrême-Asie* 7: 149–219.

Fowler, Sherry. 2000–2001. "Shifting Identities in Buddhist Sculpture: Who's Who in the Murō-ji Kondō." *Archives of Asian Art* 52: 83–104.

Fuji Masaharu 富士正晴. 1974. *Nihon no Jizō* 日本の地蔵. Tokyo: Mainichi shinbunsha.

Fujita Kōtatsu 藤田宏達. 1970. *Genshi jōdo shisō no kenkyū* 原始浄土思想の研究. Tokyo: Iwanami Shoten.

———. 1996a. "The Origin of the Pure Land." *The Eastern Buddhist* 29.1: 33–51.

———. 1996b. "Pure Land Buddhism in India." In *The Pure Land Tradition: History and Development*, edited by James Foard, Michael Solomon, and Richard K. Payne, 1–42. Berkeley Buddhist Studies Series, no. 3. Berkeley: Center for South and Southeast Asia Studies, University of California, and the Institute of Buddhist Studies.

Gabian, Annearie von. 1973. "Kṣitigarbha-kult in Zentralasien, Buchillustrationen aus den Turfan-Funden." In *Indologen-Tatung* (Verhandlungen der Indologichen Arbeitstagung im Museum für Indische Kunst Berlin 7–9, Oktober 1971), edited by Herbert Härtel and Volker Moeller, 47–71. Wiesbaden: Franz Steiner Verlag.

———. 1977. "The Purgatory of the Buddhist Uighurs: Book Illustrations from Turfan." In *Mahayanist Art after* A.D. *900*, edited by William Watson, 25–35. Colloquies on Art and Archaeology in Asia, no. 2. London: Percival David Foundation of Chinese Art.

Gao Mingdao 高明道. 1993. "Mantan hanyi shengwen pini zhong de 'xizhang' 漫談漢譯聲聞毗尼中的『錫杖』." In *Ruxue chanshi jinian lunwen ji* 如學禪師紀念論文集, edited by Ruxue chanshi huainian lu bianji weiyuanhui 如學禪師懷念錄編輯委員會, 9–19. Taipei: Faguang wenjiao jijinhui.

Gaulier, Simone, Robert Jera-Bezard, and Monique Maillard. 1976. *Buddhism in Afghanistan and Central Asia*. Parts 1 and 2. Iconography of Religions, sec. 13, fasc. 14. Leiden: E. J. Brill.

Gernet, Jacques. 1995. *Buddhism in Chinese Society: An Economic History from the Fifth to the Tenth Centuries*. Translated by Franciscus Verellen. New York: Columbia University Press.

Getz, Daniel A., Jr. 1999. "T'ien-t'ai Pure Land Societies and the Creation of the Pure Land Patriarchate." In *Buddhism in the Sung*, edited by Peter N. Gregory and Daniel A. Getz, Jr., 477–523. Honolulu: University of Hawai'i Press.

Giès, Jacques, ed. 1995. *Les arts de l'Asie centrale: La collection Paul Pelliot du musée national des arts asiatiques–Guimet*. 2 vols. Paris: Réunion des Musées Nationaux.

Gildow, Douglas. 2005. "Flesh Bodies, Stiff Corpses, and Gathered Gold: Mummy Worship, Corpse Processing, and Mortuary Ritual in Contemporary Taiwan." *Journal of Chinese Religions* 33: 1–37.

Gimello, Robert M. 1976. "Chih-yen (智儼 602–668) and the Foundations of Hua-yen (華嚴) Buddhism." Ph.D. diss., Columbia University.

———. 1978. "Random Reflections on the 'Sinicization' of Buddhism." *Society for the Study of Chinese Religions Bulletin* 5: 52–89.

———. 1983. "Li T'ung-hsuan and the Practical Dimensions of Hua-yen." In *Studies in Ch'an and Hua-yen*, edited by Robert M. Gimello and Peter N. Gregory, 321–389. Honolulu: University of Hawai'i Press.

———. 1992. "Chang Shang-ying on Wu-t'ai Shan." In *Pilgrims and Sacred Sites in China*, edited by Susan Naquin and Yü Chün-fang, 89–149. Berkeley: University of California Press.

———. 1994. "Wu-t'ai Shan 五臺山 during the Early Chin Dynasty 金朝: The Testimony of Chu Pien 朱弁." *Zhonghua foxue xuebao* 中華佛學學報 7: 501–612.

———. 1996. "Ch'eng-kuan on the Hua-yen Trinity." *Zhonghua foxue xuebao* 中華佛學學報 9: 341–411.

———. 1997. "The Mañjuśrī of a Thousand Arms and a Thousand Bowls: A Preliminary Report on an Apocryphal Image and Its Origins in an Apocryphal Tantra." Paper presented at the Conference on "Boundaries of Tantra," Flagstaff.

———. 2004. "Icons and Incantation: The Goddess Zhunti and the Role of Images in the Occult Buddhism of China." In *Images in Asian Religions: Texts and Contexts*, edited by Phyllis Granoff and Koichi Shinohara, 225–256. Vancouver: University of British Columbia Press.

Gjertson, Donald E. 1981. "The Early Chinese Buddhist Miracle Tale." *Journal of the American Oriental Society* 101.3: 287–301.

———. 1989. *Miraculous Retribution: A Study and Translation of T'ang Lin's Ming-pao chi*. Berkeley Buddhist Studies Series, no. 8. Berkeley: Centers for South and Southeast Asia Studies, University of California.

Glassman, Hank. 1999. "The Tale of Mokuren: A Translation of *Mokuren-o-sōshi*." *Buddhist Literature* 1: 120–161.

———. 2002. "The Nude Jizō at Denkoji: Notes on Women's Salvation in Kamakura Buddhism." In *Engendering Faith: Women and Buddhism in Pre-Modern Japan*, edited by Barbara Ruch, 383–413. Ann Arbor: University of Michigan Center for Japanese Studies.

Gombrich, Richard. 1998. "Organised Bodhisattvas: A Blind Alley in Buddhist Historiography." In *Sūryacandrāya: Essays in Honor of Akira Yuyama on the Occasion of His 65th Birthday*, edited by Paul Harrison and Gregory Schopen, 43–56. Swisttal-Odendorf: Indicaet Tibetica Verlag.

Gombrich, Richard, and Gananath Obeyesekere. 1988. *Buddhism Transformed: Religious Change in Sri Lanka*. Princeton: Princeton University Press.

Gómez, Luis O. 1977. "The Bodhisattva as Wonder Worker." In *Prajñāpāramitā and Related Systems: Studies in Honor of Edward Conze*, edited by Lewis Lancaster, 221–261. Berkeley Buddhist Studies Series, no. 1. Berkeley: Centers for South and Southeast Asia Studies, University of California.

———, trans. 1996. *The Land of Bliss: The Paradise of the Buddha of Measureless Light: Sanskrit and Chinese Versions of the Sukhāvatīvyūha Sūtras*. Studies in the Buddhist Traditions. Honolulu: University of Hawai'i Press.

Gonda, Jan. 1980. *Vedic Ritual: The Non-Solemn Rites*. Leiden: E. J. Brill.

Granoff, Phyllis. 1968–1969. "A Portable Buddhist Shrine from Central Asia." *Archives of Asian Art* 22: 81–95.

Gregory, Peter N. 1983. "The Teaching of Men and Gods: The Doctrinal and Social Basis of Lay Buddhist Practice in the Hua-yen Tradition." In *Studies in Ch'an and Hua-yen*, edited by Robert M.Gimello and Peter N. Gregory, 253–319. Honolulu: University of Hawai'i Press.

———. 1991. *Tsung-mi and the Sinification of Buddhism*. Princeton: Princeton University Press.

———. 1999. "The Vitality of Buddhism in the Sung." In *Buddhism in the Sung*, edited by Peter N. Gregory and Daniel A. Getz, Jr., 19–20. Kuroda Institute Studies in East Asian Buddhism, no. 13. Honolulu: University of Hawai'i Press.

Gregory, Peter N., and Patricia Buckley Ebrey. 1993. "The Religious and Historical Landscape." In *Religion and Society in T'ang and Sung China*, edited by Peter N. Gregory and Patricia Buckley Ebrey, 1–44. Honolulu: University of Hawai'i Press.

Gregory, Peter N., and Daniel A. Getz, Jr., eds. 1999. *Buddhism in the Sung*. Kuroda Institute Studies in East Asian Buddhism, no. 13. Honolulu: University of Hawai'i Press.

Gu Zhengmei 古正美. N.d. "Tangdai Wenshushili zai Zhongguo yu nanhai de fazhan xingzhi yu qingkuang 唐代文殊室利在中國與南海的發展性質與情況."

Guo Shaolin 郭紹林. 1993. *Tangdai shidafu yu fojiao* 唐代士大夫與佛教. Taipei: Wenshizhe chubanshe.

Guo Xiangying 郭相穎, ed. 1993. *Dazu shike yanjiu wenji* 大足石刻研究文集. Chongqing: Chongqing chubanshe.

———, ed. 1999a. *Dazu shike mingwenlu* 大足石刻銘文錄. Chongqing: Chongqing chubanshe.

———. 1999b. *Dazu shike diaosu quanji* 大足石刻雕塑全集. 4 vols. Chongqing: Chongqing chubanshe.

Guoli gugong bowuyuan 國立故宮博物院. 2000. *Guanyin tezhan* 觀音特展. *Visions of Compassion: Images of Guanyin in Chinese Art*. Taipei: Guoli gugong bowuyuan.

Gurevich, Aaron. 1992. "Oral and Written Culture of the Middle Ages: Two 'Peasant Visions' of the Late Twelfth to the Early Thirteenth Centuries." In *Historical Anthropology of the Middle Ages*, edited by Jana Howlett, 50–64. Chicago: University of Chicago Press.

Hadani Ryōtai 羽溪了諦. 1904. *Seiiki no bukkyō* 西域の仏教. Reprint, Kyoto: Horinkan, 1914.

———. 1937. "Chūa bukkyōkai no tokugisō 中亜仏教会の特異相." *Bukkyō kenkyū* 仏教研究 1.1: 23–49.

Han Wei 韓偉, Chen Yuexin 陳悅新, et al. 2001. *Zhongguo shiku diaosu quanji 5: Shaanxi, Ningxia* 中國石窟雕塑全集 5：陝西．寧夏. Chongqing: Chongqing chubanshe.

Hansen, Valerie. 1995. *Negotiating Daily Life in Traditional China: How Ordinary People Used Contracts, 600–1400*. New Haven and London: Yale University Press.

Harper, Donald. 1985. "A Chinese Demonography of the Third Century B.C." *Harvard Journal of Asiatic Studies* 45: 459–498.

———. 1994. "Resurrection in Warring States Popular Religion." *Taoist Resources* 5.2: 13–28.

———. 1995. "Warring States, Ch'in, and Han Periods." *The Journal of Asian Studies* 54.1: 152–160.

———. 1996. "Spellbinding." In *Religions of China in Practice*, edited by Donald S. Lopez, 241–250. Princeton: Princeton University Press.

———. 1998. *Early Chinese Medical Literature: The Mawangdui Medical Manuscripts*. London and New York: Kegan Paul International.

———. 1999a. "Ten Bamboo slips." In *The Golden Age of Chinese Achaeology: Celebrated Discoveries from the People's Republic of China*, edited by Xiao Neng Yang, 349–351. New Haven: Yale University Press.

———. 1999b. "Warring States, Natural Philosophy and Occult Thought." In *The Cambridge History of Ancient China*, edited by Michael Loewe and Edward Shaughnessy, 852–856. Cambridge: Cambridge University Press.

———. 2004. "Contracts with the Spirit World in Han Common Religion: The Xuning Prayer and Sacrifice Documents of A.D. 79." *Cahiers d'Extrême-Asie* 14: 227–267.

Harrison, Paul M. 1987. "Who Gets to Ride in the Great Vehicle? Self-Image and Identity among the Followers of the Early Mahāyāna." *Journal of the International Association of Buddhist Studies* 10.1: 67–89.

———. 1995a "Searching for the Origins of the Mahāyāna: What Are We Looking For?" *The Eastern Buddhist*, n.s., 28.1: 48–69.

———. 1995b "Some Reflections on the Personality of the Buddha." *Ōtani gakuhō* 大谷学報 74.4: 1–29.

———. 2000. "Mañjuśrī and the Cult of the Celestial Bodhisattvas." *Zhonghua foxue xuebao* 中華佛學學報 13.2: 157–193.

Hart, James A. 1983. "The Speech of Prince Chin: A Study of Early Chinese Cosmology." *JAAR Thematic Studies* 50.2: 35–65.

Harvey, Peter. 1990. *An Introduction to Buddhism: Teachings, History and Practices*. Cambridge: Cambridge University Press.

Hatta Yukio 八田幸雄. 1968. "Taizōgai mandala Jizō-in 胎蔵界マンダラ地蔵院." *Mikkyō bunka* 密教文化 85: 56–78.

Hawkes, David, trans. 1959. *Ch'u Tz'u: The Songs of the South*. Boston: Beacon Press.

Hayami Tasuku 速水侑. 1975. *Jizō shinkō* 地蔵信仰. Tokyo: Hanawa shobō.

———. 1982. *Kannon shinkō* 観音信仰. Tokyo: Yūzankaku shuppan.

He Hannan 何漢南. 1957. "Xi'an xijiao qingli chu yi pi Tangdai zaoxiang 西安西郊清理出一批唐代造像." *Wenwu cankao ziliao* 文物參考資料 6: 89.

Heng Ching, trans. 1974. *Sutra of the Past Vows of Earth Store Bodhisattva*. New York: Buddhist Text Translation Society, The Institute of Advanced Studies of World Religions.

Hervouet, Yves, ed. 1978. *A Sung Bibliography*. Hong Kong: Chinese University Press.

Hirakawa Akira. 1963. "The Rise of Mahāyāna Buddhism and Its Relationship to the Worship of Stupas." *Memiors of the Research Department of the Tōyō Bunko* 22: 57–106.

Ho Puay Bin. 1995. "The Ideal Monastery: Daoxuan's Description of the Central Jetavana Vihāra." *East Asian History* 10: 1–18.

Hoernle, A. F. Rudolf. 1916. *Manuscript Remains of Buddhist Literature Found in Chinese Turkestan.* London: Oxford University Press.

Honda Megumu. 1968. "Annoted Translation of the *Daśabhūmika-sūtra.*" In *Studies in South, East, and Central Asia: Presented as a Memorial Volume to the Late Professor Raghu Vira,* edited by Denis Sinor, 115–276. New Delhi: International Academy of Indian Culture.

Hoshino Toshio 星野俊英. 1961. "'Jizō bosatsu giki' kō 地蔵菩薩儀軌攷." *Tōyōzan gakuhō* 東洋山学報 7: 103–115.

Hou Xudong 侯旭東. 1998. *Wu, liu shiji beifang minzhong fojiao xinyang: yi zaoxiangji wei zhongxin de kaocha* 五、六世紀北方民眾佛教信仰：以造像記為中心的考察. Beijing: Zhongguo shehui kexue chubanshe.

Howard, Angela F. 1986. *The Imagery of the Cosmological Buddha.* Leiden: E. J. Brill.

———. 1988. "Tang Buddhist Sculpture of Sichuan: Unknown and Forgotten." *Museum of Far Eastern Antiquities* 60: 1–71.

———. 1989. "Buddhist Sculpture of Pujiang, Sichuan: A Mirror of the Direct Link between Southwest China and India in High Tang." *Archives of Asian Art* 42: 49–61.

———. 1990. "Tang and Song Images of Guanyin from Sichuan." *Orientations* 21.1: 49–57.

———. 1998. "The Development of Buddhist Sculpture in Sichuan: The Making of An Indigenous Art." In *The Flowering of a Foreign Faith: New Studies in Chinese Buddhist Art,* edited by Janet Baker, 118–133. Mumbai: Mārg Publications.

———. 2001. *Summit of Treasures: Buddhist Cave Art of Dazu, China.* Trumbull: Weatherhill.

Hu Liangxue 胡良學, and Chen Jing 陳靜. 1998a. "Dazu Shizhuan shan, Miaogao shan moyan zaoxiang de diaocha yanjiu 大足石篆山、妙高山摩岩造像的調查研究." *Sichuan wenwu* 四川文物 1: 42–47.

———. 1998b. "Dazu Shizhuan shan, Miaogao shan moyan zaoxiang de diaocha yanjiu (xu) 大足石篆山、妙高山摩岩造像的調查研究(續)." *Sichuan wenwu* 四川文物 2: 27–32.

Hu Liangxue 胡良學, and Jiang Decai 蔣德才. 1997. "Dazu shike de Dizang zaoxiang chushi 大足石刻的地藏造像初識." *Sichuan wenwu* 四川文物 2: 39–43.

Hu Wenhe 胡文和. 1994. *Sichuan daojiao fojiao shiku yishu* 四川道教佛教石窟藝術. Chengdu: Sichuan renmin chubanshe.

Huang Chi-chiang. See Huang Qijiang.

Huang Qijiang 黃啟江. 1998. "Mituo jingtu de zhuixun — Beisong wangsheng xifang zhuzuo de tantao 彌陀淨土的追尋—北宋往生西方著作的探討." *Gugong xueshu jikan* 故宮學術季刊 16.1: 59–86.

Huang Zheng 黃徵, and Wu Wei 吳偉, eds. 1995. *Dunhuang yuanwen ji* 敦煌願文集. Changsha: Yuelu shushe.

Hubbard, James B. 1986. "Salvation in the Final Period of the Dharma: The Inexhaustible Storehouse of the San-chieh-chiao." Ph.D. diss., University of Wisconsin.

———. 1991. "Chinese Reliquary Inscriptions and the San-chieh-chiao." *Journal of the International Association of Buddhist Studies* 14.2: 253–280.

———. 1996. "*Mo Fa,* the Three Levels Movement, and the Theory of the Three Periods." *Journal of the International Association of Buddhist Studies* 19.1: 1–17.

———. 2001. *Absolute Delusion, Perfect Buddhahood: The Rise and Fall of a Chinese Heresy*. Honolulu: University of Hawai'i Press.

Hucker, Charles O. 1985. *A Dictionary of Official Titles in Imperial China*. Stanford: Stanford University Press.

Huimen 慧門, ed. 1989. *Dizang pusa shengde huibian* 地藏菩薩聖德彙編. Taipei: Mile chubanshe.

Hurvitz, L. 1957. "Render unto Caesar in Early Chinese Buddhism." *Sino-Indian Studies* 5.3/4: 2–36.

Idema, Wilt L. 2000. "Guanyin's Acolytes." In *Linked Faiths: Essays on Chinese Religions and Traditional Culture in Honour of Kristofer Schipper*, edited by Jan A. M. De Meyer and Peter M. Engelfriet, 205–226. Leiden: E. J. Brill.

Ikeda Daisaku. 1976. *The Flower of Chinese Buddhism*. New York: Weatherhill.

Ishikawa Junichirō 石川純一郎. 1995. *Jizō no sekai* 地蔵の世界. Tokyo: Jiji tsūshinsha.

Jaini, Padmanabh S. 1988. "Stages in the Bodhisattva Career of the Tathāgata Maitreya." In *Maitreya, the Future Buddha*, edited by Alan Sponberg and Helen Hardacre, 54–90. Cambridge: Cambridge University Press.

Jan Yün-hua. 1981. "The Bodhisattva Idea in Chinese Literature: Typology and Significance." In *The Bodhisattva Doctrine in Buddhism*, edited by Leslie S. Kawamura, 125–152. Waterloo: Wilfred Laurier University Press.

———. 1995. "Zhongguo fojiao dui xiaodao de shourong ji houguo 中國佛教對孝道的受容及後果." In *Cong Yindu fojiao dao Zhongguo fojiao* 從印度佛教到中國佛教, 42–55. Taipei: Dongda tushu.

Jin Shen 金申. 2004. *Fojiao meishu congkao* 佛教美術叢考. Beijing: Kexue chubanshe.

Jiuhua shan fojiao shi bianweihui 九華山佛教史編委會, ed. 1993. *Jin Dizang yanjiu* 金地藏研究. Hefei: Huangshan shushe.

———, ed. 1996. *Jin Dizang yanjiu xuji* 金地藏研究續集. Hefei: Huangshan shushe.

Jochim, C. 1988. "Great and Little, Grid and Group: Defining the Poles of the Elite-Popular Continuum in Chinese Religion." *Journal of Chinese Religions* 16: 18–24.

Johnston, Sarah Iles. 1999. *Restless Dead: Encounters between the Living and the Dead in Ancient Greece*. Berkeley: University of California Press.

Jōji Okazaki. 1977. *Pure Land Buddhist Painting*. Tokyo: Kodansha International and Shibundo.

Jorgensen, John. 1987. "The 'Imperial' Lineage of Ch'an Buddhism: The Role of Confucian Ritual and Ancestor Worship in Ch'an's Search for Legitimation in the Mid-Tang Dynasty." *Papers in Far Eastern History* 35: 89–133.

Ju Tingyi 菊廷一. 1999. "Bazhong Nankan 25 hao Dizang kan qianyi 巴中南龕25號地藏龕淺議." *Sichuan wenwu* 四川文物 5: 45–49.

Kajitani Ryōji 梶谷亮治. 1974. "Nihon ni okeru jūō zu no seiritsu to tenkai 日本における十王図の成立と展開." *Bukkyō geijutsu* 仏教芸術 97: 84–98.

Kamata Shigeo 鎌田茂雄. 1987. *Chūgoku yondai reizan no tabi: kō no naka no bosatsu tachi* 中国四大霊山の旅：光の中の菩薩たち. Tokyo: Kōsei Shuppansha. In Chinese: *Si da mingshan de gushi* 四大名山的故事, translated by Guan Shiqian 關世謙. Taipei: Yuanming chubanshe, 1999.

Kanaoka Shūyū 金岡秀友. 1977. "Jizō, Enma no ittai setsu—shisōshi teki keihu 地

藏. 閻魔の一体説—思想史的系譜." In *Egami Namio kyōju koki kinen ronshū—Minzoku bunka hen* 江上波夫教授古稀記念論集–民族. 文化篇, edited by the Editorial Committee for the Compilation of the Volume, 121–140. Tokyo: Yamakawa shuppansha.

Karetzky, Patricia Eichenbaum. 2004. *Guanyin*. New York: Oxford University Press.

Katz, Paul R. 2003. "Local Elites and Sacred Sites in Hsin-chuang: The Growth of the Ti-tsang An during the Japanese Occupation." In *Belief, Ritual and Society: Papers from the Third International Conference on Sinology, Anthropology Section*, edited by Mei-rong Lin, 179–227. Taipei: Academia Sinica.

Kawahara Yoshio 河原由雄. 1974. "Tonkō ga Jizō zu shiryō 敦煌画地蔵図資料." *Bukkyō geijutsu* 仏教芸術 97: 99–123.

Kawakatsu Masatarō 川勝政太郎. 1974. "Sekizō Jizō 石造地蔵." *Bukkyō geijutsu* 仏教芸術 97: 25–50.

Kawamura, Leslie S., ed. 1981. *The Bodhisattva Doctrine in Buddhism*. Waterloo: Wilfred Laurier University.

Kieschnick, John. 1997. *The Eminent Monk: Buddhist Ideals in Medieval Chinese Hagiography*. Honolulu: University of Hawai'i Press.

———. 1999. "The Symbolism of the Monk's Robe in China." *Asia Major*, 3rd ser., 12.1: 9–32.

———. 2003. *The Impact of Buddhism on Chinese Material Culture*. Princeton: Princeton University Press.

———. 2005. "Buddhist Vegetarianism in China." In *Of Tripod and Palate: Food, Politics, and Religion in Traditional China*, edited by Roel Sterckx, 186–212. New York: Palgrave Macmillan.

Kikutake Jun'ichi 菊竹淳一. 1975. "Tonkō no bukkyō banga—daikan to Pari koku toshokan no zōhin wo chūshin toshite 敦煌の仏教版画—大館とパリ国図書館の蔵品を中心として." *ARS Buddhica* 101: 3–35.

Kim Wonyong, ed. 1986. *Korean Art Treasures*. Seoul: Yekyong Publications.

Kleeman, Terry. 1994. "Licentious Cults and Bloody Victuals: Sacrifice, Reciprocity, and Violence in Traditional China." *Asia Major* 7.1: 185–211.

———. 2005. "Feasting without the Victuals: The Evolution of the Daoist Communal Kitchen." In *Of Tripod and Palate: Food, Politics, and Religion in Traditional China*, edited by Roel Sterckx, 140–162. New York: Palgrave Macmillan.

Klimkeit, Hans-Joachim. 1993. *Gnosis on the Silk Road: Gnostic Texts from Central Asia*. San Franciscon: Harper Collins.

Knapp, Keith Nathaniel. 2005. *Selfless Offspring: Filial Children and Social Order in Medieval China*. Honolulu: University of Hawai'i Press.

Kohn, Livia. 1998. "Counting Good Deeds and Days of Life: The Quantification of Fate in Medieval China." In *Asiatische Studien Études Asiatiques LII.3.1998*, edited by Johannes Bronkhorst et al., 833–870. Berlin: Peter Lang.

———. 2003. *Monastic Life in Medieval Daoism: A Cross-Cultural Perspective*. Honolulu: University of Hawai'i Press.

Konishi Eiko 小西瑛子. 1971. "'Jizō bosatsu reigenki' ni tsuite 《地蔵菩薩霊験記》について." *Gengōji bukkyō minzoku shiryō kenkyūjo nenpō* 元興寺仏教民俗資料研究所年報 5: 35–45.

Kucera, Karil. 1995. "Lessons in Stone: Baodingshan and Its Hell Imagery." *Bulletin of the Museum of Far Eastern Antiquities* 67: 81–157

———. 2002. "Cliff Notes: Text and Image at Baodingshan." Ph.D. diss., University of Kansas.

Kuo, Li-ying. 1994a. *Confession et contrition dans le bouddhisme chinois du ve au xe siècle.* Paris: École française d'Extrême-Orient.

———. 1994b. "Divination, jeux de hasard et purification dans le bouddhisme chinois: Autour d'un *sūtra* apocryhe chinios, le *Zhanchajing*." In *Bouddhisme et cultures locales: Quelques cas de réciproques adaptations*, edited by Fukui Fumimasa and Gérard Fussman, 145–167. Paris: École française d'Extrême-Orient. In Chinese: "Zhongguo fojiao zhong de zhanbu, youxi he qingjing——Hanwen weijing 'Zhancha jing' yanjiu 中國佛教中的占卜，游戲和清淨—漢文偽經《占察經》研究," translated by Geng Sheng 耿昇 in *Faguo hanxue di er ji* 法國漢學第二輯, 193–223. Beijing: Qinghua daxue chubanshe, 1997.

Kwon, Cheeyun Lilian. 1999. "The Ten Kings of Seikado Library." Ph.D. diss., Princeton University.

La Vallée Poussin, Louis de. 1930. "Notes Bouddhiques XVIII: Opinions sur les Relations des deux Véhicules au point de vue du Vinaya." *Académie Royale de Belgique: Bulletins de la Class des Lettres et des Sciences Morales et Politiques*, 5th ser., 16: 20–39.

LaFleur, William R. 1983. "In and Out the Rokudō: Kyōkai and the Formation of Medieval Japan." In *The Karma of Words: Buddhism and the Literary Arts in Medieval Japan*, 26–59. Berkeley: University of California Press.

———. 1992. *Liquid Life: Abortion and Buddhism in Japan.* Princeton: Princeton University Press.

Lai Chi-tim. 2002. "The Demon Statutes of *Nüqing* and the Problem of the Bureaucratization of the Netherworld in Early Heavenly Master Daoism." *T'oung Pao* 88.4–5: 251–281.

Lai Sufen Sophia. 1999. "Father in Heaven, Mother in Hell: Gender Politics in the Creation and Transformations of Mulian's Mother." In *Presence and Presentation: Women in the Chinese Literati Tradition*, edited by Sherry J. Mou, 187–213. New York: St. Martin's Press.

Lai, Whalen. 1990. "The *Chan-ch'a ching*: Religion and Magic in Medieval China." In *Chinese Buddhist Apocrypha*, edited by Robert Buswell, 175–206. Honolulu: University of Hawai'i Press.

———. 1996. "Legends of Births and the Pure Land Tradition in China." In *The Pure Land Tradition: History and Development*, edited by James Foard, Michael Solomon, and Richard K. Payne, 173–232. Berkeley Buddhist Studies Series, no. 3. Berkeley: Center for South and Southeast Asia Studies, University of California, and the Institute of Buddhist Studies.

Lancaster, Lewis R. 1981. "The Bodhisattva Concept: A Study of the Chinese Buddhist Canon." In *The Bodhisattva Doctrine in Buddhism*, edited by Leslie S. Kawamura, 153–163. Waterloo: Wilfred Laurier University.

———. 1989. "The Rock Cut Canon in China: Findings at Fang-Shan." In *The Buddhist Heritage*, edited by Tadeusz Skorupski, 143–156. Buddhica Britannica Series Continua, no. 1. Tring, UK: The Institute of Buddhist Studies.

Ledderose, Lothar. 2000. "The Bureaucracy of Hell." In *Ten Thousand Things: Module and Mass Production in Chinese Art,* 163–185. Bollingen series, no. 46. Princeton: Princeton University Press.

Lee, Jung-hee. 1984. *The Contemplating Bodhisattva Images of Asia, with Special Emphasis on China and Korea.* Los Angeles: University of California Press.

Lee Yu-Min. 1983. "The Maitreya Cult and Its Art in Early China." Ph.D. diss., Ohio State University.

———. 1984. "Ketumati Maitreya and Tuṣita Maitreya in Early China." Parts 1 and 2. *National Palace Museum Bulletin* 19.4: 1–13; 19.5: 1–13.

Lee Yuqun 李裕群. 1992. "Nan Xiangtang shan shiku xin faxian kuyan yiji ji kanxiang 南響堂山石窟新發現窟檐遺跡及龕像." *Wenwu* 文物 5: 1–15.

Levering, Miriam. 1987. "Kṣitigarbha." In Vol. 8, *Encyclopedia of Religion,* edited by Mircea Eliade, 392–393. 16 vols. New York: Macmillan.

Lévi, Sylvain. 1904. "Notes Chinoises sur l'Inde, IV. Le pays de Kharoṣṭra et l'écriture Kharoṣṭrī." *Bulletin de l'École Française d'Extrême-Orient* 4, 543–579.

———. 1905. "Notes Chinoises sur l'Inde, V. Quelques documents sur le bouddhisme indien dans l'Asie Centrale (Première partie)." *Bulletin de l'École Française d'Extrême-Orient* 5: 262–284.

Lewis, Mark Edward. 1990. "The Suppression of the Three Stages Sect: Apocrypha as a Political Issue." In *Chinese Buddhist Apocrypha,* edited by Robert Buswell, 207–238. Honolulu: University of Hawai'i Press.

Li Fangyin 黎方銀. 1990. *Dazu shiku yishu* 大足石窟藝術. Chongqing: Chongqing chubanshe.

Li Fangyin 黎方銀, and Wang Xixiang 王熙祥. 1988. "Dazu Beishan Fowan shiku de fenqi 大足北山佛灣石窟的分期." *Wenwu* 文物 8: 31–45. Reprinted in *Dazu shike yanjiu wenji* 大足石刻研究文集, edited by Guo Xiangying 郭相穎, 47–83. Chongqing: Chongqing chubanshe, 1993.

Li Jingjie 李靜杰. 1995. *Shifo xuancui* 石佛選粹. Beijing: Zhongguo shijieyu chubanshe.

Li Ling. 1990. "Formulaic Structure of the Chu Divinatory Bamboo Slips." *Early China* 15: 71–86.

Li Song 李淞. 1999. *Shaanxi fojiao yishu* 陕西佛教藝術. Taipei: Yishu jia.

Li Wensheng 李文生. 1980. "Longmen shiku de xin faxian ji qita 龍門石窟的新發現及其它." *Wenwu* 文物 1: 1–5.

Lieu, Samuel N. C. 1979. *The Religion of Light: An Introduction to the History of Manichaeism in China.* University of Hong Kong.

———. 1998. *Manichaeism in Central Asia and China.* Leiden: E. J. Brill.

Lin Wushu 林悟殊. 1987. *Monijiao ji qi dongjian* 摩尼教及其東漸. Beijing: Zhonghua shuju.

Little, Stephen. 2003. "A Korean Gilt-Bronze Sculpture of Kshitigarbha Bodhisattva." *Orientations* 24.7: 52–56.

Liu Changdong 劉長東. 2000. *Jin Tang Mile jingtu xinyang yanjiu* 晉唐彌勒淨土信仰研究. Chengdu: Bashu shushe.

Liu Changjiu 劉長久. 1997. *Anyue shiku yishu* 安岳石窟藝術. Chengdu: Sichuan renmin chubanshe.

———. 1999. *Zhongguo shiku diaosu quanji 8: Sichuan Chongqing* 中國石窟雕塑全集 8: 四川. 重慶. Chongqing: Chongqing chubanshe.

Liu Changjiu 劉長久, Hu Wenhe 胡文和, and Li Yongqiao 李永翹. 1985. *Dazu shike yanjiu* 大足石刻研究. Chengdu: Sichuan shen shehui kexueyuan chubanshe.

Liu Shu-fen 劉淑芬. 1996. "'Foding zunsheng tuoluoni jing' he Tangdai zunsheng jingchuang de jianli—jingchuang yanjiu zhi yi 佛頂尊勝陀羅尼經和唐代尊勝經幢的建立—經幢研究之一." *Zhongyang yanjiuyuan lishi yuyan yanjiusuo jikan* 中央研究院歷史語言研究所集刊 67.1: 145–193.

———. 1997. "Jingchuang de xingzhi, xingzhi he laiyuan—jingchuang yanjiu zhi er 經幢的形制，性質和來源—經幢研究之二." *Zhongyang yanjiuyuan lishi yuyan yanjiusuo jikan* 68.3: 643–786.

Liu Ts'un-yan. 1976. "Traces of Zoroastrian and Manichaean Activities in Pre-T'ang China." In *Selected Papers from the Hall of Harmonious Wind*, 3–55. Leiden: E. J. Brill.

Loewe, Michael. 1979. *Ways to Paradise: The Chinese Quest for Immortality*. Reprint, Taipei: SMC Publishing, 1994.

———. 1994. *Divination, Mythology and Monarchy in Han China*. University of Cambridge Oriental Publications, no. 48. Reprint, Taipei: SMC Publishing, 1996.

Lopez, Donald S. 1995. *Curators of the Buddha: The Study of Buddhism under Colonialism*. Chicago: University of Chicago Press.

———. 2005. "Buddha." In *Critical Terms For the Study of Buddhism*, edited by Donald S. Lopez, 13–36. Chicago: University of Chicago Press.

Lü Jianfu 呂建福. 1995. *Zhongguo mijiao shi* 中國密教史. Beijing: Zhongguo shehui kexue chubanshe.

Lü Tiegang 呂鐵鋼, ed. 1999. *Fangshan shijing yanjiu* 房山石經研究. 3 vols. Hong Kong: Zhongguo fojiao wenhua chuban youxian gongsi.

Luo Huaqing 羅華慶. 1993. "Dunhuang Dizang tuxiang he Dizang 'shiwang ting' yanjiu 敦煌地藏圖像和地藏『十王廳』研究." *Dunhuang yanjiu* 敦煌研究 2: 5–14.

Luo Shiping 羅世平. 1998. "Dizang shiwang tuxiang de yicun ji qi xinyang 地藏十王圖像的遺存及其信仰." *Tang yanjiu* 唐研究 4: 373–414.

Luo Weiguo 羅偉國. 1998. *Hua shuo Dizang* 話說地藏. Shanghai: Shanghai shudian.

Lye, Hun Yun. 2003. "Feeding Ghosts: A Study of the Yuqie Yankou Rite." Ph.D. diss., University of Virginia.

Ma Yan 馬彥, and Ding Mingyi 丁明夷. 1990. "Guangyuan Qianfo ya shiku diaocha ji 廣元千佛崖石窟調查記." *Wenwu* 文物 6: 1–23.

Maeda Shigeki. 1995. "The Evolution of the Way of the Celestial Master: Its Early View of Divinities." *Acta Asiatica* 68: 54–68.

Mair, Victor H. 1983. *Tun-huang Popular Narratives*. Cambridge: Cambridge University Press.

———. 1986. "Records of Transformation Tableaux *(pien-hsiang)*." *Toung-pao* 72: 3–43.

———. 1988. *Painting and Performance: Chinese Picture Recitation and Its Indian Genesis*. Honolulu: University of Hawai'i Press.

———. 1989. *Tang Transformation Texts*. Cambridge, MA, and London: Council of East Asian Studies, Harvard University.

Makita Tairyō 牧田諦亮. 1970. *Rikuchō koitsu Kanzeon ōgenki no kenkyū* 六朝古逸観世音応験記の研究. Kyoto: Hyōrakuji shoten.

———. 1975. *Gikyō kenkyū* 疑経研究. Kyoto: Kyōto daigaku jinbun kagaku kenkyūjo.

Malandra, Geri H. 1993. *Unfolding a Maṇḍala: The Buddhist Caves at Ellora*. Albany: State University of New York Press.

Manabe Kōsai 真鍋廣濟. 1960. *Jizō bosatsu no kenkyū* 地蔵菩薩の研究. Kyoto: Sanmitsudō.

Markel, Stephen. 1995. *Origins of the Indian Planetary Deities*. Studies in Asian Thought and Religion, no. 16. Lewiston, NY: Edwin Mellen Press.

Mather, Richard B. 1968. "Vimalakīrti and Gentry Buddhism." *History of Religions* 8.1: 60–73.

Matsumoto Bunzaburō 松本文三郎. 1942. *Shina bukkyō ibutsu* 支那仏教遺物. Tokyo: Kōbundō.

Matsumoto Eiichi 松本栄一. 1922. "Inro bosatsu shinkō ni tsuite 引路菩薩信仰に就いて." *Kokka* 国華 387: 51–54.

———. 1933. "Jizō bosatsu jūō zu to Inro bosatsu 地蔵菩薩十王図と引路菩薩." *Kokka* 国華 515: 265–270.

———. 1937. *Tonkō ga no kenkyū* 敦煌画の研究. 2 vols. Tokyo: Tōhō bunka gakuin.

Matsunaga, Alicia. 1969. *The Buddhist Philosophy of Assimilation: The Historical Development of the Honji-Suijaku Theory*. Tokyo: Sophia University and Charles Tuttle.

Matsushima Gen 松島健. 1986. *Jizō bosatsu zō* 地蔵菩薩像. *Nihon no bijutsu* 日本の美術 239. Tokyo: Shibundō.

McBride, Richard D. 2004. "Is There Really 'Esoteric' Buddhism?" *Journal of the International Association of Buddhist Studies* 27.2: 329–356.

McNair, Amy. 1996. "The Fengxiansi Shrine and Longmen in the 670s." *The Museum of Far Eastern Antiquities* 68: 325–392.

McRae, John R. 1995. "Chinese Religions: The State of the Field (Part II), Living Religious Traditions: Buddhism." *Journal of Asian Studies* 54.2: 354–371.

Mengcan 夢參. N.d. *Dizang zhancha lun xiuxing shouce* 地藏占察輪修行手冊. Taipei: Fangguang xinshu.

———. 1993. *Zhancha shan'e yebao jing jiangji* 占察善惡業報經講記. Recorded by Wu Bitao 吳碧濤. Taipei: Yuanming chubanshe.

Michihata Ryōshū 道端良秀. 1935. "Dōshaku zenshi to sangaikyō 道綽禅師と三階教." *Ōtani gakuhō* 大谷学報 15.1: 29–49.

———. 1985a. *Chūgoku bukkyō to jukyō rinri kō to no kōshō* 中国仏教と儒教倫理孝との交渉. Tokyo: Kabushiki kaisha shoen.

———. 1985b. *Chūgoku jōdokyōshi no kenkyū* 中国浄土教史の研究. Tokyo: Kabushiki kaisha shoen.

Mikami Tsugio 三上次男. 1967. "Tō kanho gannen mei no hizō to Jizō zō 唐咸亨元年銘の碑像と地蔵像." *Kobijutsu* 古美術 18: 42–46

Mitamura Keiko. 2002. "Daoist Hand Signs and Buddhist Mudras." In *Daoist Identity: History, Lineage, and Ritual*, edited by Livia Kohn and Harold D. Roth, 235–255. Honolulu: University of Hawai'i Press.

Mizuno Seiichi 水野清一, and Nagahiro Toshio 長広敏雄. 1937. *Kyōdōsan sekkutsu: Kahoku Kanam-shō zakai ni okeru Hokusei jidai no sekkutsu jiin* 響堂山石窟: 河北

河南省境における北齊時代の石窟寺院. Kyoto: Academy of Oriental Culture, Kyōto Institute.

———. 1941. *Ryūmon sekkutsu no kenkyū: Kanan Rakuyō* 龍門石窟の研究: 河南洛陽. Tokyo: Zauhokankokai.

———. 1951. *Yun-gang, the Buddhist Cave-Temples of the Fifth Century A.D. in North China: Detailed Report of the Archaeological Survey Carried Out by the Mission of the Tohobunka Kenkyusho 1938–45 [by] Seiichi Mizuno and Nagahiro Toshio.* Kyoto: Jimbunkagaku kenkyusho, Kyoto University.

Mochizuki Shinjō 望月信成. 1989. *Jizō bosatsu—sono gen to shinkō wo saguru* 地蔵菩薩–その源と信仰をさぐる. Tokyo: Gakuseisha.

Mochizuki Shinkō 望月信亨. 1946. *Bukkyō kyōten seiritsushi ron* 仏教教典成立史論. Kyoto: Hōzōkan.

———. 1958–1963. *Bukkyō daijiten* 仏教大辞典. 3d ed. 10 vols. Tokyo: Sekai seiten kankō kyōkai.

———. 1975. *Chūgoku jōdo kyōrishi* 中国浄土教理史. Kyōto: Hōzōkan.

Moon Myong-dae 文明大. 1984. *Hankook-ye Mi 16: Chosun Bul-wha* 韓國의美 16: 朝鮮佛畫. Seoul: Chungang-Ilbosa.

Morgan, David, ed. 1996. *Icons of American Protestantism: The Art of Warner Sallman.* New Haven: Yale University Press.

———. 1998. *Visual Piety: A History and Theory of Popular Religious Images.* Berkeley: University of California Press.

———. 2001. "Protestant Visual Practice and American Mass Culture." In *Practicing Religion in the Age of the Media*, edited by Stewart M. Hoover and Lynn Schofield Clark, 37–62. New York: Columbia University Press.

Morgan, David, and Sally M. Promey, eds. 2001. *The Visual Culture of American Religions.* Berkeley and Los Angeles: University of California Press.

Morohashi Tetsuji 諸橋轍次. 1955–1960. *Daikanwa jiten* 大漢和辞典. 13 vols. Tokyo: Daishūkan Shoten.

Moroto Fumio 諸戸文男. 1986. "Chūgoku shishū Daisoku sekikoku no hibō Jizō bosatsu zō 中国四州大足石刻の被帽地蔵菩薩像." *Kikan tōzai kōshō* 季刊東西交渉 19: 34–37.

Murase, Mikeko. 1971. "Kuan-yin as Savior of Men: Illustration of the Twenty-fifth Chapter of the *Lotus Sūtra* in Chinese Painting." *Artibus Asiae* 33: 39–74.

Nakano Teruo 中野照男. 1974. "Chōsen no Jizō jūō zu ni tsuite—Nihon denraihin wo chūsin to shite—朝鮮の地蔵十王図について—日本伝来品を中心として—." *Bukkyō geijutsu* 仏教芸術 97: 124–139.

Nattier, Jan. 1988. "The Meanings of the Maitreya Myth: A Typological Analysis." In *Maitreya, the Future Buddha*, edited by Alan Sponberg and Helen Hardacre, 23–47. Cambridge: Cambridge University Press.

———. 1990. "Church Language and Vernacular Language in Central Asian Buddhism." *Numen* 37: 195–219.

———. 1991. *Once Upon a Future Time: Studies in a Buddhist Prophecy of Decline.* Berkeley: Asian Humanities Press.

———. 1992. "The *Heart Sūtra:* A Chinese Apocryphal Text?" *Journal of the International Association of Buddhist Studies* 15.2: 153–223.

———. 2000. "The Realm of Akṣobhya: A Missing Piece in the History of Pure Land Buddhism." *Journal of the International Association of Buddhist Studies* 23.1: 71–102.

———. 2003a. *A Few Good Men: The Bodhisattva Path According to the Inquiry of Ugra (Ugraparipṛcchā): A Study and Translation.* Honolulu: University of Hawai'i Press.

———. 2003b. "The Indian Roots of Pure Land Buddhism: Insights from the Oldest Chinese Versions of the *Larger Sukhāvativyūha*." *Pacific World: Journal of the Institute of Buddhist Studies*, 3d ser., 5: 179–201.

Nickerson, Peter Samuel. 1996a. "Taoism, Death, and Bureaucracy in Early Medieval China." Ph.D. diss., University of California, Berkeley.

———. 1996b. "Abridged Codes of Master Lu for the Daoist Community." In *Religions of China in Practice*, edited by Donald S. Lopez, Jr., 347–359. Princeton: Princeton University Press.

———. 1997. "The Great Petition for Selpuchral Plaints." In *Early Daoist Scriptures*, edited by Stephen R. Bokenkamp, 230–274. Berkeley: University of California Press.

———. 2002. "'Opening the Way': Exorcism, Travel, and Soteriology in Early Daoist Mortuary Practice and Its Antecedents." In *Daoist Identity : History, Lineage, and Ritual*, edited by Livia Kohn and Harold D. Roth, 58–77. Honolulu: University of Hawai'i Press.

Nishimoto Teruma 西本照真. 1998. *Sangaikyō no kenkyū* 三階教の研究. Tokyo: Shunjūsha.

Oda Yoshihisa 小田義久. 1976. "Godō daishin kō 五道大神考." *Tōhō shūkyō* 東方宗教 48: 14–29.

Ōmura Seigai 大村西崖. 1918. *Mikkyō hattatsushi* 密教発達史. Reprint, Taipei: Wuling chubanshe, 1993.

———. 1922. *Shina bijutsushi chōsohen* 支那美術史彫塑篇. 3 vols. Tokyo: Bukkyō kankōkai Toshobu.

Ono Gemmyō 小野玄妙. 1933–1936. *Bussho kaisetsu daijiten* 仏書解説大辞典. 13 vols. Tokyo: Daitō shuppansha.

Orzech, Charles D. 1989. "Seeing Chen-yen Buddhism: Traditional Scholarship and the Vajrayāna in China." *History of Religions* 29.2: 87–114.

———. 1994. "Esoteric Buddhism and the *Shishi* in China." In *The Esoteric Buddhist Tradition*, edited by Henrik H. Sørenson, 51–72. Seminar for Buddhist Studies Monographs, no. 2. Copenhagan and Aarhus: Seminar for Buddhist Studies.

———. 1996. "Saving the Burning-Mouth Hungry Ghost." In *Religions of China in Practice*, edited by Donald S. Lopez. Jr., 278–283. Princeton: Princeton University Press.

———. 1998. *Politics and Transcendent Wisdom: The Scripture for Humane Kings in the Creation of Chinese Buddhism.* Pennsylvania: Pennsylvania State University Press.

———. 2000. "Hidden Pure Lands: Alternative and Esoteric Visions I (China)." Paper presented at the annual meeting of the Association for Asian Studies, San Diego.

———. 2002. "*Fang Yankou* and *Pudu:* Translation, Metaphor, and Religious Identity." In *Daoist Identity: History, Lineage, and Ritual*, edited by Livia Kohn and Harold D. Roth, 213–234. Honolulu: University of Hawai'i Press.

Osabe Kazuo 長部和雄. 1982. *Tōsō mikkyō shi ronkō* 唐宋密教史論考. Kyoto: Nagata bunshōdō.

Ōshima Tatehiko 大島建彦, and Enomoto Chika 榎本千賀, eds. 2002. *Juyon kanbon Jizō bosatsu reigenki* 十四巻本地蔵菩薩霊験記. Tokyo: Miyai Shoten.

Overmyer, Daniel L. 1990. "Buddhism in the Trenches: Attitude toward Popular Religion in Chinese Scriptures Found at Tun-huang." *Harvard Journal of Asiatic Studies* 50.1: 197–222.

———. 1999. *Precious Volumes: An Introduction to Chinese Sectarian Scriptures from the Sixteenth and Seventeenth Centuries.* Cambridge: Harvard University Asia Center.

Pagel, Ulrich. 1995. *The Bodhisattvapiṭaka: Its Doctrines, Practices and Their Position in Mahāyāna Literature.* Tring, UK: The Institute of Buddhist Studies.

Pak, Young-Sook. 1977. "Kṣitigarbha as Supreme Lord of the Underworld." *Oriental Art*, n.s., 23.1: 96–104.

———. 1995. "The Role of Legend in Koryō Iconography (I): The Kṣitigarbha Triad in Engakuji." In *Function and Meaning in Buddhist Art*, edited by K. R. van Kooji and H. van der Veere, 157–165. Groningen: Egbert Forsten.

———. 1998. "The Korean Art Collection in The Metropolitan Museum of Art." In *Arts of Korea*, edited by Judith G. Smith, 402–449. New York: The Metropolitan Museum of Art.

Pal, Pratapaditya. 1972–1973. "A Note on the Maṇḍala of the Eight Bodhisattvas." *Archives of Asian Art* 26: 71–73.

Pan Guiming 潘桂明. 2000. *Zhongguo jushi fojiao shi* 中國居士佛教史. 2 vols. Beijing: Zhongguo shehui kexue chubanshe.

Pan Guiming 潘桂明, and Wu Zhongwei 吳忠衛. 2001. *Zhongguo tiantaizong tongshi* 中國天臺宗通史. Nanjing: Jiangsu guji chubanshe.

Pan Liangwen 潘亮文. 1998. "Dunhuang de Dizang pusa xiang yanjiu 敦煌的地藏菩薩像研究." Paper presented at the Fojiao wenxue yu yishu xueshu yantaohui 佛教文學與藝術學術研討會, Taipei.

———. 1999. *Zhongguo Dizang pusa xiang chutan* 中國地藏菩薩像初探. Tainan: Guoli tainan yishu xueyuan.

Pas, Julian F. 1986–1987. "Six Daily Periods of Worship: Symbolic Meaning in Buddhist Liturgy and Eschatology." *Monumenta Serica* 37: 49–82.

———. 1989. "Journey to Hell: A New Report of Shamanistic Travels to the Courts of Hell." *Journal of Chinese Religions* 17: 43–60.

———. 1995. *Visions of Sukhāvatī: Shan-Tao's Commentary on the Kuan Wu-liang-Shou-Fo-Ching.* Albany: State University of New York Press.

Pintchman, Tracy. 1994. *The Rise of the Goddess in the Hindu Tradition.* Albany: State University of New York Press.

Piotrovsky, Mikhail. 1993. Lost Empire of the Silk Road—Buddhist Art from Khara Khoto (X-XIIIth Century). Electa: Thyssen-Bornemisza Foundation. In Chinese: *Silu shang xiaoshi de wangguo: Xixia Heishui cheng de fojiao yishu* 絲路上消失的王國: 西夏黑水城的佛教藝術, translated by Xu Yangzhu 許洋主. Taipei: Guoli lishi bowuguan, 1996.

Poo Mu-Chou. 1997. "The Completion of an Ideal World: The Human Ghost in Early Medieval China." *Asia Major*, 3rd ser., 10.1–2: 74–75.

———. 1998. *In Search of Personal Welfare: A View of Ancient Chinese Religion*. Albany: State University of New York Press.

———. 2004. "The Concept of Ghost in Ancient Chinese Religion." In Vol. 1, *Religion and Chinese Society*, edited by John Lagerwey, 173–191. Hong Kong and Paris: Chinese University Press and École française d'Extrême-Orient.

Powell, William. 1987. "Mt. Jiuhua: The Nine-Florate Realm of Dicang Pusa." *Asian Cultural Studies* 16: 130–116. Reprinted in *Jin Dizang yanjiu* 金地藏研究, edited by Jiuhua shan fojiao shi bianweihui 九華山佛教史編委會, 170–202. Hefei: Huangshan shushe, 1993.

———. 1993. "Literary Diversions on Mount Jiuhua: Cults, Communities and Culture." In *The Sacred Mountains of Asia*, edited by John Einarsen, 22–26. Boston: Shambala.

Ray, Reginald. 1994. *Buddhist Saints in India: A Study in Buddhist Values and Orientations*. New York: Oxford University Press.

Reader, Ian, and George Tanabe. 2004. *Practically Religious: Worldly Benefits and the Common Religion of Japan*. Honolulu: University of Hawai'i Press.

Redfield, Robert. 1956. *The Little Community and Peasant Society and Culture*. Chicago: University of Chicago Press.

Reinders, Eric. 1997. "Ritual Topography: Embodiment and Vertical Space in Buddhist Monastic Practice." *History of Religions* 36.3: 244–264.

Ren Jiyu 任繼愈, ed. 1991. *Daozang tiyao* 道藏提要. Beijing: Zhongguo shehui kexue chubanshe.

Riegel, Jeffery K. 1989–1990. "Kou-mang and Ju-shou." *Cahiers d'Extrême-Asie* 5: 55–79.

Ritzinger, Justin, and Marcus Bingenheimer. 2006. "Whole Body Relics in Chinese Buddhism—Previous Research and Historical Overview." *The Indian International Journal of Buddhist Studies* 7: 37–94.

Robinson, Richard. 1965–1966. "The Ethic of the Householder Bodhisattva." *Bhāratī: Bulletin of the College of Indology* 9.2: 25–56.

———. 1967. *Early Mādhyamika in India and China*. Reprint, Delhi: Motilal Banarsidass, 1978.

Rösch, Petra. 2006. "The Changing Audience of Water-Moon Guanyin." Paper presented at the Fifth Chung-hwa Internation Buddhist Conference on "The Bodhisattva Avalokiteśvara (Guanyin) and Modern Society," Taipei.

Rudova, Maria L. 1993. "The Chinese Style Paintings from Khara Khoto." In *Lost Empire of the Silk Road: Buddhist Art from Khara Khoto (X–XIIth Century)*, edited by Mikhail Piotrovsky, 89–99. Electa: Thyssen-Bornemisza Foundation.

Sakai Tadao 酒井忠夫. 1937. "Taisan shinkō no kenkyū 太山信仰の研究." *Shichō* 史潮 7.2: 70–118.

Sakamoto Kaname 坂本要, ed. 1990. *Jigoku no sekai* 地獄の世界. Tokyo: Keisuisha.

Sakurai Tokutarō 桜井徳太郎, ed. 1983. *Jizō shinkō* 地蔵信仰. Vol. 10, Minshū shūkyōshi sōsho 民衆宗教史叢書. Tokyo: Yūzankaku shuppan.

Sangren, P. Steven. 1984. "Great Tradition and Little Tradition Reconsidered: The Question of Cultural Integration in China." *Journal of Chinese Studies* 1: 1–24.

Sasaguchi Rei. 1975. "The Image of the Contemplating Bodhisattva in Chinese Buddhist Sculpture of the Sixth Century." Ph.D. diss., Harvard University.

Sasaki Nobutsuna 佐々木信綱, ed. 1954. *Konjaku monogatari* 今昔物語. Vol. 3. *Nihon koten zensho* 日本古典全書, no. 88. Tokyo: Asahi shinbunsha.

Sasaki Shizuka 佐々木閑 1997. "A Study on the Origins of Mahāyāna Buddhism." *The Eastern Buddhist*, n.s., 30.1: 79–113.

Satō Taishun 佐藤泰舜. 1982. "Rikuchō jidai no Kannon shinkō 六朝時代の観音信仰." In *Kannon shinkō* 観音信仰, edited by Hayami Tasuku 速水侑, 17–38. Tokyo: Yūzankaku shuppan.

Saunders, E. Dale. 1960. *Mudrā: A Study of Symbolic Gestures in Japanese Buddhist Sculpture.* Reprint, Princeton: Princeton University Press, 1985.

Sawada Mizuho 沢田瑞穂. 1968. *Jigoku hen—Chūgoku no meikaisetsu* 地獄変–中国の冥界説. Kyoto: Hōzōkan.

Schipper, Kristofer. 1978. "The Taoist Body." *History of Religions* 17.3–4: 355–386.

———. 1982. *The Taoist Body*. Translated by Karen C. Duval. Berkeley: University of California Press.

Schipper, Kristofer, and Franciscus Verellen, eds. 2005. *The Taoist Canon: A Historical Companion to the Daozang*. Chicago: University of Chicago Press.

Schopen, Gregory. 1975. "The Phrase '*sa pṛthivīpradeśaś caityabhūto bhavet*' in the *Vajracchedikā*: Notes on the Cult of the Book in Mahāyāna." *Indo-Iranian Journal* 17: 147–181.

———. 1977. "Sukhāvatī as a Generalized Religious Goal in Sanskrit Mahāyāna Sūtra Literature." *Indo-Iranian Journal* 19: 177–210.

———. 1978. "The *Bhaiṣajyaguru-sūtra* and the Buddhism of Gilgit." Ph.D. diss., Australian National University.

———. 1979. "Mahāyāna in Indian Inscriptions." *Indo-Iranian Journal* 21: 1–19

———. 1984. "Filial Piety and the Monk in the Practice of Indian Buddhism: A Question of 'Sinicization' Viewed from the Other Side." *T'oung Pao* 70: 110–126.

———. 1985. "Two Problems in the History of Indian Buddhism: The Layman/Monk Distinction and the Doctrines of the Transference of Merit." *Studien zur Indologie und Iranistik* 10: 9–47.

———. 1987. "The Inscription on the Kusan Image of Amitābha and the Character of the Early Mahāyāna in India." *Journal of the International Association of Buddhist Studies* 10: 99–138.

———. 1989. "The Stūpa Cult and the Extant Pāli Vinaya." *Journal of the Pali Text Society* 13: 83–100.

———. 1991a. "Archaeology and Protestant Presuppositions in the Study of Indian Buddhism." *History of Religions* 31.1: 1–23.

———. 1991b. "Monks and the Relic Cult in the *Mahāparinibbānasutta*: An Old Misunderstanding in Regard to Monastic Buddhism." In *From Benares to Beijing: Essays on Buddhism and Chinese Religion in Honour of Prof. Jan Yün-hua*, edited by Koichi Shinohara and Gregory Schopen, 187–201. Oakville, Canada: Moasic Press.

———. 1996. "Brooding Bodhisattvas and Despondent Laymen: The 'Pensive Pose' in Early Buddhist Art and Literature." Paper presented at the symposium "The Ambiguity of Avalokiteshvara and Questions of Bodhisattvas in Buddhist Traditions," Austin.

———. 2005. "The *Bodhigarbhalaṅkāralakṣa* and *Vimaloṣṇīṣa Dhāraṇīs* in Indian Inscriptions: Two Sources for the Practice of Buddhism in Medieval India." In *Figments and Fragments of Mahayana Buddhism in India: More Collected Papers*, 314–344. Honolulu: University of Hawai'i Press.

Schwartz, Benjamin I. 1985. *The World of Thought in Ancient China*. Cambridge, MA: Harvard University Press.

Seidel, Anna. 1982. "Tokens of Immortality in Han Graves." *Numen* 24: 79–122.

———. 1987a. "Chinese Concepts of the Soul and the Afterlife." In *Death, Afterlife, and the Soul*, edited by Lawrence E. Sullivan, 183–188. New York: Macmillan.

———. 1987b. "Traces of Han Religion in Funerary Texts Found in Tombs." In *Dōkyō to shūkyō bunka* 道教と宗教文化, edited by Akizuki Kan'ei 秋月観暎, 21–57. Tokyo: Hirakawa shuppansha.

———. 1987c. "Post-Mortem Immortality or the Taoist Resurrection of the Body." In *Gilgul: Essays on Transformation, Revolution, and Permanence in the History of Religions*, edited by S. Shaked, D. Shulman, and G. G. Stroumsa, 223–237. Leiden: E. J. Brill.

———. 1988. "Early Taoist Ritual." *Cahiers d'Extrême-Asie* 4: 199–204.

———. 1997. "Taoism: The Unofficial High Religion of China." *Taoist Resources* 7: 39–72.

Shanxi sheng bowuguan 山西省博物館, ed. 1988. *Baoning si mingdai shuilu hua* 寶寧寺明代水陸畫. Beijing: Wenwu chubanshe.

Sharf, Robert H. 2001a. "Introduction: Prolegomenon to the Study of Japanese Buddhist Icons." In *Living Images: Japanese Buddhist Icons in Context*, edited by Robert H. Sharf and Elizabeth Horton Sharf, 1–18. Stanford: Stanford University Press.

———. 2001b. "Visualization and Mandala in Shingon Buddhism." In *Living Images: Japanese Buddhist Icons in Context*, edited by Robert H. Sharf and Elizabeth Horton Sharf, 151–197. Stanford: Stanford University Press.

———. 2002a. *Coming to Terms with Chinese Buddhism: A Reading of the Treasure Store Treatise*. Kuroda Institute Studies in East Asian Buddhism, no. 14. Honolulu: University of Hawai'i Press.

———. 2002b. "On Pure Land Buddhism and Ch'an/Pure Land Syncreticism in Medieval China." *T'oung Pao* 88.4–5: 282–331.

Shengyan 聖嚴. 1975. *Meimatsu Chūgoku bukkyō no kenkyū* 明末中国仏教の研究. Reprint, Taipei: Dongchu chubanshe, 1993.

Shinohara Koichi. 1988. "Two Sources of Chinese Buddhist Biographies: Stupa Inscriptions and Mircale Stories." In *Monks and Magicians: Religious Biographies in Asia*, edited by Phyllis Granoff and Koichi Shinohara, 119–229. Oakville, Canada: Mosaic Press.

———. 1990. "Daoxuan's Collection of Miracle Stories about 'Supernatural Monks' (*Shen-seng gan-tong lu*): An Analysis of Its Sources." *Zhonghua foxue xuebao* 中華佛學學報 3: 319–379.

———. 1991. "Ji shen-zhou san-bao Gan-tong-lu: Some Explanatory Notes." In *Kalyāṇna-mitta: Professor Hajime Nakamura Felicitation Volume*, edited by V. N. Jha, 203–224. Delhi: Sri Satguru Publications.

———. 1998. "Gaoli's Discovery of a Miraculous Image: The Evolution of Ashoka Image Stories in Medieval China." In *The Flowering of a Foreign Faith: New Studies in Chinese Buddhist Art*, edited by Janet Baker, 20–27. Mumbai: Mārg Publications.

———. 1999. "From Local History to Universal History: The Construction of the Sung T'ien-t'ai Lineage." In *Buddhism in the Sung*, edited by Peter N. Gregory and Daniel A. Getz, Jr., 524–576. Kuroda Institute Studies in East Asian Buddhism, no. 13. Honolulu: University of Hawai'i Press.

———. 2004. "Stories of Miraculous Images and Paying Respect to the Three Jewels: A Discourse on Image Worship in Seventh-Century China." In *Images in Asian Religions: Texts and Contexts*, edited by Phyllis Granoff and Koichi Shinohara, 180–222. Vancouver: University of British Columbia Press.

Silk, Jonathan Alan. 1994. "The Origins and Early History of the *Mahāratnakūṭa* Tradition of Mahāyāna Buddhism with a Study of the *Ratnarāśisūtra* and Related Materials." Ph.D. diss., University of Michigan.

———. 1997. "The Composition of the *Guan Wuliangshoufo jing:* Some Buddhist and Jaina Parallels to Its Narrative Frame." *Journal of Indian Philosophy* 25: 181–256.

Smith, Richard J. 1991. *Fortune-Tellers and Philosophers: Divination in Traditional Chinese Society.* Reprint, Taipei: SMC Publishing.

Snellgrove, David. 1987. *Indo-Tibetan Buddhism: Indian Buddhists and Their Tibetan Successors.* 2 vols. Boston: Shambala.

Soper, Alexander C. 1959. *Literary Evidence for Early Buddhist Art in China.* Ascona, Switzerland: Artibus Asiae Publishers.

Sørenson, Henrik H. 1989a. *A Survey of the Religious Sculptures of Anyue.* East Asian Institute Occasional Papers, no. 3. Copenhagen: East Asian Institute, University of Copenhagen.

———. 1989b. "On Recent Publications and Field-work Related to Religious Sculptures in the Province of Sichuan." *Studies in Central and East Asian Religions* 2: 176–178.

———. 1991. "A Study of the Ox-herding Theme as Sculptures at Mt. Baoding in Dazu County, Sichuan." *Artibus Asiae* 51.3–4: 207–233.

———. 1995a. "Buddhist Sculptures from the Song Dynasty at Mingshan Temple in Anyue, Sichuan." *Artibus Asiae* 55.3–4: 281–302.

———. 1995b. "Divine Scrutiny of Human Morals in an Early Chinese Buddhist Sūtra: A Study of the *Si tianwang jing* (T. 590)." *Studies in Central and East Asian Religions* 8: 44–83.

———. 1996. Review of *The Scripture on the Ten Kings and the Making of Purgatory in Medieval Chinese Buddhism*, by Stephen F. Teiser. *Studies on Central and East Asian Religions* 9: 114–121.

———. 1997. "Report on Recent Fieldwork in Sichuan (1997)." *Studies in Central and East Asian Religions* 2: 59–63

———. 1998. "The Buddhist Sculptures at Feixian Pavilion in Pujiang, Sichuan." *Artibus Asiae* 58.1–2: 33–67.

Soymié, Michel. 1962. "Jizō no shishi ni tsuite 地蔵の獅子について." Tōhō shūkyō 東方宗教 19: 37–52.

———. 1966. "Notes d'iconographie chinoise: Les acolytes de Ti-tsang (I)." *Arts Asiatiques* 14: 45–78.

———. 1967. "Notes d'iconographie chinoise: Les acolytes de Ti-tsang (II)." *Arts Asiatiques* 16: 141–170.

———. 1979. "Les dix jours de jeûne de Kṣitigarbha." In *Contributions aux etudes sur Touen-Houang*, 135–160. Paris: Droz. In Chinese: "Dunhuang xiaben zhong de Dizang shizhai ri 敦煌寫本中的地藏十齋日" in *Faguo xuezhe Dunhuang xue lunwen xuancui* 法國學者敦煌學論文選萃, translated by Geng Shen 耿昇, 391–429. Beijing: Zhonghua shuju, 1993.

Spiro, Melford E. 1970. *Buddhism and Society: A Great Tradition and Its Burmese Vicissitudes.* New York: Harper and Row.

Sponberg, Alan, and Helen Hardacre, eds. 1988. *Maitreya, the Future Buddha.* Cambridge: Cambridge University Press.

Stein, Rolf A. 1979. "Religious Taoism and Popular Religion from the Second to Seventh Centuries." In *Facets of Taoism*, edited by Anna Seidel and Holmes Welch, 53–81. New Haven: Yale University Press.

———. 1986. "Avalokiteśvara/Kouan-yin, un exemple de transformation d'un dieu en deesse." *Cahiers d'Extreme-Asie* 2: 17–77.

Stevenson, Daniel B. 1986. "The Four Kinds of Samādhi in Early T'ien-t'ai Buddhism." In *Traditions of Meditation in Chinese Buddhism*, edited by Peter N. Gregory, 45–97. Kuroda Institute Studies in East Asian Buddhism, no. 4. Honolulu: University of Hawai'i Press.

———. 1995a. "Death-Bed Testimonials of the Pure Land Faithful." In *Buddhism in Practice*, edited by Donald S. Lopez, Jr., 592–602. Princeton: Princeton University Press.

———. 1995b. "Pure Land Buddhist Worship and Meditation in China." In *Buddhism in Practice*, edited by Donald S. Lopez, Jr., 340–408. Princeton: Princeton University Press.

———. 2004. "Feeding Hungry Ghosts." In *Buddhist Scriptures*, edited by Donald S. Lopez, Jr., 416–422. London: Penguin Books.

Strickmann, Michel. 1982. "India in the Chinese Looking Glass." In *The Silk Road and the Diamond Path: Esoteric Buddhist Art on the Trans-Himalayan Trade Routes*, edited by Deborah Klimburg-Slater, 53–63. Los Angeles: UCLA Art Council.

———. 1983. "Homa in East Asia." In *Agni: The Vedic Ritual of the Fire Altar*, edited by Frits Staal, 418–455. 2 vols. Berkeley: Asian Humaities Press.

———. 1990. "The *Consecration Sūtra:* A Buddhist Book of Spells." In *Chinese Buddhist Apocrypha*, edited by Robert Buswell, 75–118. Honolulu: University of Hawai'i Press.

———. 2002. *Chinese Magical Medicine.* Stanford: Stanford University Press.

———. 2005. *Chinese Poetry and Prophecy.* Stanford: Stanford Univeristy Press.

Strong, John S. 1983. "Filial Piety and Buddhism: The Indian Antecedents to a Chinese Problem." In *Traditions in Contacts and Change*, edited by P. Slater, 171–186. Waterloo: Wilfred Laurier University Press.

———. 2004. *Relics of the Buddha.* Princeton: Princeton University Press.

Stuart, Rev. G. A. 1928. *Chinese Materia Medica.* Shanghai: Presbyterian Mission Press.

Suchan, Thomas. 2003. "The Eternally Flourishing Stronghold: An Iconographic

Study of the Buddhist Sculpture of the Fowan and Related Sites at Beishan, Dazu, ca. 892–1155." Ph.D. diss., Ohio State University.

———. 2005. "Dynamic Duos: Tang and Song Imagery of Paired Bodhisattvas from Sichuan." Paper presented at the Fourth International Convention of Asia Scholars, Shanghai.

Sullivan, Laurence. 1990 "'Seeking an End to the Primary Text' or 'Putting an End to the Text as Primary.'" In *Beyond the Classics? Essays in Religious Studies and Liberal Education*, edited by F. E. Reynolds and S. L. Burkhalter, 41–59. Atlanta: Scholars Press.

Takamine Ryōshū 高峰了州. 1963. *Kegon shisō shi* 華厳思想史. Kyoto: Hyakukaen 百華苑. In Chinese: *Huayan sixiang shi* 華嚴思想史, translated by Shi Huiyue 釋慧嶽. Taipei: Zhonghua fojiao wenxian bianzhuanshe, 1979.

Tanaka Hisao 田中久夫. 1989. *Jizō shinkō to minzoku* 地蔵信仰と民俗. Tokyo: Toshō shuppan.

Tanaka, Kenneth K. 1990. *The Dawn of Chinese Pure Land Buddhist Doctrine: Ching-ying Hui-yüan's Commentary on the Visualization Sutra*. Albany: State University of New York Press.

Tang Yongtong 湯用彤. 1987. *Han Wei Liangjin Nanbeichao fojiao shi* 漢魏兩晉南北朝佛教史. 2 vols. Changsha: Shangwu yinshuguan. Reprint, Banqiao: Luotuo chubanshe, 1938.

Teiser, Stephen F. 1986. "Ghosts and Ancestors in Medieval Chinese Religion: The Yü-lan-p'en Festival as Mortuary Ritual." *History of Religions* 26.1: 47–67.

———. 1988a. "'Having Once Died and Returned to Life': Representations of Hell in Medieval China." *Harvard Journal of Asiatic Studies* 48.2: 433–464.

———. 1988b. *The Ghost Festival in Medieval China*. Princeton: Princeton University Press.

———. 1992. "Hymns for the Dead in the Age of the Manuscript." *Gest Library Journal* 5.1: 26–56.

———. 1993. "The Growth of Purgatory." In *Religion and Society in T'ang and Sung China*, edited by Patricia B. Ebrey and Peter N. Gregory, 115–145. Honolulu: University of Hawai'i Press.

———. 1994. *The Scripture of the Ten Kings and the Making of Purgatory in Medieval Chinese Buddhism*. Kuroda Institute Studies in East Asian Buddhism, no. 9. Honolulu: University of Hawai'i Press.

———. 1995. "Chinese Religions: The State of the Field (Part II), Living Religious Traditions: Popular Religion." *Journal of Asian Studies* 54.2: 378–395.

———. 1997. "Prayers for Rebirth: Beliefs about the Pure Land in Liturgical Texts from Dunhuang." Paper presented at the Third Chung-hwa International Conference on Buddhism, Taipei.

———. 2004. "Folk Religion: An Overview." In Vol. 1, *Encylopedia of Buddhism*, edited by Robert E. Buswell, 288–290. New York: Macmillan.

Teng, Ssu-yu, and Knight Biggerstaff. 1971. *An Annotated Bibliography of Selected Chinese Reference Works*. Cambridge, MA: Harvard University Press.

Ter Haar, Barend J. 1998. *Ritual and Mythology of the Chinese Triads: Creating an Identity*. Leiden: E. J. Brill.

———. 2000. "The Rise of the Guanyin Cult: The Taoist Connection." In *Linked Faiths: Essays on Chinese Religions and Traditional Culture in Honour of Kristofer Schipper*, edited by Jan A. M. De Meyer and Peter M. Engelfriet, 184–204. Leiden: E. J. Brill.

Thomas, F. W. 1935–1963. *Tibetan Literary Texts and Documents concerning Chinese Turkestan*. London: Royal Asiatic Society.

Thompson, Laurence G. 1989. "On the Prehistory of Hell in China." *Journal of Chinese Religions* 17: 27–41.

Tiso, F. V. 1993. "The Bodhisattva as a Buddhist Saint." In *Premier Colloque Étienne Lamotte*, 141–148. Louvain-la-Neuve: Université Catholique de Louvain, Institut Orientaliste.

Tōdō Kyōshun 藤堂恭俊. 1962. "The Critical Views, or the Sense of Uneasiness, in Chinese Buddhism and Their Relief—Especially in the First Half of the 6th Century A.D." *Indogaku bukkyōgaku kenkyū* 印度学仏教学研究 10.2: 782–777.

———. 1970. "Hokugi: Bukkyō ni okeru shōmyō to sono shakai-haikei 北魏：仏教における称名とその社会背景." In *Hokugi bukkyō no kenkyū* 北魏仏教の研究, edited by Ōchō Enichi 横超慧日, 108–114. Kyoto: Heirakuji shoten.

Tokiwa Daijō 常盤大定. 1943. "Bushū shinji no ichi kenkyū 武周新字の一研究." Reprinted in *Shina bukkyō no kenkyū* 支那仏教の研究 3: 395–430.

Tokuno Kyoko. 1990. "The Evaluation of Indigenous Scriptures in Chinese Buddhist Bibliographical Catalogues." In *Chinese Buddhist Apocrypha*, edited by Robert Buswell, 31–74. Honolulu: University of Hawai'i Press.

———. 1994. "Byways in Chinese Buddhism: The "Books of Trapuṣa" and Indigenous Scriptures." Ph.D. diss., University of California, Berkeley.

Tsiang, Katherine R. 2000. "Miraculous Flying Stupas in Qingzhou Sculpture." *Orientations* 31.10: 45–53.

Tso Sze-bong 曹仕邦. 1982. "The Chinese Transformation of the Vinaya." Ph.D. diss., Australian National University.

———. 1992. *Zhongguo fojiao yijing shi lunji* 中國佛教譯經史論集. Taipei: Dongchu chubanshe.

Tsuchiya Masaaki. 2002. "Confession of Sins and Awareness of Self in the *Taiping jing*." In *Daoist Identity: History, Lineage, and Ritual*, edited by Livia Kohn and Harold D. Roth, 39–57. Honolulu: University of Hawai'i Press.

Tsui Chi, trans. 1943–1946. "*Mo ni Chiao Hsia Pu Tsan* 摩尼教下部讚: The Lower (Second?) Section of the Manichaean Hymns." *Bulletin of the School of Oriental and African Studies* 11: 174–219.

Tsukamoto Zenryū 塚本善隆. 1931. "Inro bosatsu shinkō ni tsuite 引路菩薩信仰について." *Tōhō gakuhō* 東方学報 1: 130–182.

———. 1942. *Shina bukkyōshi kenkyū: Hokugi hen* 支那仏教史研究：北魏篇. Tokyo: Kōbundō.

Unschuld, Paul U. 1985. *Medicine in China: A History of Ideas*. Berkeley: University of California Press.

Visser, Marinus Willem de. 1914. *The Bodhisattva Ti-Tsang (Jizō) in China and Japan*. Berlin: Oesterheld.

———. 1931. *The Bodhisattva Ākāśagarbha (Kokūzo) in China and Japan*. Amsterdam: Koninklijke Akademie Van Wetenschappen.

Vostrikov, A. I. 1970. *Tibetan Historical Literature.* Translated from the Russian by Harish Chandra Gupta. Soviet Indology Series, no. 4. Calcutta: Indian Studies Past and Present.

Wakamori Tarō 和歌森太郎. 1984. "Jizō shinkō ni tsuite 地蔵信仰について." In *Jizō shinkō* 地蔵信仰, edited by Sakurai Tokutarō 桜井徳太郎, 45–71. Vol. 10, Minshū shūkyō shi sōsho 民衆宗教史叢書. Tokyo: Yūzankaku shuppan.

Waley, Arthur. 1931. *Catalogue of Paintings Recovered from Tun-huang by Sir Aurel Stein.* London: The British Museum.

———. 1960. *Ballads and Stories from Tun-huang: An Anthology.* London: Allen and Unwin.

Wang Chongmin 王重民, ed. 1957. *Dunhuang bianwen ji* 敦煌變文集. 2 vols. Beijing: Renmin wenxue chubanshe.

———. 1982. *Dunhuang yishu zongmu suoyin* 敦煌遺書總目索引. Taipei: Yuanliu chubanshe.

Wang Huimin 王惠民. 2004. "Dunhuang 321 ku, 74 ku shilun jingbian kaoshi 敦煌321窟、74窟十輪經變考釋." *Yishu shi yanjiu* 藝術史研究 6: 309–336.

———. 2005. "Tang qianqi Dunhuang Dizang tuxiang kaocha 唐前期敦煌地藏圖像考察." *Dunhuang yanjiu* 敦煌研究 3: 18–25.

Wang Juan 汪娟. 1998. *Dunhuang lichan wen yanjiu* 敦煌禮懺文研究. Taipei: Fagu wenhua.

———. 1999. "Lidai Dizang chanyi xilun 歷代地藏懺儀析論." *Foxue yanjiu zhongxin xuebao* 佛學研究中心學報 4: 169–207.

Wang Shuqing 王書慶, ed. 1995. *Dunhuang foxue, foshi pian* 敦煌佛學. 佛事篇. Gansu: Gansu minzu chubanshe.

Wang Yi 汪毅. 1989. *Zhongguo fojiao yu Anyue shike yishu* 中國佛教與安岳石刻藝術. Beijing: Zhongguo lüyou chubanshe.

Wang-Toutain, Françoise. 1994. "Une peinture de Dunhuang conservée a la Bibliothèque Nationale de France." *Arts Asiatiques* 49: 53–69.

———. 1998. *Le Bodhisattva Kṣitigarbha en Chine du Ve au XIIe Siècle.* Paris: École française d'Extrême-Orient.

———. 2001. "The Fate of the Venerable Jin Dizang: From the Korean Monk to the *Bodhisattva* Kṣitigarbha." Paper presented at the annual meeting of the Association of Asian Studies, Chicago.

Ward, Benedicta. 1982. *Miracles and the Medieval Mind: Theory, Record and Event.* Philadephia: University of Pennsylvania Press.

Watanabe Ryūsei 渡辺隆生. 1973. "Jizō kenkyū to sono kyōten 地蔵研究とその経典." *Sanzō* 三蔵 49: 91–99.

Weinstein, Stanley. 1987. "Chinese Buddhism." In Vol. 2, *The Enclyclopedia of Religion*, edited by Mircea Eliade, 482–487. New York: Macmillan.

Wen Yucheng 溫玉成. 1988. "Luoyang Longmen Shuangku 洛陽龍門雙窟." *Kaogu xuebao* 考古學報 1: 101–131.

Williams, Joanna. 1973. "The Iconography of Khotanese Painting." *East and West* 23: 109–154.

Williams, Paul. 1989. *Mahāyāna Buddhism: The Doctrinal Foundations.* London: Routledge.

Whitfield, Roderick. 1982–1985. *The Art of Central Asia: The Stein Collection in the British Museum*. Photographs by Takahashi Bin. 3 vols. Tokyo: Kodansha.

Wong, Dorothy. 1998–1999. "Four Sichuan Buddhist Steles and the Beginnings of Pure Land Imagery in China." *Archives of Asian Art* 51: 56–79.

———. 2001. "Maitreya Buddha Statues at the University of Pennsylvania Museum." *Orientations* 32.2: 24–31.

Wright, Arthur F. 1959. *Buddhism in Chinese History*. Stanford: Stanford University Press.

———. 1990. "Fo-t'u-teng: A Biography." In *Studies in Chinese Buddhism*, edited by Robert M. Somers, 34–68. New Haven and London: Yale University Press.

Wu Minxia 吳敏霞. 1996. "Cong Tang muzhi kan Tangdai shisu fojiao xinyang 從唐墓志看唐代世俗佛教信仰." *Fojiao yanjiu* 佛教研究 5: 218–225.

Xiao Dengfu 蕭登福. 1989. *Han Wei Liuchao fodao liang jiao zhi tiantang diyu shuo* 漢魏六朝佛道兩教之天堂地獄說. Taipei: Xuesheng shuju.

———. 1993a. *Daojiao xindou fuyin yu fojiao mizong* 道教星斗符印與佛教密宗. Taipei: Xinwenfeng chuban gongsi.

———. 1993b. *Daojiao yu mizong* 道教與密宗. Taipei: Xinwenfeng chuban gongsi.

———. 1995. *Daojiao yu fojiao* 道教與佛教. Taipei: Dongda tushu.

———. 1996. *Daofo shiwang diyu shuo* 道佛十王地獄說. Taipei: Xinwenfeng chuban gongsi.

Xinran 心然. 1995. *Dizang wang pusa lingyan shiji* 地藏王菩薩靈驗事蹟. Taipei: Heyu chubanshe.

Yabuki Keiki 矢吹慶輝. 1927. *Sangaikyō no kenkyū* 三階教の研究. Tokyo: Iwanami Shoten.

Yamada Toshiaki. 1994. "Repentance Rituals in Taoism and Chinese Buddhism." In *Bouddhisme et cultures locales: Quelques cas de réciproques adaptations*, edited by Fukui Fumimasa and Gérard Fussman, 169–172. Paris: École française d'Extrême-Orient.

Yang Fuxue 楊富學. 1995. "Xiyu, Dunhuang wenxian suojian Huihu zhi fojing fanyi 西域、敦煌文獻所見回鶻之佛經翻譯." *Dunhuang yanjiu* 敦煌研究 4: 1–36.

Yang Xiong 楊雄, ed. 1993. *Dunhuang shiku yishu: Mogao ku di sishiwu ku* 敦煌石窟藝術: 莫高窟第四十五窟. Nanjing: Jiangsu meishu chubanshe.

Yao Congxin 姚崇新. 2002. "Guangyuan de Dizang zaoxiang ji zuhe 廣元的地藏造像及組和." *Yishu shi yanjiu* 藝術史研究 4: 305–323.

Yao Shengmin 姚生民. 1997. "Chunhua Tangdai kejing shiku 淳化唐代刻經石窟." *Zhongguo wenwu bao* 中國文物報, 27 February.

Yinshun 印順. 1989. "Dizang pusa zhi shengde ji qi famen 地藏菩薩之聖德及其法門." In *Dizang pusa shengde huibian* 地藏菩薩聖德彙編, edited by Huimen 慧門, 1–53. Taipei: Mile chubanshe.

Yü Chün-fang. 1992. "P'u-t'o Shan: Pilgrimage and the Creation of the Chinese Potalaka." In *Pilgrims and Sacred Sites in China*, edited by Susan Naquin and Yü Chün-fang, 190–245. Berkeley: University of California Press.

———. 1994. "Guanyin: The Chinese Transformation of Avalokiteshvara." In *Latter Days of the Law: Images of Chinese Buddhism 850–1850*, edited by Marsha Weidner, 151–181. Lawrence, KS: Spencer Museum of Art.

———. 2001. *Kuan-yin: The Chinese Transformation of Avalokiteśvara*. New York: Columbia University Press.

Yusa Noboru 遊佐昇. 1989. "Tōdai ni mirareru Kyūku tenson shinkō ni tsuite 唐代に見られる救苦天尊信仰について." *Tōhō Shūkyō* 東方宗教 73: 19–40.

Zang Weixi 臧維熙. 1993. "Jiuhua shan Jin Dizang kaolue 九華山金地藏考略." In *Jin Dizang yanjiu* 金地藏研究, edited by Jiuhua shan fojiao shi bianweihui 九華山佛教史編委會, 30–47. Hefei: Huangshan shushe.

Zhang Boyuan 張伯元. 1998. "Anxi Yulin ku 'liudao lunhui tu' kaoshi 安西榆林窟『六道輪回圖』考釋." *Dunhuang yanjiu* 敦煌研究 1: 20–23.

Zhang Gong 張弓. 2003. "Tangdai shiren de 'shi ru zhong fo' 唐代士人的「始儒終佛」." In *Di qi jie ru fo huitong xueshu yantaohui lunwenji* 第七屆儒佛會通學術研討會論文集, 54–63. Taipei: Huafan daxue zhexuexi.

Zhang Yan 張硯, and Wang Fumin 王福民. 1994. "Shaanxi Yaoxian Yaowang shan moya zaoxiang diaocha jianbao 陝西耀縣藥王山摩崖造像調查簡報." *Zhongyuan wenwu* 中原文物 2: 8–16.

Zhang Zong 張總. 2003. *Dizang xinyang yanjiu* 地藏信仰研究. Beijing: Zongjiao wenhua chubanshe.

Zhang Zong 張總, and Wang Baoping 王保平. 2003. "Shaanxi Chunhua Jinchuan wan sanjie jiao kejing shiku 陝西淳化金川灣三階教刻經石窟." *Wenwu* 文物 5: 65–74.

Zhao Yiwu 趙以武. 1989. *Wuliang wenhua shulun* 五涼文化述論. Gansu: Gansu renmin chubanshe.

Zhengyan 證嚴. 2003. *Fomen daxiao Dizang jing* 佛門大孝地藏經. Taipei: Ciji wenhua chubanshe.

Zhihui 智慧. 2002. "Daoxuan's Vision of Jetavana: Imagining a Utopian Monastery in Early Tang." Ph.D. diss., University of Arizona.

Zhiru 智如. 2000. "The Emergence of the Sahā Triad in Contemporary Taiwan: Iconic Representation and Humanistic Buddhism." *Asia Major* 13.2: 83–105.

———. 2001–2002. "The Kṣitigarbha Connection: A Missing Piece in the Chinese History of Pure Land Buddhism." *Studies of Central and East Asian Religions* 12–13: 41–93.

———. 2005. "The Maitreya Connection in the Tang Development of Dizang Worship." *Harvard Journal of Asiatic Studies* 65.1: 99–132.

Zhong Han 鐘漢. 2000. *Fo pusa shengri youlai* 佛菩薩生日由來. Taipei: Daqian chubanshe.

Zhongguo meishu quanji bianji weiyuanhui 中國美術全集編輯委員會. 1988. *Sichuan shike diaosu* 四川石刻雕塑. Vol. 12, *Zhongguo meishu quanji* 中國美術全集. Beijing: Renmin meishu chubanshe.

Zhuang Mingxing 莊明興. 1999. *Zhongguo zhonggu de Dizang xinyang* 中國中古的地藏信仰. Taipei: Guoli taiwan daxue chuban weiyuanhui.

Zieme, Peter. 1990. "Ein alttürkisches Fragment des *Kṣitigarbha-Sūtras* aus Bäzäklik." *Altorientalische Forschungen* 17.2: 379–384.

Zu Baoquan 祖保泉, and Tao Litian 陶禮天. 2002. *Sikong Biaosheng shiwenji jianjiao* 司空表聖詩文集箋校. Hefei: Anhui daxue chubanshe.

Zürcher, Erik. 1972. *The Buddhist Conquest of China: The Spread and Adaptation of Buddhism in Early Medieval China*. Leiden: E. J. Brill.

———. 1977. "Late Han Vernacular Elements in the Earliest Buddhist Translations." *Journal of the Chinese Language Teachers Association* 12.3: 177–203.

———. 1981. "Eshatology and Messianism in Early Chinese Buddhism." In *Leyden Studies in Sinology: Papers Presented at the Conference Held in Celebration of the Fiftieth Anniversary of the Sinological Institute of Leyden University*, edited by W. L. Idema, 34–56. Leiden: E. J. Brill.

———. 1982a. "Perspectives in the Study of Chinese Buddhism." *Journal of the Royal Asiatic Society* 2: 161–176.

———. 1982b. "'Prince Moonlight': Messianism and Eschatology in Early Medieval Chinese Buddhism." *T'oung Pao* 68.1–3: 1–75.

———. 1990. "Han Buddhism and the Western Region." In *Thought and Law in Qin and Han China*, edited by W. L Idema and E. Zürcher, 158–182. Leiden: E. J. Brill.

———. 1991. "A New Look at the Earliest Chinese Buddhist Texts." In *From Benares to Beijing: Essays on Buddhism and Chinese Religion in Honour of Prof. Jan Yün-hua*, edited by Koichi Shinohara and Gregory Schopen, 277–304. Oakville, Canada: Mosaic Press.

Zysk, Kenneth G. 1989. "Mantra in *Āyurveda:* A Study of the Use of Magico-Religious Speech in Ancient Indian Medicine." In *Understanding Mantras*, edited by Harvey P. Alper, 123–143. Albany: State University of New York.

Index

Bold page numbers refer to illustrations.

About the Author

ZHIRU, A BUDDHIST NUN ordained in the Chinese tradition, received her M.A. from the University of Michigan and holds a doctorate in East Asian Buddhism from the University of Arizona. She has authored a number of articles on medieval Chinese Buddhist cults and contemporary Buddhism in Taiwan. She is currently professor in the Department of Religious Studies at Pomona College.

Kuroda Institute
Studies in East Asian Buddhism

Studies in Ch'an and Hua-yen
Robert M. Gimello and Peter N. Gregory, editors

Dōgen Studies
William R. LaFleur, editor

The Northern School and the Formation of Early Ch'an Buddhism
John R. McRae

Traditions of Meditation in Chinese Buddhism
Peter N. Gregory, editor

Sudden and Gradual: Approaches to Enlightenment in Chinese Thought
Peter N. Gregory, editor

Buddhist Hermeneutics
Donald S. Lopez, Jr., editor

Paths to Liberation: The Margā and Its Transformations in Buddhist Thought
Robert E. Buswell, Jr., and Robert M. Gimello, editors

Sōtō Zen in Medieval Japan
William M. Bodiford

The Scripture on the Ten Kings and the Making of Purgatory in Medieval Chinese Buddhism
Stephen F. Teiser

The Eminent Monk: Buddhist Ideals in Medieval Chinese Hagiography
John Kieschnick

Re-Visioning "Kamakura" Buddhism
Richard K. Payne, editor

Original Enlightenment and the Transformation of Medieval Japanese Buddhism
Jacqueline I. Stone

Buddhism in the Sung
Peter N. Gregory and Daniel A. Getz, Jr., editors

Coming to Terms with Chinese Buddhism: A Reading of The Treasure Store Treatise
Robert H. Sharf

Ryōgen and Mount Hiei: Japanese Tendai in the Tenth Century
Paul Groner

Tsung-mi and the Sinification of Buddhism
Peter N. Gregory

Approaching the Land of Bliss: Religious Praxis in the Cult of Amitābha
Richard K. Payne and Kenneth K. Tanaka, editors

Going Forth: Visions of Buddhist Vinaya
William M. Bodiford, editor

Burning for the Buddha: Self-Immolation in Chinese Buddhism
James A. Benn

The Buddhist Dead: Practices, Discourses, Representations
Bryan J. Cuevas and Jacqueline I. Stone, editors

The Making of a Savior Bodhisattva: Dizang in Medieval China
Zhiru